The
Journal
of
Frances
Anne
Butler

The
Journal
of
Frances
Anne
Butler

better
known
as
Fanny
Kemble

Two volumes in one

BENJAMIN
BLOM
INC.
Publishers
New York

First Published 1835
Reissued 1970 by
Benjamin Blom, Inc., Bronx, New York 10452

Library of Congress Catalog Card Number 79-91530

Printed in United States of America
at Westbrook Lithographers, Inc.
Westbury, New York

JOURNAL

BY

FRANCES ANNE BUTLER.

IN TWO VOLUMES.

VOL. I.

LONDON:

JOHN MURRAY, ALBEMARLE STREET.

MDCCCXXXV.

PREFACE.

A PREFACE appears to me necessary to this book, in order that the expectation with which the English reader might open it should not be disappointed.

Some curiosity has of late been excited in England with regard to America: its political existence is a momentous experiment, upon which many eyes are fixed, in anxious watching of the result; and such accounts as have been published of the customs and manners of its societies, and the natural wonders and beauties of its scenery, have been received and read with considerable interest in Europe. This being the case, I should be loth to present these volumes to the English public without disclaiming both the intention and the capability of adding the slightest detail

of any interest to those which other travellers have already furnished upon these
subjects.

This book is, what it professes to be, my
personal journal, and not a history or a
description of men and manners in the
United States.

Engaged in an arduous profession, and
travelling from city to city in its exercise,
my leisure, and my opportunities, would
have been alike inadequate to such a task.
The portion of America which I have
visited has been a very small one, and, I
imagine, by no means that from which the
most interesting details are to be drawn. I
have been neither to the south nor to the
west ; consequently have had no opportunity of seeing two large portions of the
population of this country, — the enterprising explorers of the late wildernesses on the
shores of the Mississippi, — and the black
race of the slave states, both classes of men
presenting peculiarities of infinite interest
to the traveller : the one, a source of

energy and growing strength, the other, of disease and decay, in this vast political body.

My sphere of observation has been confined to the Atlantic cities, whose astonishing mercantile prosperity, and motley mongrel societies, though curious under many aspects, are interesting but under few.

What I registered were my immediate impressions of what I saw and heard ; of course, liable to all the errors attendant upon first perceptions, and want of time and occasion for maturer investigation. The notes I have added while preparing the text for the press; and such opinions and details as they contain are the result of a longer residence in this country, and a somewhat better acquaintance with the people of it.

Written, as my journal was, day by day, and often after the fatigues of a laborious evening's duty at the theatre, it has infinite sins of carelessness to answer for ; and but that it would have taken less time and trouble to re-write the whole book, or rather write a better, I would have endeavoured to correct them, — though, indeed, I was something of Alfieri's mind about it: — "Quanto poi allo stile, io penso di lasciar fare alla penna, e di pochissimo lasciarlo scostarsi da quella triviale e spontanea naturalezza, con cui ho scritto quest' opera, dettata dal cuore e non dall' ingegno; e che sola può convenire a così umile tema."

However, my purpose is not to write an apology for my book, or its defects, but simply to warn the English reader, before he is betrayed into its perusal, that it is a purely egotistical record, and by no means a history of America.

JOURNAL.

Wednesday, August 1st, 1832.

ANOTHER break in my journal, and here I am on board the Pacific, bound for America, having left home, and all the world behind.—Well !   *

*   *   *   *   *

We reached the quay just as the ship was being pulled, and pushed, and levered to the entrance of the dock ;—the quays were lined with people, among them were several known faces, — Mr. ——, Mr. ——.   M—— came on board to take my letters, and bid me good-by.   *   *

*   *   *   *   *

I had a bunch of carnations in my hand, which I had snatched from our drawing-room chimney ; — English flowers ! — dear English flowers ! they will be withered long before I again see land, but I will keep them until I once more stand upon the soil on which they grew.   *   *

*   *   *   *   *

VOL. I.

The sky had become clouded, and the wind blew
cold.   *   *   *

          *   *   *   *   *

Came down and put our narrow room to rights.

          *   *   *   *   *

Worked at my Bible cover till dinner time.
We dined at half-past three.— The table was excellent — cold dinner, because it was the first day
— but every thing was good; and champagne, and
dessert, and every luxury imaginable, rendered it
as little like a ship-dinner as might be.   The man
who sat by me was an American; very good-
natured, and talkative.   Our passengers are all
men, with the exception of three; a nice, pretty-
looking girl, who is going' out with her brother;
a fat old woman, and a fat young one.   I cried
almost the whole of dinner-time.   *   *

     *   *   *   *   *

After dinner the ladies adjourned to their own
cabin, and the gentlemen began to debate about
regulating the meal hours.   They adopted the
debating society tone, called my poor dear father
to the chair, and presently I heard, oh horror!
(what I had not thought to hear again for six
weeks,) the clapping of hands.   They sent him in
to consult us about the dinner-hour: and we
having decided four o'clock, the debate continued

with considerable merriment. Presently my father, Colonel ——, and Mr. ——, came into our cabin:—the former read us Washington Irving's speech at the New York dinner. Some of it is very beautiful, all of it is in good feeling—it made me cry. Oh my home, my land, England, glorious little England! from which this bragging big baby was born, how my heart yearns towards your earth! I sat working till the gentlemen left us, and then wrote journal. *   *

*   *   *   *   *

I am weary and sad, and will try to go and sleep.—It rains: I cannot see the moon.

Thursday, 2d.

It rained all night, and in the morning the wind had died away, and we lay rocking, becalmed on the waveless waters. At eight o'clock they brought me some breakfast, after which I got up; while dressing, I could not help being amused at hearing the cocks crowing, and the cow lowing, and geese and ducks gabbling, as though we were in the midst of a farm-yard. At half-past ten, having finished my toilet, I emerged; and Miss —— and I walked upon deck. The sea lay

still, and grey, without ridge or sparkle, a sheet of
lead; the sky was of the same dull colour. The
deck was wet and comfortless. We were but just
off Holyhead: two or three ships stood against
the horizon, still as ourselves. The whole was
melancholy:—and sadder than all, sat a poor
woman, dressed in mourning, in a corner of the
deck; she was a steerage passenger, and I never
saw so much sorrow in any face. Poor thing!
poor thing! was her heart aching for home, and
kindred left behind her? It made mine ach to
look at her. We walked up and down for an
hour. I like my companion well; she is a nice,
young quiet thing, just come from a country home.
Came down, and began getting out books for my
German lesson, but turning rather awful, left my
learning on the floor, and betook myself to my
berth. Slept nearly till dinner time. At dinner
I took my place at table, but presently the misery
returned; and getting up, while I had sufficient
steadiness left to walk becomingly down the
room, I came to my cabin; my dinner followed
me thither, and, lying on my back, I very comfortably discussed it. Got up, devoured some
raspberry tart, and grapes, and being altogether
delightful again, sat working and singing till
tea-time: after which, wrote journal, and now to

bed. How strange it seems to hear these Americans speaking in English of *the English !* — " Oh, hame, hame, hame wad I be," — but it is not time to sing that yet.

Friday, 3d.

Breakfasted at eight; got up, and dressed, and came upon deck. The day was lovely, the sea one deep dark sapphire, the sky bright and cloudless, the wind mild and soft, too mild to fill our sails, which hung lazily against the masts, — but enough to refresh the warm summer's sky, and temper the bright sun of August that shone above us. Walked upon deck with Miss —— and Captain Whaite: the latter is a very intelligent, good-natured person; rough and bluff, and only seven and twenty; which makes his having the command of a ship rather an awful consideration. At half-past eleven got my German, and worked at it till half-past one, then got my work; and presently we were summoned on deck by sound of bell, and oyes! oyes! oyes! — and a society was established for the good demeanour and sociability of the passengers. My father was in the chair. Mr. —— was voted secretary, Dr. —— attorney-general;

a badge was established, rules and regulations
laid down, a code framed, and much laughing
and merriment thence ensued. Worked till dinner-time. After dinner, went on deck, took a
brisk walk for half an hour with Captain Whaite.
Established myself to work, and presently we
were all summoned to attend a mock trial of
Colonel ——, which made us all laugh most
exceedingly. We adopted titles — I chose my
family appellation of Puddledock: many of the
names were very absurd, and as a penalty ensued
upon not giving every body their proper designa-
tion, much amusement arose from it. When the
trial was over, we played at dumb crambo, and
earth, air, and water, with infinite zeal, till tea-
time. After tea, we were summoned on deck to
see the ship make a tack. The wind was against
us, the sea inky black, the pale clear moon stood
high against the sail — presently, with a whooping and yaw-awling that mocks description, the
fair ship was turned away from the wind, the sails
veered round, and she set in another course.
We remained on deck, the gentlemen gathered
round us, and singing began : — it went round
and round by turns, some of our voices were
very sweet, and, upon the whole, 't was time pleasantly spent. Came to bed at ten.

Wednesday, 15*th.*

Here's a lapse! thanks to head winds, a rolling
sea, and their result, sickness, sadness, sorrow.
I've been better for the last two days, thank
God! and take to my book again. Rose at eight,
dawdled about, and then came up stairs. Breakfasted, sat working at my Bible cover till lunch-
time. — Somebody asked me if I had any of Mrs.
Siddons's hair; I sent for my dressing-box, and
forthwith it was overhauled, to use the appropriate
phrase, by half the company, whom a rainy day
had reduced to a state of worse than usual want
of occupation. The rain continued all day; we
ladies dined in the round-house, the room down
stairs being too close. The Captain and Colonel
—— joined us afterwards, and began drinking
champagne, and induced us to do the same. As
evening came on, the whole of the passengers collected in the round-house. Mr. ——, Mr. D——,
and I wrote a rhapsody; afterwards they fell to
singing; while they did so, the sky darkened
tremendously, the rain came pelting down, the
black sea swelled, and rose, and broke upon the
ship's sides into boiling furrows of foam, that fled
like ghosts along the inky face of the ocean. The

ship scudded before the blast, and we managed to keep ourselves warm by singing. After tea, for the first time since I have been on board, got hold of a pack of cards, (oh me, that it ever should come to this !) and initiated Miss —— in the mysteries of the intellectual game. Mercy ! how my home rose before me as I did so. Played till I was tired; dozed, and finally came to bed. Bed ! quotha ! 't is a frightful misapplication of terms. Oh for a bed ! a real bed; any manner of bed, but a bed on shipboard ! And yet I have seen some fair things : I have seen a universe of air and water ; I have seen the glorious sun come and look down upon this rolling sapphire ; I have seen the moon throw her silver columns along the watery waste ; I have seen one lonely ship in her silent walk across this wilderness, meet another, greet her, and pass her, like a dream, on the wide deep ; I have seen the dark world of waters at midnight open its mysterious mantle beneath our ship's prow, and show below another dazzling world of light. I have seen, what I would not but have seen, though I have left my very soul behind me. England, dear, dear England ! oh, for a handful of your earth !

Thursday, 16*th.*

Another day, another day! the old fellow posts
as well over water as over land! Rose at about half-
past eight, went up to the round-house; breakfasted, and worked at my Bible cover. As soon as
our tent was spread, went out on deck: took a
longish walk with Mr.———. I like him very
much; his face would enchant Lavater, and his
skull ecstacise the Combes. Lay down under our
rough pavilion, and heard the gentlemen descant
very learnedly upon freemasonry. A book called
" Adventures of an Irish Gentleman," suggested
the conversation; in which are detailed, some of
the initiatory ceremonies, which appear to me so
incredibly foolish, that I can scarce believe them,
even making mankind a handsome allowance for
absurdity. I soon perceived that the discussion
was likely to prove a serious one, for in America,
it seems, 'tis made a political question; and our
Boston friend, and the Jacksonite, fell to rather
sharply about it. The temperance of the former,
however, by retreating from the field, spared us
further argumentation. One thing I marvel at:—
are the institutions of men stronger to bind men,
than those of God; and does masonry effect good,

which Christianity does not? — a silly query, by
the way; for doubtless men act the good, but
forbear to act the evil, before each other's eyes;
which they think nothing of doing, or leaving
undone, under those of God.

Gossiped till lunch-time; afterwards took up
Childe Harold, — commend me to that! I thought
of dear H——. She admires Byron more than I
do; and yet how wildly I did, how deeply I do
still, worship his might, majesty, and loveliness.
We dined up stairs, and after dinner, I and
Mr. —— took a long walk on deck ; talking
flimsy morality, and philosophy; the text of which
were generalities, but all the points individualities :
I was amused in my heart at him and myself.
He'd a good miss of me at ——: heaven knows,
I was odious enough ! and therein his informer
was right. The day was bright, and bitter cold, —
the sea blue, and transparent as that loveliest line
in Dante,

"Dolce color di oriental zaffiro,"

with a lining of pearly foam, and glittering spray,
that enchanted me. Came and sat down again : —
wrote doggerel for the captain's album, about the
captain's ship, which, when once I am out of her,

I'll swear I love infinitely. Read aloud to them some of Byron's short poems, and that glorious hymn to the sea, in Childe Harold:—mercy, how fine it is! Lay under our canvass shed till nine o'clock:— the stars were brilliant in the intense blue sky, the wind had dropped, the ship lay still — we sang a song or two, supped, and came in; where, after inditing two rhapsodies, we came to bed.

Friday, 17th.

On my back all day : mercy, how it ached too! the ship reeled about like a drunken thing. I lay down and began reading Byron's life. As far as I have gone (which is to his leaving England) there is nothing in it but what I expected to find, — the fairly sown seeds of the after-harvest he bore. Had he been less of an egotist, would he have been so great a poet?— I question it. His fury and wrath at the severe injustice of his critics reminds me, by the by, of those few lines in the Athenæum, which I read the other day, about poetical shoemakers, dairy-maids, plough-men, and myself. After all, what matters it?— "If this thing be of God," the devil can't overthrow it; if it be not, why the printer's devil may. What can it signify what is said? If truth be truth to the end of reckoning, why, that share of her, if any, which I possess, must endure when recorded as long as truth endures. I almost wonder Byron was moved by criticism : I should have thought him at once too highly armed, and too self-wrapped, to care for it; — however, if a wasp's sting have such virtue in it, 'tis as well it should have been felt as keenly as it was. — Ate nothing but figs and raisins; in the evening some of our gentlemen came into our cabin, and sat with us; I, in very desperation and sea-sickness, began embroidering one of my old nightcaps, wherein I persevered till sleep overtook me.

Saturday, 18*th.*

Rose at about half-past eight, dawdled about as usual, breakfasted in the round-house—by the by, before I got out of bed, read a few more pages of Byron's life. I don't exactly understand the species of sentimental *galimatias* Moore talks about Byron's writing with the same penfull of ink, " Adieu, adieu, my native land!" and "Hurra ! Hodgson, we are going." It proves nothing except what I firmly believe, that we must not look for the real feelings of writers in their

works — or rather, that what they give us, and
what we take for heart feeling, is head weav-
ing — a species of emotion engendered somewhere
betwixt the bosom and the brain, and bearing
the same proportion of resemblance to reality
that a picture does ; that is — like feeling, but not
feeling — like sadness, but not sadness — like what
it appears, but not indeed that very thing : and
the greater a man's power of thus producing *sham
realities*, the greater his main qualification for
being a poet. — After breakfast, sat like Lady Alice
in the old song, embroidering my midnight coif.
Got Colonel —— to read Quentin Durward to us
as we sat working under our canvass pavilion.

    *   *   *   *   *

Our company consists chiefly of traders in cloth
and hardware, clerks, and counting-house men — a
species with but few peculiarities of interest to me,
who cannot talk pounds, shillings, and pence, as
glibly as less substantial trash. Most of them have
crossed this trifling ditch half a dozen times in their
various avocations. But though they belong to the
same sort generally, they differ enough individually
for the amusement of observation. That poor wi-
dower, whose remarks on the starry inside of the
sea attracted my attention the other evening, put
into my hands to-day a couple of pretty little books

enough; a sort of hotch-potch, or to speak more sweetly, pot-pourri praise of women — passages selected from various authors who have done us the honour to remember us in their good commendations. There were one or two most eloquent and exquisite passages from Jeremy Taylor — one on love that enchanted me. I should like to copy it. What a contrast to that exquisite thing of Shelley's, " What is Love ? " and yet they are both beautiful, powerful, and true. I could have helped them to sundry more passages on this subject, particularly from my oracle. Mr. —— read to us after lunch, and we sat very happily under our *yawning* till the rain drove us in. No wind, the sea one rippleless sheet of lead, and the sky just such another. Our main-top gallant-mast had been split in one of our late blows, and I went out in the rain to see them restore the spar. Towards evening the wind faired and freshened, in consequence of which, our gentlemen's spirits rose; and presently, in spite of the rain, they were dancing, singing, and romping like mad things on the quarter-deck. It was Saturday —holiday on board ship—the men were all dismissed to their grog. Mr. —— and I sang through a whole volume of Moore's melodies; and at ten o'clock (for the first time since our second day on board) we of the petticoats adjourned to the gentlemen's cabin to drink " sweethearts and wives," according to the approved sailors' practice. It made me sad to hear them, as they lifted their glasses to their lips, pass round the toast, " Sweethearts and wives ! " I drank in my heart — " Home and dear H——." One thing amused me a good deal : — the Captain proposed as a toast, " The Ladies — God bless them," which accordingly was being duly drunk when I heard, close to my elbow, a devout, half audible — " and the Lord deliver us ! " This from a man with a face like one of Retsch's most grotesque etchings, and an expression half humorous, half terrified, sent me into fits of laughter. They sang a song or two, and at twelve we left them to their meditations, which presently reached our ears in the sound, not shape, of " Health to Bacchus," in full chorus, to which tune I said my prayers.

Sunday, 19*th.*

Did not rise till late — dressed and came on deck. The morning was brilliant ; the sea, bold, bright, dashing its snowy crests against our ship's sides, and flinging up a cloud of glittering spray round the prow. I breakfasted — and then amused myself with finding the lessons, collects, and psalms for the whole ship's company. After lunch, they spread our tent, a chair was placed for my father, and the little bell being rung, we collected in our rude church. It affected me much, this praying on the lonely sea, in the words that at the same hour were being uttered by millions of kindred tongues in our dear home. There was something, too, impressive and touching in this momentary union of strangers, met but for a passing day, to part perhaps never to behold each other's faces again, in the holiest of all unions, that of Christian worship. Here I felt how close, how strong that wondrous tie of common faith that thus gathered our company, unknown and unconnected by any one worldly interest or bond, to utter the same words of praise and supplication, to think perhaps the same thoughts of humble and trustful dependence on God's great goodness in this our pilgrimage to foreign lands, to yearn perhaps with the same affection and earnest imploring of blessings towards our native soil and its beloved ones left behind. — Oh, how I felt all this as we spoke aloud that touching invocation, which is always one of my most earnest prayers, "Almighty God, who hast promised when two or three are gathered together in thy name," &c. * * * The bright cloudless

sky and glorious sea seemed to respond, in their
silent magnificence, to our *Te Deum.*—I felt
more of the excitement of prayer than I have
known for many a day, and 't was good—oh! very,
very good ! *   *   *   *
*   *   *   *   *

' Tis good to behold this new universe, this
mighty sea which he hath made, this glorious cloudless sky, where hang, like dew drops, his scattered
worlds of light—to see all this and say,—

" These are thy glorious works, parent of good ! "

After prayers, wrote journal. Some sea weed
floated by the ship to-day, borne from the gulf
stream; I longed to have it, for it told of land :
gulls too came wheeling about, and the little pet-
terels like sea-swallows skimmed round and round,
now resting on the still bosom of the sunny sea,
now flickering away in rapid circles like black
butterflies. They got a gun, to my horror, and
wasted a deal of time in trying to shoot these
feathered mariners; but they did not even succeed
in scaring them. We went and sat on the forecastle
to see the sun set : he did not go down cloudless,
but dusky ridges of vapour stretched into ruddy
streaks along the horizon, as his disk dipped into

the burnished sea. The foam round the prow,
as the ship made way with all sail set before a
fair wind, was the most lovely thing I ever saw.
Purity, strength, glee, and wondrous beauty were
in those showers of snowy spray that sprang up
above the black ship's sides, and fell like a cataract
of rubies under the red sunlight. We sat there
till evening came down; the sea, from brilliant
azure grew black as unknown things, the wind
freshened, and we left our cold stand to walk, or
rather run, up and down the deck to warm ourselves. This we continued till, one by one, the
stars had lit their lamps in heaven: their wondrous brilliancy, together with the Aurora Borea-
lis, which rushed like sheeted ghosts along the sky,
and the stream of fire that shone round the ship's
way, made heaven and sea appear like one vast
world of flame, as though the thin blue veil of
air and the dark curtain of the waters were but
drawn across a universe of light. Mercy, how
strange it was! We stood at the stern, watching
the milky wake the ship left as she stole through
the eddying waters. Came back to our gipsy en-
campment, where, by the light of a lantern, we
supped and sang sundry scraps of old songs. At
ten came to bed.   *   *   *   *   *
           *   *   *   *   *

Took an observation of the sun's altitude at noon, and saw them hoist a main-top-royal sail, which looked very pretty as it was unreefed against the clear sky.

Monday, 20th.

Calm — utter calm — a roasting August sun, a waveless sea, the sails flapping idly against the mast, and our black cradle rocking to and fro without progressing a step. They lowered the boat, and went out rowing — I wanted to go, but they would not let me! A brig was standing some four miles off us, which, by the by, I was the first to see, except our mate, in my morning watch, which began at five o'clock, when I saw the moon set and the sun rise, and feel more than ever convinced that absolute reality is away from the purpose of works of art. The sky this morning was as like the sea-shore as ever sand and shingle were, the clouds lying along the horizon in pale dusky yellow layers, and higher up, floating in light brown ribbed masses, like the sands which grow wrinkled under the eternal smiling of the sea. Against the dim horizon, which blended with the violet-coloured sky, the mate then showed me, through the glass, the brig

standing on the sea's edge, for all the world like
one of the tiny birds who were wheeling and
chirping round our ship's stern.   I have done
more in the shape of work to-day than any
since the two first I spent on board; translated
a German fable without much trouble, read a
canto in Dante, ending with a valuation of fame.
" O spirito gentil !" how lived fair wisdom in your
soul — how shines she in your lays ! — Wrote
journal, walked about, worked at my cap, in
the evening danced merrily enough, quadrilles,
country dances, La Boulangére, and the monaco ;
fairly danced myself tired.   Came to bed.   But
oh ! not to sleep — mercy, what a night ! The
wind blowing like mad, the sea rolling, the ship
pitching, bouncing, shuddering, and reeling, like
a thing possessed. I lay awake, listening to her
creaking and groaning, till two o'clock, when,
sick of my sleepless berth, I got up and was
going up stairs, to see, at least, how near drowning
we were, when D ——, who was lying awake too,
implored me to lie down again.   I did so for the
hundred and eleventh time, complaining bitterly
that I should be stuffed down in a loathsome berth,
cabined, cribbed, confined, while the sea was
boiling below, and the wind bellowing above
us.   Lay till daylight, the gale increasing

furiously ; boxes, chairs, beds, and their contents, wooden valuables, and human invaluables, rolling about and clinging to one another in glorious confusion. At about eight o'clock, a tremendous sea took the ship in the waist, and rushing over the deck, banged against our sky-light, and bounced into our cabin. Three women were immediately apparent from their respective cribs, and poor H—— appeared in all her lengthy full-length, and came and took refuge with me. As I held her in my arms, and put my cloak round her, she shook from head to foot, poor child !—I was not the least frightened, but rather excited by this invasion of Dan Neptune's; but I wish to goodness I had been on deck.—Oh, how I wish I had seen that spoonful of salt water flung from the sea's boiling bowl ! I heard afterwards, that it had nearly washed away poor Mr. ——, besides handsomely ducking and frightening our military man. Lay all day on my back, most wretched, the ship heaving like any earthquake; in fact, there is something irresistibly funny in the way in which people seem dispossessed of their power of volition by this motion, rushing hither and thither in all directions but the one they purpose going, and making as many angles, fetches, and sidelong deviations from the point they aim at, as if the devil had tied a string to their legs and jerked it every now and then in spite — by the by, not a bad illustration of our mental and moral struggles towards their legitimate aims. Another horrible night! oh horror!

Wednesday, 22*d*.

A fair wind — a fine day — though very, very cold and damp. It seems, in our squall last night, we had also a small piece of mutiny. During the mate's watch, and while the storm was at the worst, the man who was steering left the helm, and refused to obey orders; whereupon Mr. Curtis took up a hatchet, and assured him he would knock his brains out, — which the captain said, had it been his watch, he should have done on the spot, and without further warning. — We are upon the Newfoundland banks, though not yet on soundings. Stitched my gown — worked at my nightcap — walked about: — Mr. —— read Quentin Durward to us while we worked. The extreme cold made us take refuge in our cabin, where I sat working and singing till dinner-time. Dined at table again; afterwards came back to our cabin — began writing journal, and was interrupted by hearing a bustle in the dinner-room. The gentlemen were all standing up, and presently I heard Walter Scott's name passed round:—it made me lay down my pen. Oh! how pleasant it sounded—that unanimous blessing of strangers upon a great and good man, thus far from him—from all but our own small community. The genuine and spontaneous tribute to moral worth and mental power! Poor, poor Sir Walter! And yet no prayer that can be breathed to bless, no grateful and soul-felt invocation can snatch him from the common doom of earth-born flesh, or buy away one hour's anguish and prostration of body and spirit, before the triumphant infirmities of our miserable nature. I thought of Dante's lines, that I read but a day ago; and yet — and yet — fame is something. His fame is good — is great — is glorious. To be enshrined in the hearts of all virtuous and wise men, as the friend of virtue and the teacher of wisdom; to have freely given pleasure, happiness, forgetfulness, to millions of his fellow-creatures; to have made excellence lovely, and enjoyment pure and salutary; to have taught none but lessons of honour and integrity; to have surrounded his memory, and filled the minds of all men with images fair, and bright, and wonderful, yet left around his name no halo, and in the hearts of others no slightest cloud to blot these enchanting creations; to have done nothing but good with God's good gifts—is not this fame worth something? 'T is worth man's love, and God's approval—'t is worth toiling for, living for, and dying for. He has earned it fairly—he is a great and good man—peace be with him in his hour of mortal sorrow, and eternal peace hereafter in the heaven to which he surely goes. — They then drank Washington Irving,—a gentle spirit, too. After working for some time more, came on deck, where we danced with infinite glee, disturbed only by the surpassing uproar of Colonel ——.

    *   *   *   *   *
    *   *   *   *   *

The only of our crew whom I cotton to fairly, are the ——, and that good-natured lad, Mr. ——; though the former rather distress me by their abundant admiration, and the latter by his inveterate Yorkshire, and never opening his mouth when he sings, which, as he has a very sweet voice, is a cruel piece of selfishness, keeping half his tones, and all his words for his own private satisfaction.

Thursday, 23d.

On soundings, and nearly off them again — a fine day; — worked at my nightcap — another, by the by, having finished one — exemplary! — Walked about, ate, drank, wrote journal — read some of it to the ——, who seemed much gratified by my doing so. I go on with Byron's life. He is too much of an egotist. I do not like him a bit the better for knowing his prose mind; — far from thinking it redeems any of the errors of his poetical man, I think I never read any thing professing to be a person's undisguised feelings and opinions with so much heartlessness — so little goodness in it. His views of society are like his views of human nature; or rather, by the by, reverse the sentence, to prove the fallacy in judgment; and though his satire is keen and true, yet he is nothing but satirical — never, never serious and earnest, even with himself. Oh! I have a horror of that sneering devil of Goëthe's; and he seems to me to have possessed Byron utterly. A curious thought, or rather a fantastical shadow of a thought, occurred to me to-day in reading a chapter in the Corinthians about the resurrection. I mean to be buried

with H——'s ring on my finger; will it be there
when I rise again? — What a question for the
discussers of the needle's point controversy. My
father read to us, this afternoon, part of one of
Webster's speeches. It was very eloquent, but
yet it did not fulfil my idea of perfect oratory
— inasmuch as I thought it too pictorial: — there
was too much scenery and decoration about it, to
use the cant of my own trade; — there was too
much effect, theatrical effect in it, from which
Heaven defend me, for I do loathe it *in* its place,
and fifty times worse out of it. Perhaps Webster's speaking is a good sample, in its own line,
of the leaven wherewith these times are leavened.
I mean only in its defects — for its merits are
sterling, and therefore of all time.

But this oil and canvass style of thinking, writing, and speaking, is bad. I wish our age were
more sculptural in its genius — though I have not
the power in any thing to conform thereto, I have
the grace to perceive its higher excellence; yet
Milton was a sculptor, Shakspeare a painter. How
do we get through that? — My reason for object-
ing to Webster's style — though the tears were
in my eyes several times while my father read —
is precisely the same as my reason for not altogether liking my father's reading, — 't is slightly

theatrical — something too much of passion, something too much of effect — but perhaps I am mistaken; for I do so abhor the slightest approach to the lamps and orange peel, that I had almost rather hear a "brazen candlestick turned on a wheel," than all the music of due emphasis and inflection, if allied to a theatrical manner. — Dined at table again. They abound in toasts, and, among others, gave "The friends we have left, and those we are going to!" My heart sank. I am going to no friend; and the "stranger," with which the Americans salute wayfarers through their land, is the only title I can claim amongst them. After dinner, walked about — danced — saw the sun sink in a bed of gorgeous stormy clouds; — worked and walked till bedtime. — I was considerably amused, and my English blood a little roused at a very good-natured and well-meant caution of Mr. ——, to avoid making an enemy of Colonel ——. He is, they say, a party man, having influence which he may exert to our detriment.

Friday, 24th.

Rose late after a fair night's sleep — came up to the round-house. After breakfast, worked and

walked for an immense time. Read a canto in
Dante: just as I had finished it, " A sail ! a sail !"
was cried from all quarters. Remembering my
promise to dear H——, I got together my writing
materials, and scrawled her a few incoherent
lines full of my very heart. The vessel bore
rapidly down upon us, but as there was no pro-
spect of either her or our lying-to, Mr. —— tied
my missive, together with one Mr. —— had just
scribbled, to a lump of lead, and presently we all
rushed on deck to see the ship pass us. She was
an English packet, from Valparaiso, bound to
London; her foremast had been carried away,
but she was going gallantly before the wind. As
she passed us, Mr. —— got up into the boat to
have a better chance of throwing. I saw him
fling powerfully, — the little packet whizzed
through the air, but the distance was impossible,
and the dark waters received it within twenty
feet of the ship, which sailed rapidly on, and
had soon left us far behind. I believe I
screamed, as the black sea closed over my poor
letter.   *   *   *   *

    *   *   *   *   *

    *   *   *   *   *

Came down to my cabin and cried like a wretch
—came up again, and found them all at lunch.

Went and lay on the bowsprit, watching the fair ship courtesying through the bright sea with all her sail set, a gallant and graceful sight. Came in—wrote journal—translated a German fable. Worked at my cap, while my father went on with Webster's speech. I am still of the same mind about it, though some of the passages he read to-day were finer than any I had heard before. He gets over a shallow descent with admirable plausibility—and yet I think I would rather be descended from a half heathen Saxon giant, than from William Penn himself. We dined at table again; D—— could not : she was ill. After dinner, sat working for some time;—I had a horrid sick headache,—walked on deck. The wind and sea were both rising ; we stood by the side of the ship, and watched the inky waters swelling themselves, and rolling sullenly towards us, till they broke in silver clouds against the ship, and sprang above her sides, covering us with spray. The sky had grown mirk as midnight, and the wind that came rushing over the sea, was hot from the south. We staid out till it grew dark. At ten, the crazy old ship, in one of her headlong bounces, flung my whole supper in my lap ; the wind and water were riotous ; the ship plunged and shuddered. After screwing my

courage to a game of speculation, I was obliged to
leave it, and my companions. Came down and
went to bed. — Oh horror ! loathsome life ! —

Saturday and Sunday.

Towards evening got up and came on deck : —
tremendous head wind, going off our course;
pray Heaven we don't make an impromptu
landing on Sable Island ! Sat on the ship's side,
watching the huge ocean gathering itself up into
pitchy mountains, and rolling its vast ridges, one
after another, against the good ship, who dipped,
and dipped, and dived down into the black chasm,
and then sprang up again, and rode over the
swelling surges like an empress. The sky was
a mass of stormy black, here and there edged
with a copper-looking cloud, and breaking in one
or two directions into pale silvery strata, that had
an unhealthy lightning look : a heavy black squall
lay ahead of us, like a dusky curtain, whence
we saw the rain, fringe-like, pouring down against
the horizon. The wind blew furiously. I got
cradled among the ropes, so as not to be pitched
off when the ship lurched, and enjoyed it all
amazingly. It was sad and solemn, and, but for
the excitement of the savage-looking waves, that

every now and then lifted their overwhelming
sides against us, it would have made me melancholy : but it stirred my spirits to ride over
these huge sea-horses, that came bounding and
bellowing round us. Remained till I was chilled
with the bitter wind, and wet through with
spray;— walked up and down the deck for some
time, — had scarce set foot within the round
house, when a sea took her in midships, and
soused the loiterers. Sat up, or rather slept
up, till ten o'clock, and then went down to bed.
I took up Pelham to-day for a second — 't is
amazingly clever, and like the thing it means to
be, to boot. Heard something funny that I wish
to remember — at a Methodist meeting, the singer
who led the Psalm tune, finding that his
concluding word, which was Jacob, had not
syllables enough to fill up the music adequately
ended thus — Ja-a-a-a — Ja-a-a-a — fol-de-riddle
— cob !—

Monday, 26*th.*

Read Byron's life ; — defend me from my
friends ! Rose tolerably late ; after breakfast, took
a walk on deck — lay and slept under our sea-
tent ; read on until lunch-time — dined on deck,

— after dinner walked about with H—— and
the captain; we had seated ourselves on the ship's
side, but he being called away, we rushed off to
the forecastle to enjoy the starlight by ourselves.
We sat for a little time, but were soon found out;
Mr. —— and Mr. —— joined us, and we sat till
near twelve o'clock, singing and rocking under the
stars. Venus—"The star of love, all stars above,"
— threw a silver column down the sea, like the
younger sister of the moon's reflection. By the
by, I saw to-day, and with delight, an American
sunset. The glorious god strode down heaven's
hill, without a cloud to dim his downward path;
— as his golden disk touched the panting sea, I
turned my head away, and in less than a minute
he had fallen beneath the horizon — leapt down
into the warm waves, and left one glow of amber
round half the sky; upon whose verge, where the
violet curtain of twilight came spreading down to
meet its golden fringe,

> " The maiden,
> With white fire laden,
> Whom mortals call the moon,"

stood, with her silver lamp in her hand, and her
pale misty robes casting their wan lustre faintly

around her. Oh me, how glorious it was! how
sad, how very, very sad I was!   *

　　*　　　*　　　*　　　*　　　*

　　*　　　*　　　*　　　*　　　*

Dear, yet forbidden thoughts, that from my soul,
While shines the weary sun, with stern control
I drive away; why, when my spirits lie
Shrouded in the cold sleep of misery,
Do ye return, to mock me with false dreaming,
Where love, and all life's happiness is beaming?
Oh visions fair! that one by one have gone
Down, 'neath the dark horizon of my days;
Let not your pale reflection linger on
In the bleak sky, where live no more your rays.
Night! silent nurse, that with thy solemn eyes
Hang'st o'er the rocking cradle of the world,
Oh! be thou darker to my dreaming eyes;
Nor, in my slumbers, be the past unfurl'd.
Haunt me no more with whisperings from the dead,
The dead in heart, the chang'd, the withered:
Bring me no more sweet blossoms from my spring,
Which round my soul their early fragrance fling,
And, when the morning, with chill icy start,
Wakes me, hang blighted round my aching heart:
Oh night, and slumber, be ye visionless,
Dark as the grave, deep as forgetfulness!

　　*　　　*　　　*　　　*　　　*

　　*　　　*　　　*　　　*　　　*

Night, thou shalt nurse me, but be sure, good nurse,
While sitting by my bed, that thou art silent,

I will not let thee sing me to my slumbers
With the sweet lullabies of former times,
Nor tell me tales, as other gossips wont,
Of the strange fairy days, that are all gone.

Wednesday, 28*th.*

Skipped writing on Tuesday — so much the better— a miserable day spent between heart-ache and side-ache.　　*　　　*　　　*
　*　　　*　　　*　　　*　　　*

Rose late, breakfasted with H——, afterwards went and sat on the forecastle, where I worked the whole morning, woman's work, stitching. It was intensely hot till about two o'clock, when a full east wind came on, which the sailors all blessed, but which shook from its cold wings a heavy, clammy, chilly dew, that presently pierced all our clothes, and lay on the deck like rain. At dinner we were very near having a scene: the Bostonian and the Jacksonite falling out again about the President; and a sharp, quick, snapping conversation, which degenerated into a snarl on one side, and a growl on the other, for a short time rather damped the spirits of the table. Here, at least, General Jackson seems very unpopular, and half the company echoed in earnest what I said in jest to end the dispute, " Oh hang General Jackson !" After dinner, returned to the forecastle with H—— to see the sun set; her brother followed us thither.   *

   *   *   *   *   *

Finished my work, and then, tying on sundry veils and handkerchiefs, danced on deck for some time; — I then walked about with ——, by the light of the prettiest young moon imaginable.   *

   *   *   *   *   *

Afterwards sat working and stifling in the round-house till near ten, and then, being no longer able to endure the heat, came down, undressed, and sat luxuriously on the ground in my dressing-gown drinking lemonade. At twelve went to bed; the men kept up a horrible row on deck half the night; singing, dancing, whooping, and running over our heads.   *   *   *

   *   *   *   *   *

The captain brought me to-day a land-swallow, which having flown out so far, came hovering exhausted over the ship, and suffered itself to be caught. Poor little creature ! how very much more I do love all things than men and women ! I felt sad to death for its weary little wings and frightened heart, which beat against my hand, without its having strength to struggle. I made a cage in a basket for it, and gave it some seed, which it will not eat — little carnivorous wretch ! I must catch some flies for it.

Thursday, 29*th.*

My poor little bird is dead. I am sorry ! I could mourn almost as much over the death of a soulless animal, as I would rejoice at that of a brute with a soul. Life is to these winged things a pure enjoyment; and to see the rapid pinions folded, and the bright eye filmed, conveys sadness to the heart, for 'tis almost like looking on — what indeed is not — utter cessation of existence. Poor little creature ! I wished it had not died — I would but have borne it tenderly and carefully to shore, and given it back to the air again !

* * * * *

I sat down stairs in my cabin all day; the very spirit of doggerel possessed me, and I poured forth rhymes as rapidly as possible, and they were as bad as possible. — Wrote journal ; in looking over my papers, fell in with the Star of Seville — some of it is very good. I'll write an English tragedy next. Dined at table — our heroes have drunk wine, and are amicable. After dinner, went on deck, and took short walk; saw a the sun set, which he did like a god, as he is, leaving the sky like a geranium curtain, which overshadowed the sea with rosy light — beautiful! Came down and sat on the floor like a Turkish woman, stitching, singing, and talking, till midnight; supped — and to bed. My appetite seems like the Danaïdes' tub, of credible memory.

  *   *   *   *   *

  *   *   *   *   *

Friday, 30th.

On soundings. A fog and a calm. Sky yellow, sea grey, dripping, damp, dingy, dark, and very disagreeable. Sat working, reading, and talking in our own cabin all day. Read part of a book called Adventures of a Younger Son. The gentlemen amused themselves with fishing, and brought up sundry hake and dog-fish. I examined the heart of one of the fish, and was surprised at the long continuance of pulsation after the cessation of existence. In the evening, sang, talked, and played French blind man's buff; — sat working till near one o'clock, and reading Moore's Fudge Family, — which is good fun. It's too hard to be becalmed within thirty hours of our destination.

*   *   *   *   *

*   *   *   *   *

Why art thou weeping
Over the happy, happy dead,
Who are gone away,
From this life of clay,
From this fount of tears,
From this burthen of years,
From sin, from sorrow,
From sad " to-morrow,"
From struggling and creeping :
Why art thou weeping,
Oh fool, for the dead ?

Why art thou weeping,
Over the steadfast faithful dead,
Who can never change,
Nor grow cold and strange,
Nor turn away,
In a single day,
From the love they bore,
And the faith they swore,
Who are true for ever,
Will slight thee never,
But love thee still,
Through good and ill,
With the constancy
Of eternity :
Why art thou weeping,
Oh fool, for the dead ?

They are your only friends;
For where this foul life ends,
Alone beginneth truth, and love, and faith;
All which sweet blossoms are preserved by death.

Saturday, 31*st*.

Becalmed again till about two o'clock, when a fair wind sprang up, and we set to rolling before it like mad. How curious it is to see the ship, like a drunken man, reel through the waters, pursued by that shrill scold the wind. Worked at my handkerchief, and read aloud to them Mrs. Jameson's book. *   *   *
*   *   *   *   *

Set my foot half into a discussion about Portia, but withdrew it in time. Lord bless us! what foul nonsense people do talk, and what much fouler nonsense it is to answer them. Got very sick, and lay on the ground till dinner-time; went to table, but withdrew again while it was yet in my power to do so gracefully. Lay on the floor all the evening, singing for very sea-sickness; suddenly it occurred to me, that it was our last Saturday night on board; whereupon I indited a song to the tune of " To Ladies' eyes around, boys"—and having duly instructed Mr. —— how to "speak the speech," we went to sup-per. *Last*— *last*—dear, dear, what is there in

that word! I don't know one of this ship's company, don't care for some of them — I have led
a loathsome life in it for a month past, and yet
the *last* Saturday night seemed half sad to me.
Mr. ——— sang my song and kept my secret: the
song was encored, and my father innocently
demanded the author; I gave him a tremendous
pinch, and looked very silly. Merit, like murder, will out; so I fancy that when they drank
the health of the author, the whole table was
aware of the genius that sat among them. They
afterwards sang a clever parody of " To all ye
ladies now at land," by Mr. ———, the " canny
Scot," who has kept himself so quiet all the way.
Came to bed at about half-past twelve; while un-
dressing, I heard the captain come down stairs
and announce that we were clear of Nantucket
shoal, and within one hundred and fifty miles of
New York, which intelligence was received with
three cheers. They continued to sing and shout
till very late.

SATURDAY NIGHT SONG.

Come fill the can again, boys,
One parting glass, one parting glass ;
Ere we shall meet again, boys,
Long years may pass, long years may pass.

We'll drink the gallant bark, boys,
That's borne us through, that's borne us through,
Bright waves and billows dark, boys,
Our ship and crew, our ship and crew.

We'll drink those eyes that bright, boys,
With smiling ray, with smiling ray,
Have shone like stars to light, boys,
Our wat'ry way, our wat'ry way.
We'll drink our English home, boys,
Our father land, our father land,
And the shores to which we're come, boys,
A sister strand, a sister strand.

Sunday, September 2d.

Rose at half-past six : the sun was shining
brilliantly ; woke H—— and went on deck with
her. The morning was glorious, the sun had
risen two hours in the sky, the sea was cut
by a strong breeze, and curled into ridges that
came like emerald banks crowned with golden
spray round our ship; she was going through
the water at nine knots an hour. I sat and
watched the line of light that lay like a fairy
road to the east—towards my country, my dear,
dear home.　　＊　　＊　　＊　　＊
　　＊　　＊　　＊　　＊　　＊

Breakfasted at table for the first time since
I've been on board the ship—I did hope, the

last. After breakfast, put my things to rights,
tidied our cabin for prayers, and began looking out the lessons; while doing so, the joyful sound, " Land, land !" was heard aloft. I
rushed on deck, and between the blue waveless
sea, and the bright unclouded sky, lay the wished-
for line of darker element. 'T was Long Island:
through a glass I descried the undulations of
the coast, and even the trees that stood relieved
against the sky. Hail, strange land ! my heart
greets you coldly and sadly ! Oh, how I thought
of Columbus, as with eyes strained and on
tiptoe our water-weary passengers stood, after a
summer's sail of thirty days, welcoming their
mother earth ! The day was heavenly, though
intensely hot, the sky utterly cloudless, and by
that same token, I do not love a cloudless sky.
They tell me that this is their American weather
almost till Christmas; that 's nice, for those who
like frying. Commend me to dear England's
soft, rich, sad, harmonious skies and foliage — commend me to the misty curtain of silver vapour
that hangs over her September woods at morning,
and shrouds them at night; — in short, I am
home-sick before touching land. After lunch,
my father read prayers to us, and that excellent
sermon of dear Mr. Thurstone's on taking the

sacrament. After prayers, came on deck; there were two or three sails in sight — hailed a schooner which passed us — bad news of the cholera — pleasant this — walked about, collected goods and chattels, wrote journal, spent some time in seeing a couple of geese take a sea-swim with strings tied to their legs. After dinner, sat in my cabin some time — walked on deck; when the gentlemen joined us we danced the sun down, and the moon up. The sky was like the jewel-shop of angels; I never saw such brilliant stars nor so deep an azure to hang them in. The moon was grown powerful, and flooded the deck, where we sat playing at blind man's buff, magic music, and singing, and talking of shore till midnight, when we came to bed. I must not forget how happy an omen greeted us this morning. As we stood watching the "*dolce color di oriental zaffiro*," one of the wild wood pigeons of America flew round our mizen-mast, and alighted on the top-sail yard; — this was the first living creature which welcomed us to the New World, and it pleased my superstitious fancy. I would have given any thing to have caught the bird, but after resting itself awhile, it took flight again and left us. We were talking to-day to one of our steerage passengers, a Hud-

dersfield manufacturer, going out in quest of a
living, with five children of his own to take care
of, and two nephews. The father of the latter,
said our Yorkshireman, having married a second
time, and these poor children being as it were
" *thristen* (thrust) out into the world loike—whoy
oi jist took care of them." Verily, verily, he
will have his reward—these tender mercies of
the poor to one another are beautiful, and most
touching.

Monday, September 3d.

I had desired the mate to call me by sunrise,
and accordingly, in the midst of a very sound and
satisfactory sleep, Mr. Curtis shook me roughly by
the arm, informing me that the sun was just about
to rise. The glorious god was quicker at his
toilet than I at mine; for though I did but put on
a dressing-gown and cloak, I found him come out
of his eastern chamber, arrayed like a bridegroom,
without a single beam missing. I called H——,
and we remained on deck watching the clouds like
visions of brightness and beauty, enchanted creations of some strange spell-land—at every moment
assuming more fantastic shapes and gorgeous tints.
Dark rocks seemed to rise, with dazzling sum-

mits of light, pale lakes of purest blue spread
here and there between — the sun now shining
through a white wreath of floating silver, now
firing, with a splendour that the eye shrank from,
the edges of some black cloudy mass. Oh, it
was surpassing ! — We were becalmed, however,
which rather damped all our spirits, and half
made the captain swear. Towards mid-day we
had to thank Heaven for an incident. A brig had
been standing aft against the horizon for some
hours past, and we presently descried a boat
rowing from her towards us. The distance was
some five miles, the sun broiling, we telescoped
and stood on tiptoe, they rowed stoutly, and in
due time boarded us. She was an English brig
from Bristol, had been out eleven weeks, distressed
by contrary winds, and was in want of provisions.
The boat's crew was presently surrounded, grog
was given the men, porter to the captain and
his companion. Our dear captain supplied them
with every thing they wanted, and our poor steerage passengers sent their mite to the distressed
crew in the shape of a sack of potatoes ; they
remained half an hour on board, we clustering
round them, questioning and answering might
and main. As H—— said, they were new faces
at least, and though two of the most ill-favoured

physiognomies I ever set eyes on, there was something refreshing even in their ugly novelty. After this the whole day was one of continual excitement, nearing the various points of land, greeting vessels passing us, and watching those bound on the same course. At about four o'clock a schooner came alongside with a news collector ; he was half devoured with queries ; news of the cholera, reports of the tariff and bank questions were loudly demanded: poor people, how anxiously they looked for replies to the first ! Mr. ——, upon whose arm I leant, turned pale as death while asking how it had visited Boston. Poor fellow ! poor people all ! my heart ached with their anxiety. As the evening darkened, the horizon became studded with sails; at about eight o'clock we discovered the Highlands of Neversink, the entrance to New York harbour, and presently the twin lights of Sandy Hook glimmered against the sky. We were all in high spirits, a fresh breeze had sprung up, we were making rapidly to land; the lovely ship, with all sail set, courtesying along the smooth waters. The captain alone seemed anxious, and was eagerly looking out for the pilot. Some had gathered to the ship's side, to watch the progress of Colonel ——, who had left us and gone into the news-boat, which was dancing like a fairy by the side of our dark vessel. Cheering resounded on all sides, rockets were fired from the ship's stern, we were all dancing, when suddenly a cry was echoed round of " A pilot, a pilot!" and close under the ship's side a light graceful little schooner shot like an arrow through the dim twilight, followed by a universal huzza; she tacked, and lay to, but proved only a news-boat: while, however, all were gathered round the collector, the pilot-boat came alongside, and the pilot on board; the captain gave up the cares and glories of command, and we danced an interminable country dance. All was excitement and joyous confusion; poor Mr. —— alone seemed smitten with sudden anxiety; the cholera reports had filled him with alarm, lest his agent should have died, and his affairs on his arrival be in confusion and ruin — poor fellow! I was very sorry for him. We went down to supper at ten, and were very merry, in spite of the ship's bumping twice or thrice upon the sands. Came up and dawdled upon deck — saw them cast anchor; away went the chain, down dropped the heavy stay, the fair ship swung round, and there lay new York before us, with its clustered lights shining like a distant constellation against the dark outline of land. Remained on deck till very late — were going to bed, when the gentlemen entreated us to join their party once more; we did so, sang all the old songs, laughed at all the old jokes, drank our own and each other's health, wealth, and prosperity, and came to bed at two o'clock. Our cradle rocks no longer, but lies still on the still waters; we have reached our destination; thank God! I did so with all my soul.

Tuesday, September 4th,
New York, America.

It is true, by my faith! it is true; there it is written, here I sit, I am myself and no other, this is New York and nowhere else — Oh! "singular, strange!" Our passengers were all stirring and about at peep of day, and I got up myself at half past six. Trunks lay scattered in every direction around, and all were busily preparing to leave the good ship Pacific. Mercy on us! it made me sad to leave her and my shipmates. I feel like a wretch swept down a river to the open sea, and catch at the last boughs that hang over the banks to stay me from that wide loneliness. The morning was real Manchester. I believe some of the passengers had brought the fog and rain in their English clothes, which they

were all putting on, together with best hats,
dandy cravats, &c.—to make a *sensation*. A fog
hung over the shores of Staten Island and Long
Island, in spite of which, and a dreary, heavy,
thick rain, I thought the hilly outline of the former very beautiful; the trees and grass were
rather sunburnt, but in a fair spring day I should
think it must be lovely. We breakfasted, and
packed ourselves into our shawls and bonnets,
and at half-past nine the steam-boat came alongside to take us to shore: it was different from
any English steam-boat I ever saw, having three
decks, and being consequently a vessel of very
considerable size. We got on board her all in
the rain and misery, and as we drifted on, our
passengers collected to the side of the boat and
gave "The dear old Lady" three cheers. Poor
ship! there she lay—all sails reefed, rocking in
melancholy inaction, deserted by her merry inmates, lonely and idle—poor Pacific! I should
like to return in that ship; I would willingly skip
a passage in order to do so. All were looking at
the shores; some wondering and admiring, others
recognising through the rain and mist, as best
they might; I could not endure to lift my eyes
to the strange land, and even had I done so, was
crying too bitterly to see any thing. Mr. ——

and Mr. —— went to secure apartments for us at the American Hotel; and after bidding good-by to the sea, we packed ourselves into a hackney coach, and progressed. The houses are almost all painted glaring white or red; the other favourite colours appear to be pale straw colour and grey. They have all green venetian shutters, which give an idea of coolness, and almost every house has a tree or trees in its vicinity, which looks pretty and garden-like. We reached our inn,—the gentlemen were waiting for us, and led us to our drawing-room. I had been choking for the last three hours, and could endure no more, but sobbed like a wretch aloud.   *   *

   *   *   *   *   *

There was a piano in the room, to which I flew with the appetite of one who has lived on the music of the speaking-trumpet for a month; that, and some iced lemonade and cake, presently restored my spirits. I went on playing and singing till I was exhausted, and then sat down and wrote journal. Mr. —— went out and got me Sir Humphry Davy's Salmonia, which I had been desiring, and he had been speaking of on board ship.

At five o'clock we all met once more together to dinner. Our drawing-room being large and pleasant, the table was laid in it. 'T is curious how an acquaintanceship of thirty days has contrived to bind together in one common feeling of kindness and good-fellowship persons who never met before, who may never meet again. To-morrow we all separate to betake ourselves each to our several path; and as if loath to part company, they all agreed to meet once more on the eve of doing so, probably for ever. How strongly this clinging principle is inherent in our nature! These men have no fine sympathies of artificial creation, and this exhibition of *adhesiveness* is in them a real and heart-sprung feeling. It touched me — indeed it may well do so; for friends of thirty days are better than utter strangers, and when these my shipmates shall be scattered abroad, there will be no human being left near us whose face we know, or whose voice is familiar to us. Our dinner was a favourable specimen of eating as practised in this new world; every thing good, only in too great a profusion, the wine drinkable, and the fruit beautiful to look at: in point of flavour it was infinitely inferior to English hothouse fruit, or even fine espalier fruit raised in a good aspect. Every thing was wrapped in ice, which is a most luxurious necessary in this hot climate; but the

things were put on the table in a slovenly, out-
landish fashion; fish, soup, and meat, at once,
and puddings, and tarts, and cheese, at another
once; no finger glasses, and a patched table-
cloth,—in short, a want of that style and neatness which is found in every hotel in England.
The waiters, too, reminded us of the half-savage
Highland lads that used to torment us under that
denomination in Glasgow — only that they were
wild Irish instead of wild Scotch. The day had
cleared, and become intensely hot, towards evening softening and cooling under the serene influences of the loveliest moon imaginable. The
streets were brilliantly lighted, the shops through
the trees, and the people parading between them,
reminded me very much of the Boulevards. We
left the gentlemen, and went down stairs, where
I played and sang for three hours. On opening
the door, I found a junta of men sitting on the
hall floor, round it, and smoking. Came up for
coffee; most of the gentlemen were rather elated,
— we sang, and danced, and talked, and seemed
exceeding loath to say good-by. I sat listening
to the dear Doctor's theory of the nature of
the soul, which savoured infinitely more of the
spirituality of the bottle than of immaterial existences. I heard him descant very tipsily upon

the vital principle, until my fatigue getting fairly
the better of my affection for him, I bade our
remaining guests good night, and came to bed.

Wednesday, 5th.

I have been in a sulky fit half the day, because
people will keep walking in and out of our room,
without leave or licence, which is coming a great
deal too soon to Hope's idea of Heaven. I am
delighted to see my friends, but I like to tell them
so, and not that they should take it for granted.
When I made my appearance in my dressing
gown, (my clothes not being come, and the day
too hot for a silk pelisse,) great was my amazement
to find our whole ship's company assembled at the
table. After breakfast they dispersed, and I sat
writing journal, and playing, and singing. Colonel —— and Mr. —— called. Our Boston
friends leave us to-day for their homes. I am
sorry to lose them, though I think H—— will be
the better for rest. Mrs. —— called to see D——
to-day. I remember her name, as one of the first
things I do remember. A visit from a Mr. ——,
one of the directors of the Custom-House, and
W—— P——, brother to the proprietor of the
Park theatre, who is a lawyer of considerable re-

putation here. The face of the first was good, the
other's clever. I said nothing, as usual, and let
them depart in peace. We dined at half-past two,
with the H——s and Mr. ——. At half-past
three we walked down to the quay to convoy them
to their steamboat, which looked indeed like a
" castle on the main." We saw them on board,
went down and looked at the state cabin, which
was a magnificent room, and would have done
charmingly for a galoppade. We bade our new
friends, whom I like better than some old ones,
good-by, and walked briskly on to the battery, to
see them as they passed it. The sun was intensely
hot; and as I struggled forward, hooked up to this
young Sheffield giant, I thought we were the living illustration of Hood's " Long and Short" of
it. We gained the battery, and saw the steam-boat
round; our travellers kept the deck with " hat
and glove and handkerchief," as long as we could
see them. This battery is a beautiful marine parade, commanding the harbour and entrance of
the bay, with Governor's Island, and its dusky red
fort, and the woody shores of New Jersey and
Long Island. A sort of public promenade, formed
of grass plots, planted with a variety of trees,
affords a very agreeable position from whence to
enjoy the lovely view. My companion informed

me that this was a fashionable resort some time ago; but. owing to its being frequented by the lowest and dirtiest of the rabble, who in this land of liberty roll themselves on the grass, and otherwise annoy the more respectable portion of the promenaders, it has been much deserted lately, and is now only traversed by the higher classes as a thoroughfare. The trees and grass were vividly and luxuriantly green; but the latter grew rank and long, unshorn and untidy. " Oh," thought I, " for a pair of English shears, to make these green carpets as smooth and soft and thick as the close piled Genoa velvet." It looked neglected and slovenly. Came home up Broadway, which is a long street of tolerable width, full of shops, in short the American Oxford Road, where all people go to exhibit themselves and examine others. The women that I have seen hitherto have all been very gaily dressed, with a pretension to French style, and a more than English exaggeration of it. They all appear to me to walk with a French shuffle, which, as their pavements are flat, I can only account for by their wearing shoes made in the French fashion, which are enough in themselves to make a waddler of the best walker that ever set foot to earth. Two or three were pretty girls; but the town being quite empty, these are probably bad specimens of the graces and charms that adorn Broadway in its season of shining. Came home and had tea; after which my father, I, and Mr. —— crossed the Park (a small bit of grass enclosed in white palings, in plain English, a green) to the theatre. Wallack was to act in the Rent Day. Mercy, how strange I felt as I once more set foot in a theatre; the sound of the applause set my teeth on edge. The house is pretty though rather gloomy, well formed, about the size of the Haymarket, with plenty of gold carving, and red silk about it, looking rich and warm. The audience was considerable, but all men; scarce, I should think, twenty women in the dress circle, where, by the by, as well as in the private boxes, I saw men sitting with their hats on. The Rent Day is a thorough melodrama, only the German monster has put on a red waistcoat and top boots. Nathless this is a good thing of a bad sort: the incidents, though not all probable, or even as skilfully tacked together as they might be, are striking and dramatically effective, and the whole piece turns on those home feelings, those bitterest realities of every-day life, that wring one's heart, beyond the pain that one allows works of fiction to excite. As for the imitation of Wilkie's pictures, the first was very pretty, but the second I did not see, my face being buried in my handkerchief, besides having a quarter less seven fathom of tears over it, at the time. I cried most bitterly during the whole piece; for as in his very first scene Wallack asks his wife if she will go with him to America, and she replies, " What! leave the farm ?" I set off from thence and ceased no more. The manager's wife and another woman were in the box, which was his, and I thought we should have carried away the front of it with our tears. Wallack played admirably : I had never seen him before, and was greatly delighted with his acting. I thought him handsome of a rustic kind, the very thing for the part he played, a fine English yeoman : he reminded me of ——. At the end of the play, came home with a tremendous headache : sat gossiping and drinking lemonade. Presently a tap at the door came, and through the door came Mr. ——. I shook hands with him, and began expatiating on the impertinence of people's not enquiring down stairs whether we were at home or not before they came up — I don't believe he took my idea. Mr. —— came in to bid us good-by: he starts to-morrow for Baltimore. He is a nice, good-tempered young Irishman, with more tongue than brains, but still clever enough : I am sorry he is going. Came to bed-

room at eleven, remained up till one, unpacking
goods and chattels. Mercy on me, what a cargo
it is! They have treated us like ambassadors,
and not one of our one and twenty huge boxes
have been touched.

Thursday, 6th.

Rose at eight. After breakfast, began writing
to my brother; while doing so they brought
up Captain ——'s and Mr. ——'s cards. I
was delighted to see our dear Captain again,
who, in spite of his glorious slip-slop, is a glorious fellow. They sat some time. Colonel ——
called, — he walks my father off his legs. When
they were all gone, finished letter and wrote
journal. Unpacked and sorted things. Opened
with a trembling heart my bonnet box, and found
my precious *Dévy* squeezed to a crush — I pulled
it out, rebowed, and reblonded, and reflowered it,
and now it looks good enough " pour les *tha*uv-
ages mam*the*lle Fannie." Worked at my muslin
gown; in short, did a deal. A cheating German
woman came here this morning with some bewitching canezous and pelerines: I chose two that
I wanted, and one very pretty one that I didn't;
but as she asked a heathen price for 'em, I took

only the former; — dear good little me ! * We
dined at five. After dinner, sang and played
to my father, " all by the light of the moon."
The evening was, as the day had been, lovely;
and as I stood by his side near the open window,
and saw him inhaling the pure fresh air, which he
said invigorated and revived him, and heard him
exclaim upon the beauty of our surroundings, half
of my regret for this exile melted away. *

    *   *   *   *   *

    *   *   *   *   *

He said to me, " Is there not reason to be grateful to God, when we look at these fair things ? " —
and indeed, indeed, there is : yet these things are
not to me what they were. He told me that he had
begun a song on board ship for the last Saturday
night, but that not feeling well he had given it up,
but the very same ideas I had made use of had
occurred to him.   *   *   *

    *   *   *   *   *

* I do not know how it is to be accounted for, but in spite
of much lighter duties, every article of dress, particularly
silks, embroideries, and all French manufactures, are more
expensive here than in England. The extravagance of the
American women in this part of their expenditure is, considering the average fortunes of this country, quite extraordinary. They never walk in the streets but in the most
showy and extreme toilette, and I have known twenty, forty,
and sixty dollars paid for a bonnet to wear in a morning
saunter up Broadway.

This is not surprising; the ideas were so obvious that there was no escaping them. My father is ten years younger since he came here, already.　　*　　　*　　　*　　　*　　　*
　　　*　　　*　　　*　　　*　　　*

Colonel —— came in after tea, and took my father off to the Bowery theatre. I remained with D—— singing, and stitching, and gossiping till twelve o'clock. My father has been introduced to half the town, and tells me that far from the democratic *Mister*, which he expected to be every man's title here, he had made the acquaintance of a score of municipal dignitaries, and some sixty colonels and major-generals — of militia. Their omnibuses are vehicles of rank, and the *Ladies* Washington, Clinton, and Van Rensalear*, rattle their crazy bones along the pavement for all the world like any other old women of quality.

These democrats are as title-sick as a banker's wife in England. My father told me to-day, that Mr. ——, talking about the state of the country, spoke of the lower orders finding their level: now this enchants me, because a republic is a natural anomaly; there is nothing republican in the construction of the material universe; there

* These are the titles of three omnibuses which run up and down Broadway all the day long.

be highlands and lowlands, lordly mountains as barren as any aristocracy, and lowly valleys as productive as any labouring classes. The feeling of rank, of inequality, is inherent in us, a part of the veneration of our natures; and like most of our properties seldom finds its right channels — in place of which it has created artificial ones suited to the frame of society into which the civilised world has formed itself. I believe in my heart that a republic is the noblest, highest, and purest form of government; but I believe that according to the present disposition of human creatures, 't is a mere beau ideal, totally incapable of realisation. What the world may be fit for six hundred years hence, I cannot exactly perceive ; but in the mean time, 't is my conviction that America will be a monarchy before I am a skeleton.

One of the curses of living at an inn in this unceremonious land: — Dr. —— walked in this evening accompanied by a gentleman, whom he forthwith introduced to us. I behaved very *ill*, as I always do on these occasions; but 't is an impertinence, and I shall take good care to certify such to be my opinion of these free and easy proceedings. The man had a silly manner, but he may be a genius for all that. He abused General Jackson, and said the cholera was owing to his presidency; for that Clay had predicted, that when he came into

power, battle, pestilence, and famine, would come
upon the land: which prophecy finds its accomplishment thus: they have had a war with the Indians, the cholera has raged, and the people, flying from the infected cities to the country, have
eaten half the farmers out of house and home.
This hotel reminds me most extremely of our
"iligant" and untidy apartments in dear, nasty
Dublin, at the Shelbourne. The paper in our
bed-room is half peeling from the walls, our beds
are without curtains, then to be sure there are
pier looking-glasses, and one or two pieces of
showy French furniture in it. 'T is customary,
too, here, I find, for men to sleep three or four in
a room; conceive an Englishman shown into a
dormitory for half-a-dozen; I can't think how
they endure it; but, however, I have a fever at
all those things. My father asked me, this evening, to write a sonnet about the wild pigeons
welcoming us to America; I had thought of it
with scribbling intent before, but he wants me
to get it up here, and that sickened me.

Friday, 7th.

Rose at eight: after breakfast tidied my dressing-box, mended and tucked my white muslin
gown — wrote journal: while doing so, Colonel

—— came to take leave of us for a few days; he is
going to join his wife in the country. Mr. ——
called and remained some time; while he was
here, the waiter brought me word that a Mr. ——
wanted to see me. I sent word down that my
father was out, knowing no such person, and supposing the waiter had mistaken whom he asked
for; but the gentleman persisted in seeing me, and
presently in walked a good-looking elderly man,
who introduced himself as Mr. ——, to whom my
father had letters of introduction. He sat himself
down, and pottered a little, and then went away.
When he was gone, Mr. —— informed me that
this was one of *the* men of New York, in point of
wealth, influence, and consideration. He had
been a great auctioneer, but had retired from
business, having, among his other honours, filled
the office of Mayor of New York. My father and
Mr. —— went to put our letters in the post : I
practised and needle-worked till dinner-time ;
after dinner, as I stood at the window looking at
the lovely sky, and the brilliant earth, a curious
effect of light struck me. Within a hundred yards
of each other, the Town Hall lay, with its white
walls glowing in the sunset, while the tall grey
church-steeple was turning pale in the clear moonlight. That Town Hall is a white-washed anomaly,

and yet its effect is not altogether bad. I took a
bath at the house behind it, which is very con-
veniently arranged for that purpose, with a French
sort of gallery, all papered with the story of
Psyche in lead-coloured paper, that reminded me
of the doughy immortals I used to admire so much,
at the inns at Abbeville and Montreuil. The
house was kept by a foreigner — I knew it. My
father proposed to us a walk, and we accordingly
sallied forth. We walked to the end of Broadway,
a distance of two miles, I should think, and then
back again. The evening was most lovely. The
moon was lighting the whole upper sky, but every
now and then, as we crossed the streets that led
to the river, we caught glimpses of the water, and
woody banks, and the sky that hung over them;
which all were of that deep orange tint, that I
never saw, but in Claude's pictures. After walking nearly a mile up Broadway, we came to Canal
Street: it is broader and finer than any I have yet
seen in New York; and at one end of it, a Christian church, copied from some Pagan temple or
other, looked exceedingly well, in the full flood of
silver light that streamed from heaven. There
were many temptations to look around, but the
flags were so horribly broken and out of order,

that to do so was to run the risk of breaking one's neck : — this is very bad.* The street was very much thronged, and I thought the crowd a more civil and orderly one, than an English crowd. The men did not jostle or push one another, or tread upon one's feet, or kick down one's shoe heels, or crush one's bonnet into one's face, or turn it round upon one's head, all which I have seen done in London streets. There is this to be said : this crowd was abroad merely for pleasure, sauntering along, which is a thing never seen in London; the proportion of idle loungers who frequent the streets there being very inconsiderable, when compared with the number of people going on business through the town. I observed that the young men to-night invariably made room for women to pass, and many of them, as they drew near us, took the segar from their mouth, which I thought especially courteous.† They were all

---

* The New Yorkers have begun to see the evil of their ways, as far as regards their carriage-road in Broadway ; — which is now partly Macadamised. It is devoutly to be hoped, that the worthy authorities will soon have as much compassion on the feet of their fellow-citizens, as they have begun to have for their brutes.

† The roughness and want of refinement, which is legitimately complained of in this country is often however mitigated by instances of civility, which would not be found commonly elsewhere. As I have noticed above, the demean-

smoking, to a man, except those who were spitting, which helped to remind me of Paris, to which the whole place bore a slight resemblance. The shops appear to me to make no show whatever, and will not bear a comparison with the brilliant display of the Parisian streets, or the rich magnificence of our own, in that respect. The women dress very much, and very much like French women gone mad; they all of them seem to me to walk horribly ill, as if they wore tight shoes. Came in rather tired, took tea, sang an immensity, wrote journal, looked at the peerless moon, and now will go to bed.

Saturday, 8th.

Stitching the whole blessed day ; and as I have now no maid to look after them, my clothes run some chance of being decently taken care of, and kept in order. Mr. —— and his daughter called ;

---

our of men towards women in the streets is infinitely more courteous here than with us ; women can walk, too, with perfect safety, by themselves, either in New York, Philadelphia, or Boston : on board the steam-boats no person sits down to table until the ladies are accommodated with seats ; and I have myself in church benefited by the civility of men who have left their pew, and stood, during the whole service, in order to afford me room.

I like him; he appears very intelligent; and the expression of his countenance is clever and agreeable. His daughter was dressed up in French clothes, and looked very stiff; but, however, a first visit is an awkward thing, and nothing that isn't thorough-bred ever does it quite well. When they were gone, Mr. —— called. By the by, of Mr. ——, while he was speaking, he came to the word *calculate*, and stopping half way, substituted another for it, which made me laugh internally. Mercy on me ! how sore all these people are about Mrs. Trollope's book, and how glad I am I did not read it. She must have spoken the truth though, for lies do not rankle so.

" Qui ne nous touche point, ne nous fait pas rougir."

Worked till dinner-time. —— dined with us : what a handsome man he is ; but oh, what a within and without actor. I wonder whether I carry such a brand in every limb and look of me ; if I thought so, I 'd strangle myself. An actor shall be self-convicted in five hundred. There is a ceaseless striving at effect, a straining after points in talking, and a lamp and orange-peel twist in every action. How odious it is to me ! Absolute and unmitigated vulgarity I can put up with, and welcome ; but good Heaven defend me from the

genteel version of vulgarity, to see which in perfection, a country actor, particularly if he is also
manager, and sees occasionally people who be-
speak plays, is your best occasion.   My dear
father, who was a little elated, made me sing to
him, which I greatly gulped at.   When he was
gone, went on playing and singing.   Wrote journal, and now to bed.   I'm dead of the sideache. *

Sunday, 9th.

Rose at eight.   While I was dressing, D——
went out of the room, and presently I heard
sundry exclamations :   " Good God, is it you !
How are you ?   How have you been ?"   I opened
the door, and saw my uncle.   *   *
After breakfast, went to church with my father :
on our way thitherward, met the Doctor, and the
Doctor's friend, and Mr. ——, to whom I have
taken an especial fancy.   The church we went to

---

* Saw a woman riding to-day ; but she has gotten a black
velvet beret upon her head. — Only think of a beret on horseback !   The horses here are none of them properly broken :
their usual pace being a wrong-legged half-canter, or a species
of shambling trot, denominated, with infinite justice, a *rack*.
They are all broken with snaffles instead of curbs, carry their
noses out, and pull horribly ; I have not yet seen a decent
rider, either man or woman.

is situated half way between the Battery and our
hotel. It is like a chapel in the exterior, being
quite plain, and standing close in among the
houses; the interior was large and perfectly
simple. The town is filling, and the church was
well attended. 'Tis long since I have heard the
church service so well read; with so few vices of
pronunciation, or vulgarisms of emphasis. Our
own clergy are shamefully negligent in this point;
and if Chesterfield's maxim be a good one in all
cases, which it is, surely in the matter of the
service of God's house 't is doubly so; they lose
an immense advantage, too, by their slovenly and
careless way of delivering the prayers, which
are in themselves so beautiful, so eloquent, so full
of the very spirit of devotion; that whereas, now, a
congregation seems but to follow their leader, in
gabbling them over as they do; were they solemnly, devoutly, and impressively read, many
would feel and understand, what they now repeat
mechanically, without attaching one idea to the
words they utter. There was no clerk to assist
in the service, and the congregation were as neg-
lectful of the directions in the prayer-book, and as
indolent and remiss in uttering the responses, as
they are in our own churches; indeed, the absence
of the clerk made the inaudibility of the congre-

gation's portion of the service more palpable than
it is with us.   The organ and chanting were very
good; infinitely superior to the performances of
those blessed little parish cherubim, who mono-
polise the praises of God in our churches, so
much to the suffering of all good Christians not
favoured with deafness.   The service is a little
altered — all prayers for our King, Queen, House
of Lords, Parliament, &c., of course omitted: in
lieu of which, they pray for the President and all
existing authorities.   Sundry repetitions of the
Lord's Prayer, and other passages, were left out;
they correct our English, too, substituting the
more modern phraseology of *those*, for the dear
old-fashioned *them*, which our prayer-book uses:
as, " spare thou *those*, O God," instead of " spare
thou *them*, O God, which confess their faults."
Wherever the word wealth occurs, too, these
zealous purists, connecting that word with no idea
but dollars and cents, have replaced it by a term
more acceptable to their comprehension, — prosperity, — therefore they say, " In all time of our
prosperity, (*i. e.* wealth,) in all time of our tribu-
lation," &c.   I wonder how these gentlemen
interpret the word commonwealth, or whether,
in the course of their reading, they ever met with
the word deprived of the final th ; and if so, what

they imagined it meant.* Our prayers were desired for some one putting out to sea; and a very
touching supplication to that effect was read, in
which I joined with all my heart. The sermon
would have been good, if it had been squeezed
into half the compass it occupied; it was upon the
subject of the late terrible visitations with which
God has tried the world, and was sensibly and
well delivered, only it had " damnable iteration."
The day was like an oven; after church, came
home. Mr. —— called, also Mr. ——, the
Boston manager, who is longer than any human
being I ever saw. Presently after, a visit from
" his honour the Recorder," a twaddling old
lawyer by the name of ——, and a silent young
gentleman, his son. They were very droll. The
lawyer talked the most; at every half sentence,
however, quoting, complimenting, or appealing to
" his honour the Recorder," a little, good-tempered, turnippy-looking man, who called me a
female; and who, the other assured me, was the

* The spirit of independence, which is the common atmo-
spheric air of America, penetrates into the churches, as well
as elsewhere. In Boston, I have heard the Apostles' creed
mutilated and altered; once by the omission of the passage
" descended into hell," and another time, by the substitu-
tion of the words " descended into the place of departed
spirits."

Chesterfieldian of New York (I don't know precisely what that means): what fun! Again I
had an opportunity of perceiving how thorough a
chimera the equality is, that we talk of as American. "There's no such thing," with a vengeance!
Here they were, talking of their aristocracy and
democracy; and I'm sure, if nothing else bore
testimony to the inherent love of *higher things*
which I believe exists in every human creature,
the way in which the lawyer dwelt upon the Duke
of Montrose, to whom, in Scotch kindred, he is
allied at the distance of some miles, and Lady
Loughborough, whom Heaven knows how he got
hold of, would have satisfied me, that a my Lord,
or my Lady, are just as precious in the eyes of
these levellers, as in those of Lord and Lady-
loving John Bull himself. They staid pottering a
long time. One thing his "honour the Recorder"
told me, which I wish to remember : that the
only way of preserving universal suffrage from
becoming the worst of abuses, was of course to edu-
cate the people*, for which purpose a provision is

* Unfortunately, this precaution does not fulfil its purpose; universal suffrage is a political fallacy : and will be one
of the stumbling-blocks in the path of this country's great.
ness. I do not mean that it will lessen her wealth, or injure
her commercial and financial resources; but it will be an in-

made by government; thus: a grant of land is given, the revenue of which being estimated, the population of the State are taxed to precisely the same amount; thus furnishing, between the government and the people, an equal sum for the education of all classes.* I do nothing but look out of window all the blessed day long: I did not think in my old age to acquire so Jezebel a trick; but the park (as they entitle the green opposite our windows) is so very pretty, and the streets so gay, with their throngs of smartly dressed women, and so amusing with their abundant proportion of black

---

superable bar to the progress of mental and intellectual cultivation — 't is a plain case of action and re-action. If the mass, *i. e.* the inferior portion, (for when was the mass not inferior?) elect their own governors, they will of course elect an inferior class of governors, and the government of such men will be an inferior government; that it may be just, honest, and rational, I do not dispute; but that it ever will be enlarged, liberal, and highly enlightened, I do not, and cannot, believe.

* I do not know, whether his honour the Recorder's information applied only to the state of New York, or included all the others; 't is not one of the least strange features, which this strange political process, the American government, presents, that each state is governed by its own laws; thus forming a most involved and complicated whole, where each part has its own individual machinery; or, to use a more celestial phraseology, its own particular system.

and white caricatures, that I find my window the
most entertaining station in the world.   Read
Salmonia : the natural-history part of it is curious and interesting; but the local descriptions
are beyond measure tantalising; and the " bites,"
five thousand times more so.   Our ship-mate,
Mr. ——, called : I was glad to see him.   Poor
man ! how we did *reel* him off his legs to be
sure, — what fun it was !   My father dined out :
D—— and I dined *tête-à-tête*.   Poor D——
has not been well to-day : she is dreadfully bitten
by the musquitoes, which, I thank their discrim-
ination, have a thorough contempt for me, and
have not come near me : the only things that bother
me are little black ants, which I find in my wash-
hand basin, and running about in all directions.   I
think the quantity of fruit brings them into the
houses.   After dinner, sat looking at the blacks parading up and down ; most of them in the height of
the fashion, with every colour in the rainbow about
them.   Several of the black women I saw pass
had very fine figures ; (the women here appear to
me to be remarkably small, my own being, I
should think, the average height ;) but the contrast of a bright blue, or pink crape bonnet, with
the black face, white teeth, and glaring blue
whites of the eyes, is beyond description gro-

tesque. The carriages here are all, to my taste, very ugly; hung very high from the ground, and of all manner of ungainly, old-fashioned shapes. Now this is where, I think, the Americans are to be quarrelled with: they are beginning at a time when all other nations are arrived at the highest point of perfection, in all matters conducive to the comfort and elegance of life: they go into these countries; into France, into our own dear little snuggery, from whence they might bring models of whatever was most excellent, and give them to their own manufacturers, to imitate or improve upon. When I see these awkward, uncomfortable vehicles swinging through the streets, and think of the beauty, the comfort, the strength, and lightness of our English-built carriages and cabs, I am much surprised at the want of emulation and enterprise, which can be satisfied with inferiority, when equality, if not superiority, would be so easy.* At seven o'clock, D—— and I

* Whoever pretends to write any account of " Men and Manners" in America must expect to find his own work give him the lie in less than six months; for both men and manners are in so rapid a state of progress that no record of their ways of being and doing would be found correct at the expiration of that term, however much so at the period of its writing. Broadway is not only partly Macadamised since first we arrived here, but there are actually to be seen in it

walked out together. The evening was very beautiful, and we walked as far as Canal Street and back. During our promenade, two fire engines passed us, attended by the usual retinue of shouting children; this is about the sixth fire since yesterday evening. They are so frequent here, that the cry " Fire, fire !" seems to excite neither alarm nor curiosity, and except the above mentioned pains-taking juveniles, none of the inhabitants seem in the least disturbed by it.* We prosecuted our walk down to the Battery, but just as we reached it, we had to return, as 't was tea-time. I was sorry: the whole scene was most lovely. The moon shone full upon the trees and intersecting walks of the promenade, and threw a bright belt of silver along the water's edge. The fresh night wind came over the broad estuary, rippling it, and stirring the boughs with its delicious breath. A building, which was once

---

now, two or three carriages of decent build, with hammer-cloths, foot-boards, and even once or twice lately I have seen footmen standing on those foot-boards !!!

* Perhaps one reason for the perfect coolness with which a fire is endured in New York is the dexterity and courage of the firemen: they are, for the most part, respectable tradesmen's sons, who enlist in this service, rather than the militia; and the vigilance and activity with which their duty is discharged deserves the highest praise.

a fort, from whence the Americans fired upon our ships, is now turned into a sort of *café*, and was brilliantly lighted with coloured lamps, shining among the trees, and reflected in the water. The whole effect was pretty, and very Parisian. We came home, and had tea, after which Mr. —— came in. He told us, that we must not walk alone at night, for that we might get spoken to, and that a friend of his, seeing us go out without a man, had followed us the whole way, in order to see that nothing happened to us : this was very civil. Played and sang, and strove to make that stupid lad sing, but he was shy, and would not open his mouth, even the accustomed hair's breadth. At about eleven he went away; and we came to bed at twelve.

Monday, 10*th.*

Rose at eight. After breakfast wrote journal, and practised for an hour. —— called. I remember taking a great fancy to him about eight years ago, when I was a little girl in Paris; but, mercy, how he is aged ! I wonder whether I am beginning to look old yet, for it seems to me that all the world's in wrinkles. My father went out

with him. Read a canto in Dante; also read
through a volume of Bryant's poetry, which Mr.
—— had lent us, to introduce us to the American
Parnassus. I liked a great deal of it very well;
and I liked the pervading spirit of it much more,
which appears to me hopeful and bright, and what
the spirit of a poet should be; for in spite of all
De Stael's sayings, and Byron's doings, I hold that
melancholy is *not* essentially the nature of a poet.
Though instances may be adduced of great poets
whose Helicon has been but a bitter well of tears,
yet, in itself, the spirit of poetry appears to me to
be too strong, too bright, too full of the elements
of beauty and of excellence, too full of God's own
nature, to be dark or desponding; and though
from the very fineness of his mental constitution
a poet shall suffer more intensely from the baseness
and the bitterness which are the leaven of life,
yet he, of all men, the most possesses the power
to discover truth, and beauty, and goodness, where
they do exist; and where they exist not, to create
them. If the clouds of existence are darker, its
sunshine is also brighter to him; and while others,
less gifted, lose themselves in the labyrinth of life,
his spirit should throw light upon the darkness,
and he should walk in peace and faith over the
stormy waters, and through the uncertain night;

standing as 't were above the earth, he views with clearer eyes its mysteries; he finds in apparent discord glorious harmony, and to him the sum of all is good; for, in God's works, good still abounds to the subjection of evil. 'T is this trustful spirit that seems to inspire Bryant, and to me, therefore, his poetry appears essentially good. There is not much originality in it. I scarce think there can be in poems so entirely descriptive : his descriptions are very beautiful, but there is some sameness in them, and he does not escape self-repetition; but I am a bad critic, for which I thank God ! I know the tears rolled down my cheeks more than once as I read; I know that agreeable sensations and good thoughts were suggested by what I read ; I thought some of it beautiful, and all of it wholesome (in contradistinction to the literature of this age), and I was well pleased with it altogether. Afterwards read a sort of satirical burlesque, called " Fanny," by Hallek : the wit being chiefly confined to local allusions and descriptions of New York manners, I could not derive much amusement from it. * * * *

* * * * *

* * * * *

When my father came home, went with him to call on Mrs. ———. What I saw of the house

appeared to me very pretty, and well adapted to
the heat of the season. A large and lofty room,
paved with India matting, and furnished with white
divans, and chairs, no other furniture encumbering
or cramming it up; it looked very airy and cool.
Our hostess did not put herself much out of the
way to entertain us, but after the first " how do
you do," continued conversing with another visiter,
leaving us to the mercy of a very pretty young
lady, who carried on the conversation at an
average of a word every three minutes. Neither
Mr. —— nor his eldest daughter were at home ;
the latter, however, presently came in, and relieved
her sister and me greatly. We sat the proper
time, and then came away.   *   *

*   *   *   *   *

This is a species of intercourse I love not any
where. I never practised it in my own blessed
land, neither will I here. We dined at six : after
dinner played and sang till eight, and then walked
out with D—— and my father, by the most
brilliant moonlight in the world. We went down
to the Battery ; the aquatic Vauxhall was lighted
up very gaily, and they were sending up rockets
every few minutes, which, shooting athwart the
sky, threw a bright stream of light over the
water, and falling back in showers of red stars,

seemed to sink away before the steadfast shining
of the moon, who held high supremacy in heaven.
The bay lay like molten silver under her light,
and every now and then a tiny skiff, emerging
from the shade, crossed the bright waters, its dark
hull and white sails relieved between the shining
sea and radiant sky. Came home at nine, tea'd
and sat embroidering till twelve o'clock, industrious little me.

Tuesday, 11*th.*

This day week we landed in New York; and
this day was its prototype, rainy, dull, and dreary;
with occasional fits of sunshine, and light delicious
air, as capricious as a fine lady. After breakfast,
Colonel —— called. Wrote journal, and practised till one o'clock. My father then set off
with Colonel —— for Hoboken, a place across
the water, famous once for duelling, but now the
favourite resort of a turtle-eating club, who go
there every Tuesday to cook and swallow turtle.
The day was as bad as a party of pleasure could
expect, (and when were their expectations of bad
weather disappointed?) nathless, my father, at
the Colonel's instigation, *persevered,* and went
forth, leaving me his card of invitation, which

made me scream for half an hour ; the wording as follows : — " Sir, the Hoboken Turtle Club will meet at the grove, for *spoon exercise*, on Tuesday, the 11th inst., by order of the President." Mr. —— and the Doctor paid us a visit of some length.   *   *   *   *
         *   *   *   *   *

When they were gone, read a canto in Dante, and sketched till four o'clock. I wish I could make myself draw. I want to do every thing in the world that can be done, and, by the by, that reminds me of my German, which I must *persecute*. At four o'clock sent for a hair-dresser, that I might in good time see that I am not made an object on my first night. He was a Frenchman, and after listening profoundly to my description of the head-dress I wanted, replied, as none but a Frenchman could, " *Madame, la difficulté n'est pas d'executer votre coiffure mais de la bien concevoir.*" However, he conceived and executed sundry very smooth-looking bows, and, upon the whole, dressed my hair very nicely, but charged a dollar for so doing ; O nefarious. D—— and I dined *tête-à-tête ;* the evening was sulky — I was in miserable spirits.   *   *   *
         *   *   *   *   *

Sat working till my father came home, which he did at about half past six. His account of his dinner was any thing but delightful; to be sure he has no taste for rainy ruralities, and his feeling description of the damp ground, damp trees, damp clothes, and damp atmosphere, gave me the *rheumatiz*, letting alone that they had nothing to eat but turtle, and that out of iron spoons,— " Ah, you vill go a pleasuring." * * *

* * * * *

He had a cold before, and I fear this will make him very ill. He went like wisdom to take a vapour bath directly. —— came, and sat with us till he returned. Had tea at eight, and embroidered till midnight. The wind is rioting over the earth. I should like to see the Hudson now. The black clouds, like masses of dark hair, are driven over the moon's pale face, the red lights and fire engines are dancing up and down the streets, the church bells are all tolling — 't is sad and strange.

> 'T is all in vain, it may not last,
> The sickly sunlight dies away,
> And the thick clouds that veil the past,
> Roll darkly o'er my present day.
>
> Have I not flung them off, and striven
> To seek some dawning hope in vain;
> Have I not been for ever driven
> Back to the bitter past again?

What though a brighter sky bends o'er
Scenes where no former image greets me,
Though lost in paths untrod before,
Here, even here, pale Memory meets me.

Oh life — oh blighted bloomless tree!
Why cling thy fibres to the earth?
Summer can bring no flower to thee,
Autumn no bearing, spring no birth.

Bid me not strive, I'll strive no more,
To win from pain my joyless breast;
Sorrow has ploughed too deeply o'er
Life's Eden — let it take the rest!

Wednesday, 12th.

Rose at eight.   After breakfast, heard my father
say Hamlet.   How beautiful his whole conception
of that part is, and yet it is but an actor's conception too.   *   *   *   *
            *   *   *   *   *

I am surprised at any body's ever questioning the
real madness of Hamlet: I know but one passage
in the play which tells against it, and there are a
thousand that go to prove it.   But leaving all
isolated parts out of the question, the entire colour
of the character is the proper ground from which
to draw the right deduction.   Gloomy, despond-

ing, ambitious, and disappointed in his ambition, full of sorrow for a dead father, of shame for a living mother, of indignation for his ill-filled inheritance, of impatience at his own dependent position; of a thoughtful, doubtful, questioning spirit, looking with timid boldness from tho riddles of earth and life, to those of death and the mysterious land beyond it; weary of existence upon its very threshold, and withheld alone from self-destruction by religious awe, and that pervading uncertainty of mind which stands on the brink, brooding over the unseen may-be of another world; in love, moreover, and sad and dreamy in his affection, as in every other sentiment; for there is not enough of absolute passion in his love to make it a powerful and engrossing interest; had it been such, the entireness and truth of Hamlet's character would have been destroyed. 'T is love indeed, but a pulseless, powerless love; gentle, refined, and tender, but without ardour or energy; such are the various elements of Hamlet's character, at the very beginning of the play: then see what follows. A frightful and unnatural visitation from the dead; a horrible and sudden revelation of the murder of the father, for whom his soul is in mourning; thence burning hatred and thirst of vengeance against his uncle; double

loathing of his mother's frailty; above all, that
heaviest burden that a human creature can have
put upon him, an imperative duty calling for fulfilment, and a want of resolution and activity to
meet the demand; thence an unceasing struggle
between the sluggish nature and the upbraiding
soul; an eternal self-spurring and self-accusing,
from which mental conflict, alone sufficient to un-
seat a stronger mind, he finds relief in fits of
desponding musing, the exhaustion of over-
wrought powers.   Then comes the vigilant and
circumspect guard he is forced to keep upon every
word, look, and action, lest they reveal his terrible
secret; the suspicion and mistrust of all that surround him, authorised by his knowledge of his
uncle's nature; his constant watchfulness over the
spies that are set to watch him; then come, in the
course of events, Polonius's death, the uninten-
tional work of his own sword, the second appa-
rition of his father's ghost, his banishment to
England, still haunted by his treacherous friends,
the miserable death of poor Ophelia, together
with the unexpected manner of his first hearing of
it — if all these — the man's own nature, sad and
desponding — his educated nature (at a German
university), reasoning and metaphysical — and the
nature he acquires from the tutelage of events,

bitter, dark, amazed, and uncertain; if these do not make up as complete a madman as ever walked between heaven and earth, I know not what does.* Wrote journal, and began to practise; while doing so, —— called; he said that he was accompanied by some friends who wished to see me, and were at the door. I 've heard of men's shutting the door in the face of a dun, and going out the back way to escape a bailiff—but how to get rid of such an attack as this I knew not, and was therefore fain to beg the gentlemen would walk in, and accordingly in they walked, four as fine grown men as you would wish to see on a summer's day. I was introduced to this regiment man by man, and thought, as my Sheffield friend would say, "If *them* be American manners, defend me from them." They are traders, to be sure; but I never heard of such wholesale introduction in my life. They sat a little while, behaved very

---

* I have lately read Goethe's Wilhelm Meister. In that wonderful analysis of the first work of our master-mind by his German peer, all has been said upon this subject that the most philosophical reason, or poetical imagination, can suggest; and who that has read it can forget that most appropriate and beautiful simile, wherein Hamlet's mind is likened to an acorn planted in a porcelain vase — the seed becomes living — the roots expand — and the fragile vessel bursts into a thousand shivers.

like Christians, and then departed. Captain ——
and —— called, — the former to ask us to come
down and see the Pacific, poor old lady ! When
they were gone, practised, read a canto in Dante,
and translated verbatim a German fable, which
kept me till dinner-time. After dinner, walked
out towards the Battery. —— joined us. It was
between sunset and moonrise, and a lovelier light
never lay upon sea, earth, and sky. The horizon
was bright orange colour, fading as it rose to pale
amber, which died away again into the modest
violet colour of twilight; this possessed the main
sky wholly, except where two or three masses of
soft dark purple clouds floated, from behind which
the stars presently winked at us with their bright
eyes. The river lay as still as death, though
there was a delicious fresh air : tiny boats were
stealing like shadows over the water ; and every
now and then against the orange edge of the sky
moved the masts of some schooner, whose hull
was hidden in the deep shadow thrown over it by
the Jersey coast. A band was playing in the
Castle garden, and not a creature but ourselves
seemed abroad to see all this loveliness. Fashion
makes the same fools all the world over; and
Broadway, with its crowded dusty pavement, and
in the full glare of day, is preferable, in the eyes

of the New York promenaders, to this cool and beautiful walk. Came home at about nine. On the stairs met that odious Dr. ——, who came into the drawing-room without asking or being asked, sat himself down, and called me " Miss Fanny." I should like to have thrown my tea at him ! —— sent up his name and presently followed it. I like to see any of our fellow-passengers, however little such society would have pleased me under any other circumstances ; but necessity " makes us acquainted with strange bedfellows ; " and these my ship-mates will, to the end of time, be my very good friends and boon companions. My father went to the Park theatre, to see a man of the name of Hacket give an American entertainment after Matthews's at-home fashion. I would not go, but staid at home looking at the moon, which was glorious.   *   *   *

  *   *   *   *   *

  *   *   *   *   *

To-night, as I stood watching that surpassing sunset, I would have given it all — gold, and purple, and all — for a wreath of English fog stealing over the water.

Thursday, 13*th.*

Rose late : there was music in the night, which is always a strange enchantment to me. After breakfast, wrote journal. At eleven, Captain —— and —— called for us; and my uncle having joined us, we proceeded to the slip, as they call the places where the ships lie, and which answer to our docks. Poor dear Pacific ! I ran up her side with great glee, and was introduced to Captain ——, her old commander ; rushed down into my berth, and was actually growing pathetic over the scene of my sea-sorrows, when Mr. ——- clapped his hands close to me, and startled me out of my reverie. Certainly my *adhesiveness* must either be very large, or uncommonly active just now, for my heart yearned towards the old timbers with exceeding affection. The old ship was all drest out in her best, and after sitting for some time in our cabin, we adjourned to the larger one and lunched. Mr. —— joined our party ; and we had one or two of our old ship songs, with their ridiculous burdens, with due solemnity. Saw Mr. ——, but not dear M. ——. Visited the forecastle, whence I have watched such glorious sunsets, such fair uprisings of the

starry sisterhood; now it looked upon the dusty
quay and dirty dock water, and the graceful sails
were all stripped away, and the bare masts and
rigging shone in the intense sunlight.   Poor good
ship, I wish to Heaven my feet were on her deck,
and her prow turned to the east.   I would not
care if the devil himself drove a hurricane at our
backs.   Visited the fish and fruit markets * : it
was too late in the day to see either to advantage,
but the latter reminded me of Aladdin's treasure :
the heaps of peaches, filling with their rich
downy balls high baskets ranged in endless rows,
and painted of a bright vermilion colour, which
threw a ruddy ripeness over the fruit.   The enormous baskets (such as are used in England to
carry linen) piled with melons, the wild grapes,
the pears and apples, all so plenteous, so fragrant,

* The fish of these waters may be excellent in the water ;
but owing to the want of care and niceness with which they
are kept after being caught, they are very seldom worth eating
when brought to table.   They have no turbot or soles, a
great national misfortune : their best fish are rock-fish, bass,
shad, (an excellent herring, as big as a small salmon,) and
sheep's head.   Cod and salmon I have eaten ; but from the
above cause they were never comparable to the same fish at
an English table.   The lobsters, crabs, and oysters are all
gigantic, frightful to behold, and not particularly well-
flavoured : their size makes them tough and coarse.

so beautiful in form and colour, leading the mind to the wondrous bounteousness which has dowered this land with every natural treasure — the whole enchanted me. ——, to my horror, bought a couple of beautiful live wild-pigeons, which he carried home, head downwards, one in each coat pocket. We parted from him at the park gate, and proceeded to Murray Street, to look at the furnished house my father wishes to take. Upon enquiry, however, we found that it was already let. The day was bright and beautiful, and my father proposed crossing the river to Hoboken, the scene of the turtle-eating expedition. We did so accordingly: himself, D——, Mr. ——, and I. Steamers go across every five minutes, conveying passengers on foot and horseback, gigs, carriages, carts, any thing and every thing. The day was lovely — the broad, bright river was gemmed with a thousand sails. Away to the right it stretched between richly wooded banks, placid and blue as a lake; to the left, in the rocky doorway of the narrows, two or three ships stood revealed against the cloudless sky. We reached the opposite coast, and walked. It was nearly three miles from where we landed to the scene of the " *spoon-exercise*." The whole of our route lay through a beautiful wild plantation,

or rather strip of wood, I should say, for 't is
nature's own gardening which crowns the high
bank of the river; through which trellice-work of
varied foliage, we caught exquisite glimpses of the
glorious waters, the glittering city, and the opposite banks, decked out in all the loveliest contrast
of sunshine and shade. As we stood in our leafy
colonnade looking out upon this fair scene, the
rippling water made sweet music far down below
us, striking with its tiny silver waves the smooth
sand and dark-coloured rocks from which they
were ebbing. Many of the trees were quite new
to me, and delighted me with their graceful forms
and vivid foliage. The broad-leaved catalpa, and
the hickory with its bright coral-coloured berries.
Many lovely, lowly things, too, grew by our path-
side, which we gathered as we passed, to bring
away, but which withered in our hands ere we
returned. Gorgeous butterflies were zig-zagging
through the air, and for the first time I longed to
imprison them. In pursuing one, I ran into the
midst of a slip of clover land, but presently
jumped out again, on hearing the swarms of grass-
hoppers round me. Mr. —— caught one; it
was larger and thicker than the English grass-
hopper, and of a dim mottled brown colour, like
the plumage of our common moth; but presently

on his opening his hand to let it escape, it spread
out a pair of dark purple wings, tipped with pale
primrose colour, and flew away a beautiful but-
terfly, such as the one I had been seduced by.
The slips of grass ground on the left of our path
were the only things that annoyed me : they were
ragged, and rank, and high, — they wanted mow-
ing; and if they had been mowed soft, and thick,
and smooth, like an English lawn, how gloriously
the lights and shadows of this lovely sky would
fall through the green roof of this wood upon
them.   There is nothing in nature that, to my
fancy, receives light and shade with as rich an
effect as sloping lawn land.   Oh ! England,
England ! how I have seen your fresh emerald
mantle deepen and brighten in a summer's day.
About a hundred yards from the place where they
dined on Tuesday, with no floor but the damp
earth, no roof but the dripping trees, stands a sort
of *café ;* a long, low, pretty Italianish-looking
building.   The wood is cleared away in front of
it, and it commands a lovely view of the Hudson
and its opposite shores : and here they might
have been sheltered and comfortable, but I suppose it was not yet the appointed day of the
month with them for eating their dinner within
walls ; and, rather than infringe on an established

rule, they preferred catching a cold apiece. The
place where they met in the open air is extremely
beautiful, except, of course, on a rainy day. The
shore is lower just here; and though there are
trees enough to make shade all round, and a thick
screen of wood and young undergrowth behind,
the front is open to the river, which makes a bend
just below, forming a lake-like bay, round which
again the coast rises into rocky walls covered with
rich foliage. Upon one of these promontories, in
the midst of a high, open knoll, surrounded and
overhung by higher grounds covered with wood,
stood the dwelling of the owner of the land, high
above the river, overlooking its downward course
to the sea, perched like an eagle's aërie, half-way
between heaven and the level earth, but beautifully encircled with waving forests, a shade in
summer and a shelter in winter. My father,
D——, and my bonnet sat down in the shade.
Mr. —— and I clambered upon some pieces of
rock at the water's edge, whence we looked out
over river and land — a fair sight. "Oh!" I exclaimed, pointing to the highlands on our left,
through whose rich foliage the rifted granite
looked cold and grey, "what a place for a
scramble! there must be lovely walks there."
"Ay," returned my companion, "and a few

rattle-snakes too." * We found D——, my father, and my bonnet buffeting with a swarm of musquitoes; this is a great nuisance. We turned our steps homeward. I picked up a nut enclosed like a walnut in a green case. I opened it; it was not ripe; but in construction exactly like a walnut, with the same bitter filmy skin over the fruit, which is sweet and oily, and like a walnut in flavour also. Mr. —— told me it was called a marrow-nut. The tree on which it grew had foliage of the acacia kind. We had to rush to meet the steam-boat, which was just going across: the whole walk reminded me of that part of Oattands which, from its wild and tangled wood-land, they call America.   *   *   *
   *   *   *   *   *

There must have been something surpassingly beautiful in our surroundings, for even Mr. ——, into whose composition I suspect much of the poetical element does not enter, began expatiating on the happiness of the original possessors of these fair lands and waters, the Indians — the Red

* My friend was entertaining himself, at the expense of my credulity, in making this assertion. The rattle-snakes and red Indians have fled together before the approach of civilisation; and it would be as difficult to find the one as the other in the vicinity of any of the large cities of the northern states.

Children of the soil, who followed the chase through these lovely wildernesses, and drove their light canoes over these broad streams — " great nature's happy commoners,"—till the predestined curse came on them, till the white sails of the invaders threw their shadow over these seas, and the work of extermination began in these wild fastnesses of freedom. The destruction of the original inhabitants of a country by its discoverers, always attended, as it is, with injustice and cruelty, appears to me one of the most mysterious dispensations of Providence.

The chasing, enslaving, and destroying creatures, whose existence, however inferior, is as justly theirs, as that of the most refined European is his; who, for the most part, too, receive their enemies with open-handed hospitality, until taught treachery by being betrayed, and cruelty by fear; the driving the child of the soil off it, or, what is fifty times worse, chaining him to till it; all the various forms of desolation which have ever followed the landing of civilised men upon uncivilised shores; in short, the theory and practice of discovery and conquest, as recorded in all history, is a very singular and painful subject of contemplation.

'T is true that cultivation and civilisation, the

VOL.

arts and sciences that render life useful, the knowledge that ennobles, the adornments that refine
existence, above all, the religion that is the most
sacred trust and dear reward, all these, like pure
sunshine and healthful airs following a hurricane,
succeed the devastation of the invader; but the
sufferings of those who are swept away are not
the less; and though I believe that good alone is
God's result, it seems a fearful proof of the evil
wherewith this earth is cursed, that good cannot
progress but over such a path. No one, beholding
the prosperous and promising state of this fine
country, could wish it again untenanted of its
enterprising and industrious possessors; yet even
while looking with admiration at all that they
have achieved, with expectation amounting to certainty to all that they will yet accomplish, 't is
difficult to refrain from bestowing some thoughts
of pity and of sadness upon those whose homes
have been overturned, whose language has passed
away, and whose feet are daily driven further from
those territories of which they were once sole and
sovereign lords. How strange it is to think, that
less than one hundred years ago, these shores,
resounding with the voice of populous cities, —
these waters, laden with the commerce of the wide
world, — were silent wildernesses, where sprang and

fell the forest leaves, where ebbed and flowed the
ocean tides from day to day, and from year to
year in uninterrupted stillness; where the great
sun, who looked on the vast empires of the East,
its mouldering kingdoms, its lordly palaces, its
ancient temples, its swarming cities, came and
looked down upon the still dwelling of utter loneliness, where nature sat enthroned in everlasting
beauty, undisturbed by the far-off din of worlds
" beyond the flood." *

* It is two years since I visited Hoboken for the first
time; it is now more beautiful than ever. The good taste
of the proprietor has made it one of the most picturesque
and delightful places imaginable; it wants but a good carriage-road along the water's edge (for which the ground lies
very favourably) to make it as perfect a public promenade
as any European city can boast, with the advantage of such a
river, for its principal object, as none of them possess.

I think the European traveller, in order to form a just
estimate both of the evils and advantages deriving from the
institutions of this country, should spend one day in the
streets of New York, and the next in the walks of Hoboken.
If in the one, the toil, the care, the labour of mind and body,
the outward and visible signs of the debasing pursuit of
wealth, are marked in melancholy characters upon every man
he meets, and bear witness to the great curse of the country;
in the other, the crowds of happy, cheerful, enjoying beings
of that order, which, in the old world, are condemned to
ceaseless and ill-requited labour, will testify to the blessings
which counterbalance that curse. I never was so forcibly
struck with the prosperity and happiness of the lower orders

Came home rather tired : my father asked
Mr. —— to dine with us, but he could not. After

---

of society in this country as yesterday returning from Hoboken.   The walks along the river and through the woods,
the steamers crossing from the city, were absolutely thronged
with a cheerful, well-dressed population abroad, merely for
the purpose of pleasure and exercise. Journeymen, labourers,
handicraftsmen, trades-people, with their families, bearing all
in their dress and looks evident signs of well-being and con-
tentment, were all flocking from their confined avocations,
into the pure air, the bright sunshine, and beautiful shade of
this lovely place.   I do not know any spectacle which could
give a foreigner, especially an Englishman, a better illustration of that peculiar excellence of the American government
— the freedom and happiness of the lower classes.   Neither
is it to be said that this was a holyday, or an occasion of
peculiar festivity — it was a common week-day — such as
our miserable manufacturing population spends from sun-rise
to sun-down, in confined, incessant, unhealthy toil — to earn,
at its conclusion, the inadequate reward of health and happiness so wasted.   The contrast struck me forcibly — it rejoiced my heart; it surely was an object of contemplation, that
any one who had a heart must have rejoiced in.   Presently,
however, came the following reflections : —_These people
are happy — their wants are satisfied, their desires fulfilled —
their capacities of enjoyment meet with full employment —
they are well fed — well clothed — well housed — moderate
labour insures them all this, and leaves them leisure for such
recreations as they are capable of enjoying; but how is it with
me ? — and I mean not *me myself* alone, but all who, like myself, have received a higher degree of mental cultivation,
whose estimate of happiness is, therefore, so much higher,
whose capacity for enjoyment is so much more expanded and

dinner, sat working till ten o'clock, when ——
came to take leave of us. He is going off to-
morrow morning to Philadelphia, but will be back
for our Tuesday's dinner. The people here are
all up and about very early in the morning. I went
out at half-past eight, and found all Broadway
abroad.

---

cultivated; — can I be satisfied with a race in a circular rail-
road car, or a swing between the lime-trees? where are my
peculiar objects of pleasure and recreation? where are the
picture-galleries — the sculptures — the works of art and
science — the countless wonders of human ingenuity and
skill — the cultivated and refined society — the intercourse
with men of genius, literature, scientific knowledge — where
are all the sources from which I am to draw my recreations?
They are not. The heart of a philanthropist may indeed be
satisfied, but the intellectual man feels a dearth that is inex-
pressibly painful; and in spite of the real and great pleasure
which I derived from the sight of so much enjoyment, I
could not help desiring that enjoyment of another order were
combined with it. Perhaps the two are incompatible; if so,
I would not alter the present state of things if I could.

The losers here are decidedly in the minority. Indeed, so
much so, as hardly to form a class; they are a few individuals,
scattered over the country, and of course their happiness
ought not to come into competition with that of the mass of
the people; but the Americans, at the same time that they
make no provision whatever for the happiness of such a portion of their inhabitants, would be very angry if one were to
say it was a very inconsiderable one, and yet that is the
truth.

Friday, 1*4th.*

Forget all about it, except that I went about the
town with Colonel ——.   *   *   *
      *   *   *   *   *
went to see his Quaker wife, whom I liked very
much.   *   *   *   *   *
      *   *   *   *   *

Drove all about New York, which more than ever
reminded me of the towns in France : passed the
Bowery theatre, which is a handsome, finely-pro-
portioned building, with a large brazen eagle
plastered on the pediment, for all the world like an
insurance mark, or the sign of the spread eagle :
this is nefarious ! We passed a pretty house,
which Colonel —— called an old mansion ; mercy
on me, him, and it ! Old ! I thought of Warwick
Castle, of Hatfield, of Checquers, of Hopwood,
— old, and there it stood, with its white pillars
and Italian-looking portico, for all the world like
one of our own cit's yesterday-grown boxes. Old,
quotha ! the woods and waters, and hills and skies
alone are old here; the works of men are in the very
greenness and unmellowed imperfection of youth;
true, 'tis a youth full of vigorous sap and glorious
promise ; spring, laden with blossoms, foretelling

abundant and rich produce, and so let them be proud of it. But the worst of it is, the Americans are not satisfied with glorying in what they are, — which, considering the time and opportunities they have had, is matter of glory quite sufficient,— they are never happy without comparing this their sapling to the giant oaks of the old world, — and what can one say to that? *Is* New York like London? No, by my two troths it is not; but· the oak was an acorn once, and New York will surely, if the world holds together long enough, become a lordly city, such as we know of beyond the sea.

Went in the evening to see Wallack act the Brigand; it was his benefit, and the house was very good. He is perfection in this sort of thing, yet there were one or two blunders even in his melo-dramatic acting of this piece; however, he looks very like the thing, and it is very nice to see — once.

Saturday, 15*th.*

Sat stitching all the blessed day. So we are to go to *Philadelphia* before *Boston.* I'm sorry. The H——s will be disappointed, and I shall get no riding, *che seccatura!* At five dressed, and

went to the ——, where we were to dine. This is
one of the first houses here, so I conclude that
I am to consider what I see as a tolerable sample
of the ways and manners of being, doing, and suffering of the *best society* in New York. There
were about twenty people; the women were in a
sort of French demi-toilette, with bare necks, and
long sleeves, heads frizzed out after the very last
petit courier, and thread net handkerchiefs and
capes; the whole of which, to my English eye,
appeared a strange marrying of incongruities.
The younger daughter of our host is beautiful; a
young and brilliant likeness of Ellen Tree, with
more refinement, and a smile that was, not to say
a ray, but a whole focus of sun rays, a perfect
blaze of light; she was much taken up with a
youth, to whom, my neighbour at dinner informed
me, she was engaged.   *   *   *
        *   *   *   *   *

The women here, like those of most warm climates,
ripen very early, and decay proportionably soon.
They are, generally speaking, pretty, with good
complexions, and an air of freshness and brilliancy, but this, I am told, is very evanescent; and
whereas, in England, a woman is in the full bloom
of health and beauty from twenty to five-and-
thirty, here they scarcely reach the first period

without being faded and looking old.* They marry very young, and this is another reason why age comes prematurely upon them. There was a fair young thing at dinner to-day, who did not look above seventeen, and she was a wife. As for their figures, like those of French women, they are too well dressed for one to judge exactly what they are really like: they are, for the most part, short and slight, with remarkably pretty feet and ankles; but there's too much pelerine and petticoat, and " de quoi" of every sort to guess any thing more.   *   *   *   *

　　　*   *   *   *   *

　　　*   *   *   *   *

There was a Mr. ——, the magnus Apollo of New York, who is a musical genius : sings as well as any gentleman need sing, pronounces Italian well, and accompanies himself without false chords; all which renders him *the* man round whom (as round H——, G——, Lord C——, and that pretty Lord O——, in our own country,)

---

* The climate of this country is the scape-goat upon which all the ill looks and ill health of the ladies is laid; but while they are brought up as effeminately as they are, take as little exercise, live in rooms like ovens during the winter, and marry as early as they do, it will appear evident that many causes combine with an extremely variable climate, to sallow their complexions, and destroy their constitutions.

the women listen and languish. He sang the
Phantom Bark : the last time I heard it was from
the lips of Moore, with two of the loveliest faces
in all the world hanging over him, Mrs. N——,
and Mrs. B——. By the by, the man who sat
next me at dinner was asking me all manner of
questions about Mrs. N——; among others, whether she was " as pale as a poetess ought to be ! "
Oh ! how I wish Corinne had but heard that
herself ! what a deal of funny scorn would have
looked beautiful on her rich brown cheek and
brilliant lips. The dinner was plenteous, and
tolerably well dressed, but ill served : there were
not half servants enough, and we had neither
water-glasses nor finger-glasses. Now, though I
don't eat with my fingers, (except peaches, whereat
I think the aborigines, who were paring theirs
like so many potatoes, seemed rather amazed,) yet
do I hold a finger-glass at the conclusion of my
dinner a requisite to comfort. After dinner we
had coffee, but no tea, whereat my English taste
was in high dudgeon. The gentlemen did not
sit long, and when they joined us, Mr. ——, as I
said before, uttered sweet sounds. By the by, I
was not a little amused at Mrs. —— asking me
whether I had heard of his singing, or their
musical soirees, and seeming all but surprised that

I had no revelations of either across the Atlantic.
Mercy on me! what fools people are all over the
world! The worst is, they are all fools of the
same sort, and there is no profit whatever in travelling. Mr. B——, who is an Englishman,
happened to ask me if I knew Captain ——,
whereupon we immediately struck up a conversation, and talked over English folks and doings
together, to my entire satisfaction. The ——
were there: he is brother to that wondrous ruler
of the spirits whom I did so dislike in London,
and his lady is a daughter of Lord ——.   *

        *   *   *   *   *

        *   *   *   *   *

I was very glad to come home. I sang to them
two or three things, but the piano was pitched too
high for my voice; by the by, in that large, lofty,
fine room, they had a tiny, old-fashioned, be-
curtained cabinet piano stuck right against the wall,
unto which the singer's face was turned, and into
which his voice was absorbed. We had hardly
regained our inn and uncloaked, when there came
a tap at the door, and in walked Mr. —— to ask
me if we would not join them (himself and the
——) at supper. He said that, besides five being
a great deal too early to dine, he had not half
dinner enough; and then began the regular English

quizzing of every thing and every body we had left
behind.   Oh dear, oh dear ! how thoroughly
English it was, and how it reminded me of H——— ;
of course, we did not accept their invitation, but
it furnished me matter of amusement.   How we
English folks do cling to our own habits, our own
views, our own things, our own people ; how, in
spite of all our wanderings and scatterings over
the whole face of the earth, like so many Jews, we
never lose our distinct and national individuality ;
nor fail to lay hold of one another's skirts, to laugh
at and depreciate all that differs from that country,
which we delight in forsaking for any and all
others.

Sunday, 16th.

Rose at eight. After breakfast, walked to church
with the C———s and Mr. B———.   They went
to Grace church for the music ; we stopped short
to go to the ——— pew in the Episcopal church.
The pew was crammed, I am sorry to say, owing
to our being there, which they had pressed so
earnestly, that we thought ourselves bound to accept
the invitation.   The sermon was tolerably good ;
better than the average sermons one hears in London, and sufficiently well delivered.   After church,

I—— called, also two men of the name of M——,
large men, very ! also Mr. B—— and Mr. C—— :
when they were all gone, wrote journal, and began
a letter to J——. Dined at five ; after dinner,
went on with my letter to J——, and wrote an
immense one to dear H——, which kept me pen
in hand till past twelve.   A tremendous thunder
storm came on, which lasted from nine o'clock till
past two in the morning : I never saw but one such
in my life; and that was our memorable Weybridge
storm, which only exceeded this in the circumstance
of my having seen a thunderbolt fall during that
paroxysm of the elements.   But this was very
glorious, awful, beautiful, and tremendous.   The
lightning played without the intermission of a
second, in wide sheets of purple glaring flame that
trembled over the earth for nearly two or three
seconds at a time ; making the whole world, river,
sky, trees, and buildings, look like a ghostly universe cut out in chalk.   The light over the water,
which absolutely illumined the shore on the other
side with the broad glare of full day, was of a
magnificent purple colour.   The night was pitchy
dark, too ; so that between each of these ghastly
smiles of the devil, the various pale steeples and
buildings, which seemed at every moment to leap
from nothing into existence, after standing out in

fearful relief against a back-ground of fire, were
hidden like so many dreams in deep and total
darkness.   God's music rolled along the heavens ;
the forked lightnings now dived from the clouds
into the very bosom of the city, now ran like
tangled threads of fire all round the blazing sky.
" The big bright rain came dancing to the earth,"
the wind clapped its huge wings, and swept through
the dazzling glare ; and as I stood, with eyes half
veiled (for the light was too intense even upon the
ground to be looked at with unshaded eyes),
gazing at this fierce holyday of the elements — at
the mad lightning — at the brilliant shower, through
which the flashes shone like daylight — listening to
the huge thunder, as its voice resounded, and its
heavy feet rebounded along the clouds — and the
swift spirit-like wind rushing triumphantly along,
uttering its wild pæan over the amazed earth ; —
I felt more intensely than I ever did before
the wondrous might of these, God's powerful
and beautiful creatures ; the wondrous might,
majesty, and awfulness of him their Lord, beneath
whose footstool they lie chained, by his great goodness made the ministers of good to this our lowly
dwelling-place.   I did not go to bed till two ; the
storm continued to rage long after that.

Monday, 17*th.*

Rose at eight. At twelve, went to rehearsal. The
weather is intolerable; I am in a state of perpetual fusion. The theatre is the coolest place I
have yet been in, I mean at rehearsal; when the
front is empty, and the doors open, and the stage
is so dark that we are obliged to rehearse by candlelight. That washed-out man who failed in London
when he acted Romeo with me is to be my Fazio;
let us hope he will know some of his words to-
morrow night, for he is at present most innocent
of any such knowledge. After rehearsal, walked
into a shop to buy some gauze: the shopman
called me by my name, entered into conversation
with us; and one of them, after showing me a
variety of things which I did not want, said, that
they were most anxious to show me every attention,
and render my stay in this country agreeable. A
Christian, I suppose, would have met these benevolent advances with an infinitude of thankfulness,
and an outpouring of grateful pleasure; but for
my own part, though I had the grace to smile and
say, " Thank you," I longed to add, " but be so
good as to measure your ribands, and hold your
tongue." I have no idea of holding parley with

clerks behind a counter, still less of their doing so with me.   So much for my first impression of the courtesy of this land of liberty.   I should have been much better pleased if they had called me " Ma'am," which they did not.   We dined at three.   V—— and Colonel —— called after dinner.   At seven, went to the theatre.   It was my dear father's first appearance in this new world, and my heart ached with anxiety.   The weather was intensely hot, yet the theatre was crowded : when he came on, they gave him what every body here calls an immense reception ; but they should see our London audience get up, and wave hats and handkerchiefs, and shout welcome as they do to us.   The tears were in my eyes, and all I could say was, " They might as well get up, I think." My father looked well, and acted beyond all praise; but oh, what a fine and delicate piece of work this is ! There is not one sentence, line, or word of this part which my father has not sifted grain by grain ; there is not one scene or passage to which he does not give its fullest and most entire substance, toge- ther with a variety that relieves the intense study of the whole with wonderful effect.   *   *

      *   *   *   *   *

  *   *   *   *   *

I think that it is impossible to conceive Hamlet

more truly, or execute it more exquisitely than
he does. The refinement, the tenderness, the
grace, dignity, and princely courtesy with which
he invests it from beginning to end, are most
lovely ; and some of the slighter passages, which,
like fine tints to the incapable eyes of blindness,
must always pass unnoticed, and, of course,
utterly uncomprehended, by the discriminating
public, enchanted me.   *   *   *

*   *   *   *   *

*   *   *   *   *

His voice was weak from nervousness and the
intolerable heat of the weather, and he was not
well dressed, which was a pity.   *   *

*   *   *   *   *

*   *   *   *   *

The play was well got up, and went off very well.
The —— were there, a regiment of them ; also
Colonel —— and Captain ——. After the play,
came home to supper.

Tuesday, 18*th.*

Rose at eight. At eleven, went to rehearsal. Mr.
Keppel is just as nervous and as imperfect as
ever : what on earth will he, or shall I, do to-
night ! Came home, got things out for the

theatre, and sat like any stroller stitching for dear life at my head-dress. Mr. H—— and his nephew called : the latter asked me if I was at all apprehensive ? No, by my troth, I am not ; and that not because I feel sure of success, for I think it very probable the Yankees may like to show their critical judgment and independence by damning me ; but because, thank God, I do not care whether they do or not : the whole thing is too loathsome to me, for either failure or success to affect me in the least, and therefore I feel neither nervous nor anxious about it. We dined at three : after dinner, J—— came ; he sat some time. When he was gone, I came into the drawing-room, and found a man sitting with my father, who presented him to me by some inaudible name. I sat down, and the gentleman pursued his conversation as follows : — " When Clara Fisher came over, Barry wrote to me about her, and I wrote him back word : ' My dear fellow, if your bella donna is such as you describe, why, we 'll see what we can do ; we will take her by the hand.' " This was enough for me. I jumped up, and ran out of the room ; because a newspaper writer is my aversion. At half-past six, went to the theatre. They acted the farce of Popping the Question first, in order, I suppose, to get the people to their places before the play began. Poor Mr. Keppel was gasping for breath; he moved my compassion infinitely; I consoled and comforted him all I could, gave him some of my lemonade to swallow, for he was choking with fright; sat myself down with my back to the audience, and up went the curtain. Owing to the position in which I was sitting, and my plain dress, most unheroine-like in its make and colour, the people did not know me, and would not have known me for some time, if that stupid man had done as I kept bidding him, gone on; but instead of doing so, he stood stock still, looked at me, and then at the audience, whereupon the latter caught an inkling of the truth, and gave me such a reception as I get in Covent Garden theatre every time I act a new part. The house was very full; all the —— were there, and Colonel ——. Mr. Keppel was frightened to death, and in the very second speech was quite out: it was in vain that I prompted him; he was too nervous to take the word, and made a complete mess of it. This happened more than once in the first scene; and at the end of the first act, as I left the stage, I said to D——, "It's all up with me, I can't do any thing now;" for having to prompt my Fazio, frightened by his fright, annoyed by his forgetting his crossings and posi-

tions, utterly unable to work myself into any thing
like excitement, I thought the whole thing must
necessarily go to pieces. However, once rid of
my encumbrance, which I am at the end of the
second act, I began to move a little more freely,
gathered up my strength, and set to work comfortably by myself; whereupon, the people applauded, I warmed, (warmed, quotha? the air was
steam,) and got through very satisfactorily, at least
so it seems. My dresses were very beautiful; but
oh, but oh, the musquitoes had made dreadful
havoc with my arms, which were covered with
hills as large and red as Vesuvius in an eruption.
After the play, my father introduced me to Mr.
B——, Lord S——'s brother, who was behind
the scenes; his brother's place, by the by. Came
home, supped.   *   *   *   *

*   *   *   *   *

*   *   *   *   *

Came to bed at half past twelve; weary, and half
melted away. The ants swarm on the floors, on
the tables, in the beds, about one's clothes; the
plagues of Egypt were a joke to them: horrible !
it makes one's life absolutely burdensome, to
have creatures creeping about one, and all over
one, night and day, this fashion; to say nothing
of those cantankerous stinging things, the musquitoes.

Wednesday 19*th*.

D—— did not call me till ten o'clock, whereat I was in furious dudgeon. Got up, breakfasted, and off to rehearsal; Romeo and Juliet. Mr. Keppel has been dismissed, poor man! I'm sorry for him: my father is to play Romeo with me, I'm sorrier still for that. After rehearsal, came home, dawdled about my room: Mr. —— called: he is particularly fond of music. My father asked him to try the piano, which he accordingly did, and was playing most delightfully, when in walked Mr. ——, and by and by Colonel ——, with his honour the Recorder, and General —— of the militia. I amused myself with looking over some exquisite brown silk stockings, wherewith I mean to match my gown. When they were all gone, dawdled about till time to dress. So poor dear H—— can't come from Philadelphia for our dinner — dear, I'm quite sorry! At five our party assembled: we were but thin in numbers, and the half empty table, together with the old ship faces, made it look, as some one observed, as if it was blowing hard. Our dinner was neither good nor well served, the wine not half iced. At the end of it, my father gave Captain —— his claret jug, wherewith that worthy seemed much satisfied. 　　　*　　　*

*　　　*　　　*　　　*　　　*

We left the table soon; came and wrote journal.   When the gentlemen joined us, they were
all more or less " how com'd you so indeed ? "
Mr. —— and Mr. —— particularly.   They put
me down to the piano, and once or twice I
thought I must have screamed.   On one side
vibrated dear Mr. ——, threatening my new gown
with a 'cup of coffee, which he held at an awful
angle from the horizontal line ; singing with every
body who opened their lips, and uttering such
dreadfully discordant little squeals and squeaks,
that I thought I should have died of suppressed
laughter.   On the other side, rather *concerned*, but
not quite so much so, stood the Irishman ; who,
though warbling a little out of tune, and flourishing somewhat luxuriantly, still retained enough of
his right senses to discriminate between Mr. ——'s
yelps and singing, properly so called ; and accordingly pished ! — and pshawed ! — and oh
Lorded ! — and good heavened ! away, — staring
at the perpetrator with indignant horror through
his spectacles, while his terrified wig stood on end
in every direction, each particular hair appearing
vehemently possessed with the centrifugal force.
They all went away in good time, and we came
to bed.

—— To bed — to sleep —
To sleep!—perchance to be bitten! ay—there's the scratch:
And in that sleep of ours what bugs may come,
Must give us pause.

Thursday, 20th.

Rose at eight. After breakfast, went to rehearse
Romeo and Juliet. Poor Mr. Keppel is fairly
laid on the shelf; I'm sorry for him! What a
funny passion he had, by the by, for going down
upon his knees. In Fazio, at the end of the
judgment scene, when I was upon mine, down he
went upon his, making the most absurd, devout
looking *vis-à-vis* I ever beheld: in the last scene,
too, when he ought to have been going off to
execution, down he went again upon his knees,
and no power on earth could get him up again,
for Lord knows how long. Poor fellow, he
bothered me a good deal, yet I'm sincerely sorry
for him. At the end of our rehearsal, came
home. The weather is sunny, sultry, scorching,
suffocating. Ah! Mr. —— called. This is an
indifferent imitation of bad fine manners amongst
us; "he speaks small, too, like a gentleman."
He sat for a long time, talking over the opera,
and all the prima donnas in the world. When he
was gone, Mr. —— and Mr. —— called.   *

*   *   *   *   *

The latter asked us to dinner to-morrow, to meet Dr. ——, who, poor man, dares neither go to the play nor call upon us, so strict are the good people here about the behaviour of their pastors and masters. By the by, Essex called this morning to fetch away the Captain's claret jug: he asked my father for an order ; adding, with some hesitation, " It must be for the gallery, if you please, sir, for people of colour are not allowed to go to the pit, or any other part of the house." I believe I turned black myself, I was so indignant. Here's aristocracy with a vengeance ! —— called with Forrest, the American actor. Mr. Forrest has rather a fine face, I think. We dined at three : after dinner, wrote journal, played on the piano, and frittered away my time till half-past six. Went to the theatre : the house was very full, and dreadfully hot. My father acted Romeo beautifully : I looked very nice, and the people applauded my *gown* abundantly. At the end of the play I was half dead with heat and fatigue : came home and supped, lay down on the floor in absolute meltiness away, and then came to bed.

Friday, 21st.

Rose at eight.   After breakfast went to rehearsal.   The School for Scandal ; Sir Peter, I
see, keeps his effects to himself; what a bore this
is, to be sure !   Got out things for the theatre.
While eating my lunch, Mr. —— and his cousin,
a Mr. —— (one of the cleverest lawyers here),
called   *   *   *   *
      *   *   *   *   *
      *   *   *   *   *

They were talking of Mr. Keppel.   By the by,
of that gentleman ; Mr. Simpson sent me this
morning, for my decision, a letter from Mr. Keppel,
soliciting another trial, and urging the hardness
of his case, in being condemned upon a part
which he had had no time to study.   My own
opinion of poor Mr. Keppel is, that no power on
earth or in heaven can make him act decently ;
however, of course, I did not object to his trying
again ; he did not swamp me the first night, so I
don't suppose he will the fifth.   We dined at
five.   Just before dinner, received a most delicious
bouquet, which gladdened my very heart with its
sweet smell and lovely colours: some of the
flowers were strangers to me.   After dinner,

Colonel —— called, and began pulling out heaps of newspapers, and telling us a long story about Mr. Keppel, who, it seems, has been writing to the papers, to convince them and the public that he is a good actor, at the same time throwing out sundry hints, which seem aimed our way, of injustice, oppression, hard usage, and the rest on 't.

*   *   *   *   *

*   *   *   *   *

Mr. —— called to offer to ride with me; when, however, the question of a horse was canvassed, he knew of none, and Colonel ——'s whole regiment of " beautiful ladies' horses " had also neither a local habitation nor a name.   *

*   *   *   *   *

*   *   *   *   *

When they were gone, went to the theatre ; the house was very good, the play, the School for Scandal. I played pretty fairly, and looked very nice. The people were stupid to a degree, to be sure ; poor things ! it was very hot. Indeed, I scarce understand how they should be amused with the School for Scandal; for though the dramatic situations are so exquisite, yet the wit is far above the generality of even our own audiences, and the tone and manners altogether are so thoroughly English, that I should think it must be for

the most part incomprehensible to the good people here. After the play, came home. Colonel S—— supped with us, and renewed the subject of Mr. Keppel and the theatre. My father happened to say, referring to a passage in that worthy's letter to the public, " I shall certainly enquire of Mr. Keppel why he has so used my name ;" to which Colonel S—— replied, as usual, " No, now let me advise, let me beg you, Mr. Kemble, just to remain quiet, and leave all this to me." This was too much for mortal woman to bear. I immediately said, " Not at all : it is my father's affair, if any body's ; and he alone has the right to demand any explanation, or make any observation on the subject ; and were I he, I certainly should do so, and that forthwith." I could hold no longer.   *   *   *   *
        *   *   *   *   *
        *   *   *   *   *

Came to bed in tremendous dudgeon. The few *critiques* that I have seen upon our acting, have been, upon the whole, laudatory. One was sent to me from a paper called The Mirror, which pleased me very much ; not because the praise in it was excessive, and far beyond my deserts, but that it was written with great taste and feeling, and was evidently not the produce of a common press hack. There appeared to me in all the others the true provincial dread of praising too much, and being *led* into approbation by previous opinions ; a sort of jealousy of critical freedom, which, together with the established *nil admirari* of the press, seems to keep them in a constant dread of being thought enthusiastic. They need not be afraid : enthusiasm may belong to such analysis as Schlegel's or Channing's, but has nothing in common with the paragraphs of a newspaper ; the inditers of which, in my poor judgment, seldom go beyond the very threshold of criticism, *i. e.* the discovery of faults. I am infinitely amused at the extreme curiosity which appears to me to be the besetting sin of the people here. A gentleman whom you know (as for instance, in my case,) very slightly, will sit down by your table during a morning visit, turn over every article upon it, look at the cards of the various people who have called upon you, ask half-a-dozen questions about each of them, as many about your own private concerns, and all this, as though it were a matter of course that you should answer him, which I feel greatly inclined occasionally not to do.

Saturday, 22d.

Rose at eight. After breakfast, dawdled about till near one o'clock : got into a hackney coach * with D——, and returned all manner of cards.

* * * * *

* * * * *

Went into a shop to order a pair of shoes. The shopkeepers in this place, with whom I have hitherto had to deal, are either condescendingly familiar, or insolently indifferent in their manner. Your washerwoman sits down before you, while you are *standing* speaking to her ; and a shop-boy bringing things for your inspection, not only sits down, but keeps his hat on in your drawing-room. The worthy man to whom I went for my shoes was so amazingly ungracious, that at first

---

* The hackney coaches in this country are very different from those perilous receptacles of dust and dirty straw, which disgrace the London stands. They are comfortable within, and clean without ; and the horses harnessed to them never exhibit those shocking specimens of cruelty and ill usage which the poor hack horses in London present. Indeed (and it is a circumstance which deserves notice, for it bespeaks general character,) I have not seen, during a two years' residence in this country, a single instance of brutality towards animals, such as one is compelled to witness hourly in the streets of any English town.

I thought I would go out of the shop; but recollecting that I should probably only go farther and fare worse, I gulped, sat down, and was measured. All this is bad: it has its origin in a vulgar misapprehension, which confounds ill breeding with independence, and leads people to fancy that they elevate themselves above their condition by discharging its duties and obligations discourteously.†   *   *   *   *

*   *   *   *   *

*   *   *   *   *

Came home: wrote journal, practised, dressed for dinner. At five, went into our neighbour's: Dr. ——, the rector of Grace Church, was the only stranger. I liked him extremely: he sat by me at dinner, and I thought his conversation suf-

† There is a striking difference in this respect between the trades-people of New York and those of Boston and Philadelphia; and in my opinion the latter preserve quite self-respect enough to acquit their courtesy and civility from any charge of servility. The only way in which I can account for the difference, is the greater impulse which trade receives in New York, the proportionate rapidity with which fortunes are made, the ever-shifting materials of which its society is composed, and the facility with which the man who has served you behind his counter, having amassed an independence, assumes a station in the first circle, where his influence becomes commensurate with his wealth. This is not the case either in Boston or Philadelphia; at least, not to the same degree.

ficiently clever, with an abundance of goodness,
and liberal benevolent feeling shining through it.
We retired to our room, where Mrs. —— made
me laugh extremely with sundry passages of her
American experiences. I was particularly amused
with her account of their stopping, after a long
day's journey, at an inn somewhere, when the
hostess, who remained in the room the whole
time, addressed her as follows: " D' ye play?"
pointing to an open piano-forte. Mrs. —— replied that she did so sometimes; whereupon the
free and easy landlady ordered candles, and
added, " Come, sit down and give us a tune,
then;" to which courteous and becoming invitation Mrs. —— replied by taking up her candle,
and walking out of the room. The pendant to
this is Mr. ——'s story. He sent a die of his
crest to a manufacturer to have it put upon his
gig harness. The man sent home the harness,
when it was finished, but without the die; after
sending for which sundry times, Mr. —— called
to enquire after it himself, when the reply was : —

" Lord ! why I did'nt know you wanted it."

" I tell you, I wish to have it back."

" Oh, pooh ! you can't want it much, now —
do you?"

" I tell you, sir, I desire to have the die back immediately."

" Ah well, come now, what 'll you take for it ? "

" D' ye think I mean to sell my crest ? why you might as well ask me to sell my name."

" Why you see, a good many folks have seen it, and want to have it on their harness, as it 's a pretty looking concern enough."

So much for their ideas of a crest. This, though, by the by, happened some years ago.

After the gentlemen joined us, my father made me sing to them, which I did with rather a bad grace, as I don't think any body wished to hear me but himself. *   *   *   *

  *   *   *   *   *

  *   *   *   *   *

Dr. —— is perfectly enchanting. They left us at about eleven. Came to bed.

Sunday, 23d.

Rose at eight. After breakfast, went to church with D——. There is no such thing, I perceive, as a pew-opener ; so, after standing sufficiently long in the middle of the church, we established ourselves very comfortably in a pew, where we remained unmolested. The day was most lovely, and my eyes were constantly attracted to the church windows, through which the magnificent willows of the burial-ground looked like golden-green fountains rising into the sky.   *   *

  * * * * *

  * * * * *

The singing in church was excellent, and Dr. ——'s sermon very good, too: he wants stern-ness ; but that is my particular fancy about a clergyman, and by most people would be accounted no want.   It was not sacrament Sunday; D—— was disappointed, and I mistaken.   Mr. —— walked home with us.   After church, wrote jour-nal.   —— called, and sat with us during dinner, telling us stories of the flogging of slaves, as he himself had witnessed it in the south, that forced the colour into my face, the tears into my eyes, and strained every muscle in my body with positive rage and indignation : he made me per-fectly sick with it.   When he was gone, my father went to Colonel ——'s.   I played all through Mr. ——'s edition of Cinderella, and then wrote three long letters, which kept me up till nearly one o'clock.   Oh, bugs, fleas, flies, ants, and musquitoes, great is the misery you inflict upon me !   I sit slapping my own face all day, and lie thumping my pillow all night : 't is a perfect nuisance to be devoured of creatures *before* one's in the ground ; it isn't fair.   Wrote to Mr. ——, to ask if he would ride with me on Tuesday. I am dying to be on horseback again.   *

*   *   *   *   *

*   *   *   *   *

Monday, 24th.

Rose at eight: went and took a bath.   After breakfast, went to rehearsal : Venice Preserved, with Mr. Keppel, who did not appear to me to know the words even, and seemed perfectly bewildered at being asked to do the common business of the piece.   " Mercy on me ! what will he do to-night?" thought I.   Came home and got things ready for the theatre.   Received a visit from poor Mr. ——, who has got the lumbago, as Sir Peter would say, " on purpose," I believe, to prevent my riding out to-morrow.   Dined at three: after dinner, played and sang through Cinderella; wrote journal: at six, went to the theatre.   My gown was horribly ill-plaited, and I looked like a blue-bag.   The house was very full, and they received Mr. K—— with acclamations and shouts of applause.   When I went on, I was all but tumbling down at the sight of my Jaffier, who looked like

the apothecary in Romeo and Juliet, with the
addition of some devilish red slashes along his
thighs and arms. The first scene passed well and
so : but, oh, the next, and the next, and the next
to that. Whenever he was not glued to my side
(and that was seldom), he stood three yards behind me ; he did nothing but seize my hand, and
grapple to it so hard, that unless I had knocked
him down (which I felt much inclined to try), I could
not disengage myself. In the senate scene, when
I was entreating for mercy, and *struggling*, as
Otway has it, for my life, he was prancing round
the stage in every direction, flourishing his dagger
in the air : I wish to Heaven I had got up and
run away ; it would but have been natural, and
have served him extremely right. In the parting
scene, — oh what a scene it was ! — instead of
going away from me when he said " farewell for
ever," he stuck to my skirts, though in the same
breath that I adjured him, in the words of my
part, not to leave me, I added, aside, " Get away
from me, oh *do !*" When I exclaimed, " Not
one kiss at parting," he kept embracing and kissing me like mad ; and when I ought to have been
pursuing him, and calling after him, " Leave thy
dagger with me," he hung himself up against the
wing, and remained dangling there for five

minutes. I was half crazy! and the good people sat and swallowed it all : they deserved it, by my troth, they did. I prompted him constantly, and once, after struggling in vain to free myself from him, was obliged, in the middle of my part, to exclaim, " You hurt me dreadfully, Mr. Keppel!" He clung to me, cramped me, crumpled me, — dreadful! I never experienced any thing like this before, and made up my mind that I never would again. I played of course like a wretch, finished my part as well as I could, and, as soon as the play was over, went to my father and Mr. Simpson, and declared to them both my determination not to go upon the stage again, with that gentleman for a hero. Three trials are as many as, in reason, any body can demand, and come what come may, *I* will not be subjected to this sort of experiment again. At the end of the play, the clever New Yorkians actually called for Mr. Keppel! and this most worthless clapping of hands, most worthlessly bestowed upon such a worthless object, is what, by the nature of my craft, I am bound to care for; I spit at it from the bottom of my soul! Talking of applause, the man who acted Bedamar to-night thought fit to be two hours dragging me off the stage; in consequence of which I had to scream, " Jaffier,

Jaffier," till I thought I should have broken a blood-vessel. On my remonstrating with him upon this, he said, " Well, you are rewarded, listen :" the people were clapping and shouting vehemently : this is the whole history of acting and actors. We came home tired, and thoroughly disgusted, and found no supper. The cooks, who do not live in the house, but come and do their work, and depart home whenever it suits their convenience, had not thought proper to stay to prepare any supper for us : so we had to wait for the readiest things that could be procured out of doors for us — this was pleasant * — very ! At

* The universal hour of dining, in New York, when first we arrived, was three o'clock; after which hour the cooks took their departure, and nothing was to be obtained fit to eat, either for love or money : this intolerable nuisance is gradually passing away; but even now, though we can get our dinner served at six o'clock, it is always dressed at three; its excellence may be imagined from that. To say the truth, I think the system upon which all houses of public entertainment are conducted in this country is a sample of the patience and long-suffering with which dirt, discomfort, and exorbitant charges may be borne by a whole community, without resistance, or even remonstrance. The best exceptions I could name to these various inconveniences are, first, Mr. Cozzen's establishment at West Point ; next, the Tremont at Boston, and, lastly, the Mansion House at Philadelphia. In each of these, wayfarers may obtain some portion of decent comfort : but they have their drawbacks ;

last appeared a cold boiled fowl, and some monstrous oysters, that looked for all the world like
an antediluvian race of oysters, " for in those days
there were giants." Six mouthfuls each : they
were well-flavoured ; but their size displeased my
eye, and I swallowed but one, and came to bed.

Friday, 28th.

A letter from England, the first from dear ——.
D—— brought it me while I was dressing, and
oh, how welcome, how welcome it was !   *

*   *   *   *   *

After breakfast went to rehearsal : Much Ado
about Nothing.   Came home, wrote journal, put
out things for the theatre, dined at three.   After
dinner, —— called.

---

in the first, there are no private sitting rooms ; and in the
last, the number of servants is inadequate to the work.   The
Tremont is by far the best establishment of the sort existing
at present.   Mr. A——, the millionaire of New York, is
about to remedy this deficiency, by the erection of a magnificent hotel in Broadway.   One thing, however, is certain ;
neither he nor any one else will ever succeed in having a decent house, if the servants are not a little superior to the
Irish savages who officiate in that capacity in most houses,
public and private, in the northern states of America.

*   *   *   *   *

*   *   *   *   *

Mr. —— called, and sat with us till six o'clock.

*   *   *   *   *

*   *   *   *   *

I constantly sit thunderstruck at the amazing number of unceremonious questions which people here think fit to ask one, and, moreover, expect one to answer. Went to the theatre; the house was not good. The Italians were expected to sing for the first time; they did not, however, but in the mean time thinned our house.

I would give the world to see Mr. —— directing the public taste, by an oeiliad, and leading the public approbation, by a gracious tapping of his supreme hand upon his ineffable snuff-box; he reminds me of high life below stairs. The play went off very well; I played well, and my dresses looked beautiful; my father acted to perfection. I never saw any thing so gallant, gay, so like a gentleman, so full of brilliant, buoyant, refined spirit; he looked admirably, too. Mr. —— was behind the scenes: speaking to me of my father's appearance in Pierre, he said he reminded him of Lord ——. I could not forbear asking him how long he had been away from England: he replied, four years. Truly, four years will furnish him

matter of astonishment when he returns. Swallow Street is grown into a line of palaces; the
Strand is a broad magnificent avenue, where all
the wealth of the world seems gathered together;
and Lord ——, the " observed of all observers,"
is become a red-faced, fat old man.   " Och,
Time! can't ye be aisy now ! "

Sunday, 30th.

Rose late, did not go to church; sat writing
letters all the morning.   Mr. —— and Mr. ——
called.   What a character that Mr. —— is.
Colonel —— called, and wanted to take my
father out ; but we were all inditing epistles to go
to-morrow by the dear old Pacific.   At three
o'clock, went to church with Mrs. —— and Mr.
——.   I like Dr. —— most extremely.   His
mild, benevolent, Christian view of the duties
and blessings of life is very delightful; and the
sound practical doctrine he preaches " good for
edification."   *   *   *   *

     *   *   *   *   *

It poured with rain, but they sent a coach for us
from the inn; came home, dressed for dinner.
D—— and I dined *tête-à-tête*.   After dinner, sat
writing letters for Mr. ——'s bag till ten o'clock :

came to my own room, undressed, and began a volume to dear ——. * * *

* * * * *

* * * * *

I did not get to bed till three o'clock : in spite of all which I am as fat as an overstuffed pincushion.

* * * * *

* * * * *

Select specimens of American pronunciation : —

vaggaries,	vagaries.
ad infínnitum,	ad infinitem.
vitúpperate,	vituperate.

Monday, October 1st.

While I was out, Captain —— called for our letters. Saw Mr. ——, and bade him good-by : they are going away to-day to Havre, to Europe; I wish I was a nail in one of their trunks. After breakfast, went to rehearse King John : what a lovely mess they will make of it, to be sure. When my sorrows were ended, my father brought me home : found a most lovely nosegay from Mr. —— awaiting me. Bless it! how sweet it smelt, and how pretty it looked. Spent an hour delightfully in putting it into water. Got things ready for to-night, practised till dinner, and wrote journal. My father received a letter to-day, informing him that a cabal was forming by the friends of Miss Vincent and Miss Clifton (native talent!) to hiss us off the New York stage, if possible; if not, to send people in every night to create a disturbance during our best scenes: the letter is anonymous, and therefore little deserving of attention. After dinner, practised till time to go to the theatre. The house was very full; but what a cast! what a play! what botchers! what butchers! In his very first scene, the most christian king stuck fast; and there he stood, shifting his truncheon from hand to hand, rolling his eyes, gasping for breath, and struggling for words, like a man in the night-mare. I thought of Hamlet — "Leave thy damnable faces"—and was obliged to turn away. In the scene before Angiers, when the French and English heralds summon the citizens to the walls, the Frenchman applied his instrument to his mouth, uplifted his chest, distended his cheeks, and appeared to blow furiously; not a sound! he dropped his arm, and looked off the stage in discomfiture and indignation, when the perverse trumpet set up a blast fit to waken the dead, — the audience roared: it reminded me of the harp in the old ballad, that

" began to play alone." Chatillon, on his return
from England, begged to assure us that with
King John was come the mother queen, an *Anty*
stirring him to blood and war. When Cardinal
Pandulph came on, the people set up a shout,
as usual: he was dreadfully terrified, poor thing;
and all the time he spoke kept giving little nervous twitches to his sacred petticoat, in a fashion
that was enough to make one die of laughter.
He was as obstinate, too, in his bewilderment as
a stuttering man in his incoherency; for once, when
he stuck fast, having twitched his skirts, and
thumped his breast in vain for some time, I
thought it best, having to speak next, to go on;
when, lo and behold! in the middle of my speech,
the " scarlet sin " recovers his memory, and shouts
forth the end of his own, to the utter confusion of
my august self and the audience. I thought they
never would have got through my last scene:
king gazed at cardinal, and cardinal gazed at
king; king nodded and winked at the prompter,
spread out his hands, and remained with his
mouth open: cardinal nodded and winked at the
prompter, crossed his hands on his breast, and
remained with his mouth open; neither of them
uttering a syllable! What a scene! O, what a

glorious scene! Came home as soon as my part was over. Supped, and sat up for my father. Heard his account of the end, and came to bed.*

Wednesday, 3d.

Rose late. After breakfast, went to rehearsal: what a mess I do make of Bizarre! Ellen Tree and Mrs. Chatterly were angels to what I shall be, yet I remember thinking them both bad enough. After all, if people generally did but know the difficulty of doing well, they would be less damnatory upon those who do ill. It is not easy to act well. After rehearsal, went to Stewart's with D——. As we were proceeding up Broadway

* It is fortunate for the managers of the Park Theatre, and very unfortunate for the citizens of New York, that the audiences who frequent that place of entertainment are chiefly composed of the strangers who are constantly passing in vast numbers through this city. It is not worth the while of the management to pay a good company, when an indifferent one answers their purpose quite as well: the system upon which theatrical speculations are conducted in this country is, having one or two "stars" for the principal characters, and nine or ten sticks for all the rest. The consequence is, that a play is never decently acted, and at such times as stars are scarce, the houses are very deservedly empty. The terrestrial audiences suffer much by this mode of getting up plays; but the celestial performers, the stars propped upon sticks, infinitely more.

to Bonfanti's*, I saw a man in the strangest attitude imaginable, absolutely setting at us : presently he pounced, and who should it be but ——. He came into Bonfanti's with us, and afterwards insisted on escorting us to our various destinations ; not, however, without manifold and deep lamentations on his slovenly appearance and dirty gloves. The latter, however, he managed to exchange *chemin faisant* for a pair of new ones, which he extracted from his pocket and drew on, without letting go our arms, which he squeezed most unmercifully during the operation. We went through a part of the town which I had never seen before. The shops have all a strange fair-like appearance, and exhibit a spectacle of heterogeneous disorder, which greatly amazes the eye of a Londoner. The comparative infancy in which most of the adornments of life are yet in this country, renders it impossible for the number of distinct trades to exist, that do among us, where the population is so much denser, and where the luxurious indulgences of the few find ample occupation for the penurious industry of the many. But here, one man drives several trades ; and in every shop you meet with a strange incongruous mixture of articles

* Stewart — Bonfanti. The name of shopkeepers in Broadway : the former's is the best shop in New York.

for sale, which would be found nowhere in England, but in the veriest village huckster's. Comparatively few of the objects for sale can be exposed in the windows, which are unlike our shop windows, narrow and ill adapted for the display of goods : but piles of them lie outside the doors, choking up the pathway, and coloured cloths, flannels, shawls, &c., are suspended about in long draperies, whose vivid colours flying over the face of the houses give them an untidy, but at the same time a gay, flaunting appearance. We went into a shop to buy some stockings, and missing our *preux chevalier*, I turned round to look for him ; when I perceived him beautifying most busily before a glass in a further corner of the shop. He had seized on a sort of house brush, and began brooming his hat : the next operation was to produce a small pocket comb and arrange his disordered locks ; lastly, he transferred the services of the brush of all work from his head to his feet, and having dusted his boots, drawn himself up in his surtout, buttoned its two lower buttons, and given a re forming grasp to his neckcloth, he approached us, evidently much advanced in his own good graces. We went to the furrier's, and brought away my dark boa. Came home, put out things for packing up, and remained so engaged till time to dress for dinner. Mr. and Mrs. —— and Mr. —— dined with us.

* * * * *

* * * * *

Mr. —— is an Englishman of the high breed, and sufficiently pleasant. After dinner we had to withdraw into our bed-room, for the house is so full that they can't cram any thing more into an inch of it.

Joined the gentlemen at tea. Mr. —— had gone to the theatre : Mr. —— and I had some music. He plays delightfully, and knows every note of music that ever was written ; but he had the barbarity to make me sing a song of his own composing to him, which is a cruel thing in a man to do. He went away at about eleven, and we then came to bed. My father went to see Miss Clifton, at the Bowery theatre.

Thursday, 4th.

Rose late. After breakfast, went to rehearsal: my Bizarre is getting a little more into shape. After rehearsal, came home. Mr. —— and Mr. —— called, and sat some time with me. The former is tolerably pleasant, but a little too fond of telling good stories that he has told before. Put out things

for the theatre: dined at three.   Colonel ——
called. Wrote journal: while doing so, was called
out to look at my gown, which the worthy milliner
had sent home.

> I am, I am an angel! Witness it, heaven !
> Witness it earth, and every being witness it!
> The gown was spoil'd !   Yet by immortal patience
> I did not even fly into a passion.

She took it back to alter it.   Presently arrived my
wreath, and that had also to be taken back; for
't was nothing like what I had ordered.   Now all
this does not provoke me; but the thing that does,
is the dreadful want of manners of the trades-people
here.   They bolt into your room without knocking,
nod to you, sit down, and without the preface of
either Sir, Ma'am, or Miss, start off into " Well
now, I 'm come to speak about so and so." At six,
went to the theatre; play, the Hunchback: the
house was crammed from floor to ceiling.   I had
an intense headache, but played tolerably well.   I
wore my red satin, and looked like a bonfire. Came
home and found Smith's Virginia, and two volumes
of Graham's America, which I want to read. They
charge twelve dollars for these : every thing is
horribly dear here.   Came to bed with my head
splitting.

Friday, 5th.

Played Bizarre for the first time. Acted so-so, looked very pretty, the house was very fine, and my father incomparable : they called for him after the play. Colonel —— and Mr. —— called in while we were at supper.

Saturday, 6th.

Rose late : when I came in to breakfast, found Colonel —— sitting in the parlour. He remained for a long time, and we had sundry discussions on topics manifold. It seems that the blessed people here were shocked at my having to hear the coarseness of Farquhar's Inconstant — humbug ! †   *

＊   ＊   ＊   ＊   ＊

* Were the morality that I constantly hear uttered a little more consistent, not only with right reason, but with itself, I think it might be more deserving of attention and respect. But the mock delicacy, which exists to so great a degree with regard to theatrical exhibitions, can command neither the one nor the other. To those who forbid all dramatic representations, as exhibitions of an unhealthy tendency upon our intellectual and moral nature, I have no objections, at present, to make. Unqualified condemnation, particularly when adopted on such grounds, may be a sincere, a respectable, perhaps a right, opinion. I have but one reply to offer to it : the human mind requires recreation ; is not a theatre, (always supposing it to be, not what theatres too

At twelve, went out shopping, and paying bills ; called upon Mrs. ――, and sat some time with

---

often are, but what they ought to be,) is not a theatre a better, a higher, a more noble, and useful place of recreation than a billiard-room, or the bar of a tavern ?, Perhaps in the course of the moral and intellectual improvement of mankind, *all* these will give way to yet purer and more refined sources of recreation ; but in the mean time, I confess, with its manifold abuses, a play-house appears to me worthy of toleration, if not of approbation, as holding forth (when directed as it should be) a highly intellectual, rational, and refined amusement.

However, as I before said, my quarrel is not with those who condemn indiscriminately all theatrical exhibitions ; they may be right : at all events, so sweeping a sentence betrays no inconsistency. But what are we to say to individuals, or audiences, who turn with affected disgust from the sallies of Bizarre and Beatrice, and who applaud and laugh, and are delighted at the gross immorality of such plays as the Wonder, and Rule a Wife and have a Wife ; the latter particularly, in which the immorality and indecency are not those of expression only, but of conception, and mingle in the whole construction of the piece, in which not one character appears whose motives of action are not most unworthy, and whose language is not as full of coarseness, as devoid of every generous, elevated, or refined sentiment. (The tirades of Leon are no exception ; for in the mouth of a man who marries such a woman as Marguerita, by such means, and for such an end, they are mere mockeries.)   I confess that my surprise was excited when I was told that an American audience would not endure that portion of Beatrice's wit, which the London censors have spared, and that Othello was all but a proscribed play ; but it was infinitely

her and Mrs. ———; left a card at Mrs. ———'s,
and came home, prepared things for our journey,

---

more so, when I found that the same audience tolerated, or
rather encouraged with their presence and applause, the
coarse production of Mrs. Centlivre and Beaumont and
Fletcher. With regard to the Inconstant, it is by far the
most moral of Farquhar's plays; that, perhaps, is little
praise, for the Recruiting Officer, and the Beau's Stratagem,
are decidedly the reverse. But in spite of the licentiousness
of the writing, in many parts, the construction, the motive,
the action of the play is not licentious; the characters are
far from being utterly debased in their conception, or de-
praved in the sentiments they utter (excepting, of course,
the companions of poor Mirable's last revel); the women,
those surest criterions, by whose principles and conduct
may be formed the truest opinion of the purity of the social
atmosphere, the women, though free in their manners and
language, (it was the fashion of their times, and of the times
before them, when words did not pass for deeds, either good
or bad,) are essentially honest women; and Bizarre, coarse
as her expressions may appear, has yet more *real* delicacy
than poor Oriana, whose womanly love causes her too far to
forget her womanly pride. Of the catastrophe of this play,
and its frightfully pointed moral, little need be said to prove
that its effect is likely to be far more wholesome, because
far more homely, than that of most theatrical inventions; invention, indeed, it is not, and its greatest interest, as perhaps
its chief utility, is drawn from the circumstance of its being
a faithful representation of a situation of unequalled horror,
in which the author himself was placed, and from which he
was rescued precisely as he extricates his hero. Of the
truth and satirical power of the dialogue, none who understand it can dispute, and if, instead of attaching themselves

and dressed for dinner.　On our way to Mr.
———'s, my father told me he had been seeing Miss

---

to the farcical romping of Bizarre and her ungallant lover,
the modest critics of this play had devoted some attention
to the dialogues between young and old Mirable, their nice
sense of decency would have been less shocked, and they
might have found themselves repaid by some of the most
pointed, witty, and pithy writing in the English dramatic
literature.　I am much obliged to such of my friends as
lamented that I had to personate Farquhar's impertinent
heroine; for my own good part, I would as lief be such an
one, as either Jane Shore, Mrs. Haller, Lady Macbeth, or
the wild woman Bianca.　I know that great crimes have a
species of evil grandeur in them; they spring only from a
powerful soil, they are in their very magnitude respectable.
I know that mighty passions have in their very excess a
frightful majesty, that asserts the vigour of the natures from
which they rise; and there is as little similarity between
them, and the base, degraded, selfish, cowardly tribe of petty
larceny vices with which human societies abound, as there is
between the caterpillar blight, that crawls over a fertile dis-
trict, gnawing it away inch-meal, and the thunderbolt that
scathes, or the earthquake that swallows the same region, in
its awful mission of destruction.　But I maintain that freedom of expression and manner is by no means an indication
of laxity of morals, and again repeat that Bizarre is free in
her words, but not in her principles.　The authoress of the
most graceful and true analysis of Shakspeare's female characters has offered a better vindication of their manners
than I could write; I can only say, I pity sincerely all those
who, passing over the exquisite purity, delicacy, and loveliness of their conception, dwell only upon modes of expression which belong to the times in which their great creator

Clifton, the girl they want him to teach to act; (to
teach to act, quotha ! ! !) he says, she is very pretty,

---

lived. With respect to the manner in which audiences are
affected by what they hear on the stage, I cannot but think
that gentlemen who wish their wives and daughters to hear
no language of an exceptionable nature, had better make
themselves acquainted with what they take them to see, or
at all events, avoid, when in the theatre, attracting their
attention to expressions which their disapprobation serves
only to bring into notice, and which had much better escape
unheard, or at least unheeded. Voluminous as this note
has become, I cannot but add one word with respect to the
members of the profession to which I have belonged. Many
actresses that I have known, in the performance of unvir-
tuous or unlovely characters, (I cannot, however, help remembering that they were also secondary parts,) have thought
fit to impress the audience with the wide difference between
their assumed and real disposition, by acting as ill, and looking as cross as they possibly could, which could not but be a
great satisfaction to any moral audience. I have seen this done
by that fine part in Milman's Fazio, Aldabella, repeatedly,
and not unfrequently by the Queen in Hamlet, Margarita in
Rule a Wife and have a Wife, (I scarcely wonder at that,
though,) and even by poor Shakspeare's Lady Falconbridge.
I think this is a mistake: the audience, I believe, never
forget that the actress is not indeed the wicked woman she
seems. In one instance that might have been the case,
perhaps. I speak of a great artist, whose efforts I never
witnessed, but whose private excellence I have a near right
to rejoice in, and who was as true in her performance of the
wretch Millwood, as in her personifications of Shakspeare's
grandest creations.

indeed, with fine eyes, a fair, delicate skin, and a handsome mouth; moreover, a tall woman, and yet from the front of the house her effect is nought. What a pity, and a provoking ! A pleasant dinner, very. Mr. —— the poet, one Dr. ——, Colonel ——, and Mr. —— : the only woman was a Miss ————

*　　*　　*　　*

　*　　*　　*　　*　　*

　*　　*　　*　　*　　*

——'s face reminded me of young —— : the countenance was not quite so good, but there was the same radiant look about the eyes and forehead. His expression was strongly sarcastic ; I liked him very much, notwithstanding. When we left the men, we had the pleasure of the children's society, and that of an unhappy kitten, whom a little pitiless urchin of three years old was carrying crumpled under her arm like a pincushion. The people here make me mad by abusing Lawrence's drawing of me. If ever there was a refined and intellectual work, where the might of genius triumphing over every material impediment has enshrined and embodied spirit itself, it is that. Talking of Lawrence, (poor Lawrence !) Mrs. —— said, " Ah, yes ! your picture by—a—Sir—something—Lawrence !" Oh, fame ! oh, fame ! Oh, vanity and vexation of spirit ! does your eternity and your

infinitude amount to this? There are lands where
Shakspeare's name was never heard, where Raphael and Handel are unknown; to be sure, for
the matter of that, there are regions (and those
wide ones too) where Jesus Christ is unknown.
At nine o'clock, went to the Richmond Hill theatre, to see the opening of the Italian company.
The house itself is a pretty little box enough, but
as bad as a box to sing in. We went to Mr.
————'s box, where he was kind enough to give us
seats. The first act was over, but we had all the
benefit of the second. I had much ado not to
laugh ; and when Mr. ————, that everlasting gigler,
came and sat down beside me, I gave myself up
for lost. However, I did behave in spite of two
blue bottles of women, who by way of the sisters
buzzed about the stage, singing enough to set one's
teeth on edge. Then came a very tall Dandini ;
by the by, that man had a good bass voice, but
Mr. ———— said it was the finest he had heard since
Zucchelli. O tempora ! O mores ! Zucchelli, that
prince of delicious baritones ! However, as I said,
the man has a good bass voice ; there was also a
sufficiently good Pompolino. Montresor banged
himself about, broke his time, and made some
execrable flourishes in the Prince, whereat the
enlightened New Yorkians applauded mightily.

But the Prima Donna ! but the Cenerentola ! Cospetto di Venere, what a figure, and what a face ! Indeed she was the very thing for a lower housemaid, and I think the Prince was highly to blame for removing her from the station nature had evidently intended her for. She was old and ugly, and worse than ugly, unpardonably common-looking, with a cast in her eye, and a foot that, as Mr. ―― observed, it would require a *pretty considerable* large glass slipper to fit. Then she sang ― discords and dismay, how she did sing ! I could not forbear stealing a glance at ―― : he applauded the **sestett** vehemently ; but when it came to that most touching " *nacqui al'affanno* " he wisely interposed his handkerchief between the stage and his gracious countenance. I thought of poor dear ―― and her sweet voice, and her refined taste, and shuddered to hear this favourite of hers bedevilled by such a Squalini. Now is it possible that people can be such fools as to fancy this good in spite of their senses, or such earless asses (that 's a bull I suppose), as to suffer themselves to be persuaded that it is ? Though why do I ask it ? Oh yes, " very easily possible." Do not half the people in London spend money and time without end, enduring nightly penances ― listening to what hey can't understand, and couldn't appreciate if they did? I suppose if I shall allow a hundred out of the whole King's Theatre audience to know any thing whatever about music, I am wide in my grant of comprehension. There was that virtuous youth, Mr. ——, who evidently ranks as one of the cognoscenti here, who exclaimed triumphantly at the end of one of the perpetrations, " Well, after all, there 's nothing like Rossini." Handel, Haydn, Mosart, Beethoven, and Weber, are *not*, that is certain.* I wish I could have seen Mr. ——

* The Russians and Danes are rich in the possession of an original and most touching national music; Scotland, Ireland, and Wales, are alike favoured with the most exquisite native melodies, probably, in the world. France, thºugh more barren in the wealth of sweet sounds, has a few fine old airs, that redeem her from the charge of utter sterility. Austria, Bohemia, and Switzerland, each claim a thousand beautiful and characteristic mountain songs; Italy is the very palace of music, Germany its temple; Spain resounds with wild and martial strains, and the thick groves of Portugal with native music, of a softer and sadder kind. All the nations of Europe, I presume all those of all the world, possess some kind of national music, and are blessed by Heaven with some measure of perception as to the loveliness of harmonious sounds. England alone, England and her descendant America, seems to have been denied a sense, to want a capacity, to have been stinted of a faculty, to the possession of which she vainly aspires. The rich spirit of Italian music, the solemn soul of German melody, the wild free Euterpe of the Cantons, have in vain been summoned by turns to teach her how to listen; 't is all in vain — she

during that finale. Coming out, were joined by
Mr. ———— : brought him home in the carriage
with us. Gave him " Ye mariners of Spain," and
some cold tongue, to take the taste of the Cenerentola out of his mouth. He stayed some time.
I like him enough : he is evidently a clever man,
though he does murder the King's English. (By
the by, does *English*, the tongue, belong, in America, to the King or the President — I wonder ?
I should rather think, from my limited observations, that it was the individual property of every
freeborn citizen of the United States.) Now, what
on earth can I say to the worthy citizens, if they
ask me what I thought of the Italian opera ! That
it was very amusing — yes, that will do nicely ;
that will be true, and not too direct a condemnation
of their good taste.

---

does listen painfully ; she has learnt by dint of time, and
much endurance, the technicalities of musical science ; she
pays regally her instructors in the divine pleasure, but all in
vain : the spirit of melody is not in her ; and in spite of hosts
of foreign musicians, in spite of the King's Theatre, in spite
of Pasta, in spite of music-masters paid like ministers of
state, in spite of singing and playing young ladies, and criti-
cising young gentlemen, England, to the last day of her
life, will be a dunce in music, for she hath it not in her ;
neither, if I am not much mistaken, hath her daughter.

Sunday, 7th.

Rose late. Young —— breakfasted with us. How unfortunately plain he is! His voice is marvellously like his father's, and it pleased me to hear him speak therefore. He was talking to my father about the various southern and western theatres, and bidding us expect to meet strange coadjutors in those lost lands beyond the world. On one occasion he said, when he was acting Richard the Third, some of the underlings kept their hats on while he was on the stage, whereat —— remonstrated, requesting them in a whisper to uncover, as they were in the presence of a king; to which admonition he received the following characteristic reply: " Fiddlestick! I guess we know nothing about kings in this country." Colonel —— called too; but D—— and I went off to church, and left my father to entertain them. Met Mr. —— and Mr. ——, who were coming to fetch us: went to Mr. ——'s pew. The music was very delightful; but decidedly I do not like music in church. The less my senses are appealed to in the house of prayer the better for me and my devotions. Although I have experienced excitement of a stern and martial, and sometimes of a

solemn, nature, from music, yet these melt away,
and its abiding influence with me is of a much
softer kind : therefore, in church, I had rather dis-
pense with it, particularly when they sing psalms,
as they did to-day, to the tune of " Come dwell
with me, and be my love." I did not like the
sermon much; there was effect in it, painting,
which I dislike. Staid the sacrament, the first I
have taken in this strange land. Mr. —— walked
home with us : when he was gone, Mr. —— and
Mr. —— called. When they had all taken their
departure, settled accounts, wrote journal, wrote
to my mother, came and put away sundry things,
and dressed for dinner. My father dined with
Mr. —— : D—— and I dined *tête-à-tête*. Colonel —— came twice through the pouring rain
to look after our baggage for to-morrow; such
charity is unexampled.

Monday, 8*th.*

Rose (oh, horror !) at a quarter to five. Night
was still brooding over the earth. Long before I
was dressed the first voice I heard was that of
Colonel ——, come to look after our luggage, and
see us off. To lend my friend a thousand pounds
(if I had it) I could; to lend him my horse, per-

haps I might; but to get up in the middle of the night, and come dawdling in the grey cold hour of the morning upon damp quays, and among dusty packages, except for my own flesh and blood, I could not. Yet this worthy man did it for us; whence I pronounce that he must be half a Quaker himself, for no common episcopal benevolence could stretch this pitch. Dressed, and gathered together my things, and at six o'clock, just as the night was folding its soft black wings, and rising slowly from the earth, we took our departure from that mansion of little ease, the American, and our fellow-lodgers the ants, and proceeded to the Philadelphia steam-boat, which started from the bottom of Barclay Street. We were recommended to this American hotel as the best and most comfortable in New York; and truly the charges were as high as one could have paid at the Clarendon, in the land of comfort and taxation. The wine was exorbitantly dear; champagne and claret about eleven shillings sterling a bottle; sherry, port, and madeira, from nine to thirteen. The rooms were a mixture of French finery, and Irish disorder and dirt; the living was by no means good; the whole house being conducted on a close scraping system of inferior accommodations and extravagant charges. On a sudden influx of visiters,

sitting-rooms were converted into bed-rooms, containing four and five beds. The number of servants was totally inadequate to the work; and the
articles of common use, such as knives and spoons,
were so scantily provided, that when the public
table was very full one day, the knives and forks
for our dinner were obliged to be washed from
theirs; and the luxury of a carving knife was not
to be procured at all on that occasion: it is true
that they had sometimes as many as two hundred
and fifty guests at the ordinary. The servants,
who, as I said before, were just a quarter as many
as the house required, had no bed-rooms allotted
to them, but slept *about* any where, in the public
rooms, or on sofas in drawing-rooms, let to private families.   In short, nothing can exceed the
want of order, propriety, and comfort in this establishment, except the enormity of the tribute it
levies upon pilgrims and wayfarers through the
land.*   And so, as I said, we departed therefrom
nothing loath.

The morning was dull, dreary, and damp, which

---

* It is but justice to state, that this house has passed
into other hands, and is much improved in every respect.
Strangers, particularly Englishmen, will find a great convenience in the five o'clock ordinary, now established there
which is, I am told, excellently conducted and appointed.

I regretted very much. The steam-boat was very large and commodious, as all these conveyances are. I enquired of one of the passengers what the power of the engine was: he replied that he did not exactly know, but that he thought it was about forty-horse power; and that, when going at speed, the engine struck thirty times in a minute: this appeared to me a great number in so short a time; but the weather shortly became wet and drizzly, and I did not remain on deck to observe. My early rising had made me very sleepy, so I came down to the third deck to sleep. These steam-boats have three stories; the upper one is, as it were, a roofing or terrace on the leads of the second, a very desirable station when the weather is neither too foul nor too fair; a burning sun being, I should think, as little desirable there as a shower of rain. The second floor or deck has the advantage of the ceiling above, and yet, the sides being completely open, it is airy, and allows free sight of the shores on either hand. Chairs, stools, and benches, are the furniture of these two decks. The one below, or third floor, downwards, in fact, the *ground floor*, being the one near the water, is a spacious room completely roofed and walled in, where the passengers take their meals, and resort if the weather is unfavourable.

At the end of this room is a smaller cabin for the use of the ladies, with beds and a sofa, and all the conveniences necessary, if they should like to be sick; whither I came and slept till breakfast time. Vigne's account of the pushing, thrusting, rushing, and devouring on board a western steam-boat at meal times had prepared me for rather an awful spectacle; but this, I find, is by no means the case in these more civilised parts, and every thing was conducted with perfect order, propriety, and civility. The breakfast was good, and served and eaten with decency enough. Came up on the upper deck, and walked about with my father. The width of the river struck me as remarkable; but the shores were flat, and for the most part uninteresting, except for the rich and various tints which the thickets of wood presented, and which are as superior in brilliancy and intenseness to our autumnal colouring as their gorgeous skies are to ours. Opposite the town of Amboy, the Raritan opens into a magnificent lake-like expanse round the extreme point of Staten Island.*   As

* The whole of this passage is in fact a succession of small bays, forming a continuation to the grand bay of New York, and dividing Staten Island from the mainland of New Jersey; the Raritan river does not properly begin till Amboy, where it empties itself into a bay of its own name.

the shores on either side, however, were not very
interesting, I finished reading Combe's book.
There is much sound philosophy in it; but I do
not think it altogether establishes the main point
that he wishes to make good — the truth of phrenology, and the necessity of its being adopted as
the only science of the human mind. His general
assertions admit of strong individual exceptions,
which, I think, go far towards invalidating the
generality. However, 't is not a full developement
of his own system, but, as it were, only an introduction to it; and his own admissions of the obscurity and uncertainty in which that system is
still involved necessarily enforces a suspension of
judgment, until its practical results have become
more manifest, and in some measure borne witness
to the truth of his theory.—At about half-past
ten we reached the place where we leave the river,
to proceed across a part of the State of New Jersey
to the Delaware. The landing was beyond measure wretched: the shore shelved down to the
water's edge; and its marshy, clayey, sticky soil,
rendered doubly soft and squashy by the damp
weather, was strewn over with broken potsherds,
stones, and bricks, by way of pathway; these,
however, presently failed, and some slippery planks
half immersed in mud were the only roads to the

coaches that stood ready to receive the passengers of the steam-boat. Oh, these coaches! English eye hath not seen, English ear hath not heard, nor hath it entered into the heart of Englishmen to conceive the surpassing clumsiness and wretchedness of these leathern inconveniences. They are shaped something like boats, the sides being merely leathern pieces, removable at pleasure, but which, in bad weather, are buttoned down to protect the inmates from the wet. There are three seats in this machine; the middle one, having a movable leathern strap, by way of adossier, runs between the carriage doors, and lifts away to permit the egress and ingress of the occupants of the other seats. Into the one facing the horses D—— and I put ourselves; presently two young ladies occupied the opposite one; a third lady, and a gentleman of the same party, sat in the middle seat, into which my father's huge bulk was also squeezed; finally, another man belonging to the same party ensconced himself between the two young ladies. Thus the two seats were filled, each with three persons, and there should by rights have been a third on ours; for this nefarious black hole on wheels is intended to carry nine. However, we profited little by the space, for, letting alone that there is not really and truly room for more than

two human beings of common growth and proportions on each of these seats, the third place
was amply filled up with baskets and packages of
ours, and huge *undoubleableup* coats and cloaks of
my father's. For the first few minutes I thought
I must have fainted from the intolerable sensation
of smothering which I experienced. However,
the leathers having been removed, and a little
more air obtained, I took heart of grace, and re-
signed myself to my fate. Away wallopped the
four horses, trotting with their front, and galloping
with their hind legs; and away went we after them,
bumping, thumping, jumping, jolting, shaking,
tossing, and tumbling, over the wickedest road, I
do think the cruellest, hard-heartedest road that
ever wheel rumbled upon. Thorough bog and
marsh, and ruts wider and deeper than any christian ruts I ever saw, with the roots of trees pro-
truding across our path; their boughs every now
and then giving us an affectionate scratch through
the windows; and, more than once, a half-demo-
lished trunk or stump lying in the middle of the
road lifting us up, and letting us down again, with
most awful variations of our poor coach body from
its natural position. Bones of me! what a road!*

---

* I had always heard that the face of nature was gigantic
in America; and truly we found the wrinkles such for so
young a country. The ruts were absolute abysses.

Even my father's solid proportions could not keep their level, but were jerked up to the roof and down again every three minutes.   Our companions seemed nothing dismayed by these wondrous performances of a coach and four, but laughed and talked incessantly, the young ladies, at the very top of their voices, and with the national nasal twang.* The conversation was much of the *genteel* shopkeeper kind; the wit of the ladies, and the gallantry of the gentlemen, savouring strongly of tapes and yard measures, and the shrieks of laughter of the whole set enough to drive one into a frenzy. The ladies were all pretty; two of them particularly so, with delicate fair complexions, and beau-

* The southern, western, and eastern states of North America have each their strong peculiarities of enunciation, which render them easy of recognition.   The Virginian and New England accents appear to me the most striking; Pennsylvania and New York have much less brogue; but through all their various tones and pronunciations a very strong nasal inflection preserves their universal brotherhood. They all speak through their noses, and at the top of their voices.   Of dialects, properly so called, there are none; though a few expressions, peculiar to particular states, which generally serve to identify their citizens; but these are not numerous, and a jargon approaching in obscurity that of many of our counties is not to be met with.   The language used in society generally is unrefined, inelegant, and often ungrammatically vulgar; but it is more vulgar than unintelligible by far.

tiful grey eyes : how I wish they could have held
their tongues for two minutes. We had not long
been in the coach before one of them complained
of being dreadfully sick.* This, in such a space,
and with seven near neighbours ! Fortunately she
was near the window; and during our whole fourteen miles of purgatory she alternately leaned
from it overcome with sickness, then reclined lan-
guishingly in the arms of her next neighbour, and
then, starting up with amazing vivacity, joined her
voice to the treble duet of her two pretty companions, with a superiority of shrillness, that might
have been the pride and envy of Billingsgate.
'T was enough to bother a rookery ! The country
through which we passed was woodland, flat, and
without variety, save what it derived from the
wondrous richness and brilliancy of the autumnal
foliage. Here indeed decay is beautiful; and nature appears more gorgeously clad in this her
fading mantle, than in all the summer's flush of
bloom in our less favoured climates. † I noted

---

* This appears to me to be a most frequent ailment among
the American ladies : they must have particularly bilious constitutions. I never remember travelling in a steam-boat, on
the smoothest water, without seeing sundry " afflicted fair
ones" who complained bitterly of *sea-sickness* in the river.

† In spite of its beauty, or rather on that very account,
an American autumn is to me particularly sad. It presents

several beautiful wild flowers growing among the underwood; some of which I have seen adorning with great dignity our most cultivated gardens.* None of the trees had any size or appearance of age: they are the second growth, which have sprung from the soil once possessed by a mightier race of vegetables. The quantity of mere underwood, and the number of huge black stumps rising in every direction a foot or two from the soil, bear witness to the existence of fine forest timber. The few cottages and farm houses which we passed reminded me of similar dwellings in France and Ireland; yet the peasantry here have not the same excuse for disorder and dilapidation as either the Irish or French. The farms had the same deso-

---

an union of beauty and decay, that for ever reminds me of that loveliest disguise death puts on, when the cheek is covered with roses, and the eyes are like stars, and the life is perishing away; even so appear the gorgeous colours of the withering American woods. 'T is a whole forest dying of consumption.

* The magnolia and azalia are two of these; and, earlier in the summer, the whole country looks like fairy-land, with the profuse and lovely blossoms of the wild laurel, an evergreen shrub unequalled for its beauty, and which absolutely over-runs every patch of uncultivated ground. I wonder none of our parks have yet been adorned with it: it is a hardy plant, and I should think would thrive admirably in England.

late, untidy, untended look : the gates broken, the fences carelessly put up, or ill repaired; the farming utensils sluttishly scattered about a littered yard, where the pigs seemed to preside by undisputed right; house-windows broken, and stuffed with paper or clothes; dishevelled women, and barefooted, anomalous looking human young things;—none of the stirring life and activity which such places present in England and Scotland; above all, none of the enchanting mixture of neatness, order, and rustic elegance and comfort, which render so picturesque the surroundings of a farm, and the various belongings of agricultural labour in my own dear country.* The fences struck me

* In the opening chapter of that popular work, Eugene Aram, are the following words : — " It has been observed, and there is a world of homely, ay, and of legislative knowledge in the observation, that wherever you see a flower in a cottage garden, or a bird-cage at the window, you may feel sure that the cottagers are better and wiser than their neighbours." The truth of this observation is indisputable. But for such " humble tokens of attention to something beyond the *sterile labour* of life" you look in vain during a progress through this country. In New England alone, neatness and a certain endeavour at rustic elegance and adornment, in the cottages and country residences, recall those of their father-land; and the pleasure of the traveller is immeasurably heightened by this circumstance. If the wild beauties of uncultivated nature lead our contemplations to our great Maker, these lowly witnesses of the industry and natural refinement of

as peculiar; I never saw any such in England.
They are made of rails of wood placed horizon-
tally, and meeting at obtuse angles, so forming a
zig-zag wall of wood, which runs over the country
like the herring-bone seams of a flannel petticoat.
At each of the angles two slanting stakes, considerably higher than the rest of the fence, were
driven into the ground, crossing each other at the
top, so as to secure the horizontal rails in their
position.*   There was every now and then a soft

---

the laborious cultivator of the soil warm our heart with
sympathy for our kind, and the cheering conviction that,
however improved by cultivation, the sense of beauty, and
the love of what is lovely, have been alike bestowed upon all
our race; 't is a wholesome conviction, which the artificial
divisions of society too often cause us to lose sight of.   The
labourer, who, after "sweating in the eye of Phœbus" all
the day, at evening trains the fragrant jasmine round his
lowly door, is the very same man who, in other circumstances, would have been the refined and liberal patron of
those arts which reflect the beauty of nature.

* In all my progress I looked in vain for the refreshing
sight of a hedge — no such thing was to be seen; and their
extreme rarity throughout the country renders the more
cultivated parts of it arid-looking and comparatively dreary.
These crooked fences in the south, and stone walls to the
north, form the divisions of the fields, instead of those delicious "hedge-rows green," where the old elms delight to
grow, where the early violets and primroses first peep sheltered forth, where the hawthorn blossoms sweeten the sum-

vivid strip of turf, along the road-side, that made me long for a horse. Indeed the whole road would have been a delightful ride, and was a most bitter drive. At the end of fourteen miles we turned into a swampy field, the whole fourteen coachfuls of us, and, by the help of Heaven, bag and baggage were packed into the coaches which stood on the rail-way ready to receive us. The carriages were not drawn by steam, like those on the Li-

---

mer, the honeysuckle hangs its yellow garlands in the autumn, and the red " hips and haws" shine like bushes of earthly coral in the winter.

But the Americans are in too great a hurry to plant hedges : they have abundance of native material ; but a wooden fence is put up in a few weeks, a hedge takes as many years to grow ; and, as I said before, an American has not time to be a year about any thing. When first the country was settled, the wood was an encumbramce, and it was cut down accordingly; that is by no means the case now ; and the only recommendation of these fences is, therefore, the comparative rapidity with which they can be constructed. One of the most amiable and distinguished men of this country once remarked to me, that the Americans were in too great a hurry about every thing they undertook to bring any thing to perfection. And certainly, as far as my observation goes, I should *calculate* that an American is born, lives, and dies twice as fast as any other human creature. I believe one of the great inducements to this national hurry is, that " time is money," which is true; but it is also true, sometimes, that " most haste makes worst speed."

verpool rail-way, but by horses, with the mere advantage in speed afforded by the iron ledges, which,
to be sure, compared with our previous progress
through the ruts, was considerable. Our coachful
got into the first carriage of the train, escaping,
by way of especial grace, the dust which one's
predecessors occasion. This vehicle had but two
seats, in the usual fashion; each of which held
four of us. The whole inside was lined with blazing
scarlet leather, and the windows *shaded* with stuff
curtains of the same refreshing colour; which,
with full complement of passengers, on a fine,
sunny, American summer's day, must make as
pretty a little miniature hell as may be, I should
think. The baggage waggon, which went before
us, a little obstructed the view. The road was
neither pretty nor picturesque; but still fringed
on each side with the many-coloured woods, whose
rich tints made variety even in sameness. This
rail-road is an infinite blessing; 't is not yet finished,
but shortly will be so, and then the whole of that
horrible fourteen miles will be performed in comfort and decency in less than half the time. In
about an hour and a half we reached the end of
our rail-road part of the journey, and found another steam-boat waiting for us, when we all embarked on the Delaware. Again, the enormous
width of the river struck me with astonishment

and admiration. Such huge bodies of water mark out the country through which they run, as the future abode of the most extensive commerce, and greatest maritime power in the universe. The banks presented much the same features as those of the Raritan, though they were not quite so flat, and more diversified with scattered dwellings, villages, and towns. We passed Bristol and Burlington, stopping at each of them to take up passengers.* I sat working, having finished my book, not a little discomfited by the pertinacious staring of some of my fellow-travellers. One woman, in particular, after wandering round me in every direction, at last came and sat down opposite me, and literally gazed me out of countenance. One improvement they have adopted on board these boats is to forbid smoking, except in the fore part of the vessel. I wish they would suggest that, if the gentlemen would refrain from spitting about too, it would be highly agreeable to the female part of the community. The universal practice here of this disgusting trick makes me absolutely sick: every place is made a perfect piggery of —

* These are two very pretty villages of Quaker origin; situated in the midst of a fertile and lovely country, and much resorted to during the summer season by the Philadelphians.

street, stairs, steam-boat, every where—and behind
the scenes; and on the stage at rehearsal I have
been shocked and annoyed beyond expression by
this horrible custom.   To-day, on board the boat,
it was a perfect shower of saliva all the time; and
I longed to be released from my fellowship with
these very obnoxious chewers of tobacco.*   At
about four o'clock we reached Philadelphia, having
performed the journey between that and New York
(a distance of a hundred miles) in less than ten
hours, in spite of bogs, ruts, and all other impediments.   The manager came to look after us and
our goods, and we were presently stowed into a
coach which conveyed us to the Mansion House,
the best reputed inn in Philadelphia.   On asking
for our bed-rooms, they showed D—— and myself
into a double-bedded room. On my remonstrating
against this, the chamber-maid replied, that they
were not accustomed to allow lodgers so *much room*

* It has happened to me after a few hours' travelling in a
steam-boat to find the white dress, put on fresh in the morning, covered with yellow tobacco stains; nor is this very
offensive habit confined to the lower orders alone. I have seen
gentlemen spit upon the carpet of the room where they were
sitting, in the company of women, without the slightest remorse; and I remember once seeing a gentleman, who was
travelling with us, very deliberately void his tobacco juice
into the bottom of the coach, instead of through the windows, to my inexpressible disgust.

as a room apiece. However, upon my insisting, they gave me a little nest just big enough to turn about in, but where, at least, I can be by myself. Dressed, and dined at five; after dinner, wrote journal till tea-time, and then came to bed.

Tuesday, 9th.

Rose at half-past eight. Went and took a bath. On my way thither, drove through two melancholy looking squares, which reminded me a little of poor old Queen Square in Bristol. The ladies' baths were closed, but as I was not particular, they gave me one in the part of the house usually allotted to the men's use. I was much surprised to find two baths in one room, but it seems to me that the people of this country have an aversion to solitude, whether eating, sleeping, or under any other circumstances.

*　　*　　*　　*　　*

*　　*　　*　　*　　*

I made acquaintance with a bewitching Newfoundland puppy whom I greatly coveted. Came home, dressed, and breakfasted. After breakfast, righted my things, and wrote journal. Took a walk with my father through some of the principal streets. The town is perfect silence and solitude, compared

with New York; there is a greater air of age about
it too, which pleases me. The red houses are not
so fiercely red, nor the white facings so glaringly
white; in short, it has not so new and flaunting a
look, which is a great recommendation to me. The
city is regularly built, the streets intersecting each
other at right angles. We passed one or two
pretty buildings in pure white marble, and the
bank in Chestnut Street, which is a beautiful little
copy of the Parthenon. The pure, cold, clear-
looking marble, suits well with the severe and un-
adorned style of architecture; and is in harmony,
too, with the extreme brilliancy of the sky, and
clearness of the atmosphere of this country.* We

* I wish that somebody would be so obliging as to impress
people in general with the extreme excellence of a perception
of the *fitness of things*. Besides the intrinsic beauty of works
of art, they have a beauty derived from their appropriateness
to the situations in which they are placed, and their harmony
with the objects which surround them: this minor species of
beauty is yet a very great one. If it were more studied, and
better understood, public buildings would no longer appear
as if they had fallen out of the clouds by chance; parks and
plantations would no more have the appearance of nurseries,
where the trees were classed by kind, instead of being massed
according to their various forms and colours; and Gothic and
classic edifices would not so often seem as if they had forsaken their appropriate situations, to rear themselves in
climates, and among scenery, with which they in no way har-
monise.

passed another larger building, also a bank, in the Corinthian style, which did not please me so much. The shops here are much better looking than those at New York : the windows are larger, and more advantageously constructed for the display of goods; and there did not appear to be the same anomalous mixture of vendibles, as in the New York shops. The streets were very full of men hurrying to the town house, to give their votes. It is election time, and much excitement subsists with regard to the choice of the future President.*

---

* Politics of all sorts, I confess, are far beyond my limited powers of comprehension. Those of this country, as far as I have been able to observe, resolve themselves into two great motives, — the aristocratic desire of elevation and separation, and the democratic desire of demolishing and levelling. Whatever may be the immediate cause of excitement or discussion, these are the two master-springs to which they are referable. Every man in America is a politician; and political events, of importance only because they betray the spirit which would be called into play by more stirring occasions, are occurring incessantly, and keeping alive the interest which high and low alike take in the evolutions of their political machine. Elections of state officers, elections of civil authorities, all manner of elections (for America is one perpetual contest for votes), are going on all the year round; and whereas the politics of men of private stations in other countries are kept quietly by them, and exhibited only on occasions of general excitement, those of an American are as inseparable from him as his clothes, and mix up with his daily discharge of his commonest daily avocations. I was

The democrats or radicals are for the re-election of General Jackson, but the aristocratic party, which here at all events is the strongest, are in favour of H enry Clay. Here is the usual quantity of shouting and breaking windows that we are accustomed to on these occasions. I saw a caricature of Jackson and Van Buren, his chief supporter, which was entitled " The King and his Minister." Van Buren held a crown in his hand, and the devil was approaching Jackson with a sceptre. — Came in at half-past four, dressed for dinner : they gave us an excellent one. The master of this house was, it seems, once a man of independent fortune, and a great *bon vivant*. He has retained from thence a fellow-feeling for his guests, and does by

---

extremely amused at seeing over a hat shop in New York one day, " Anti-Bank Hat Store," written in most attractive characters, as an inducement for all good democrats to go in and purchase their beavers of so republican a hatter. The universal-suffrage system is of course the cause of this general political mania ; and during an election of mayor or aldermen the good shopkeepers of New York are in as fierce a state of excitement as if the choice of a perpetual dictator were the question in point. Politics is the main subject of conversation among American men in society ; but, as I said before, the immediate object of discussion being most frequently some petty local interest or other, strangers cannot derive much pleasure from, or feel much sympathy in, the debate.

them as he would be done by. After dinner, worked till tea-time; after tea, wrote journal, and now I 'll go to bed. We are attended here by a fat old lively negro, by name Henry ; who canters about in our behalf with great alacrity, and seems wrapt in much wonderment at many of our proceedings. By the by, the black who protected our baggage from the steam-boat was ycleped *Oliver Cromwell.* I have begun Grahame's History of America, and like it " mainly," as the old plays say.

Wednesday, 10*th.*

Rose at eight. After breakfast, trimmed a cap, and wrote to dear ——. The streets were in an uproar all night, people shouting and bonfires blazing; in short, electioneering fun, which seems to be pretty much the same all the world over. Clay has it hollow here, they say : I wonder what Colonel —— will say to that. At twelve o'clock, sallied forth with D—— to rehearsal. The theatre is very pretty ; not large, but well sized, and I should think, favourably constructed for the voice.

* * * * *

* * * * *

Unless Aldabella is irresistibly lovely, as well as wicked, there is no accounting for the conduct of Fazio. My own idea of her, as well as Milman's description, is every thing that can be conceived of splendid in beauty, sparkling in wit, graceful in deportment, gorgeous in apparel, and deep and dangerous in crafty wiliness; in short, the old serpent in the shape of Mrs. ———. I wish Mrs. ——— would act that part: I could act it well enough, but she would both act and look it, to the very life. After rehearsal, walked about the town in quest of some *coques de perle* for my Bianca dress: could not procure any. I like this town extremely : there is a look of comfort and cleanliness, and withal of age about it, which pleases me. It is quieter, too, than New York, and though not so gay, for that very reason is more to my fancy ; the shops, too, have a far better appearance. New York always gave me the idea of an irregular collection of temporary buildings, erected for some casual purpose, full of life, animation, and variety, but not meant to endure for any length of time; a fair, in short. This place has a much more substantial, sober, and city-like appearance. Came home at half-past two. In the hall met Mr. ———, who is grown ten years younger since I saw him last: it always delights me to see one of my fellow-passengers, and I am much disappointed in not finding ——— here. Dined at three ; after dinner, read my father some of my journal ; went on with letter to ———, and then went and dressed myself. Took coffee, and adjourned to the theatre. The house was very full, but not so full as the Park on the first night of his acting in New York, which accounts for the greater stillness of the audience. I watched my father narrowly through his part to-night with great attention and some consequent fatigue, and the conclusion I have come to is this : that though his workmanship may be, and is, far finer *in the hand*, than that of any other artist. I ever saw, yet its very minute accuracy and refinement renders it unfit for the frame in which it is exhibited. Whoever should paint a scene calculated for so large a space as a theatre, and destined to be viewed at the distance from which an audience beholds it, with the laborious finish and fine detail of a miniature, would commit a great error in judgment. Nor would he have the least right to complain, although the public should prefer the coarser, yet far more effective work of a painter, who, neglecting all refinement and niceness of execution, should merely paint with such full colouring, and breadth and boldness of touch, as to produce in the wide space he is called upon to fill, and upon the remote senses he appeals to, the *effect* of that which he intends to represent. Indeed he

is the better artist of the two, though probably
not the most intellectual man. For it is the part
of such an one to know exactly what will best convey to the mass of mind and feeling to which he
addresses himself the emotions and passions which
he wishes them to experience.* Now the great

* I have often thought that the constant demand for
small theatres, which I have heard made by persons of the
higher classes of society in England, was a great proof of
the decline of the more imaginative faculties among them ;
and the proportionate increase of that fastidious and critical
spirit, which is so far removed from every thing which con-
stitutes the essence of poetry. The idea of illusion in a
dramatic exhibition is confined to the Christmas spectators
of old tragedies and new pantomimes; the more refined portions of our English audiences yawn through Shakspeare's
historical plays, and *quiz* through those which are histories
of human nature and its awful passions. They have forgotten what human nature really is, and cannot even *imagine it*.
They require absolute reality on the stage, because their incapable spirits scoff at poetical truth, and that absolute
reality, in our days, consists in such representations as the
Rent Day ; or (crossing the water, for we dearly love what
is foreign) the homely improbabilities of Victorine, Henriette,
and a pack of equally worthless subjects of exhibition. Indeed, theatres have had an end; for the refined, the highly
educated, the first classes of society, they have had an end ; it
will be long, however, before the mass is sufficiently refined
to lose all power of imagination ; and while our aristocracy
patronise French melodramas, and seek their excitement in
the most trashy sentimentalities of the modern *école roman-
tique*, I have some hopes that our plebeian pits and galleries

beauty of all my father's performances, but particularly of Hamlet, is a wonderful accuracy in the
detail of the character which he represents; an
accuracy which modulates the emphasis of every
word, the nature of every gesture, the expression
of every look; and which renders the whole a
most laborious and minute study, toilsome in the
conception and acquirement, and most toilsome
in the execution. But the result, though the natural one, is not such as he expects, as the reward
of so much labour. Few persons are able to follow
such a performance with the necessary attention,
and it is almost as great an exertion to see it *un-
derstandingly*, as to act it. The amazing study of
it requires a study in those who are to appreciate
it, and, as I take it, this is far from being what the
majority of spectators are either capable or desir-
ous of doing; the actor loses his pains, and they
have but little pleasure. Those who perform, and
those who behold a play, have but a certain proportion of power of exciting, and capability of being excited. If, therefore, the actor expends his

---

may still retain their sympathy for the loves of Juliet and
the sorrows of Ophelia. I would rather a thousand times
act either of those parts to a set of Manchester mechanics,
than to the most select of our aristocracy, for they are " nothing, if not critical."

power of exciting, and his audience's power of being excited, upon the detail of the piece, and continues through five whole acts to draw from both, the main and striking points, those of strongest appeal, those calculated most to rouse at once, and gratify the emotions of the spectator, have not the same intensity or vigour that they would have had, if the powers of both actor and audience had been reserved to give them their fullest effect. A picture requires light and shadow; and the very relief that throws some of the figures in a fine painting into apparent obscurity, in reality enhances the effect produced by those over which the artist has shed a stronger light. Every note in the most expressive song does not require a peculiar expression; and an air sung with individual emphasis on each note would be utterly unproductive of the desired effect. All things cannot have all their component parts equal, and " nothing pleaseth but rare accidents." This being so, I think that acting the best which skilfully husbands the actor's and spectator's powers, and puts forth the whole of the one, to call forth the whole of the other, occasionally only; leaving the intermediate parts sufficiently level, to allow him and them to recover the capability of again producing, and again receiving, such impressions. It is constant that our finest nerves deaden and dull from over-excitement, and require repose, before they regain their acute power of sensation. At the same time, I am far from advocating that most imperfect conception and embodying of a part which Kean allows himself: literally acting detached passages alone, and leaving all the others, and the entire character, indeed, utterly destitute of unity, or the semblance of any consistency whatever. But Kean and my father are immediately each other's antipodes, and in adopting their different styles of acting, it is evident that each has been guided as much by his own physical and intellectual individuality, as by any fixed principle of art. The one, Kean, possesses particular physical qualifications; an eye like an orb of light, a voice, exquisitely touching and melodious in its tenderness, and in the harsh dissonance of vehement passion terribly true; to these he adds the intellectual ones of vigour, intensity, amazing power of concentrating effect: these give him an entire mastery over his audience in all striking, sudden, impassioned passages; in fulfilling which, he has contented himself, leaving unheeded what he probably could not compass, the unity of conception, the refinement of detail, and evenness of

execution.*   My father possesses certain physical
defects, a faintness of colouring in the face and
eye, a weakness of voice ; and the corresponding
intellectual deficiencies, a want of intensity, vigour,
and concentrating power: these circumstances have
led him (probably unconsciously) to give his attention and study to the finer and more fleeting
shades of character, the more graceful and delicate
manifestations of feeling, the exquisite variety of
all minor parts, the classic keeping of a highly
wrought whole ; to all these, polished and refined
tastes, an acute sense of the beauty of harmonious

---

* Kean is gone — and with him are gone Othello, Shylock,
and Richard. I have lived among those whose theatrical
creed would not permit them to acknowledge him as a great
actor; but they must be bigoted, indeed, who would deny
that he was a great genius, a man of most original and striking powers, careless of art, perhaps because he did not need
it ; but possessing those rare gifts of nature, without which
art alone is as a dead body.   Who that ever heard will ever
forget the beauty, the unutterable tenderness of his reply to
Desdemona's entreaties for Cassio, " Let him come when
he will, I can deny thee nothing ; " the deep despondency of
his " Oh, now farewell ; " the miserable anguish of his " Oh,
Desdemona, away, away" ?   Who that ever saw will ever
forget the fascination of his dying eyes in Richard : when
deprived of his sword, the wondrous power of his look
seemed yet to avert the uplifted arm of Richmond.   If he
was irregular and unartist-like in his performances, so is
Niagara, compared with the water-works of Versailles.

proportions, and a native grace, gentleness, and refinement of mind and manner, have been his prompters; but they cannot inspire those startling and tremendous bursts of passion, which belong to the highest walks of tragedy, and to which he never gave their fullest expression. I fancy my aunt Siddons united the excellences of both these styles. But to return to my father's Hamlet: every time I see it, something strikes me afresh in the detail. Nothing in my mind can exceed the exquisite beauty of his last " Go on — I follow thee," to the ghost. The full gush of deep and tender faith, in spite of the awful mystery, to whose unfolding he is committing his life, is beautiful beyond measure. It is distinct, and wholly different from the noble, rational, philosophic conviction, " And for my soul, what can it do to that?" It is full of the unutterable fondness of a believing heart, and brought to my mind, last night, those holy and lovely words of scripture, " Perfect love casteth out fear:" it enchanted me.* There is

* I have acted Ophelia three times with my father, and each time, in that beautiful scene where his madness and his love gush forth together like a torrent swollen with storms, that bears a thousand blossoms on its troubled waters, I have experienced such deep emotion as hardly to be able to speak. The exquisite tenderness of his voice, the wild compassion and forlorn pity of his looks, bestowing that on others,

one thing in which I do not believe my father ever has been, or ever will be, excelled; his high and noble bearing, his gallant, graceful, courteous deportment ; his perfect good-breeding on the stage; unmarked alike by any peculiarity of time, place, or self (except peculiar grace and beauty).   He appears to me the beau ideal of the courtly, thorough-bred, chivalrous gentleman from the days of the admirable Crichton down to those of George the Fourth.   Coming home after the play, the marble buildings in the full moonlight reminded me of the Ghost in Hamlet : they looked like pale majestic spirits, cold, calm, and colourless.

Thursday, 11*th*.

Rose rather late. After breakfast, wrote journal ;

---

which, above all others, he most needed; the melancholy restlessness, the bitter self-scorning ; every shadow of expression and intonation was so full of all the mingled anguish that the human heart is capable of enduring, that my eyes scarce fixed on his ere they filled with tears ; and long before the scene was over, the letters and jewel cases I was tendering to him were wet with them.   The hardness of professed actors and actresses is something amazing : after acting this part, I could not but recall the various Ophelias I have seen, and commend them for the astonishing absence of every thing like feeling which they exhibited.   Oh, it made my heart sore to act it.

at twelve, went to rehearsal.   *   *   *

  *   *   *   *   *

After rehearsal, came home, habited, and went to the riding-school to try some horses. *Merci de moi !* what quadrupeds ! How they did wallop and shamble about; poor half-broken dumb brutes ! they know no better; and as the natives here are quite satisfied with their shuffling, rollicking, mongrel pace, half trot, half canter, why it is not worth while to break horses in a christian-like fashion for them.* I found something that I think my father can ride with tolerable comfort, but must go

---

* I am speaking now only of the common saddle-horses that one sees about the streets and roads. The southern breed of race-horses is a subject of great interest and care to all sporting men here : they are very beautiful animals, of a remarkably slight and delicate make. But the perfection of horses in this county are those trained for trotting : their speed is almost incredible. I have been whirled along in a light-built carriage by a pair of famous professed trotters, who certainly got over the ground at the rate of a moderate going steam-engine, and this without ever for a moment breaking into a gallop. The fondness of the Americans for this sort of horses, however, is one reason why one can so rarely obtain a well mouthed riding-horse. These trotters are absolutely carried on the bit, and require only a snaffle, and an arm of iron to hold them up. A horse well set upon his haunches is not to be met with; and owing to this mode of breaking, their action is entirely from the head and shoulders; and they both look and feel as if they would tumble down on their noses.

again to-morrow and see after something for myself. Came home: the enchanting Mr. Head has
allowed me a piano-forte; but in bringing it into
the room, the stupid slave broke one of its legs
off, whereat I was like to faint, for I thought Mr.
Head would wish me hanged therefore. Nothing
can exceed the civility of the people here, and the
house is extremely well kept, quiet, and comfortable. Came home in high delight with this Quaker
city, which is indeed very pretty and pleasant.
Played on the piano: dressed for dinner. After
dinner, practised till tea-time, finished journal,
discussed metaphysics with D——, for which I
am a fool; wrote to-day's journal, and now to bed.
I have a dreadful cold and cough, and have done
nothing but hack and snivel the whole day long:
this is a bad preparation for to-morrow's work.
Howsoever ——

Friday, 12*th.*

Rose at eight. After breakfast, sat writing journal and letter to ——. At half-past eleven, went
to rehearsal. Afterwards walked down to the
riding-school with my father. The horse I was
to look at had not arrived; but my father saw the
grey. We were there for some time; and during

that whole some time a tall, thin, unhappy looking
gentleman, who had gotten up upon a great hulking
rawboned horse, kept trotting round and round,
with his legs dangling down, *sans* stirrups, at the
rate of a mile and a quarter an hour; occasionally
ejaculating in the mildest of tones, " keome —
keome up ; " whereat the lively brute, nothing persuaded, proceeded in the very same pace, at the
very same rate; and this went on till I wondered
at the man and the beast. Came home and put
out things for the theatre. My cold and cough
are dreadful. After dinner, practised : invented
and executed a substitute for the *coques de perle*
in my Bianca dress ; and lay down to rest a little
before my work. At six, went to the theatre: the
house was very full ; and D—— and my father
say that I was extremely ungracious in my acknowledgment of their greeting. I cannot tell; I did
not mean to be so ; I made them three courtesies,
and what could woman do more? Of course, I
can neither feel nor look so glad to see them, as
I am to see my own dear London people : neither
can I be as profound in my obeisance, as when my
audience is civil enough to rise to me: " there is
differences, look you." *   *   *
    *   *   *   *   *
    *   *   *   *   *

My Fazio had a pair of false black whiskers on,
which distilled a black stripe of trickling cement
down his cheeks, and kept me in agony every time
he had to embrace me. My voice was horrible
to hear; alternately like Mrs. —— and ——, and
every now and then it was all I could do to utter
at all. This audience is the most unapplausive I
ever acted to, not excepting my *excitable* friends
north of the Tweed. They were very attentive,
certainly, but how they did make me work ! 'T is
amazing how much an audience loses by this species
of hanging back, even where the silence proceeds
from unwillingness to interrupt a good performance : though in reality it is the greatest compliment an actor can receive, yet he is deprived by
that very stillness of half his power. Excitement
is reciprocal between the performer and the audience : he creates it in them, and receives it back
again from them ; and in that last scene in Fazio,
half the effect that I produce is derived from the
applause which I receive, the very noise and tumult
of which tends to heighten the nervous energy
which the scene itself begets. I know that my
aunt Siddons has frequently said the same thing.
And besides the above reason for applause, the
physical powers of an actor require, after any tremendous exertion, the rest and regathering of

breath and strength, which the interruption of the audience affords him; moreover, as 't is the conventional mode of expressing approbation in a theatre, it is chilling and uncomfortable to go toiling on, without knowing whether, as the maid-servants say, " one gives satisfaction or no." They made noise enough, however, at the end of the play. Came home, supped, and to bed: weary to death, and with a voice like a cracked bagpipe.

Saturday, 13*th.*

Rose at half-past eight. After breakfast, wrote journal; practised for an hour; got things ready for to-morrow; put on my habit, which I had no sooner done than the perverse clouds began to rain. The horses came at two, but the weather was so bad that I sent them away again. Practised for another hour, read a canto in Dante, and dressed for dinner. After dinner, worked and practised. Came to my own room, and tried to scribble something for the Mirror, at my father's request; the editors having made an especial entreaty to him, that I might write something for them, and also sit to some artist for them. I could not accomplish any thing, and they must just take something that I have by me: as for my

physiognomy, that they shall certainly not have
with my own good leave. I will never expend so
much useless time again as to sit for my picture;
nor will I let any unhappy painter again get abused
for painting me as I am, which is any thing but
what I look like. Lawrence alone could do it:
there is no other that could see my spirit through
my face; and as for the face without that, the less
that is seen of it the better. Came down to tea,
and found a young gentleman sitting with my
father; one Mr. ——. *   *   *

*   *   *   *   *

*   *   *   *   *

He was a pretty-spoken, *genteel* youth enough : he
drank tea with us, and offered to ride with me.
He is, it seems, a great fortune ; consequently, I
suppose (in spite of his inches), a great man.
Now I'll go to bed: my cough's enough to kill a
horse.

Sunday, 14*th.*

Rose late; so late that, by the time I had breakfasted, it was no longer time to go to church.

*   *   *   *   *

*   *   *   *   *

Finished my first letter to ——. Mr. —— called,

and told us that he was going about *agitating*, and
that Jackson was certainly to be re-elected. . *

*   *   *   *   *

*   *   *   *   *

At three o'clock D—— and I sallied forth to go
to church. Following the silver voices of the
Sabbath bells, as they called the worshippers to
the house of prayer, we entered a church with a
fine simple façade, and found ourselves in the
midst of a Presbyterian congregation. 'T is now'
upwards of eight years since, a school girl, I used
to attend a dissenter's chapel. The form of worship, though displeasing to me in itself, borrowed
a charm to-day from old association. How much
of the past it did recall !   *   *

*   *   *   *   *

*   *   *   *   *

Came home and dressed for dinner. After dinner
half-killed myself with laughter over an Irish version of Fazio, ycleped Grimaldi, from which the
author swears Milman has shamefully filched the
plot, characters, and even the language, I believe,
of his drama. A gentleman of the press, by
name ——, paid us an evening visit. He seems
an intelligent young man enough; and when he
spoke of the autumnal woods, by the Oneida lake,
his expressions were poetical and enthusiastic;

and he pleased me.*   He seems to think much of having had the honour of corresponding with sundry of the small literati of London. *Je lui en fais mon compliment.*   When he was gone, wrote another letter to ——, journal, and now to bed.

Monday, 15*th.*

Rose at eight; took a hot bath. The more I read of Grahame, the better I like him and his history. Those early settlers in Massachusetts

---

* Except where they have been made political tools, newspaper writers and editors have never, I believe, been admitted into good society in England. It is otherwise here : newspapers are the main literature of America; and I have frequently heard it quoted, as a proof of a man's abilities, that he writes in such and such a newspaper. Besides the popularity to be obtained by it, it is often attended with no small literary consideration ; and young men here, with talents of a really high order, and who might achieve far better things, too often are content to accept this very mediocre mode of displaying their abilities, at very little expense of thought or study, and neglect far worthier objects of ambition, and the rewards held out by a distant and permanent fame. I know that half my young gentlemen acquaintance here would reply, that they must live in the mean time, and it is a real and deep evil, arising from the institutions of this country, that every man must toil from day to day for his daily bread ; and in this degrading and spirit-loading care, all other nobler desires are smothered. It is a great national misfortune.

were fine fellows, indeed; and Cotton, one of the finest samples of a Christian priest imaginable. After breakfast, went to rehearsal. The day was cold, but beautifully bright and clear. The pure, fresh, invigorating air, and gay sunlight, together with the delightfully clean streets, and pretty mixture of trees and buildings in this nice town, caused me to rejoice, as I walked along.* After rehearsal, saw Sinclair and his wife. So — we are to act the Gamester here. Went and ordered a dress for that same, my own being at New York. Came home, put out things for the theatre, practised an hour; dined at three. After dinner, read a canto in Dante: he is my admiration! — great, great master! — a philosopher profound, as all poets should be; a glorious poet, as I wish all philosophers were. Sketched till dark. Chose a beautiful claret-coloured velvet for Mrs. Beverley; which will cost Miss Kemble eleven guineas, by this living light. At six, went to the theatre. I never beheld any thing more gorgeous than the sky

* This delightful virtue of neatness is carried almost to an inconvenient pitch by the worthy Philadelphians: the town, every now and then, appears to be in a perfect frenzy of cleanliness; and of a Saturday morning, early, the streets are really impassable, except to a good swimmer. " Cleanliness," says the old saw, " is near to godliness." Philadelphia must be very near heaven.

at sunset.   Autumn is an emperor here, clothed
in crimson and gold, and canopied with ruddy
glowing skies.   Yet I like the sad russet cloak of
our own autumnal woods; I like the sighing voice
of his lament through the vaporous curtain that
rises round his steps; I like the music of the
withered leaves that rustle in his path ; and oh,
above all, the solemn thoughts that wait upon
him, as he goes stripping the trees of their bright
foliage, leaving them like the ungarlanded columns
of a deserted palace.   The play was Romeo and
Juliet.   My father was the " youngest of that
name," for want of a better, or, rather, of a worse.
How beautiful this performance must have been,
when the youthful form made that appear natural
which now seems the triumph of art over nature.
Garrick said, that to act Romeo required a
grey head upon green shoulders.   Indeed, 'tis
difficult!   Oh, that our sapient judges did but
know half how difficult.   It is delightful to act
with my father.   One's imagination need toil but
little, to see in him the very thing he represents ;
whereas, with all other Romeos, although they
were much younger men, I have had to do double
work with that useful engine, my fancy : first, to
get rid of the material obstacle staring me in the
face, and then to substitute some more congenial

representative of that sweetest vision of youth and
love. Once, only, this was not necessary.

* * * * *

* * * * *

The audience here are, without exception, the
most disagreeable I ever played to. Not a single
hand did they give the balcony scene, or my
father's scene with the friar: they are literally
immovable. They applauded vehemently at the
end of my draught scene, and a great deal at the
end of the play; but they are, nevertheless, in-
tolerably dull; and it is all but impossible to act
to them. * * * *

* * * * *

* * * * *

The man who acted Capulet did it better than any
Capulet I ever acted with; and the nurse, besides
looking admirably, acted her part very well: and
't is hard to please me, after poor dear old Mrs.
Davenport. The house was literally crammed
from floor to ceiling. Came home tired and
hoarse; though my voice was a good deal better
to-day. Mr. —— supped with us. My father
expected a visit from the haggling Boston manager,
and chose to have a witness to the conference.

Tuesday, 16*th.*

Rose at nine.   After breakfast, read a canto in
Dante ; wrote journal ; practised for an hour.
The Boston manager, it seems, does not approve
of our terms; and after bargaining till past two
o'clock last night with my father, the latter, wearied out with his illiberal trafficking, and coarse
vulgarity of manner, declined the thing altogether :
so, unless the gentleman thinks better of the matter, we shall not go to Boston this winter.*   At
one o'clock, habited ; and at two, rode out with
my father.   The day was most enchanting, mild,
bright, and sunny; but the roads were deplorable,
and the country utterly dull.   My horse was a
hard-mouthed, half-broken beast, without pace of
any christian kind soever ; a perfect rack on hoofs :
how it did jog and jumble me.   However, my
bones are young, and my courage good, and I
don't mind a little hard work; but the road was

* The final result of our very unfortunate dealings with
this gentleman is, that our earnings (and they are not lightly
come by), to the amount of near three thousand dollars, are
at this moment in the hands of a trustee, and Heaven and a
New England court of justice will decide whether they are
ever to come into ours.

so villanously bad, and the surrounding country
so weary, dull, stale, and unprofitable, that I was
heartily sick of my ride, when we turned towards
Fairmount, the site of some large water-works on
the Schuylkill, by which Philadelphia is supplied
with water. On our right I descried, over some
heights, a castellated building of some extent,
whose formidable appearance, at least, bespoke an
arsenal; but it was the entrance to the penitentiary instead : and presently the river, bright,
and broad, and placid as a lake, with its beautiful
banks, and rainbow-tinted woods, opened upon us.
We crossed a covered wooden bridge, and followed the water's edge. The rich colours of the
foliage cast a warm light over the transparent face
of the mirror-like stream ; and, far along the
winding shores, a mingled mantle of gorgeous-
glowing tints lay over the woody banks, and was
reflected in the still, sunny river. Indeed, it was
lovely ! But our time was growing short, and we
had to turn home; which we did by a pleasant
and more direct path. My horse, towards the
end of the ride, got more manageable; and I
doubt whether it would not be wiser to continue
to ride it than try another, which may be just as
bad, and, moreover, a *stranger*. My riding-cap
seemed to excite universal marvel wherever we

passed. We came in at five o'clock; dressed, and dined. Just as I had finished dinner, a most beautiful, fragrant, and delicious nosegay was brought to me, with a very laconic note from a Philadelphia "*friend*," dashed under, as though from a Quaker. Whoever 't is from, Jew or Gentile, Puritan or Pagan, he, she, or it hath my most unbounded gratitude. Spent an ecstatic half hour in arranging my flowers in glasses; gave orders about my Mrs. Beverley's gown, and began marking journal; while doing so, a card was brought up.   *   *   *

   *   *   *   *   *

   *   *   *   *   *

Presently Mr. —— came in, another of our Pacific fellow-sailors. It pleases me to see them: they seem to bring me nearer to England. He gave a dreadful account of his arrival in Baltimore, and of the state to which the cholera had reduced that city. Mr. —— amused me, by telling me that he had heard my behaviour canvassed with much censure by some man or other, who met me at Mr. ——, and who was horrified at my taking up a book, and then a newspaper; and, in short, being neither tragical nor comical, at a dinner-party. Of course, I must seem a very strange

animal to them all; but they seem just as strange
to me.   *   *   *   *
    *   *   *   *   *

Wednesday, 17*th.*

Rose at eight. After breakfast, put out things
for the theatre. At eleven, went to rehearsal. It
seems there has been fighting, and rushing, and
tearing of coats at the box-office; and one man
has made forty dollars by purchasing and reselling
tickets at an increased price. After rehearsal,
came home. Mr. —— called, and sat some time :
he sails for England on the twenty-fourth. England, oh England ! — yet, after all, what is there
in that name? It is not my home; it is not those
beloved ones whose fellowship is half the time
what we call *home.* Is it really and truly the
yearning of the roots for the soil in which they
grew ? Perhaps it is only the restless roving
spirit, that still would be where it is not. I know
not. His description of American life and manners (and he knows both, for he has lived constantly in this country, and his partialities are, I
believe, fairly divided between it and his own,) is
any thing but agreeable.   *   *
    *   *   *   *   *

The dignified and graceful influence which married women, among us, exercise over the tone of manners, uniting the duties of home to the charms of social life, and bearing, at once, like the orange-tree, the fair fruits of maturity with the blossoms of their spring, is utterly unknown here. Married women are either house-drudges and nursery-maids, or, if they appear in society, comparative ciphers; and the retiring, modest, youthful bearing, which among us distinguishes girls of fifteen or sixteen, is equally unknown. Society is entirely led by chits, who in England would be sitting behind a pinafore; the consequence is, that it has neither the elegance, refinement, nor the propriety which belongs to ours; but is a noisy, rackety, vulgar congregation of flirting boys and girls, alike without style or decorum.* When

---

* When we arrived in America, we brought letters of introduction to several persons in New York: many were civil enough to call upon us: we were invited out to sundry parties, and were introduced into what is there called the first society. I do not wish to enter into any description of it, but will only say that I was most disagreeably astonished; and had it been my fate to have passed through the country as rapidly as most travellers do, I should have carried away a very unfavourable impression of the *best* society of New York. Fortunately, however, for me, my visits were repeated, and my stay prolonged; and, in the course of time, I became acquainted with many individuals whose manners

Mr. —— was gone, practised till dinner time.
After dinner, practised for half an hour; marked

---

and acquirements were of a high order, and from whose intercourse I derived the greatest gratification. But they
generally did me the favour to visit me; and I still could not
imagine how it happened that I never met them at the parties
to which I was invited, and in the circles where I visited. I
soon discovered that they formed a society among themselves, where all those qualities which I had looked for
among the self-styled *best* were to be found. When I name
Miss Sedgwick, Halleck, Irving, Bryant, Paulding, and some
of less fame, but whose acquirements rendered their companionship delightful indeed, amongst whom I felt proud
and happy to find several of my own name, it will no longer
appear singular that they should feel too well satisfied with
the resources of their own society, either to mingle in that
of the vulgar *fashionables*, or seek with avidity the acquaintance of every stranger that arrives in New York. It is not
to be wondered at that foreigners have spoken as they have
of what is termed fashionable society here, or have condemned, with unqualified censure, the manners and tone
prevailing in it. Their condemnations are true and just as
regards what they see; nor, perhaps, would they be much
inclined to moderate them when they found that persons
possessing every quality that can render intercourse between
rational creatures desirable were held in light esteem, and
neglected, as either bores, blues, or dowdies, by those so
infinitely their inferiors in every worthy accomplishment.
The same separation, or, if any thing, a still stronger one, subsists in Philadelphia between the self-styled fashionables
and the really good society. The distinction there is really
of a nature perfectly ludicrous. A friend of mine was describing to me a family whose manners were unexception-

journal, till time to go to the theatre; took coffee, and away. The house was crammed again, and the play better acted than I have ever seen it out of London, though Mrs. Candour had stuck upon her head a bunch of feathers which threatened the gods ; and Lady Sneerwell had dragged all her

---

able, and whose mental accomplishments were of a high order : upon my expressing some surprise that I had never met with them, my informant replied, " Oh, no, they are not received by the Chestnut Street *set*." If I were called upon to define that society in New York and Philadelphia which ranks (by right of self-arrogation) as first and best, I should say it is a purely dancing society, where a fiddle is indispensable to keep its members awake; and where their brains and tongues seem, by common consent, to feel that they had much better give up the care of mutual entertainment to the feet of the parties assembled ; and they judge well. Now, I beg leave clearly to be understood, there is another, and a far more desirable circle; but it is not the one into which strangers find their way generally. To an Englishman, this *fashionable* society presents, indeed, a pitiful sample of lofty pretensions without adequate foundation. Here is a constant endeavour to imitate those states of European society which have for their basis the feudal spirit of the early ages, and which are rendered venerable by their rank, powerful by their wealth, and refined, and in some degree respectable, by great and general mental cultivation. Of Boston, I have not spoken. The society there is of an infinitely superior order. A very general degree of information, and a much greater simplicity of manners, render it infinitely more agreeable. But of that hereafter.

hair off her face, which needed to be as pretty as
it was, to endure such an exposure. I do not
wonder the New Yorkians did not approve of my
Lady Teazle. If, as —— tells me, Mrs. —— is
their idea of the perfection of good-breeding, well
may my delineation of a lady be condemned as
" nothing particular." Yet I am sorry I must
continue to lie under their censure, for I, unfortunately for myself, have seen ladies, " ripe and
real," who, from all I can see, hear, and understand, differ widely from the good manners of their
" beau ideal." The fact is, I am not " *genteel* "
enough, and I am conscious of it. The play went
off remarkably well. Came to bed at half-past
eleven.　　　*　　　*　　　*　　　*
　*　　　*　　　*　　　*　　　*

Thursday, 18*th.*

Here is the end of October, the very mourning-
time of the year with us, and my room is full of
flowers, and the sun is so bright and powerful,
that it is impossible to go out with a shawl, or
without a parasol. Went to rehearsal at twelve;
at two, came in and habited; and at half-past two,
rode out with my father. We took the road to
the Schuylkill at once, through Arch Street, which

is a fine, broad, long street, running parallel with
Chestnut Street.　We walked along the road under the intense sunlight that made all things look
sleepy around.　Turning between some rising
banks, through a defile where the road wound up
a hill, we caught a glimpse of a white house standing on the sunny slope of a green rise.　The undulating grounds around were all bathed in warm
light, relieved only by the massy shadows of the
thick woods that sheltered them.　It was a bit of
England.　　　*　　　　*　　　　*　　　　*
　　*　　　　*　　　　*　　　　*　　　　*

Some good farming and tidy out-houses, and de-
pendencies, completed the resemblance, and made
me think that this must be the dwelling of some
of my own country people.　How can they live
here ? Here, even in the midst of what is fair and
peaceful in nature, I think my home would haunt
me, and the far off chiming of the waves against
her white shores resound in my ears through the
smooth flowing of the Schuylkill.*　After pursuing

* The beautiful villas on the banks of the Schuylkill are
all either utterly deserted and half ruinous, or let out by the
proprietors to tavern keepers.　The reason assigned for this
is, that during that season of the year when it would be
most desirable to reside there, the fever and ague takes possession of the place, and effectually banishes all other occupants.　This very extraordinary and capricious malady is as

a level uninteresting road for some time, we turned
off to the right, and standing on the brow of a

uncertain in its residence, as unwelcome where it does fix its
abode. The courses of some of the rivers, and even whole
tracts of country away from the vicinity of the water, have
been desolated by it: from these it has passed away entirely,
and removed itself to other districts, before remarkably
healthy. Sometimes it visits particular places at intervals
of one or two seasons; sometimes it attaches itself to one
side of a river, and leaves the inhabitants of the other in the
enjoyment of perfect health; in short, it is quite as unaccountable in its proceedings as a fine lady. Many causes
have been assigned as its origin; which, however, have
varied in credibility at almost every new appearance of the
malady. The enormous quantity of decaying vegetation
with which the autumn woods are strewn, year after year,
till it absolutely forms a second soil; the dam lately erected
by the water-works, and which, intercepting the tide, causes
occasional stagnation; the unwholesome action of water
lodging in hollows in the rocks; are all reasons which have
been given to me when I have enquired about this terrible
nuisance along the banks of the Schuylkill: but there is
another, and one which appeared so obvious to me that
when first I saw it, I felt much inclined to attribute the
fever and ague to that, and to that alone. I allude to a foul
and stagnant ditch, lying between the tow-path and the
grounds of these country houses, of nearly a mile in length,
and of considerable width. When I saw the sun pouring its
intense light down into this muddy pool, covered with thick
and unwholesome incrustations, I could not help remarking
that this alone was quite sufficient to breed a malaria in the
whole neighbourhood; and that if the gentlemen proprietors
of the lands along this part of the river would drain this
very poisonous looking repository for bull frogs, their dwellings would, in all probability, be free from fever and ague.

considerable declivity, had a most enchanting
glimpse of the Schuylkill and its woody shores.
The river makes a bend just above the water-
works, and the curving banks scooping themselves
form a lovely little sunny bay. It was more like
a lake, just here, than a flowing stream. The sky
was so blessedly serene, and the air so still, that
the pure deep-looking water appeared to sleep,
while the bright hues of the heavens, and the
glowing tints of the woody shores, were mirrored
with wondrous vividness on its bosom. I never
saw such gorgeousness, and withal such perfect
harmony of colouring. The golden sky, the
mingled green, brown, yellow, crimson, and dark
maroon, that clothed the thickets; the masses of
grey granite, with the vivid, mossy green that
clung round them; the sunny purple waters; the
warm, red colour of the road itself, as it wound
down below, with a border of fresh-looking turf
on either side of it; the radiant atmosphere of rosy
light that hung over all; all combined to present
a picture of perfect enchantment. The eye was
drunk with beauty.* How I thought of Mr. ——.
Indeed a painter would have gone crazy over it,

---

* This beautiful younger world appears to me to have
received the portion of the beloved younger son — the " coat
of many colours."

and I, who am not a painter, was half crazy that I was not. Though if I had been, what would it have availed? Such colours are from God's pallet, and mortal hand may no more copy, than it could mingle them. We rode on through scenery of the same description, passing in our way a farm and dairy, where the cattle were standing, not in open pasture land, but in a corner of forest-ground, all bright with the golden shedding of the trees; it was very picturesque. A little runlet of water, too, that held the middle of a tangled ravine, ran glittering like a golden snake through the underwood, while the stems of the trees, and the light foliage on the edge of the thick woody screens were bathed in yellow sunshine. All around was beautiful, and rich, and harmonious to the eye, and should have been so to the spirit.   *   *
     *   *   *   *   *

Returned home at about half-past five, dined at six; found another beautiful nosegay waiting for me, from my unknown furnisher of sweets. This is almost as tantalising as it is civil; and I would give half my lovely flowers to find out who sends them to me. Distributed them all over the room, and was as happy as a queen. Mr. —— called. My father was obliged to go out upon business, so D—— and I had to entertain that worthy youth.

He seems to have a wonderful veneration for a
parcel of scribblers whose names were never heard
of in England, beyond the limits of their own narrow coteries.   But he speaks like an enthusiast of
the woods and waters of his glorious country, and
I excuse his taste in poetry.   Now isn't this strange,
that a man who can feel the amazing might, majesty, and loveliness of nature, can endure for a moment the mawkish scribbling of these poetasters?
Verily, we be anomalous beasts.   *   *

*   *   *   *   *

AUTUMN.

Thou comest not in sober guise,
    In mellow cloak of russet clad —
Thine are no melancholy skies,
    Nor hueless flowers pale and sad;
But, like an emperor, triumphing,
    With gorgeous robes of Tyrian dyes,
Full flush of fragrant blossoming,
    And glowing purple canopies.
How call ye this the season's fall,
    That seems the pageant of the year,
Richer and brighter far than all
    The pomp that spring and summer wear?
Red falls the westering light of day
    On rock and stream and winding shore;
Soft woody banks and granite grey
    With amber clouds are curtained o'er;

The wide clear waters sleeping lie
  Beneath the evening's wings of gold,
And on their glassy breast the sky
  And banks their mingled hues unfold.
Far in the tangled woods, the ground
  Is strewn with fallen leaves, that lie
Like crimson carpets all around
  Beneath a crimson canopy.
The sloping sun with arrows bright
  Pierces the forest's waving maze;
The universe seems wrapt in light, —
  A floating robe of rosy haze.
Oh, Autumn! thou art here a king;
  And round thy throne the smiling hours
A thousand fragrant tributes bring
  Of golden fruits and blushing flowers.

Oh! not upon thy fading fields and fells
  In such rich garb doth Autumn come to thee,
My home! — but o'er thy mountains and thy dells
  His footsteps fall slowly and solemnly.
Nor flower nor bud remaineth there to him,
  Save the faint-breathing rose, that, round the year,
Its crimson buds and pale soft blossoms dim,
  In lowly beauty constantly doth wear.
O'er yellow stubble lands, in mantle brown,
  He wanders through the wan October light;
Still as he goeth, slowly stripping down
  The garlands green that were the spring's delight.
At morn and eve thin silver vapours rise
  Around his path; but sometimes at mid-day
He looks along the hills with gentle eyes,
  That make the sallow woods and fields seem gay.

Yet something of sad sov'reignty he hath —
   A sceptre crown'd with berries ruby red;
And the cold sobbing wind bestrews his path
   With wither'd leaves that rustle 'neath his tread;
And round him still, in melancholy state,
   Sweet solemn thoughts of death and of decay,
In slow and hush'd attendance, ever wait,
   Telling how all things fair must pass away.

Tuesday, 23d.

At ten o'clock, went to rehearsal. Rehearsed the Hunchback, and then Fazio: this is tolerably hard work, with acting every night: we don't steal our money, that's one comfort. Came home, found a letter for me in a strange hand.   *

   *   *   *   *   *

Went on with my letter to —— : while doing so, was interrupted by the entrance of a strange woman, who sat herself down, apparently in much confusion. She told me a story of great distress, and claimed my assistance as a fellow-country-woman. I had not a farthing of money: D—— and my father were out; so I took the reference she gave me, and promised to enquire into her condition. The greatest evil arising from the many claims of this sort which are made upon us, wherever we go, is the feeling of distrust and suspicion which they engender, and the sort of excuse which they teach us to apply plausibly to our unwillingness to answer such demands. " Oh, ten to one, an impostor," is soon said, and instances enough may unfortunately be found to prove the probability of such a conclusion. Yet in this sweeping condemnation, one real case of misery may be included, and that possibility should make us pause, for 't is one that, if afterwards detected, may be the source of heavy condemnation, and bitter regret to ourselves. †   *   *   *   *

† This country is in one respect blessed above all others, and above all others deserving of blessing. There are no poor — I say there are none, there *need* be none ; none here need lift up the despairing voice of hopeless and helpless want, towards that Heaven which hears when men will not. No father here need work away his body's health, and his spirit's strength, in unavailing labour, from day to day, and from year to year, bowed down by the cruel curse his fellows lay upon him. No mother need wish, in the bitterness of her heart, that the children of her breast had died before they exhausted that nourishment which was the only one her misery could feel assured would not fail them. None need be born to vice, for none are condemned to abject poverty. Oh, it makes the heart sick to think of all the horrible anguish that has been suffered by thousands and thousands of those wretched creatures, whose want begets a host of moral evils fearful to contemplate ; whose existence begins in poverty, struggles on through care and toil, and heart-grinding burdens, and ends in destitution, in sickness, — alas ! too often in crime and infamy. Thrice blessed is this coun-

*　　　*　　　*　　　*　　　*
*　　　*　　　*　　　*　　　*

The fact is, that to give well, one should give equally one's trouble with one's money : the one in all cases, the other where one's enquiries are satisfactorily answered.—Received a purple bound, gilt-edged periodical, published at Boston, from Mr. ——. 　*　　*　　*　　*

　　*　　*　　*　　*　　*
　　*　　*　　*　　*　　*

The literary part of the book seems much on a par with that of similar works in England, but there was a wide difference in the excellence of the engravings. There was one from that pretty picture, the Bride's Maid ; a coarse, bad engraving,

---

try, for no such crying evil exists in its bosom; no such moral reproach, no such political rottenness. Not only is the eye never offended with those piteous sights of human suffering, which make one's heart bleed, and whose number appals one's imagination in the thronged thoroughfares of the European cities ; but the mind reposes with delight in the certainty that not one human creature is here doomed to suffer and to weep through life; not one immortal soul is thrown into jeopardy by the combined temptations of its own misery, and the heartless selfishness of those who pass it by without holding out so much as a finger to save it. If we have any faith in the excellence of mercy and benevolence, we must believe that this alone will secure the blessing of Providence on this country.

but yet how much of the sadness of the original it recalled to me. It is a painful thing to look at: it brings before one too much of the sorrow of life, of the anguish that has been endured ; that is daily, hourly, endured in this prison-house of torments. After dinner, went on writing to ——, till time to go to the theatre. The house was not as full as I had expected, though a good one enough. My father looked wonderfully well and young : there is certainly some difference in acting with him, but this part fatigues me horribly.

Wednesday, 24th.

Went to rehearsal at eleven ; at half-past one, went with D—— to find out something about my yesterday's poor woman. The worst of it is, that my trouble involves necessarily the trouble of somebody else, as I cannot go trotting and exploring about by myself. The references were sufficiently satisfactory, that is, they proved that she was poor, and in distress, and willing to work. I gave her what I could, and the man by whom she is employed seems anxious to afford her work ; so I hope she will get on a little. The " God bless you," of gratitude, even if uttered by guileful and unworthy lips, is surely yet a blessing if it

alights on those who are seeking to do good. And
if I were assured that that woman was the veriest
impostor under the sun, I still should hope her
prayer might descend with profit on my head; for
I was sincere in my desire to do well by her.
Came home, wrote a letter to ———, finished one
to ———; and went to the theatre. It seems there
have been,

> " Bloody noses and crack'd crowns,
>   And all the currents of a heady fight,"

at the box-office, and truly the house bore witness
thereto ; for it was crammed from floor to ceiling.
The play was the Hunchback. I played very
well, in spite of no green carpet, and no letter in
the letter scene, which lost one of my favourite
points ; one, by the by, that I am fond of, because
it is all my own.   *   *   *
        *   *   *   *   *
        *   *   *   *   *

Thursday, 25th.

After breakfast, went to rehearsal. Came home,
put out things for the theatre, made myself a belt;
received a whole bundle of smart annuals from
Mr. ———; spent some time in looking over their

engravings. My gown looked very handsome, but my belt was too small; had to make another. The house was good, but not great. I played only so-so: the fact is, it is utterly impossible to play to this audience at all. They are so immovable, such very stocks and stones, that one is fairly exhausted with labouring to excite them, before half one's work is done.   *   *   *   *

   *   *   *   *   *

   *   *   *   *   *

AUTUMN SONG.

The merriest time of all the year
Is the time when the leaves begin to fall,
When the chestnut-trees turn yellow and sear,
And the flowers are withering one and all;

When the thick green sward is growing brown,
And the honeysuckle berries are red,
And the oak is shaking its acorns down,
And the dry twigs snap 'neath the woodman's tread.

The merriest dance that e'er was seen
Is the headlong dance of the whirling leaves,
And the rattling stubble that flies between
The yellow ranks of the barley sheaves.

The merriest song that e'er was heard
Is the song of the sobbing autumn wind;
When the thin bare boughs of the elm are stirr'd,
And shake the black ivy round them twined.

The merriest time of all the year
Is the time when all things fade and fall,
When the sky is bleak, and the earth is drear,
Oh, that's the merriest month of all.

Friday, 26th.

While I was dressing, D——, like a good angel, came in with three letters from England in her hand.   *   *   *   *

*   *   *   *   *

The love of excellent friends is one of God's greatest blessings, and deserves our utmost thankfulness.   The counsel of sound heads and the affection of Christian spirits is a staff of support, and a spring of rejoicing through life.   *

*   *   *   *   *

A Mr., Mrs., and young Mr. ——, called upon us: they are the only inhabitants of this good city who have done us that honour.   *   *

*   *   *   *   *

As soon as my father came in, we sallied forth to see the giantess of a ship the Americans have been building, to thresh us withal.   I hooked myself up to ——, and away we strode; D—— and my father struggling after us, as best they might. The day was most beautiful; bright, sunny, and fresh.   After walking at an immense pace for some

time, we bethought us of looking for our *poursui-
vants ;* but neither sign nor vestige appeared of
them. We stood still and waited, and went on,
and stood still again. —— looked foolish at me,
and I foolish at him: at length we wisely agreed
that they had probably made the best of their way
to the Navy yard, and thither we proceeded. We
found them, according to our expectations, waiting
for us, and proceeded to enter the building where
this lady of the seas was propped upon a hundred
stays; surrounded with scaffolding, with galleries
running round from the floor to the ceiling. We
went on deck; in fact, the Pennsylvania has been
boarded by the English in our person, before she
sets foot on the sea. How I should like to see that
ship launched; how she will sweep down from her
holdings, and settle to the water, as a swan before
swimming out! How the shores will resound with
living voices, applauding her like a living creature;
how much of national pride, of anticipated triumph,
will be roused in every heart, as her huge wings
first unfold their shadow over the sea, and she
moves abroad, the glory and the wonder of the
deep! How, if this ship should ever lie in an
English harbour? If I were an American on board
of her, I would sooner blow her up with all the
" precious freighting souls" within her, than see

such a consummation. When my wonderment had a little subsided, it occurred to me that she would not, perhaps, be so available a battle ship as one of a smaller size : it must be impossible to manœuvre her with any promptitude. *

*   *   *   *   *

My father and —— indulged in sundry right English bits of bragging, as they stood at her stern, looking down the enormous deck. I wish I knew her exact measurements : she is the largest ship ever built, larger than any East Indiaman ; the largest ship in the world. How the sea will groan under her ; nathless in a storm I would rather be in the veriest nutshell that ever was flung from wave-top to wave-top. How she would sink ! she would go down like another Atlantis, poor ship ! I have an amazing horror of drowning. Came home just in time to dine. After dinner, wrote letters ; at six, went to the theatre ; play, Hunchback ; played so-so : the audience are detestable. The majority are so silent that they not only do not applaud the acting, but most religiously forbear to notice all noises in the house, in consequence of which some impudent women amused themselves with talking during the whole play, much " louder than the players." At one time their impertinent racket

so bewildered me, that I was all but out, and this
without the audience once interfering to silence
them ; perhaps, however, that would have been an
unwarrantable interference with the sacred liberties
of the people. I indulged them with a very signi-
ficant glance; and at one moment was most strongly
tempted to request them to hold their tongues.

Saturday, 27th.

The poor sick lady, whose pretty children I
met running about the stairs, sent to say she
should be very glad if I would go in and see her:
I had had sundry inward promptings to this effect
before, but was withheld by the real English
dread of intruding. At eleven, went to rehearsal:
on my return, called on Mrs. ——. *

  *   *   *   *   *

  *   *   *   *   *

She interested me most extremely : I would have
stayed long with her, but feared she might ex-
haust herself by the exertion of conversing. On
my return to my own room, I sent her Mr. ——'s
annuals, and the volume of Mrs. Hemans's poetry
he lent me. Began practising, when in walked
that interesting youth, Mr. ——, with a nosegay,
as big as himself, in his hand. Flowers, — sweet

blooming, fresh, delicious flowers,—in the last days
of October; the very sackcloth season of the
year. How they do rejoice my spirit. He sat
some time, making most excessively fine speeches
to me: while he was here, arrived another bouquet from my unknown friend; how nice, to be
sure! all but not knowing who they come from.
When my visiter was gone, wrote to —— till
dinner-time. After dinner, spent nearly the whole
afternoon in dressing my pretty flowers. Sent
some of them in to Mrs. ——. I don't know
why, but it seemed a sad present to make to her;
for I almost fear she will never see the blossoms
of another year. Yet why do I say that?—is not
heaven brighter than even this flowery earth?

*   *   *   *   *

*   *   *   *   *

Finished my letter to ——; went to the theatre.
My benefit: the Provoked Husband. The house
was very good. I played so-so, and looked very
nice. What fine breeding this play is, to be sure:
it is quite refreshing to act it; but it must be
heathen Greek to the American *exclusives*, I
should think.

Sunday, 28*th*.

Had only time to swallow a mouthful of breakfast, and off to church. I must say it requires a deal of fortitude to go into an American church: there are no pew openers, and the people appear to rush indifferently into any seats that are vacant. We went into a pew where there were two women and a man, who did not take up one half of it; but who, nevertheless, looked most ungracious at our coming into it. They did not move to make way or accommodate us, but remained, with very discourteous, unchristian-like sulkiness, spread over twice as much space as they required. The spirit of independence seems to preside paramount, even in the house of God. This congregation, by frequenting an Episcopalian temple, evidently professed the form of faith of the English church; yet they neither uttered the responses, nor observed any one of the directions in the Common Prayer-book. Thus, during portions of the worship where kneeling is enjoined, they sat or stood; and while the Creed was being read, half the auditors were reclining comfortably in their pews: the same thing with the Psalms, and all parts of the service. I suppose their love of freedom will not suffer them to be amenable to forms, or wear the exterior of humbleness and homage, even in the house of the Most High God.* The whole appearance of the congregation was that of indifference, indolence, and irreverence, and was highly displeasing to my eye. After church, came home,

* Throughout all the northern states, and particularly those of New England, the Unitarian form of faith prevails very extensively. It appears to me admirably suited to the spiritual necessities of this portion of the Americans. They are a reasoning, not an imaginative, race; moreover, they are a hard-working, not an idle, one. It therefore suits their necessities, as well as their character, to have a religious creed divested at once of mysteries at which the rational mind excepts; and of long and laborious ceremonies, which too often engross the time without the attention of the worshipper. They are poor, too, comparatively speaking; and were they so inclined, could little afford, either the splendid pageantry which the Romish priesthood require, or the less glaring, but not less expensive revenues which the Episcopalian clergy enjoy. Their form of religion is a simple one, a short one, and a cheap one. Without attempting to discuss its excellence in the abstract, it certainly appears to me to be as much fitted for this people, as the marvellous legends and magnificent shows of the Romish church were to the early European nations. The church in America is not, as with us, made a mere means of living: there are no rich benefices, or over-swelled bishoprics, to be hoped for, by the man who devotes himself to the service of God's altar: the pecuniary remuneration of the clergy depends upon the generosity of their congregations; and, for the most part, a sincere love of his vocation must be the American minister's reward, as it was his original instigation to the work.

and began writing to ——. —— called. He sat
some time mending pens for me ; and at half-past
one D——, he, and I packed ourselves into a
coach, and proceeded on to Fair Mount, where
we got out, and left the coach to wait for us.
The day was bright and bitter cold : the keen
spirit-like wind came careering over the crisping
waters of the broad river, and carried across the
cloudless blue sky the golden showers from the
shivering woods. They had not lost their beauty
yet ; though some of their crimson robes were
turned to palest yellow, and through the thin
foliage, the dark boughs, and rugged barks showed
distinctly, yet the sun shone joyfully on them, and
they looked beautiful still ; and so did the water,
curled into a thousand mimic billows, that came
breaking their crystal heads along the curving
shore, which, with its shady indentings and bright
granite promontories, seemed to lock the river in,
and gave it the appearance of a lovely lake. We
took the tow-path, by D——'s desire ; but found
(alas, that it is ever so !) that it was distance lent
enchantment to the view. For, though it was very
pretty, it had lost some of the beauty it seemed to
wear, when we looked down upon it from the
woody heights that skirt the road.

On we went, —— and I moderating our strides

to keep pace with D——; and she, puffing, panting, and struggling on to keep pace with us; yet
I was perished, and she was half melted: like all
compromises, it was but a botched business. The
wind was deliciously fresh; and I think, as we
buffeted along in its very face, we should have
made an admirable subject for Bunbury. I, with
my bonnet off, my combs out, and all my hair
flying about, hooked up to ——, who, willow-
like, bent over me, to facilitate my reaching his
arm. D—— following in the rear, her cap and
hair half over her face, her shawl and clothes
fluttering in the blast, her cheeks the colour of
crimson, which, relieved by her green bonnet,
whose sides she grappled tightly down to balk
the wind, had much the effect of a fine carnation
bursting its verdant sheath. I never saw any
thing half so absurd in my life, as we all looked.
Yet it was very pleasant and wholesome, good for
soul and body. After walking for some time, I
asked D—— the hour. It was three, and we
were to dine at four, in order to accommodate the
servants, who, in this land of liberty, make complete slaves of their masters. Horror took possession of us, — how were we ever to get back in
time? To turn back was hopeless: the endless
curvings of the shore, however much we had

admired their graceful sinuosities before, would now have appeared abominable to our straight-forward designs of home, so we agreed to climb the hill and take the upper road — and what a hill it was ! — the sun poured his intense rays down upon it ; and, what with the heat and the wind, and the steep path-way, I thought poor D—— would have died. We turned once as we reached the summit, and I never saw any thing more lovely than the scene we were leaving behind us. The beautiful blue water winding far away between its woody shores; close below the hill, a small reed-crowned island lying like a gem on the bright river, and a little beyond, the unfinished arches of a white bridge : the opposite shores were bathed with the evening light, and far away the varied colours of the autumnal woods were tinged with the golden glory of sunset. But we were pursued by the thought of four o'clock, and paused but a moment. On we struggled, and at last my frozen blood began to warm ; and by the time we reached the carriage, I was in a fine glow. Certainly exercise is, in itself, very de-lightful, but in scenes like these it is doubly so : the spirit is roused to activity by the natural uties around, and the fancy and feelings seem cquire vigour from the quick circulation of the

blood, and the muscular energy of the limbs ; it
is highly excellent.*   We jumped into the coach,
adjured the man by all the saints in the calendar

* Whatever progress phrenology may have made in the
convictions of people in general, it is much to be hoped, that
the physiological principles to which, in the developement of
their system, its professors constantly advert, may find
favour even with those who are not prepared to admit the
truth of the new philosophy of the human intellect.   While
we have bodies as well as souls, we must take care of the
health of our bodies, if we wish our souls to be healthy.   I
have heard many people mention the intimate union of spirit
and matter, displayed in the existence of a human being, as
highly degrading to the former ; however that may be, it is
certain that we by no means show our value for the one, by
neglecting and maltreating the other ; and that if instead of
lamenting over the unworthiness of the soul's fleshy partner,
we were to improve and correct, and endeavour to ennoble
it, we should do the wiser thing.   Upon a well-regulated
digestion and circulation, and a healthful nervous system,
many of our virtues depend, much of our happiness ; and it
is almost as impossible to possess a healthy and vigorous
mind in a diseased and debilitated body, as it is unusual to
see a strong and healthful body allied to an intemperate and
ill-governed spirit. We have some value for the casket which
contains our jewel : then should we not have some for that
casket to which the jewel absolutely adheres, and which cannot suffer injury itself without communicating it to that
which it contains ? Exercise, regularity, and moderation in
diet and sleep, well proportioned and varied studies and recreations,—these are none of them subjects of trivial importance to the wise.   Much of our ease and contentedness
depends upon them ; much of our well-being, much of our
well-doing.

to put wings to his chariot wheels, and sat con-
cocting plausible lies, by way of excuses, all the
way home. At last we hit upon an admirable
invention. The cause of our being so late was to
be, that we stopped to render our assistance in
reviving an unfortunate young woman, (a lovely
creature, of course,) who had thrown herself into
the Schuylkill, in consequence of some love disappointment, and who was withdrawn just in time
to be preserved. —— was to tell this story with
the gravest face he could summon for the occasion, while we went up to dress, and when we
came down we were to corroborate his statement
as correctly as good chance might enable us. We
dressed in half a minute, and found Mr. ——
sitting with my father, and —— looking amazingly
demure. It seemed, however, that no remark
had been made, nor question asked, about our
protracted perambulations, so that we had actually
thrown away all our ingenuity. This vexed me so
much, that in the middle of dinner I introduced the
topic of drowning, and, with a lamentable face,
related the circumstance ; but, alas ! one of my
auditors was occupied with a *matelotte d'anquilles*,
another with an oyster *vol-au-vent*, and all the
pretty girls in creation might have been drowned,
without the loss in any degree affecting the evi-

dent satisfaction which the above subjects of me-
ditation seemed to afford the gentlemen : what
selfish brutes men are! shocking. Our invention
was thus twice thrown away : one said " Humph ! "
and the other " Ha ! " and that was the extent of
their sympathy. After dinner, came up to my
own room, lay down, and fairly slept till coffee
was announced. Came down with half an eye
open, and found the circle augmented by the
delectable presence of Mr. ——. What an original that youth is. They talked politics, abused
republicanism, lauded aristocracy, drank tea, took
snuff, ate cakes, and pottered a deal. My father
was going fast asleep, —— was making a thousand signs to me to go to the piano, when Mr.
—— rose to depart : the other gentlemen took
the hint, and left us at half-past ten.

Tuesday, 30*th*.

At eleven o'clock, went to rehearsal : came home,
began letter to ——. Called with my father upon
Mrs. —— : the servant committed that awfullest
of blunders, letting one into the house, and then
finding out that nobody was at home.* Came

* I think it has not been my good fortune, in more than
six instances, during my residence in this country, to find

home, practised for some time: all of a sudden the door opened, and in walked Colonel —— with my father. He had just arrived from New

---

ladies " at home" in the morning. The first reason for this is, the total impossibility of having a housekeeper; the American servants steadfastly refusing to obey *two* mistresses; the being subservient to any appears, indeed, a dreadful hardship to them. Of course this compels the lady of the house to enter into all those minute daily details, which with us devolve upon the superintendent servant, and she is thus condemned, at least for some part of the morning, to the store-room or the kitchen. In consequence of this, her toilet is seldom completed until about to take her morning promenade; and I have been a good deal surprised, more than once, at being told, when I called, that " the ladies were dressing, but would be down immediately." This is French; the disorderly slouching about half the morning in a careless undress being, unluckily, quite compatible with that exquisite niceness of appearance with which the Parisian ladies edify their streets so much, and their homes so little. Another very disagreeable result of this arrangement is, that when you are admitted into a house in the morning, the rooms appear as if they never were used : there are no books lying about, no work-tables covered with evidences of constant use, and if there is a piano, it is generally closed; the whole giving one an uninhabited feel that is extremely uncomfortable. As to a morning lounge in a lady's boudoir, or a gentleman's library, the thing's unheard of; to be sure there are no loungers, where every man is tied to a counting-house from morning till night; and therefore no occasion for those very pleasant sanctums devoted to gossiping, political, literary, and scandalous.

York. He dined with us. After dinner, finished letter to ——. At six, went to the theatre. The house was very good; play, Much Ado about Nothing. I played well; but what an audience it is! I have been often recommended, in cases of nervousness on the stage, to consider the audience as just so many cabbages, and, indeed, a small stretch of fancy would enable me to do so here. Colonel —— supped with us. Found an invitation to dinner from the ——. " One exception makes a rule," say the scholars; by that same token, therefore, the Philadelphians are about the most inhospitable set of people it ever was my good fortune to fall in with.* Towards

* I am sure there is no town in Europe where my father could fix his residence for a week, without being immediately found out by most of the residents of any literary acquirements, or knowledge of matters relating to art; I am sure that neither in France, Italy, or Germany, could he take up his abode in any city, without immediately being sought by those best worth knowing in it. I confess it surprised me, therefore, when I found that, during a month's residence in Philadelphia, scarcely a creature came near us, and but one house was hospitably opened to us; as regards myself, I have no inclination whatever to speak upon the subject; but it gave me something like a feeling of contempt, not only for the charities, but for the good taste of the Philadelphians, when I found them careless and indifferent towards one whose name alone is a passport into every refined and cul-

the end of supper, we fell into a strange discussion
as to the nature of existence. A vain and fruit-
less talk, after all; for life shall be happy or sad,
not, indeed, according to its events, but according
to the nature of the individuals to whom these
events befall. Colonel —— maintained that life
was in itself desirable; abounding in blessings,
replete with comforts, a fertile land, where still,
-as one joy decays, another springs up to flourish
in its place. He said that he felt thankful every
day, and every hour of the day, for his existence;
that he feared death, only because life was an
absolute enjoyment, and that he would willingly,
to-morrow, accept the power of beginning his
again, even though he should be placed on the
world's threshold, a lonely, friendless beggar: so
sure was he that his prospects would brighten,
and friends spring up to him, and plenty reward
labour, and life become pleasant, ere it had grown
many years old. How widely human beings
differ! It was but an hour before, that I, in

---

tivated society in Europe. Every where else, in America,
our reception was very different; and I can only attribute the
want of courtesy we met with in Philadelphia to the greater
prevalence of that very small spirit of dignity which is always
afraid of committing itself.

counting how many stars I had already seen go down
below the horizon of existence—Weber, Lawrence,
Scott, all of whom I have known, — was saying to
D——, " How sad a thing, and strange, life is ! "
adding, what I repent me for, " I wish that I
were dead ! " Oh, how can any human being, who
looks abroad into the world, and within upon
himself, who sees the wondrous mystery of all
things, the unabidingness which waits on all
matter, the imperfection which clogs all spirit ;
who notes the sovereignty of change over the
inanimate creation, of disease, decay, and death
over man's body, of blindness and delusion over
his mind, of sin over his soul ; who beholds the
frailty of good men ; who feels the miserable inconsistency of his own nature ; the dust and ashes
of which our love, and what we love, is made ; the
evil that, like an unwholesome corpse, still clings
to our good ; the sorrow that, like its shadow, still
walks behind our joy ;—oh, who that sees all this
can say that this life is other than sad—most sad ?
Yet, while I write this, God forbid that I should
therefore want eyes to see, or sense to feel, the
blessings wherewith he has blessed it ; the rewards with which he sweetens our task, the flowers
wherewith he cheers our journey's road, the many
props wherewith he supports our feet in it. Yet

of all these, the sweetest, the brightest, the strongest, are those which our soul draws from him, the end of its desire, not those it finds here. And how should not that spirit yearn for its accomplishment? If we seek knowledge here, a thousand mists arise between our incapable senses and the truth; how, then, should we not wish to cast away this darkness, and soar to the fountains of all light? If we strive to employ those faculties which, being of our soul, have the strength and enduring of immortality, the objects whereon we expend them here are vague, evanescent, disappointing; how then should we not desire to find food for our capacities, abiding as themelves? If we long to love — ah, are not the creatures in whom we centre our affections frail, capable of change; perishable, born to decay? How then should we not look with unutterable yearning for that life where affection is unchangeable, eternal? Surely, if all the hopes, the fears, the aims, the tendings of our soul, have but their beginning here, it is most natural, it is most fitting, to turn to that future where they shall be fulfilled. But there ie s a road between.   *   *   *   *

*   *   *   *   *

A break—a break—a break ! So much the better ; for the two last days have been nothing but annoyance, hardwork, and heartache.　　＊　　＊

　＊　　　＊　　　＊　　　＊　　　＊

Friday, November 2d.

A bright sunny day ; too hot for a fire ; windows open, shutters closed, and the room full of flowers. How the sweet summer-time stays lingering here. Found Colonel —— in the drawing-room. After breakfast, began writing to ——. Mr. —— called : he stayed but a short time, and went out with Colonel ——. My father went out soon after, and I began to practise. Mrs. —— came in and sat with me : she played to me, and sang " Should those fond hopes ever leave thee." Her voice was as thin as her pale transparent hands. She appeared to me much better than when last I saw her ; but presently told me she had just been swallowing eighty drops of laudanum, poor thing ! When she was gone, went on practising, and writing, till my father came home. Walked with him and D—— to call on old Lady ——. The day was so hot that I could scarcely endure my boa. The election was going on ; the streets full of rabblement, the air full of huzzaing, and the sky obscured with star-spangled banners, and

villanous transparencies of " Old Hickory *,"
hung out in all directions. We went round the
Town House, and looked at the window out of
which Jefferson read the Act of Independence,
that proclaimed the separation between England
and America.† Called at a music-shop, tossed

* The familiar appellation by which the democracy designate their favourite, General Jackson. The hickory
wood is the tallest and the toughest possible, and by no
means a bad type of some of the President's physical and
moral attributes. Hickory poles, as they are called, are
erected before most of the taverns frequented by the
thorough-going Jacksonites; and they are sometimes sur-
mounted by the glorious " Cap of Liberty," that much
abused symbol, which has presided over so many scenes of
political frenzy.

† In beholding this fine young giant of a world, with all
its magnificent capabilities for greatness, I think every Englishman must feel unmingled regret at the unjust and unwise
course of policy which alienated such a child from the
parent government. But, at the same time, it is impossible
to avoid seeing that some other course must, ere long, have
led to the same result, even if England had pursued a more
maternal course of conduct towards America. No one, beholding this enormous country, stretching from ocean to
ocean, watered with ten thousand glorious rivers, combining
every variety of climate and soil, therefore, every variety of
produce and population; possessing within itself every re-
source that other nations are forced either to buy abroad, or
to create substitutes for at home; no one, seeing the internal wealth of America, the abundant fertility of the
earth's surface, the riches heaped below it, the unparalleled

over heaps of music, bought some, and ordered some to be sent home for me to look over. Came

---

facilities for the intercourse of men, and the interchange of their possessions throughout its vast extent, can for an instant indulge the thought that such a country was ever destined to be an appendage to any other in the world, or that any chain of circumstances whatever could have long maintained in dependence a people furnished with every means of freedom and greatness. But far from regretting that America has thrown off her allegiance, and regarding her as a rebellious subject, and irreverent child, England will surely, ere long, learn to look upon this country as the inheritor of her glory; the younger England, destined to perpetuate the language, the memory, the virtues of the noble land from which she is descended. Loving and honouring my country as I do, I cannot look upon America with any feeling of hostility. I not only hear the voice of England in the language of this people, but I recognise in all their best qualities, their industry, their honesty, their sturdy independence of spirit, the very witnesses of their origin — they are English; no other people in the world would have licked us as they did; nor any other people in the world built up, upon the ground they won, so sound, and strong, and fair an edifice.

With regard to what I have said in the beginning of this note, of the many reasons which combined to render this country independent of all others, I think they in some measure tell against the probability of its long remaining at unity with itself. Such numerous and clashing interests; such strong and opposite individuality of character between the northern and southern states; above all, such enormous extent of country; seem rationally to present many points

home, put out things for the theatre. Dined at
three.　　*　　　*　　　*　　　*　　　*

　　　　*　　　*　　　*　　　*　　　*

　　　　*　　　*　　　*　　　*　　　*

Received another beautiful nosegay. After dinner, went on with letter to ——— ; tried over my
music; Heber's song that I wanted is not among
them. At six, went to the theatre. The sunset
was glorious, the uprising of the moon most
beautiful. There is an intensity, an earnestness
about the colour of the sky, and the light of its
bright inhabitants here, that is lovely and solemn,
beyond any thing I ever saw. Can Italy have
brighter heavens than these? surely, nothing can
exceed the beauty of these days and nights. We
were obliged to go all manner of roundabouts to
the play-house, in order to avoid the rabble that
choked up the principal streets. I, by way of
striking salutary awe into the hearts of all rioters
who might come across our path, brandished my
father's sword out of the coach window the whole
way along. The play was Venice Preserved; my
father played Jaffier.　　*　　　*　　　*

　　　*　　　*　　　*　　　*　　　*

---

of insecurity; many probabilities of separations and break-
irgsasunder; but all this lies far on, and I leave it to those
who have good eyes for a distance.

I played pretty well.   The house was very good;
but at the end I really was half dead.   *

    *   *   *   *   *

    *   *   *   *   *

On our return home, met a procession of
electioneerers carrying triangular paper lanterns
upon poles, with " sentiments " political scribbled
thereon, which, however, I could not distinguish.
Found a most exquisite nosegay waiting for me
at home, so sweet, so brilliant, so fragrant, and
fresh.   *   *   *   *   *

      *   *   *   *   *

Found nothing for supper that I could fancy.
Drank some tea, wrote journal.   Colonel ——
came in after supper, and wondered that I had
played better to my father's Jaffier, than to Mr.
Keppel's.   Heaven bless the world, for a *con-
glomerated amalgamation* of fools !

Monday, 5th.

Guy Fawlk's day, and no squibs, no firing of
pistols, no bonfires, nor parading about of fero-
cious looking straw men. Ah ! these poor people
never had a king and two houses of parliament,
and don't know what a mercy it is they weren't
blown up before they passed the reform bill.

Now if such an accident should occur to them, they'd all be sure to be blown straight into heaven, and hang there. Rose at half-past five. Oh, I quite agree with the Scotch song,

" Up in the morning's na for me,
　Up in the morning early;
　I 'd rather watch a winter's night,
　Than rise in the morning early."

Dressed myself by candle light. Mrs. —— sent in to ask me if I would see her, but I had not time. Sent her a note, and received, in exchange, the seed of what I suspect is the wood laurel, common in this country, but unknown in ours. Started from the Mansion House (which is a very nice inn, kept by the civilest of people,) at six, and reached the quay just in time to meet the first rosy breaking of the clouds over the Delaware. 　*　　　*　　　*
　*　　　*　　　*　　　*　　　*
　*　　　*　　　*　　　*　　　*

I am sorry to leave Philadelphia. I like the town, and the little I have seen of its inhabitants, very much; I mean in private, for they are intolerable audiences. There is an air of stability, of well to do, and occasionally of age, in the town, that reminds me of England. Then, as

far as my yesterday's dinner will allow me to judge,
I should say, that not only the style of living,
but the society was superior to that which I saw
in New York.   Certainly, both the entertainment
itself, and the guests, were irreproachable ; the
first was in very good taste, the latter appeared
to me well-informed, and very agreeable.   The
morning, in spite of all ——'s persuasive pro-
phecies, was beautiful beyond description.   The
river like the smoothest glass.   The sky was
bright and cloudless, and along the shores, the
distinctness with which each smallest variation of
form, or shade of colour, was reflected in the
clear mirror of the Delaware, was singularly beautiful and fairy-like.   The tints of the woods were
what no words can convey the slightest idea of.
Now, a whole track of withered oaks, of a red
brick hue, like a forest scorched with fire ; now,
a fresh thicket of cedars, of the brightest green ;
then, wide screens of mingled trees, where the
foliage was one gorgeous mixture of vermilion,
dark maroon, tender green, golden yellow, and
deep geranium.   The whole land at a distance
appearing to lie under an atmosphere of glowing
colour, richer than any crimson mantle that ever
clothed the emperors of the olden world ; all
this, illuminated by a sun, which we should have

thought too hot for June. It was very beautiful. I did not, however, see much of it, for I was overcome with fatigue, and slept, both in the steam-boat, and in the stage-coach. When we embarked on the Raritan, I had intended lying down in the cabin, and taking my sleep fairly out, but the jolting of those bitter roads had made every one of the women sick, and the cabin was horrible beyond expression. Came up on deck, and worked till within a quarter of a mile of New York, when I went on the upper deck, and walked about with Colonel ——. I asked Captain Seymour how often the engine would strike in a minute; he told me, thirty-six times. By the by, we had a race coming down the Raritan, with the Union steamboat. The Water Witch beat her hollow; but she came so near as to make our water rough, and so impede our progress, that I thought we should have had a concussion; there is something very exciting in emulation, certainly. The sun went down in a watery, gloomy sky, though the day had been so fine; and when we got sight of the Narrows, sky, and sea, and land, were all of a dark leaden hue. Our second landing at New York was rather melancholy: shall I ever forget the first? Came up to our comfortless quarters at the American; dressed, and dined, and began

finishing my letter to dear ———, when they
brought me in another from her, by the packet
that has just come in.   *   *   *

*   *   *   *   *

*   *   *   *   *

Tuesday, 6th.

It poured with rain. Lucky we did not follow
———'s advice, else we should have been miserably progressing through rain and wretchedness,
or perhaps sticking fast in the mud. Went
and took a warm bath; came home, breakfasted; after breakfast, practised for an hour;
finished letter to ———; wrote to my mother; dined
at five. After dinner, Colonel ——— called, and
very nearly caused a blow up between me and my
father: he came preaching to me the necessity of
restoring those lines of Bianca's, in the judgment
scene, which were originally omitted, afterwards
restored by me at Milman's request, and again
cut out, on finding that they only lengthened the
scene, without producing the slightest effect. My
father appeared perfectly to agree with me, but
added, that I might as well oblige the people. I
straightforth said I would do no such thing.

People sitting before the curtain must not come and tell me what I am to do behind it. Not one out of a hundred, in the first place, understand what they are talking about; and why, therefore, am I to alter my work at their suggestion, when each particular scene has cost me more consideration than they ever bestowed upon any whole play in all their lives. Besides, it would be with me and my parts, as with the old man, his son, and his ass, in the fable of old; I should never have done altering, and yet never satisfy any body, for the most universal talent I know of, is that of finding fault. So, all things well considered, the New Yorkians must e'en be contented with the judgment of Miss O'Neill, my father, and their obedient, humble servant. Worked till tea-time; after tea, wrote letters till now, bed-time.

Wednesday, 7th.

Our breakfast was so bad, none of us could eat any thing. After breakfast, despatched letters to Mr. ——, for England. Practised for an hour, — sketched for an hour.   *   *

 * * * * *

 * * * * *

At half-past one, went out with my father to walk on the Battery, while Colonel —— and D—— went to ——, to see if we could get decent lodgings, and wholesome eatables there. The day was melancholy, grey, cold; with a full, fresh wind, whirling the rattling leaves along, and rippling the leaden waters of the wide estuary that opens before this beautiful parade. The Jersey shore and Staten Island, with their withered woods all clothed in their dark, warm, autumnal hues, at a distance reminded me of the heathery hills of Scotland; they had that dark purple richness of colouring.

  *   *   *   *   *

  *   *   *   *   *

D—— and Colonel —— joined us, and we walked up Broadway together : my father left me to go with them, and look at our proposed dwelling. It is all in vain struggling with one's fate ; 't is clear they haven't the most distant idea of the comforts of life in these parts. Darkness, dinginess, and narrowness, were the attributes of the apartments into which we were shown; then, as the Colonel had never eaten in the house, he did not know what our food might be — pleasant this ! *Resolved*, that we were better off where we are, and so returned to the American. Sketched and practised for some time longer. Mr. —— called to go with my father to Mrs. ——'s, where they were to dine. He certainly is one of the handsomest men I ever saw; but he looks half dead, and is working himself to death, it should seem.　　*　　　*

　　*　　*　　*　　*　　*
　　*　　*　　*　　*　　*

He told me that Boston was the most charming town in America.　　*　　　*　　　*
　　*　　*　　*　　*　　*

Put away things, while D—— unpacked them. Dressed for dinner. Dined at five; afterwards proceeded in the unpacking and stowing away.
　　*　　*　　*　　*　　*

I was interrupted by the announcement of an incomprehensible cognomen, which solved itself in the shape of Mr. ——, who walked in, sat down, and began talking a deal of nonsense. I worked, that I might not go to sleep. He was most exceedingly odd and dauldrummish. I think he was a little " how com'd you so indeed." He sat very near me, spoke exceedingly drowsily, and talked an amazing quantity of thickish philosophy, and moral and sentimental potter. I bore it as well as I could, till ten o'clock, when I asked him how long it was " reckoned" discreet, in this country, to prolong evening visits; whereupon he arose and took his departure.　　*　　　*

*   *   *   *   *

*   *   -   *   *   *

Worked at the ornaments of my Bianca dress,
finished one, and wrote journal.

Thursday, 8*th.*

*   *   *   *   *

After breakfast, worked at my dress till late;
Mr. —— called.   Put away goods and chattels;
put out things for the theatre.   A brother of Mr.
—— called upon us, and sat some time : when he
was gone, came back to my room to finish the
ornaments for my dress.   This day has been spent
in the thorough surroundings of my vocation; foil
stone, glass beads, and brass tape !   —— came
just before dinner ; and at the end of it, Colonel
—— called.   He read us a paragraph in one of
the Philadelphia papers, upon me, and all my
good parts ; there was actually a column of them.
It was well written, for I was absolute perfection ;
excepting, indeed, in one respect, the hauteur and
disdain with which I had treated the " *rank* and
fashion of Philadelphia."   Now this was not true,
for, to speak candidly, I did not know that there
were such things as rank and fashion in all
America.   However, the article made me laugh

extremely, for, as I could not help observing,
" there are *real* lords and ladies in my country." †

*   *   *   *   *

† I think the pretension to pre-eminence, in the various
societies of North America, is founded on these grounds. In
Boston, a greater degree of mental cultivation; in New York,
the possession of wealth; and a lady, of whom I enquired
the other day what constituted the superiority of the *aristocracy* in Philadelphia, replied, — " Why, birth, to be sure."
Virginia and Carolina, indeed, long prided themselves upon
their old family names, which were once backed by large
possessions; and for many years the southern gentlemen
might not improperly be termed the aristocracy of America;
but the estates of those who embraced the king's cause during the rebellion were confiscated; and the annulling the
laws of entail and primogeniture, and the parcelling out of
property under the republican form of government, have
gradually destroyed the fortunes of most of the old southern
families. Still, they hold fast to the spirit of their former
superiority, and from this circumstance, and the possession
of slaves, which exempts them from the drudgery of earning
their livelihood, they are a much less mercantile race of men
than those of the northern states; generally better informed,
and infinitely more polished in their manners. The few
southerners with whom I have become acquainted resemble
Europeans both in their accomplishments, and the quiet and
reserve of their manners. On my remarking, one day, to a
Philadelphia gentleman, whose general cultivation keeps
pace with his political and financial talents, how singular the
contrast was between the levelling spirit of this government,
and the separating and dividing spirit of American society,
he replied, that if his many vocations allowed him time, he
should like to write a novel illustrating the curious struggle
which exists throughout this country between its political

Came to my own room, — refurbished my green velvet bonnet. 'T is a worthy old thing that, and looks amazingly well. The cold weather is setting in very bitterly to-day ; we were obliged to have a fire. Heard my father his part : whilst saying it, he received a subpœna on some business between Mr. —— and Mr. ——. At a quarter to six, went to the theatre. Play, Fazio; house very fine; dress like a bonfire. I played well, but then my father was the Fazio. The people cried abundantly. Mrs. —— was shocked at having to play that naughty woman Aldabella (I wish they would let me try that part); and when the Duke dismissed her in the last scene, picked up her train, and flounced off in a way that made the audience for to laugh. Coming home, Mr. —— overtook us. My father asked him in, but he excused himself; before, however, we were well seated, he had repented the refusal, and came rushing back. Colonel —— came in, and they both of them supped with us, discussing many matters of pith.

---

and its social institutions. The anomaly is, indeed, striking. Democracy governs the land; whilst, throughout society, a contrary tendency shows itself, wherever it can obtain the very smallest opportunity. It is unfortunate for America, that its aristocracy must, of necessity, be always one of wealth.

Received a nosegay, as big as myself, of dahlias and other autumnal flowers.   *   *

     *   *   *   *   *

The moon is resplendent! the earth is flooded with her cold light — beautiful! By the by, *last night*, at three o'clock this morning, I was awakened by music. It was a military band playing Yankee Doodle, the national anthem of the Americans, accompanied by the tramp of a considerable body of men. They took the direction of the Park, and there halted, when I heard a single voice haranguing for a length of time, with occasional interruptions of vehement huzzas, and rolling of drums. And anon, the march struck up again, grew faint, and died into the stillness of night.   *   *   *   *

     *   *   *   *   *

I was much bounden to the Jacksonites, who are carrying it by fair means or foul. One man, I was assured, voted nine times over! He was an Irishman, and it is to be presumed, a tailor.

Saturday, 10th.

Skipped yesterday: so much the better, for though it began, like May, with flowers and sun-

shine, it ended, like December, with the sulks,
and a fit of crying. The former were furnished
me by my friends and Heaven, the latter, by myself and the devil.   *   *   *

*   *   *   *   *

*   *   *   *   *

At six o'clock, D—— roused me ; and grumpily
enough I arose. I dressed myself by candlelight in
a hurry. Really, by way of a party of pleasure,
't is too abominable to get up in the middle of the
night this fashion. At half-past six, Colonel
—— came ; and as soon as I could persuade myself into my clothes, we set off to walk to the
quay. Just as we were nearing the bottom of Barclay Street, the bell rang from the steam-boat, to
summon all loiterers on board ; and forthwith we
rushed, because in this country steam and paddles,
like wind and tide in others, wait for no man.
We got on board in plenty time, but D—— was
nearly killed with the pace at which we had
walked, in order to do so. One of the first persons we saw was Mr. ——, who was going up to
his father's place beyond West Point, by name
Hyde Park, which sounds mighty magnificent.
I did not remain long on the second deck, but
ascended to the first with Colonel ——, and
paced to and fro with infinite zeal till breakfast-

time. The morning was grey and sad looking,
and I feared we should not have a fine day:
however, towards eight o'clock the grey clouds
parted, and the blue, serene eyes of heaven
looked down upon the waters; the waves began
to sparkle, though the sun had not yet appeared;
the sky was lighter, and faint shadows began to
appear beside the various objects that surrounded
us, all which symptoms raised our hopes of the
weather. At eight o'clock, we went down to
breakfast. Nobody who has not seen it, can conceive the strange aspect of the long room of one
of these fine boats at meal-time. The crowd, the
hurry, the confusion of tongues, like the sound
of many waters, the enormous consumption of
eatables, the mingled demands for more, the
cloud of black waiters hovering down the sides
of the immense tables, the hungry, eager faces
seated at them, form altogether a most amusing
subject of contemplation, and a caricaturist would
find ample matter for his vein in almost every
other devouring countenance. As far as regards
the speed, safety, and convenience with which
these vessels enable one to perform what would
be in any other conveyance most fatiguing jour-
neys, they are admirable inventions. The way
in which they are conducted, too, deserves the

highest commendation. Nothing can exceed the comfort with which they are fitted up, the skill with which they are managed, and the order and alacrity with which passengers are taken up from, or landed at, the various points along the river. The steamer goes at the rate of fifteen miles an hour ; and in less than two minutes, when approaching any place of landing, the engine stops, the boat is lowered — the captain always convoys his passengers himself from the steamer to the shore — away darts the tiny skiff, held by a rope to the main boat; as soon as it grazes the land, its freight, animate and inanimate, is bundled out, the boat hauls itself back in an instant, and immediately the machine is in motion, and the vessel again bounding over the water like a race-horse. * Doubtless all this has many and great advantages; but to an English person, the mere cir-

* Of course the captain is undisputed master of the boat, and any disorders, quarrels, &c., which may arise, are settled by his authority. Any passenger, guilty of misbehaviour, is either confined or sent immediately on shore, no matter how far from his intended destination. I once saw very summary justice performed on a troublesome fellow who was disturbing the whole society on board one of the North River steamers. He was put into the small boat with the captain and a stout looking sailor, and very comfortably deposited on some rafts which were floating along shore, about twenty miles below West Point, whither he was bound.

cumstance of being the whole day in a crowd is a nuisance. As to privacy at any time, or under any circumstances, 't is a thing that enters not into the imagination of an American. They do not seem to comprehend that to be from sunrise to sunset one of a hundred and fifty people con- fined in a steam-boat is in itself a great misery, or that to be left by one's self and to one's self can ever be desirable. They live all the days of their lives in a throng, eat at ordinaries of two or three hundred, sleep five or six in a room, take plea- sure in droves, and travel by swarms. †   *

*   *   *   *   *

In spite, therefore, of all its advantages, this mode of journeying has its drawbacks. And the greatest of all, to me, is the being *companioned* by so many strangers, who crowd about you, pursue their conversation in your very ears, or, if they like it better, listen to yours, stare you out of all countenance, and squeeze you out of all comfort. It is perfectly intolerable to me ; but then I have

† The quantity of one's companions in these conveyances is not more objectionable than their quality sometimes. As they are the only vehicles, and the fares charged are ex- tremely low, it follows, necessarily, that all classes and sorts of people congregate in them, from the ragged Irish emigrant and the boorish back-countryman, to the gentleman of the senate, the supreme court, and the president himself.

more than even the national English abhorrence
of coming in contact with strangers. There is no
moment of my life when I would not rather be
alone, than in company; and feeling, as I often
do, the society of even those I love a burden, the
being eternally surrounded by indifferent persons
is a positive suffering that interferes with every
enjoyment, and makes pleasure three parts endurance. I think this constant living in public is one
reason why the young women here are much less
retiring and shy than English girls. Instead of
the domestic privacy in which women among us
are accustomed to live, and move, and have their
being, here they are incessantly, as Mr. ——- says,
" *en evidence*." Accustomed to the society of
strangers, mixing familiarly with persons of whom
they know nothing earthly, subject to the gaze of
a crowd from morning till night, pushing, and
pressing, and struggling in self-defence, conversing,
and being conversed with, by the chance companions of a boarding-house, a steam-boat, or the
hotel of a fashionable watering-place, they must
necessarily lose every thing like reserve or bashfulness of deportment, and become free and
familiar in their manners, and noisy and unrefined
in their tone and style of conversation.* An

---

* The manners of the young girls of America appear
singularly free to foreigners; and until they become better

English girl of sixteen, put on board one of these
Noah's arks (for verily there be clean and unclean

---

acquainted with the causes which produce so unrestrained a
deportment, they are liable to take disadvantageous and mistaken impressions with regard to them. The term which I
should say applied best to the tone and carriage of American
girls from ten to eighteen, is hoydenish; laughing, giggling,
romping, flirting, screaming at the top of their voices, running
in and out of shops, and spending a very considerable portion
of their time in lounging about in the streets. In Philadelphia and Boston, almost all the young ladies attend classes
or day schools; and in the latter place I never went out,
morning, noon, or evening, that I did not meet, in some of
the streets round the Tremont House, a whole bevy of young
school girls, who were my very particular friends, but who,
under pretext of going to, or returning from, school, appeared
to me to be always laughing, and talking, and running about
in the public thoroughfares; a system of education which we
should think by no means desirable. The entire liberty which
the majority of young ladies are allowed to assume, at an age
when in England they would be under strict nursery discipline, appears very extraordinary; they not only walk alone
in the streets, but go out into society, where they take a
determined and leading part, without either mother, aunt, or
chaperon of any sort; custom, which renders such an appendage necessary with us, entirely dispenses with it here;
and though the reason of this is obvious enough in the narrow circles of these small towns, where every body knows
every body, the manners of the young ladies do not derive
any additional charm from the perfect self-possession which
they thus acquire. Shiness appears to me to be a quality
utterly unknown to either man, woman, or child in America.
The girls, from the reasons above stated; and the boys, from

beasts in them), would feel and look like a scared thing. To return to our progress. After losing

---

being absolutely thrown into the world, and made men of business before they are sixteen, are alike deficient in any thing like diffidence; and I really have been all but disconcerted at the perfect assurance with which I have been addressed, upon any and every subject, by little men and women just half way through their teens. That very common character amongst us, a shy man, is not to be met with in these latitudes. An American conversing on board one of their steam-boats is immediately surrounded, particularly if his conversation, though strictly directed to one individual, is of a political nature; in an instant a ring of spectators is formed round him, and whereas an Englishman would become silent at the very first appearance of a listener, an American, far from seeming abashed at this "audience," continues his discourse, which thus assumes the nature of an harangue, with perfect equanimity, and feels no annoyance whatever at having unfolded his private opinions of men and matters to a circle of forty or fifty people whom they could in no possible way concern. Speechifying is a very favourite species of exhibition with the men here, by the by; and, besides being self-possessed, they are all remarkably fluent. Really eloquent men are just as rare in this country as in any other, but the " gift of the gab " appears to me more widely disseminated amongst Americans than any other people in the world. Many things go to make good speakers of them: great acuteness, and sound common sense, sufficient general knowledge, and great knowledge of the world, an intense interest in every political measure, no matter how trivial in itself, no sense of bashfulness, and a great readiness of expression. But to return to the manners of the young American girls: — It is Rousseau, I think, who says, " Dans un

sight of New York, the river becomes narrower in
its bed, and the banks on either side assume a
higher and more rocky appearance. A fine range
of basaltic rock, called the Palisadoes, rising to a
height of some hundred feet (I guess), immediately
from the water on the left, forms a natural rampart,
overhanging the river for several miles. The
colour of the basalt was greenish grey, and con-

---

pays ou les mœurs sont pures, les filles seront faciles, et les
femmes severes." This applies particularly well to the carriage of the American women. When remarking to a gentleman once the difference between the manners of my own
young countrywomen and his, I expressed my disapprobation
of the education which led to such a result, he replied, " You
forget the comparatively pure state of morals in our country,
which admits of this degree of freedom in our young women,
without its rendering them liable to insult or misconstruction."
This is true, and it is also most true, for I have seen repeated
instances of it, that those very girls, whose manners have
been most displeasing to my European ways of feeling, whom
I should have pointed out as romps and flirts pre-eminent,
not only make excellent wives, but from the very moment of
their marriage seem to forsake society, and devote themselves exclusively to household duties and retirement. But
that I have seen and known of repeated instances of this, I
could scarcely have believed it, but it is the case; and a
young American lady, speaking upon this subject, said to me,
" We enjoy ourselves before marriage ; but in your country,
girls marry to obtain a greater degree of freedom, and indulge
in the pleasures and dissipations of society." She was not,
I think, greatly mistaken.

trasted finely with the opposite shore, whose softer
undulations were yet clothed with verdure, and
adorned with patches of woodland, robed in the
glorious colours of an American autumn. While
despatching breakfast, the reflection of the sun's
rays on the water flickered to and fro upon the
cabin ceiling; and through the loop-hole windows
we saw the bright foam round the paddles sparkling
like frothed gold in the morning light. On our
return to the deck, the face of the world had
become resplendent with the glorious sunshine that
now poured from the east; and rock and river,
earth and sky, shone in intense and dazzling
brilliancy. The broad Hudson curled into a
thousand crisp billows under the fresh north-wester
that blew over it. The vaporous exhalations of
night had melted from the horizon, and the bold,
rocky range of one shore, and exquisite rolling
outline of the other, stood out in fair relief against
the deep serene of the blue heavens.   *

* * * * *

* * * * *

I remained on deck without my bonnet, walking
to and fro, and enjoying the delicious wind that
was as bracing as a shower-bath. Mr. —— most
civilly offered me, when I returned to New York,
the use of a horse, and himself as escort to a beau-

tiful ride beyond Hoboken, which proffer was very gratefully received by me. Colonel —— introduced me to an old man of the name of ——.

*   *   *   *   *

*   *   *   *   *

A jester, and a long story-teller; — a man whom it would be awful to meet when you were too late for dinner, still more awful on your progress to a rendezvous; — a man to whom a listener is a God-send, and a button an anchor of discoursing for half a day. He made me laugh once or twice heartily. As we passed the various points of the river, to which any interest, legendary or historical, attached, each of my three companions drew my attention to it; and I had, pretty generally, three variations of the same anecdote at each point of observation. On we boiled past Spitendevil creek*, where the waters of the broad Hudson join those of the East River, and circle with their silver arms the island of Manhattan. Past the last stupendous reach of the Palisadoes, which, stretching out into an endless promontory, seems to grow with the mariner's onward progress, and bears witness to the justice with which Hudson, on his exploring voyage up the river, christened it, the " weary

---

* For the origin of this curious name, see that interesting and veracious work, the history of Knickerbocker.

point." Past the thick masses of wood that mark
the shadowy site of Sleepy Hollow.* Past the
marble prison of Sing Sing; and Tarrytown, where
poor André was taken; and on the opposite shore,
saw the glimmering white buildings, among which
his tomb reposes. — By the by, for a bit of the
marvellous, which I dearly love. I am credibly
informed, that on the day the traitor Arnold died,
in England, a thunderbolt struck the tree that grew
above André's tomb here, on the shores of the
Hudson — nice, that! Crossed the broad, glorious,
Tappan Sea, where the shores receding, form a
huge basin, where the brimming waters roll in an
expanse of lake-like width, yet hold their rapid
current to the ocean, themselves a running sea.
The giant shadows of the mountains on the left,
falling on the deep basin at their feet, the triumphant sunlight that made the restless mirror that
reflected it too bright for the eye to rest upon, the
sunny shores to the right, rising and falling in every
exquisite form that hill and dale can wear, the
jutting masses of granite, glittering like the diamond
rocks of fairy-land, in the sun, the golden waves
flinging themselves up every tiny crevice, the glowing crimson foliage of the distant woods, the fresh

---

* Famous as the scene of Ichabod Crane's exploits.

vivid green of the cedars, that rifted their strong
roots in every stony cleft, and threw a semblance
of summer over these November days — all, all
was beautiful, and full of brightness. We passed
the lighthouse of Stony Point, now the peaceful
occupant of the territory, where the blood in English veins was poured out by English hands, during
the struggle between old established tyranny and
the infant liberties of this giant world. Over all
and each, the blessed sky bent its blue arch, re-
splendently clear and bright, while far away the
distant summits of the Highlands rose one above
another, shutting in the world, and almost appearing as though each bend of the river must find us
locked in their shadowy circle, without means of
onward progress.   *   *   *

         *   *   *   *   *

         *   *   *   *   *

At every moment, the scene varied; at every moment, new beauty and grandeur was revealed to us;
at every moment, the delicious lights and shadows
fell with richer depth and brightness upon higher
openings into the mountains, and fairer bends of
the glorious river. At about a quarter to eleven,
the buildings of West Point were seen, perched
upon the rock side, overhanging the water; above,
the woody rise, upon whose summit stands the large

hotel, the favourite resort of visiters during the summer season; rising again above this, the ruins of Fort Putnam, poor André's prison-house, overlooking the Hudson and its shores; and towering high beyond them all, the giant hills, upon whose brown shoulders the trees looked like bristles standing up against the sky. We left the boat, or rather she left us, and presently we saw her holding her course far up the bright water, and between the hills; where, framed by the dark mountains with the sapphire stream below and the sapphire sky above, lay the bright little town of Newburgh, with its white buildings glittering in the sunshine.   *   *   *   *

*   *   *   *   *

*   *   *   *   *

We toiled up the ascent, which, though by comparison with its overpeering fellows inconsiderable, was a sufficiently fatiguing undertaking under the unclouded weather and over the unshaded downs that form the parade ground for the cadets. West Point is a military establishment containing some two hundred and fifty pupils; who are here educated for the army under the superintendence of experienced officers.*   The buildings, in which

* If the results answer to the means employed, the pupils of West Point ought to turn out accomplished scholars in

they reside and pursue their various studies, stand upon a grassy knoll holding the top of the rocky

---

every branch of human learning, as well as ripe soldiers and skilful engineers. Their course of education consists of almost every study within the range of man's capacity; and as the school discipline is unusually strict, their hours of labour many, and of recreation very few, they should be able to boast of many " wise men" among their number. However it is here, I imagine, as elsewhere; where studies are pursued laboriously for a length of time, variety becomes a necessary relief to the mental powers, and so far the multiplicity of objects of acquirement may be excused; but surely, to combine in the education of one youth the elements of half a dozen sciences, each one of which would wear out a man's life in the full understanding of it, is not the best system of instruction. However, 't is the one now universally adopted, and tends to give more smatterers in science than scientific men to the world. The military part of their education is, however, what the pupils of West Point are most exercised in, and so far as one so ignorant of such matters as myself can judge, I should imagine the system adopted calculated to make expert artillerymen and engineers of them. Their deportment, and the way they went through their evolutions on the parade, did not appear to me very steady — there was a want of correctness of carriage, generally, and of absolute precision cf movement, which one accustomed to the manœuvring of regular troops detects immediately. There are several large pieces of ordnance kept in the gun-room, some of which were taken from the English; and I remarked a pretty little brass cannon, which almost looked like a plaything, which bore the broad arrow and the name of Saratoga.

bank of the river, and commanding a most enchanting view of its course. They are not particularly extensive; but commodious and well-or-
dered. I am told they have a good library; but
on reaching the dwelling of Mr. Cozzens, (proprietor of the hotel, which being at this season
shut, he received us most hospitably and courteously in his own house,) I felt so weary, that I
thought it impossible I should stir again for the
whole day, and declined seeing it. I had walked
on the deck at an amazing pace, and without once
sitting down from eight o'clock till eleven; and I
think must nearly have killed Colonel ——, who
was my companion during this march. However,
upon finding that it wanted full an hour till dinner-
time, it was agreed that we should go up to the
fort, and we set off under the guidance of one of
Mr. Cozzens' servants, who had orders not to go
too fast with us. Before turning into the woods
that cover the foot of the mountain, we followed
a bit of road that overhung the river; and stealing
over its sleepy-looking waters, where shone like
stars the white sails of many a tiny skiff, came the
delicious notes of a bugle-horn. The height at
which we stood above the water prevented the ear
being satisfied with the complete subject of the
musician, but the sweet, broken tones that came

rising from the far down thickets that skirted the
river, had more harmony than a distinct and perfect
strain. I stood entranced to listen — the whole
was like a dream of fairy-land : but presently our
guide struck into the woods, and the world became
screened from our sight. I had thought that I
was tired, and could not stir, even to follow the
leisurely footsteps of our cicerone; but tangled
brake and woodland path, and rocky height, soon
roused my curiosity, and my legs following there-
with, I presently outstripped our party, guide and
all, and began pursuing my upward path ; through
close growing trees and shrubs, over pale, shining
ledges of granite, over which the trickling mountain
springs had taken their silvery course ; through
swampy grounds, where the fallen leaves lay like
gems under the still pools that here and there
shone dimly in little hollow glens ; over the soft
starry moss that told where the moist earth retained
the freshening waters, over sharp, hard splinters
of rock, and rough masses of stone. Alone, alone,
I was alone and happy, and went on my way rejoicing, climbing and climbing still, till the green
mound of thick turf, and ruined rampart of the
fort arrested my progress. I coasted the broken
wall ; and lighting down on a broad, smooth table
of granite fringed with young cedar bushes, I look-

ed down, and for a moment my breath seemed to stop, the pulsation of my heart to cease — I was filled with awe. The beauty and wild sublimity of what I beheld seemed almost to crush my faculties, — I felt dizzy as though my senses were drowning, — I felt as though I had been carried into the immediate presence of God. Though I were to live a thousand years, I never can forget it. The first thing that I distinctly saw was the shadow of a large cloud, which rolled slowly down the side of a huge mountain, frowning over the height where I stood. The shadow moved down its steep sunny side, threw a deep blackness over the sparkling river, and then passed off and climbed the opposite mountain on the other shore, leaving the world in the full blaze of noon. I could have stretched out my arms, and shouted aloud — I could have fallen on my knees, and worshipped — I could have committed any extravagance that ecstasy could suggest. I stood filled with amazement and delight, till the footsteps and voices of my companions roused me. I darted away, unwilling to be interrupted. Colonel —— was following me, but I peremptorily forbade his doing so, and was clambering on alone, when the voice of our guide assuring me that the path I was pursuing was impassable, arrested my course. My

father beckoned to me from above not to pursue
my track; so I climbed through a break, which
the rocky walls of nature and the broken fortifica-
tions of art rendered tolerably difficult of access,
and running round the wall joined my father on
his high stand, where he was holding out his arms
to me. For two or three minutes we mingled exclamations of delight and surprise : he then led
me to the brink of the rampart; and looking down
the opposite angle of the wall to that which I was
previously coasting, I beheld the path I was then
following break suddenly off, on the edge of a pre-
cipice several hundred feet down into the valley :
it made me gulp to look at it. Presently I left
my father, and after going the complete round of
the ruins, found out for myself a grassy knoll commanding a full view of the scene, sufficiently far
from my party not to hear their voices, and screened
from seeing them by some beautiful young cedar
bushes; and here I lay down and cried most
abundantly, by which means I recovered my senses,
which else, I think, must have forsaken me. How
full of thoughts I was ! Of God's great might, and
gracious goodness, of the beauty of this earth, of
the apparent nothingness of man when compared
with this huge inanimate creation, of his wondrous
value, for whose delight and use all these fair things

were created. I thought of my distant home; that
handful of earth thrown upon the wide waters,
whose genius has led the kingdoms of the world
— whose children have become the possessors of
this new hemisphere. I rejoiced to think that
when England shall be, as all things must be, fallen
into the devouring past, her language will still be
spoken among these glorious hills, her name re-
vered, her memory cherished, her fame preserved
here, in this far world beyond the seas, this country
of her children's adoption. Poor old mother!
how she would remain amazed to see the huge
earth and waters where her voice is heard, in the
name of every spot where her descendants have
rested the soles of their feet: this giant inheritance of her sons, poor, poor, old England!   *

   *   *   *   *   *

Where are the poets of this land?   Why such a
world should bring forth men with minds and
souls larger and stronger than any that ever dwelt
in mortal flesh.   Where are the poets of this land?
They should be giants, too; Homers and Miltons,
and Goethes and Dantes, and Shakspeares. Have
these glorious scenes poured no inspirings into
hearts worthy to behold and praise their beauty?
Is there none to come here and worship among
these hills and waters till his heart burns within

him, and the hymn of inspiration flows from his
lips, and rises to the sky? Is there not one among
the sons of such a soil to send forth its praises to
the universe, to throw new glory round the mountains, new beauty over the waves? Is inanimate
nature, alone, here " telling the glories of God ? "
Oh, surely, surely, there will come a time when
this lovely land will be vocal with the sound of
song, when every close-locked valley and waving
wood, rifted rock and flowing stream, shall have
their praise. Yet 't is strange how marvellously
unpoetical these people are! How swallowed up
in life and its daily realities, wants, and cares!
How full of toil and thrift, and money-getting
labour! Even the heathen Dutch, among us the
very antipodes of all poetry, have found names
such as the Donder Berg for the hills, whilst the
Americans christen them Butter Hill, the Crows
Nest, and *such like*. Perhaps some hundred years
hence, when wealth has been amassed by individuals, and the face of society begins to grow
checkered, as in the old lands of Europe, when
the whole mass of population shall no longer go
running along the level road of toil and profit,
`when inequalities of rank shall exist, and the rich
man shall be able to pay for the luxury of poetry,
and the poor man who makes verses no longer

be asked, " Why don't you cast up accounts?"
when all this comes to pass, as *perhaps* some day
it may, America will have poets.   It seems strange
to me that men, such as the early settlers in Mas-
sachussets, the Puritan founders of New England,
the " Pilgrim Fathers," should not have had
amongst them some men, or at least man, in whose
mind the stern and enduring courage, the fervent,
enthusiastic piety, the unbending love of liberty,
which animated them all, become the inspiration
to poetic thought, and the suggestion of poetical
utterance.   They should have had a Milton or a
Klopstock amongst them.   Yet, after all, they had
excitement of another sort, and, moreover, the
difficulties and dangers, and distresses of a fate of
unparalleled hardship, to engross all the energies
of their minds; and I am half inclined to believe
that poetry is but a hothouse growth, and yet I
don't know : I wish somebody would explain to me
every thing in this world that I can't make out.*

* It might be a curious and interesting matter of research
to determine under what combination of external circumstances the spirit of poetry flourishes most vigorously, and
good poets have most abounded.   The extremes of poverty
and luxury seem alike inimical to its well-being; yet the latter far more so than the former, for most poets have been
poor ; some so poor, as to enrich the world, while they
themselves received so little return from its favour as miser-

We came down from the mountain at about half-past one: our party had been joined by Colonel

---

ably to perish of want. Again, the level tenor of a life alike removed from want and superfluity should seem too devoid of interest or excitement to make a good poet. Long-lived competency is more favourable to the even temper of philosophy than the fiery nature of one who must know the storms of passion, and all the fiercer elements of which the acting and suffering soul of man is made. Again, it would be curious to know, if it might be ascertained, whether those men whose inspirations have been aided alone by the comtemplation of the inanimate beauties of nature, and the phenomena of their own minds and the minds and lives of their fellows, have been as great poets as those, who, besides these sources of inspiration, fed the power within them with the knowledge of great writers and poets of other countries and times. Another question, which it would be interesting to determine, would be, under what species of government poets have been most numerous, and most honoured. As our modern exploders of old fallacies have not yet made up their minds whether such a person as Homer ever lived, it is rather a vain labour of imagination to determine whether this great king of all poets flourished under a monarchy, or in a republic; certain it is, he sang of kings and princes in right lordly style: be that as it may, we have rather better authority for believing that the Greek dramatists, those masters, and sometime models, of their peculiar branch of the art, flourished under republican governments; but with them, I think, ends the list of republican poets of great and universal fame. Rome had no poets till she had emperors. Italy was, it is true, divided into so called republics during the golden age of her literature; but they were so in name alone, the spirit of equality had long departed from the soil,

——, Governor of the College, who very courteously came toiling up to Fort Putnam, to pay his compliments to us. I lingered far behind them, returning; and, when they were out of sight, turned back, and once more ascended the ruin, to look my last of admiration and delight, and then down, down, every step bringing me out of the clouds, farther from heaven, and nearer this work i' day world. I loitered, and loitered, looking back

---

and they were merely prouder and more arbitrary aristocracies than have ever existed under any monarchy in the world. If ever France can be said to have had a poetical age, it was during the magnificent reign of Lewis the Fourteenth, that pageant that prepared the bloodiest tragedy in the pages of history. England offers the only exception that I have advanced, namely, that the republican form of government is inimical to poetry. For it was during the short and shameful period of fanatical republicanism, which blots her annals, that the glory and the might of Milton rose upon the world; he is the only great poet who ever flourished under a republic; and he was rather the poet of heaven and hell, than of earth: his subjects are either biblical or mythological; and however his stern and just spirit might advocate the cause of equality and universal freedom in the more arid regions of political and theological controversies, in his noblest and greatest capacity, he has sung of angels and archangels, the starry hierarchy of heaven, where some of the blessed wore a brighter glory than their fellows, where some were inferior to other celestial powers, and where God was King supreme, over all. In heaven, Milton dreamt of no republics, nor in hell either.

at every step; but at last the hills were shut out
by a bend in the road, and I came into the house
to throw myself down on the floor, and sleep most
seriously for half an hour; at the end of which
time, we were called to dinner. In England, if
an innkeeper gives you a good dinner, and places
the first dish on the table himself, you pay him,
and he's obliged to you. Here, an innkeeper is a
gentleman, your equal, sits at his table with you,
you pay him, and are obliged to him besides.
'T is necessary therefore for a stranger, but especially an Englishman, to understand the fashions
of the land, else he may chance to mistake that
for an impertinent familiarity, which is in fact the
received custom of the country. Mr. Cozzens
very considerately gave us our dinner in a private
room, instead of seating us at an ordinary with
all the West Point Officers. Moreover, *gave* in
the literal sense, and a very good dinner it was.
He is himself a very intelligent, courteous person,
and, during the very short time that we were his
guests, showed us every possible attention and
civility. We had scarce finished our dinner, when
in rushed a waiter to tell us that the boat was in
sight. Away we trotted, trailing cloaks, and
shawls, any-how fashion, down the hill. The
steamer came puffing up the gorge between the

mountains, and in a moment we were bundled into the boat, hauled alongside, and landed on the deck; and presently the glorious highlands, all glowing in the rosy sunset, began to recede from us. Just as we were putting off from shore, a tiny skiff, with its graceful white sail glittering in the sun, turned the base of the opposite hill, evidently making to the point whence we embarked. I have since learned that it contained a messenger to us, from a gentleman bearing our name, and distantly connected with us, proprietor of some large iron works on the shore opposite West Point. However, our kinsman was too late, and we were already losing sight of West Point, when his boat reached the shore. Our progress homeward was, if any thing, more enchanting than our coming out had been, except for leaving all this loveliness. The sun went down in splendour, leaving the world robed in glorious beauty. The sky was one glowing geranium curtain, into which the dark hills rose like shadow-land, stretching beyond, and still beyond, till they grew like hazy outlines through a dazzling mist of gold. The glory faded; and a soft violet colour spread downwards to the horizon, where a faint range of clouds lay floating like scattered rose leaves. As the day fell, the volumes of smoke from our steam-boat chimneys became streams of fiery sparks, which glittered over the water with a strange unearthly effect. I sat on deck watching the world grow dark, till my father, afraid of the night air, bade me go down; and there, in spite of the chattering of a score of women, and the squalling of half as many children, I slept profoundly till we reached New York, at a quarter to seven.

Saturday, 17*th.*

After breakfast, wrote journal : while doing so, Mr. —— called to know if I held my mind in spite of the grey look of the morning. A wan sunbeam just then lighted on the earth, and I said I would go; for I thought by about twelve it probably would clear. * *

* * * * *

* * * * *

They called for me in the carriage at eleven; and afterwards we mounted our steeds in Warren Street to escape the crowd in Broadway. We rode down to the ferry. The creature, *on top* of which I sat, was the real *potatuppy* butcher's horse. However, it did not shake me, or pull my arms much, so I was content. As to a horse properly broken, either for man or woman, I have done

looking for it in this land. We went into the
steam-boat on our horses. The mist lay thick over
the river; but the opposite shores had that grey
distinctness of colour and outline that invariably
foretells rain in England. The wind blew bitterly
keen and cold.   *   *   *

    *   *   *   *   *

Our riding party was Mr. ——, whom I like;
Mrs. ——, whom I also like, in spite of her out-
landish riding habiliments, a brother of his,   *

    *   *   *   *   *

and a young —— in white hair and spectacles.
The carriage held old Mr. ——, Miss ——, the
youngest daughter, and that beautiful youngest
boy of theirs, who is so like his handsome sister;
also sundry baskets of cake, and bottles of champagne. After landing, we set off at a brisk canter
to Weehawk. None of these people know how to
ride: they just go whatever pace their horse likes,
sitting as backward as they can in the saddle, and
tugging at the reins as hard as ever they can, to
the infinite detriment of their own hands and their
horses' mouths. When we had reached the height,
we dismounted and walked through the woods
that crown the cliffs, which here rise to an elevation of some hundred feet above the river. Our
path lay through tangled brakes, where the withered

trees and fallen red leaves, the bright cedar bushes, and pale slabs of granite, formed a fine and harmonious contrast of colouring; the whole blending beautifully together under the grey light, that made it look like one of Ruysdael's pictures. Our walk terminated at a little rocky promontory, called the Devil's Pulpit, where, as legends say, Satan was wont to preach, loud enough to drown the sound of the Sabbath bells in New York. The Hudson, far below, lay leaden and sullen; the woods along the shores looked withered and wintry; a thick curtain of vapour shrouded all the distance : the effect of the whole was very sad and beautiful; and had I been by myself I should have enjoyed it very much. But I was in company, and, moreover, in company with two punsters, who uttered their atrocities without remorse in the midst of all that was most striking and melancholy in nature. When we mounted our horses again, Mrs. ——— complained that hers pulled her wrists most dreadfully; and as they seemed none of the strongest, I exchanged steeds with her. The lady proprietress of the grounds over which we had been walking and riding invited us into the house, but being mounted I declined, and we set off for the pavilion. Just as we arrived there, it began to rain. Mercy on me and Mrs. ———! how our

arms will ache to-morrow! This worthy animal of
hers had a mouth a little worse than a donkey's.
Arrived at the pavilion, we dismounted, and swallowed sundry champagnes and lumps of plum
cake, which were singularly refreshing. We set
off again, and presently it began to pelt with rain.
We reached and crossed the ferry without getting
very wet. Arranged to ride on Wednesday, if
fine, and so home. Upon the whole, rather satisfied than otherwise with my expedition. Dressed
for dinner at once; went on with journal; Colonel —— called, and sat some time. After dinner,
embroidered till eight: teaed: — my father went
over to the theatre: I practised for two hours.

Sunday, 18*th.*

The muscles of my arms (for I have such un-
lady-like things) stand out like lumps of stone,
with the fine exercise they had yesterday. I wonder
how Mrs. ——'s shoulders and elbows feel.   *
   *   *   *   *   *

It rained so, we hackneyed to church. This is
twice Mr. —— has not been to church, which is
really very wrong, though it leaves us the pew
comfortably to ourselves. Dr. —— must be an
excellent good man — his sermons are every way

delightful; good sense, sound doctrine, and withal a most winning mildness and gentleness of manner. A benevolent good man, I am sure, he must be. Came home — copied snuff-box verses for my father; divided out my story of the Sisters into acts and scenes: began doing the same by the English tragedy; but in the midst took a fancy to make a story instead of a play of it — and so I will, I think. Dressed for dinner. At about half-past five Colonel —— and his Quaker wife came. She is a most delightful creature, with the sweetest expression of face imaginable. She reminded me several times of dear Mrs. ——. Her dress, too, the rich brown watered silk, made so plainly, recalled Mrs. —— to me very forcibly. We had a very comfortable dinner and evening. They went away at about half-past ten.

Monday, 19*th.*

After breakfast, wrote journal. Went out shopping and returning cards; called at Mrs. ——, and was let in. I like her; she is a nice person, with agreeable manners. Came home at about half-past two; put out things for the theatre; dined at three. After dinner, pottered about clothes till

time to go to the theatre. The house was very
good. My benefit — play, Much Ado about Nothing. I played very well. I am much improved
in my comedy acting. Came home in a coach — it
poured with rain. What a stupidday! The accounts of cholera in New Orleans are frightful;
they have the yellow fever there too. Poor people!
what an awful visitation!

Tuesday, 20th.

After breakfast, wrote journal. At twelve, went
and called upon Mrs. ——: the day was bright,
but bitter cold, with a keen piercing wind that
half cut one in half, and was delicious. The servant denied Mrs. ——; but we had hardly turned
from the door when both the ladies came rushing
after us, with nothing on their heads and necks,
and thin summer gowns on. They brought us
into a room where there was a fire fit to roast an
ox. No wonder the women here are delicate and
subject to cold, and die of consumption. Here
were these sitting absolutely in an oven, in clothes
fit only for the hottest days in summer, instead of
wrapping themselves up well, and trotting out,
and warming their blood wholesomely with good
hard exercise. The pretty Mrs. —— looks very

sickly, and coughs terribly. Her beauty did not strike me so much to-day. I do not admire any body who looks as if a puff of wind would break them in half, or a drop of water soak them through. I greatly prefer her sister's looks, who certainly is not pretty, but tall and straight, and healthy-looking, and springy as a young thing ought to be. Was introduced to a most enchanting young Newfoundland dog, whom I greatly coveted. Settled to ride to-morrow if fine. Called at ———'s, also at a furrier's about cap, and came home. Found ——— and ——— with my father. What a very bad expression of face the former has; sneering and false — terrible ! I looked at ——— with much respect. I like his spirit, as it shines through his works, greatly. He was a pale, sickly-looking man, without any thing at all remarkable in the expression of his countenance. While they were here, Mr. ——— called to settle about to-morrow. He is a nice person; sensible and civil, and civil in the right way. Arrangements were made for dear ———'s going, which I rejoiced in greatly. I do not like at all leaving her behind. When the folks were gone, put out things for the theatre. While doing so, Mr. ——— and Mr. and Mrs. ——— called. Great discoursing about horses and horsemanship. Dined at three. After dinner, put fur

upon my habit. At half-past five, went to the
theatre. House very good; play, Hunchback.
By the by, Colonel —— called to-day, to entreat
me to go and see his " Honour, the Recorder,"
who had sent me tickets of admission to the town
hall, to see —— receive the freedom of the city.
I could not go, because of our horseback expedition — this by the way. I played so-soish. ——was
at the play; and at the end, somebody in the house
exclaimed, " Three cheers for —— ! " whereupon a mingled chorus of applause and hisses
arose. The Vice-President looked rather silly,
and acknowledged neither the one or the other.
How well I remember the Duke of —— coming
to the orchestra to see this play, the night before
it was expected the Whigs would go out. I dare
say he knew little enough what the Hunchback
was about. I do not think the people noticed him,
however; so the feeling of the pulse must have
been unsatisfactory. Mr. —— said to Modus
to-night in the play, speaking of me, " a change
of linen will suffice for her." How absurd ! we
were all dying on the stage. Came home; supped :
— looked at silks; chose a lovely rose-coloured
one to line my Portia dress; with which good deed
my day ended.

Wednesday, 21st.

Looked at the sun, and satisfied with his promise, went to bed again, and slept till half-past
eight. After breakfast, wrote to his honour, the
Recorder, an humble apology in true Old Bailey
style. Wrote journal, and began practising. Mrs.
—— called before I was out of my bed to tell us
that the ——'s were not going, but that either her
husband or her brother-in-law would be too glad
to go in the gig with D——. This, however, the
latter refused, not choosing, as she said, to make
any young man do the penance of keeping her
company on a party of pleasure. Dear good old
D——! I was vexed and provoked; but it could
not be helped. At eleven, —— came for me. I
found Mrs. —— in the carriage waiting for me.
We adjourned to Warren Street, where were assembled all the party. While we waited for our
horses, Neptune, the beautiful Newfoundland, was
admitted, and amused himself by prancing over
tables, and chairs, and sofas, to his own infinite
delight, and the visible benefit of the furniture.
Our steeds having arrived, we mounted and began
to progress. Myself, and Mrs. ——, her husband,
his brother, ——, and papa ——, Dr. ——,

Mrs. ——'s brother, and Mr. ——, nephew, I believe, of the Irish patriot, were the equestrians of the party. After, followed Mr. —— and Mrs. ——, all be-coated and be-furred, in the stanhope. After, followed the ammunition waggon, containing a negro servant, Neptune, and sundry baskets of champagne, cake, and cherry bounce. Away we rushed down Broadway, to the infinite edification of its gaping multitudes. Mr. —— had gotten me an enchanting horse that trotted like an angel. So in spite of Major ——'s awful denunciation of " disgusting," I had a delicious hard trot all through the streets, rising in my saddle like a lady, or rather, a gentleman. My habit seemed to excite considerable admiration and approbation, and indeed it was *great*. Crossed the Brooklyn ferry in the steam-boat, and safely landed on the opposite side. The whole army defiled; the stanhope taking the van, the horses forming the main body, and the provisions bringing up the rear. Our party separated constantly, as we progressed, into various groups, but I remained chiefly with Dr. ——, Mr. ——, and old Mr. ——. By the by, those ——'s are a charming family; for Mrs. —— sits straight in her saddle, and the Doctor settled, when we started, that when he had *despatched his patients*, he would call for D—— in the gig, and come down to meet

us at the fort. Our ride thither was extremely
agreeable: the day was clear, cold, and grey; a
delightful day for riding. I trotted to my heart's
content; and kept my blood warm, and my spirits
like champagne, till we reached the fort, when, at
sight of the Narrows, and the Sandy Hook lighthouse, they sank deep, deep down.

    *   *   *   *   *

    *   *   *   *   *

The sea lay grey and still, without a wave or
scarce a ripple. A thousand light skiffs, of various shapes, lay upon the leaden waters. The sky
was a fine heap of heavy purple clouds, from behind which the sun shot down his rays, which threw
a melancholy wan lustre on the sea beneath them.
'T was a sad and beautiful scene. The colouring
of the whole was gloomily harmonious; and the
dark shores and grey expanse of water blended
solemnly with the violet-coloured curtain of the
heavens. We went over the fort. 'T is a fortifi-
cation of no great size, or, I should think, strength;
but its position, which commands the narrow entrance to the bay of New York, effectually checks
the pass, and guards the watery defile that leads
to the city of mammon. We looked at the guns
and powder magazine, walked round the walls,
and peeped into the officers' quarters, and then

descended to seek where we might eat and be satisfied. Mrs. —— is a very nice creature: she
looks the picture of good temper — never stands
still a minute; and as we rode along to-day, when,
fearing she might be cold, I asked her how she
found herself, she replied, with perfect innocence
and sincerity, " Oh, delightful !" which made us
all scream.   We knocked up the quarters of an
old woman who kept a cottage, not exactly young
love's humble shed, but good enough for our purpose.   We got sundry logs of wood, and made a
blazing fire ; moreover, the baskets were opened,
and presently we presented the interesting spectacle of a dozen people each with a lump of cake
in one hand, and a champagne glass in the other.
Mr. —— and Mrs. —— stuck to the cherry
bounce, and, as we afterwards heard, drove home
accordingly.   Having discussed, we remounted,
and set forwards home by another road ; a very
lovely one, all along the river side.   Ere we had
progressed long, we met D—— and Dr. —— in
the gig.   The nice good man had kept his word,
and gone to fetch her.   They had met Mr. ——'s
equipage going cherry-bounce pace, it seems, two
miles ahead of us. The men here are never happy
unless they are going full speed.   'T is no wonder
their horses are good for nothing : they would ruin

any horses that were good for any thing.* Such un-
skilful horsemanship I never saw : Going full tear;
crossing one another in every direction; knocking up against one another ; splashing through
puddles because they have no hand over their
horses, and either overshooting their point, or being half thrown at every turn of the road for the
same reason. Came home full speed, and arrived
at half-past four, having ridden, I should think,
nearly twenty miles. Found Mrs. —— at home.
They pressed me very much to stay dinner with
them; but my father expected me, and I would
not. That worthy youth, ——, insisted upon my
accepting his beautiful large dog, Neptune, which
I did conditionally, in case Mr. —— should fail
me, which I think a very improbable case indeed.
They ordered the carriage, and Mr. —— persisted

* It is quite curious to observe how utterly unknown a
thing a *really* well broken horse is in this country. I have
just bought one who was highly approved and recommended
by several gentlemen considered here as learned in all these
matters ; and of my own knowledge, I might hunt the Union
over and not find a better. As far as the make, and beauty,
and disposition of the animal goes, there is no fault to find ;
but this *lady's horse* never had a woman on its back, had
never been ridden but with a snaffle bit, and until she came
into my possession, did not know how to canter with her
right foot. When the Americans say a horse is well broken,
they mean it is not wild.

in seeing me home in it, much to my annoyance,
as 't was a very useless ceremony indeed. Did
not dishabit, but dined *en amazone.*   *

*   *   *   *   *

Gave D—— her muff and tippet, which are
exceedingly magnificent. After dinner, pottered
about, and dressed at once. Played on the piano
till nine, when we adjourned to ——'s. A complete " small party, my dear." Dr. —— was
there, whom I was glad to see; also Mrs. ——;
also Mr. and Miss ——; also that Mrs. ——,
who is utter horror and perturbation of spirit to
me; also ——; also ——; all our riding party,
and a world besides. After a little time, dancing
was proposed; and I stood up to waltz with Mr.
——, who observed that Dr. —— was gone, as
he never chose to be present while waltzing was
going on. I felt shocked to death that unconsciously I should have been instrumental in driving him away, and much surprised that those who
knew his disapprobation of waltzing should have
proposed it. However, he was gone, and did not
return. Therefore I waltzed myself out of my
conscientious remorse. Sang them Fanny Gray,
and Ye Mariners of Spain. Danced sundry quadrilles; and, finally, what they called a Kentucky
reel, — which is nothing more than Sir Roger de

Coverly turned Backwoodsman — and afterwards a " foursome reel." Played magic music; and, finally, at one o'clock, came home, having danced myself fairly off my legs.

Thursday, 22d.

It poured with rain all day. Dr. —— called, and gave me a sermon about waltzing. As it was perfectly good sense, to which I could reply nothing whatever in the shape of objection, I promised him never to waltz again, except with a woman, or my brother.   *   *

*,   *   *   *   *

After all, 't is not fitting that a man should put his arm round one's waist, whether one belongs to any one but one's self or not. 'T is much against what I have always thought most sacred, — the dignity of a woman in her own eyes and those of others. I like Dr. —— most exceedingly. He spoke every way to my feelings of what was right, to-day. After saying that he felt convinced, from conversations which he had heard amongst men, that waltzing was immoral in its tendency, he added, " I am married, and have been in love, and cannot imagine any thing more destructive of the deep and devoted respect which love is cal-

culated to excite in every honourable man's heart,
not only for the individual object of his affections,
but for her whole sex, than to see any and every
impertinent coxcomb in a ball-room come up to
her, and, without remorse or hesitation, clasp her
waist, imprison her hand, and absolutely whirl her
round in his arms." So spake the Doctor; and
my sense of propriety and conviction of right bore
testimony to the truth of his saying. So, farewell,
sweet German waltz ! — next to hock, the most
intoxicating growth of the Rheinland. I shall
never keep time to your pleasant measure again !
— no matter; after all, any thing is better than to
be lightly spoken of, and to deserve such mention.
Mr. —— called, and sat some time with me. He
is grown monstrously fat, and looks perfectly
radiant. He brought with him a good-looking
staring man of the name of ——. We dined at
three. After dinner, received a pretty anonymous
nosegay, with sundry very flattering doggrel. The
play was the Stranger. It poured cats and dogs,
and the streets were all grey pudding. I did not
expect to see six people in the house ; instead of
which, 'twas crowded : a satisfactory proof of our
attraction.

Friday, 23d.

At eleven, went to rehearsal — Isabella. I have forgotten all about it. They all read their parts; came home; began to practise. The two Mrs. —— called. I like them mainly, Mrs. —— particularly. While they were here, Mr. —— and a man called; they stayed but a minute. By and by, in walked Mr. and Mrs. ——; whereupon the —— departed.   *   *   *

 * * * * *

 * * * * *

While they were here, received from —— the beautiful annual he has bought for me, which is, indeed, most beautiful; and with it, literally a copy of verses, which are *not so bad neither* — only think of that ! ! ! The engravings are from things of Stanfield's, taken on the Rhine; and made my heart ache to be once more in Europe, in the old land where fairy tales are told; in the old feudal world, where every rock, and valley, and stream, are haunted with imaginings wild and beautiful: the hallowed ground of legend history; the dream-land of fancy and of poetry. Put out things for the theatre: dined at three. Colonel —— called: he brought news of the arrival of a

Liverpool packet, and prophesied letters to me.
Went to the theatre. Play, Hunchback — house
very fine again. Just as I was dressing for the
second act, three letters were brought into my
room.　　*　　　*　　　*　　　*

　*　　　*　　　*　　　*　　　*

　*　　　*　　　*　　　*　　　*

I was so much overset by them, that, with the
strange faculty I have of pouring one feeling into
another, I cried so bitterly in the parting scene
with Clifford, that I could scarcely utter the words
of my part.　　*　　　*　　　*

　*　　　*　　　*　　　*　　　*

　*　　　*　　　*　　　*　　　*

Saturday, 24th.

Our riding expedition having been put off, the
day was beautifully bright and clear. Sat stitching and pottering an infinity. My feet got so
perished that I didn't know what to do. Wrote
journal; practised for an hour; Mr. —— called.
When he was gone, went out with my father.
Called at ——'s to order home my gown for dinner-time. Left a card at Mrs. ——'s, and then
marched down to the tailor's to upbraid him about

my waistcoat, which is infamously ill made.* Coming home, met that very odious Mr. ——, who is
the perfection of genteel vulgarity. He walked
home with us. Dressed for dinner. Mme. ——
did not send my gown home in time: abominable
sempstress! so put on my blue and looked rather
dowdy. Found sundry that we know: Colonel
——; Mr. ——; my favourite aversion, Mr.
——; that signal fool, Mr. ——; Miss ——, who
looked like a hair-dresser's wax block; a Miss ——,
with lovely feet, and a terrified Bacchante-looking
head, *cum multis aliis.* I sat by one Mr. ——,
who talked without end, and cleverly enough : indeed, it was rather clever to talk so wonderfully
fast and much. After dinner, the party became

---

* The various censures which English travellers have bestowed upon various things in this country are constantly,
both in private conversation and the public prints, attributed
to *English jealousy.* I confess I have been amused at the
charge, and can only sincerely hope I may not draw down so
awful an accusation on myself, when I declare, that, during a
three years' residence in America, almost every article, of
every description, which I have had made, has been ill made,
and obliged to undergo manifold alterations. I don't pre-
tend to account for the fact, for fear the obvious reasons
might appear to find their source in that very small jealousy
of which England is guilty towards this country, in the person of her journal-scribbling travellers; but to the fact there
is and can be no denial.

much larger : Dr. ——, Mr. ——, the —— (all
but ——), that entire self-satisfaction, Mr. ——,
Mr. ——, and the knight of the rueful countenance;
three singing men, ycleped ——; and a shoal besides.   One of the Mr. —— and Miss —— sang
the duet in the Didone, that dear —— and ——
used to sing so lovelily.   They both had good
voices, but the style is but so-soish.   Presently,
three men sang that sea glee that I remember
Lord and Lady —— teaching me at ——.   What
a strange faculty of our nature this is, this leading
back of our minds to the past, through the agency
of our senses, acted upon by present influences,
the renewing life, the magical summoning up of
dead time from its grave, with the very place and
circumstance it wore.   Wondrous riddle ! what
— what are we, that are so curiously made ?   By
and by dancing was proposed, and I was much
entreated and implored to change my determination about waltzing; but I was inexorable, and
waltzed only with the ladies, who one and all dance
extremely well.   Mrs. —— looked lovely to-night.
Dr. —— says very true, she has a thorough-bred
look, which reminds me a little of our noble English ladies.   He says she is like Lady ——.   I
think she is prettier: she certainly looks like a
gem.   We danced a Kentucky reel, and sundry

quadrilles. That long *ens*, Mr. ——, was tipsy,
and went slithering about in a way to kill one; and
Mr. —— was sitting slyly in the corner, pretending to talk to D——, but in fact dying with laughter
at poor ——, who meandered about the room to
the infinite dismay and confusion of the whole
dance. Vain were the vigorous exertions of his
partner, who pulled him this way and that, and
pushed him hither and thither, to all which the
unresisting creature submitted incorrigibly. Remained dancing till half-past twelve, in fact, Sunday
morning, and then came home. They made me
sing, which I did abominably. On my return
home, found my black satin gown; every atom of
which will have to be unpicked — pleasant! The
trades-people here are really terrible; they can do
nothing, and will take no pains to do any thing:
'tis a handsome gown spoilt.*

* When you carry your complaint of careless work, or
want of punctuality, to the trades-people whom you employ
here, the unfortunate principals really excite your sympathy
by their helpless situation with regard to the free re-
publicans whom they employ, and who, with the utter com-
tempt of subordination which the cheapness of living, and
the spirit of licence (not liberty) produce among the lower
classes here, come when they please, depart when they like,
work when they choose, and if you remonstrate, take themselves off to new masters, secure of employment in your

Sunday, 25th.

My dear father's birth-day! also, by the by, a grand occasion here — the anniversary of the evacuation of the island by the British troops, which circumstance the worthy burghers have celebrated ever since with due devotion and thankfulness. Went to church: Dr. —— did not preach, which was a disappointment to me. The music was exquisite; and there was a beautiful graceful willow branch, with its long delicate fibres and golden leaves, waving against the blue sky and the

———————————

neighbour's house, if your mode of employing them displeases them. Manifold are the lamentations I have heard, of " Oh, ma'am, this is not like the old country; we can't get journeymen to work here, ma'am; we're obliged to do just as our workmen please, ma'am." One poor French dress-maker appeared to me on the verge of distraction, from the utter impossibility of keeping in any order a tribe of sewing girls, whom she seemed to pay on purpose that they might drive her crazy; and my shoemaker assured me the other day, with a most woful face, that it was election week, and that if I was as *suffering* for shoes as a lady could be, I could not have mine till the political cobblers in his employ had settled the " business of the nation" to their satisfaction. Patience is the only remedy. Whoever lives here, that has ever lived elsewhere, should come provided with it.

church window, that seemed to me like a magical
branch in a fairy tale. It struck me as strange
to-day, as I looked from the crowded gloomy
church to the bright unbounded sky, to think that
we call the one the house of God; to be sure, we
have other authority for calling the blue heavens
his throne; and oh, how glorious they did look!
The day was bright, but bitter cold. Coming
out of church, saw all our last night's party. On
my return home, found a perfect levee; Dr. ——,
Mr. ——, Mr. ——, Mr. ——, Mr. ——, a
whole regiment. When they were all gone, wrote
journal: having finished that and my lunch, set
out with my father to *fetch a walk;* which we did
to the tune of near six miles, through all the
outskirts of the town, an exceedingly low-life
ramble indeed — during which we came across a
man who was preaching in the street. He had
not a very large assembly round him, and we stood
in the crowd to hear him. By his own account,
he had been imprisoned before for a similar proceeding, and he was denouncing, most vehemently,
signal judgments on the blind and wicked corpor-
ation who had so stopped the work of righteous-
ness. The man's face was a very fine one, remarkably intelligent and handsome: he was cleanly
and well dressed, and had altogether a respectable

appearance. When we came home, it was past four. Dressed for dinner. My father dined with Mr. ——; so D—— and I had a *tête-à-tête* dinner. After which, played on the piano for some time; after which, began letter to H——; after which, wrote journal.   *   *   *

*   *   *   *   *

*   *   *   *   *

Monday, 26th.

Yesterday was evacuation day; but as yesterday was the Lord's day also, the American militia army postponed their yearly exhibition, and, instead of rushing about the streets in token of their thankfulness at the departure of the British, they quietly went to church, and praised God for that same. To-day, however, we have had firing of pop-guns, waving of star-spangled banners (some of them rather the worse for wear), infantry marching through the streets, cavalry (oh, Lord, what delicious objects they were!) and artillery prancing along them, to the infinite ecstasy and peril of a dense mob. Went to rehearsal at half-past ten. Was detained full ten minutes on the way thither, by the defiling of troops, who were progressing down Broadway. After rehearsal, came home —

put out things for the theatre. Mr. —— called : while he was here, spent a delightful half hour at the window, which, overlooking the park, commanded a full view of the magnanimous military marshalled there. O, pomp and circumstance of glorious war ! They were certainly not quite so bad as Falstaff's men, of ragged memory ; for, for aught I know to the contrary, they perhaps *all* of them had shirts to their backs. But some had gloves, and some had none ; some carried their guns one way, and some another ; some had caps of one fashion, and some of another ; some had no caps at all, but " shocking bad hats," with feathers in them.*

* This description may amaze sundry narrow-minded and prejudiced dwellers in those unhappy countries where standing armies are among the standing abuses, and the miserable stipendiaries of hoary tyrannies go about wearing the livery of their trade with a slavish unanimity becoming alone to hirelings, and salaried butchers base. But whoever should imagine that the members of an enlightened and free republic must, because they condescend to become soldiers, for the pure love of their country, behave as soldiers also, would draw foolish conclusions. Discipline, order, a peculiar carriage, a particular dress, obedience to superiors, and observance of rules, these, indeed, may all be the attributes of such miserable creatures as are content to receive wages for their blood. But for free Americans ! why should they not walk crooked, in the defence of their country, if they don't like to walk straight ? why should they not carry their guns on their shoulders instead of upright, if they please ?

The infantry were, however, comparatively respectable troops. They did not march many degrees out of the straight line, or stoop *too much*, or turn their heads round *too often*. Mr. ———— remarked, that militia were seldom more steady and orderly in their appearance. But the cavalry! oh, the cavalry! what gems without price they were! Apparently extremely frightened at the shambling *tituppy* chargers upon whose backs they clung, straggling in all directions, putting the admiring crowd in fear of their lives, and proving beyond a doubt how formidable they must appear to the enemy, when, with the most peaceable intentions in the world, they thus jeopardied the safety of their enthusiastic fellow-citizens. Bold would have been the man who did not edge backwards into the crowd, as a flock of these worthies a-horseback came down the street — some trotting, some galloping, some racking, some ambling; each and all " witching the world with wondrous horsemanship." If any thing ever might

---

and why, since they chose to defend their lives and liberties by becoming volunteers, should they not stick any feathers, of any colours that they like in their caps — black, white, or green? Is the noble occupation of war incompatible with the still nobler possession of freedom? Heaven forbid! and long live the American militia to prove their entire compatibility.

be properly called wondrous, they, their riders and accoutrements, deserve the title. Some wore boots, and some wore shoes, and one independent hero had got on grey stockings and *slippers!* Some had bright yellow feathers, and some red and black feathers! I remembered, particularly, a doctor, in a black suit, Hessian boots, a cocked hat, and bright yellow gauntlets; another fellow was dressed in the costume of one of the Der Freyschutz's corps: it looked for all the world like a *fancy* parade. The officers fulfilled completely my idea of Macheath's company of gentlemen of the road; only, I strongly suspect the latter would have been heartily ashamed of the unhappy hacks the evacuation heroes had gotten up upon. The parade terminated with a full half hour's *feu de joie.*†   *   *   *   *

† The militia has fallen into disrepute of late in New York and Philadelphia. Trainings and parades take too much of the precious time, whose minutes are cents, and hours dollars. The only instance of humour, national or individual, which I have witnessed since my abode in this country, was a sham parade got up in mimicry of the real one here described. In this grotesque procession, every man was dressed in the most absurd costume he could devise: banners with the most ludicrous inscriptions, wooden swords of gigantic dimensions, and children's twopenny guns were some of their paraphernalia; and, in the absurd and

*   *   *   *   *

*   *   *   *   *

The bands of these worthies were worthy of them ;
half a dozen fifers and drummers playing old
English jig tunes.   In spite of the folly and injustice of such a comparison, I could not keep
out of my head the last soldiers I had seen, those
fine tall fellows, the grenadier guards, that used
to delight us of a Sunday morning in St. James's
Park, and their exquisite band, and dandy-looking
officers.   Those *looked* like soldiers, whatever they
may fight like ; and allowing these excellent good
folks to be very lions, look you, I can only say
their appearance approached the sublime, by as
near as the French critic assures us the extreme

---

monstrous objects the men had made of themselves, with
false whiskers, beards, and noses, I recognised some of the
broad, coarse, powerful humour of the lower orders in the
old country.   But it is the *only* symptom of such a spirit
which I have met with.   The absolute absence of imagination, of course, is also the absolute absence of humour.   An
American can no more understand a fanciful jest than a
poetical idea; and in society and conversation, the strictest
matter of fact prevails : for any thing departing from it, though
but an inch, either towards the sublime or the ridiculous,
becomes immediately incomprehensible to your auditors, who
will stare at your enthusiasm, and sincerely ask you the
meaning of your jest.

of the ridiculous does. Dined at three; —— and —— called after dinner. My father went with Mr. —— to Tammany Hall*, where there was a grand democratic dinner, in honour of the triumph of the Jackson party, the mob men here. I sat writing to —— till time to go to the theatre. The play was Isabella; the house crammed; a regular holyday audience—shrieking, shouting, laughing, and rowing, like one of our own Christmas audiences. I acted like a wretch. My dresses looked very handsome, particularly my marriage dress; but my muslin bed-gown was so long that I set my feet through it the very first thing; and those *animaux bêtes,* who dragged me off, tore a beautiful point lace veil I had on to tatters, a thing that cost three guineas, if a farthing! My father received a most amusing letter this morning from Lord ——, asking us to come over to Jamaica and act, offering us quarters in his house, and plenty of volunteer actors (did he include himself, I wonder?) to make up a company, if we will come. I should like it very well: to pass the winter in that nice warm climate would be delightful, and I dare say we should find our stay

---

* A place devoted to political meetings, chiefly, however, I believe, those termed here " democratic."

there amusing and agreeable enough.   I wish we
could do it.

Tuesday, 27th.

After breakfast, Colonel —— called.   Put out
things for to-night.   At half-past twelve, went out
with my father and Colonel ——.   Called upon
his honour, the Recorder, but he was in court,
and not to be seen.   Walked down to the Battery.
The day was most lovely, like an early day in
June in England: my merino gown was intolerable, and I was obliged to take a parasol with me,
the sun was so powerful.   The Battery was, as
usual, totally deserted, though the sky, and shores,
and beautiful bright bay, were smiling in perfect
loveliness.   A delicious fresh breeze came wandering over the wide estuary; and graceful boats,
with their full sails glittering in the sun, glided to
and fro, swift and strong, over the smooth waters,
like summer clouds across the blue heavens — as
silently, as rapidly, as tracklessly.†   *   *

† It is the property of perfection alone to rivet the admiration of absolute ignorance; whence I conclude that the
river craft, hovering from morning till night along the waters
that surround New York, must be the most beautiful in the
world.   Their lightness, grace, swiftness, and strength, ap-

* * * * *

* * * * *

Came home at half-past one. Found a card from Mrs. ——. I 'm sorry I didn't see her. —— called, with one Mr. ——, kinsman to the authoress. * * * *

 * * * * *

 * * * * *

While they were here, Mrs. —— called to settle about to-morrow's ride. Mr. and Mrs. —— arriving, the rest departed. We dined at three. After dinner, came to my own room; wrote journal; went on with letter to ——. At half-past five, went to the theatre. Play, the Gamester; my father's benefit; the house was very good. I played pretty well. Mr. —— thoroughly bothered me, by standing six yards behind me: what a complete stroller's trick that is. So we are to act on Saturday. If I can go to the opera, all the same, I sha'n't mind so much; but I will be in most horrible dudgeon if it prevents that, for I want to hear this new prima donna. Mr. —— was behind the scenes, and —— *wrapt*, in his usual seat: he 's a delightful bit of audience.

---

pear to me unequalled. Such beautiful vessels I never saw; more beautiful ones I cannot imagine.

Received a bill of the intended performances for Thursday, Mr. ———'s benefit; and such another farce as the whole thing is I never heard of; as Mr. ——— says, "the benefit of humbug," indeed.

*   *   *   *   *

*   *   *   *   *

Came home.   While we were at supper, my father showed me a note he had received from ———, which, to use a most admirable vulgarism, struck me all of a heap.   A sort of threatening letter, desiring him, as he valued his interest, to come forward and offer to act Charles the Second for the said Mr. ———'s benefit, having already agreed to act in one piece, for said Mr. ———'s benefit.   " O monstrous! monstrous! most unnatural!"   What a vulgar wretch the man must be!

Wednesday, 28th.

Mary ———'s wedding day! Poor lassie! I looked at the bright morning sun with pleasure for her sake. After breakfast, sat reading the poems of Willis, a young man, whose works, young as they evidently are, would have won him some consideration in any but such a thorough work-day world as this. I cried a good deal over some of this man's verses.

I thought some of them beautiful; and 't is the property of beauty to stir the wells of my soul sadly, rather than cast sunshine over them. I think all things are sad. 'T is sad to hear sweet music; 't is sad to read fine poetry; 't is sad to look upon the beautiful face of a fair woman; 't is sad to behold the unclouded glory of a summer's sky. There is a deep and lingering tone in the harmony of all beauty that resounds in our souls with too full and solemn a vibration for pleasure alone. In fact, *intensity*, even of joy and delight, is in itself serious; 't is impossible to be fulfilled with emotion of any sort and not feel as though we were within the shadow of a cloud.* I remember when first I recited Juliet to my mother, she said I spoke the balcony scene almost sadly. Was not such deep, deep love too strong, too passionate, too pervading, to be uttered with the light laughing voice of pleasure? Was not that love, even in its fulness of joy, sad—awful? However, perhaps, I do but see through my own medium, and fancy it the universal one. My eyes are dark, and most things look darkly through

* In Canova's group of Cupid and Psyche, the young god is smiling like a god; but the eager parted lips with which Psyche is seeking his, wear no such expression — you might fancy they trembled, but they certainly do not smile.

them.   At about twelve o'clock Mrs. —— called
for me; and, escorted by her husband and Mr.
——, we rode forth to visit the island.   We went
to a pretty cottage belonging to Mr. ——'s father-
in-law, Dr. ——.   The day was still and grey —
a pleasant day; there was no sunshine, but neither were there any dark shadows.   My horse
had been ill ridden by somebody or another, and
was mighty disagreeable.   Our ride was pleasant
enough : there was not much variety in the country
we passed through.   Masses of granite and greenish
basalt, wild underwood, and vivid bright-looking
cedar bushes.   The Hudson lay leaden and sullen
under the wings of the restless wind.   We stood
to hear the delicious music of the water plashing
against the rocky shore, which is the pleasantest
sound in all the world.   We then rode to a place
ycleped Hell-gate*, from a dangerous current in
the East river, where ships have been lost — and
home through the mellow sunlight of a warm autumnal afternoon.   Came in at a little past four.

* The ladies of New York, and all lady-like people there,
have agreed to call this eddy *Hurl*-gate.   The superior propriety of this name is not to be questioned; for hell is a
shocking bad word, no doubt : but being infinitely more
appropriate to the place and its qualities, I have ventured to
mention it.

Devoured sundry puddings and pies; put out
clothes for the evening; dined at five. My father
dined at ——'s: I've an especial fancy for that
man. After dinner, sat making blonde tippet, and
strumming on the piano till eight. Drank tea,
dressed, and off to Mrs. ——'s " small party, my
dear." * * * *
* * * * *
* * * * *

The people here have no conscience about the
questions they ask; and, as I have one in answering, and always give them " the truth, the whole
truth, and nothing but the truth," it follows that
nothing can be more disagreeable than their queries, except my replies. Mr. —— was there; I
like him: he has something in him, and is not
vulgar or impertinent. Was introduced to a very
handsome French creole woman*, whom I liked:
she reminded me of my mother, and her son bore

---

* The ladies here have an extreme aversion to being called
women, I don't exactly understand why. Their idea is, that
that term designates only the lower or less refined classes of
female human-kind. This is a mistake which I wonder they
should fall into; for in all countries in the world, queens,
duchesses, and countesses, are called women; but in this
one alone, washerwomen, sempstresses, and housemaids are
entitled *ladies;* so that, in fact, here woman is by far the
more desirable appellation of the two.

a striking resemblance to dear ——. We stood up to dance a couple of quadrilles; but as they had not one distinct idea of what the figures were, the whole was a mess of running about, explaining, jostling, and awkward blundering.* I took greatly to the governess of the family, a German woman, with a right German face, a nice person, with quiet simple manners. The women's voices here distract me; so loud, so rapid, and with such a twang! What a pity! for they are, almost without an exception, lovely-looking creatures, with an air of refinement in their appearance, which would be very attractive, but for their style of dress, and those said tremendous shrill loud

---

* The established succession of figures which form the *one* French quadrille, in executing which the ball-rooms of Paris and London have spent so many satisfactory hours, ever since it was invented, by no means satisfies the Americans. At the close of almost every quadrille, a *fancy* figure is danced, which, depending entirely upon the directions of the leader of the band, is a very curious medley of all the rest. The company not being gifted with second sight, and of course not knowing at every step what next they may be called upon to do, go fearfully sliding along, looking at each other, asking, " how does it go on ?" some *en avant deuxing*, while others are starting off *en promenade*, the whole being a complete confusion of purpose and execution. The common French figure, the Trénis, is very seldom danced at all, — they do not appear to know it.

voices.* Came home at twelve o'clock. My favourite aversion, Mrs. ——, was there.

* This terrible nuisance has often made me wish for that "still small voice," which has become the universal tone of good society in England, and which, however inconvenient sometimes from its utter inaudibility, at least did not send one to bed with one's ears ringing and one's head splitting. I was in a society of about twelve ladies, the other evening, and the *uproar* was so excessive that I felt my eyebrows contracting from a sense of perfect bewilderment, occasioned by the noise all round me, and more than once was obliged to request the person with whom I was conversing to stop till the *noise* had subsided a little, that I might be able to distinguish what he was saying to me. Were the women here large and masculine in their appearance, this defect would appear less strange, though not less disagreeable; but they are singularly delicate and feminine in their style of beauty; and the noise they make strikes one with surprise as something monstrous and unnatural — like mice roaring. They frequently talk four or five at a time, and directly across each other; neither of which proceedings is exactly according to my ideas of good breeding.

END OF THE FIRST VOLUME.

JOURNAL

BY

FRANCES ANNE BUTLER.

IN TWO VOLUMES.

VOL. II.

LONDON:

JOHN MURRAY, ALBEMARLE STREET.

MDCCCXXXV.

JOURNAL.

My birth-day   *   *   *   *

    *   *   *   *   *

    *   *   *   *   *

After breakfast sat writing to dear —— for some time. Put out things for the theatre, and went to rehearsal. My father has received a most comical note from one ————, a Scotch gardener, florist, and seedsman; the original, by the by, of Galt's Lawrie Todd, — and original enough he must be. The note expresses a great desire that my father and myself will call upon him, for that he wishes very much to *look at us* — that the hours of the theatre are too late for him, and that besides, he wants to see us as ourselves, and not as " kings and princesses." I have entreated my father to go: this man must be worth knowing. I shall certainly keep his note. After rehearsal, came home. Wrote to ——, to dear ——. Mr. ——

called; also Colonel ——, who gave an account
of the proceedings of the committee for ——'s
benefit, which, added to the gentleman's own note
to my father, thoroughly disgusted me. And
here I do solemnly swear, never again, with my
own good will, to become acquainted with any
man in any way connected with the public press.
They are utterly unreliable people, generally;
their vocation requires that they should be so;
and the very few exceptions I must forego, for
however I might like them, I can neither respect
nor approve of their trade; for trade it is in the
vilest sense of the word.   Dined at five.   After
dinner Mr. and Mrs. —— came in.   *

  *   *   *   *   *

  *   *   *   *   *

At eight, went to the theatre.   The house was, in
consequence of the raised prices, only three parts
full.   I just caught a glimpse of Forrest in the
fourth act of Brutus.   What an enormous man he
is !   After the play came sundry songs and recitations, and then Katharine and Petruchio.   I did
not play well: the actors were very inattentive,
as well as stupid, and annoyed my father very
much.   The pit was half filled with women,
opera fashion, who, for the greater attraction of
the night, and satisfaction of themselves, were

allowed to sit out of their proper places: to be
sure they had the pleasure of the society of the
volunteer heroes, who, for the benefit of Mr. ——,
were all in full uniform. What an absurdity!
Swallowed an ice. Saw ——, also Mr. ——, and
young —— behind the scenes. Came home and
supped. Colonel —— called, and discussed, first,
the farce on the boards; then the farce before the
curtain; finally, the farce of life, which, to my
mind, is but a melancholy one.

Friday, 30th.

How the time goes ! Bless the old traveller, how
he posts along ! After breakfast, Mrs. —— and
her son, and Mr. —— called. I like the latter;
his manners are very good, and he is altogether
more like a gentleman than most men here.
When they were gone, walked out with my father
to ——'s. The day was grey, and cold, and
damp — a real November day, such as we know
them. We held the good man's note, and steered
our course by it, and in process of time entered a
garden, passed through a green-house, and arrived in an immense and most singularly arranged
seed-shop, with galleries running round it, and
the voice of a hundred canaries resounding through
it. I don't know why, but it reminded me of a

place in the Arabian Nights. " Is Mr. ——
within ?" shouted forth my father, seeing no one
in this strange-looking abode. " Yes, he is,"
was replied from somewhere, by somebody. We
looked about, and presently, with his little grey
bullet head, and shrewd piercing eyes, just appearing above the counter, we detected the master of the house. My father stepped up to him
with an air like the Duke of ——, and returning
his coarse, curiously folded note to him, said,
" I presume I am addressing Mr. —— : this,
sir," drawing me forward, " is Miss Fanny
Kemble." The little man snatched off his spectacles, rushed round the counter, rubbed his
enormous hand upon his blue stuff apron, and
held it out to us with a most hearty welcome.
He looked at us for some time, and then exclaimed, " Ha ! ye're her father. Well, ye'll
have married pretty early — ye look very young :
I should not have been sae much surprised if ye
had called her ye're wife !" I laughed, and my
father smiled at this compliment, which was recommended by a broad Scotch twang, which
always sounds sweetly in my ears. The little
man, whose appearance is that of a dwarf in some
fairy tale, then went on to tell us how Galt had
written a book all about him ; how it was, almost

word for word, his own story; how he had come
to this country in early life, with three halfpence
in his pocket, and a nail and hammer in his hand,
for all worldly substance; how he had earned
his bread by making nails, which was his business
in Scotland; how, one day, passing by some
flowers exposed for sale, he had touched a geranium leaf by accident, and, charmed with its
fragrance, bought it, having never seen one
before; how, with fifteen dollars in his pocket,
he commenced the business of a florist and gardener; and how he had refused as many thousand
dollars for his present prosperous concern; how,
when he first came to New York, the place opposite his garden, where now stands a handsome
modern dwelling-house, was the site of a shed
where he did this first bit of work; how, after
six-and-twenty years' absence from Scotland, he
returned home; how he came to his father's
house — " 'T was on a bright morning in August
— the eighth of August, just, it was — when I
went through the door. I knew all the old passages so well: I opened the parlour door, and
there, according to the good old Scottish custom,
the family were going to prayers afore breakfast.
There was the old Bible on the table, and the
old clock ticking in the corner of the room.

there was my father in his own old chair, exactly just where I had left him six-and-twenty years gone by. The very shovel and tongs by the fire were the same; I knew them all. I just sat down, and cried as sweetly as ever a man did in his life." These were, as nearly as I can recollect, his words; and oh, what a story! His manner, too, was indescribably vivid and graphic. My father's eyes filled with tears. 'He stretched out his hand, and grasped and shook the Scotchman's hand repeatedly without speaking; I never saw him more excited. I never was more struck myself with the wonderful strangeness of this bewildering life. He showed us the foot of a rude rustic-looking table. " That," he said, " was cut from out the hawthorn hedge that grows by my father's house; and this," showing us a wooden bowl, " is what I take my *parritch* in!" I asked him if he never meant to leave this country, and return to bonny Scotland. He said, No, never: he might return, but he never meant to settle any where but here. " For," added he, " I have grown what I am in it, madam, and 't is a fine country for the poor." He had been an early martyr, too, to his political opinions; and, when only nineteen years of age, had been imprisoned in Edinburgh for advocating the cause of that very reform which the people are at this moment crying jubilee over in England. He seemed to rejoice in this country, as in the wide common land of political freedom, unbounded by the limits of long-established prejudice, unbroken by the deep trenches which divide class from class in the cultivated soil of the old world. I could have listened to this strange oracle for a day; but in the midst of his discourse he was summoned to dinner; and, presenting his son to us, who presented a nosegay to me, left us to wander about his singular domain. His father, by the by, is still alive, and residing within six miles of Edinburgh, a man of ninety years and upwards. We walked about the shop, visited the birds, who are taken most admirable care of, and are extremely beautiful. I saw several mocking birds: they should sing well, for they are not pretty. Their plumage is of a dull grey colour, and they are clumsy-looking birds.* Saw two beautiful African widow birds, with their jet black hoods and trains. Saw an English blackbird, and thrush,

---

* Unromantic as these birds are in their external appearance, there is something poetical in their love of sunny skies. Many attempts have been made to rear them in England; but I am told that they will not sing there, or indeed any where but where the sun shines as it does here.

in cages. They made my heart ache. I wonder
if they ever think of the red ripe cracking cherries, the rich orchard lands, and the hawthorn-
hedged lanes in the summer sunsets of dear
England ? I did for them. We then went and
looked at a tank full of beautiful gold fish, as they
indiscriminately called them. But though the
greater number were the glittering scarlet creatures usually so denominated, some were of the
richest purple, with a soft dark bloom playing
over their sides; others, again, were perfectly
brown, with a glancing golden light shining
through their scales; others were palest silver ;
others, again, mingled the dazzling scarlet with spots
of the most beautiful gloomy violet, like dark-coloured jewels set in fire. Their tank was planted
with the roots of aquatic vegetables, which, in summer, spread their cool leaves over the water, which is
perpetually renewed by means of an escape, and
a little silvery fountain which keeps bubbling up in
the midst. They seemed very happy, and devoured sundry pieces of wafer paper, while we
admired them at our leisure. Saw an India-rubber
tree, a very young one, which had not attained its
full growth. 'T is a fine broad-leaved tree, unlike
any that I ever saw before. After dawdling about
very satisfactorily for some time, we departed

from the dwelling of Lawrie Todd. Of a verity, " truth is strange, stranger than fiction." Went to a bookseller's. I bought a Bible for little ——; my father, a Shakspeare for ——. Came home. Mr. —— called, and gossiped some time with me. Told me a bit of scandal, of which I had some slight suspicion before, *i. e.* that Mr. —— was pretty Mrs. ——'s very devoted. At half-past four dressed for dinner. Colonel —— called just as we were going to dinner. At five, my father and I went to Mrs. ——'s. A pleasant dinner. I like him enough, and I like her very much. She is extremely pretty, and very pleasant. Sat by that tall ninny, Mr. ——, who uttered inanity the whole of dinner-time. After dinner, the usual entertaining half hour among the ladies passed in looking over caricatures. When the men joined us, Mr. —— came and sat down by me, and in the course of a few minutes, poor Lord —— having by chance been mentioned, we fell into English talk ; and it appears that he knows sundry of my gracious *patrons ;* among the rest, the ——s. He had been at —— ; and it pleased me to speak of it again. But what in the name of all wonders could possess him with the idea that Lady —— was guilty of editing the Comic Annual. Was asked to sing, and sang

" Ah no ben mio" pretty well.   Mr. —— sang
a thing of his own very well, though it was not
in itself worth much.   Discussed all manner of
prima donnas with him.   At half-past nine,
D—— came for me, and we proceeded to the
——s. The people here never tell one when they
mean to dance; the consequence is, that one is
completely put out about one's toilet.   I was in a
black satin dress; and dancing in these hot rooms,
might as well have been in a pall.   *

    *   *   *   *   *

    *   *   *   *   *

In the middle of the evening, Dr. —— asked if I
would allow him to introduce to me one Mr. ——,
a very delightful man, full of abilities, *and* writer
in such and such a paper.   I immediately called
to mind my resolution, and refused.   In the mean
time, Mrs. ——, less scrupulous, and without asking my leave, brought the gentleman up, and introduced him.   I was most ungracious and forbid-
ding, and meant to be so.   I am sorry for this,
but I cannot help it : he is ——'s brother, too,
which makes me doubly sorry. As he is an agreeable man, and ——'s brother, I esteem and reverence him; but as he belongs to the press
gang, I will not know him. The room was full
of pretty women, one prettier than another.   I
danced myself half dead, and came home. By

the by, was introduced to young ——, who, at
the corner of a street, with a red cap on his head,
might pass for a capital hickory pole. Mrs. ——'s
bed-room, where we left our cloaks, made my
heart ache. 'T was exactly like my dear little
bed-room at home; the bed, the furniture, and
the rose-coloured lining, all the same.

Saturday, December 1st, 1832.

First day of the last month of the year — go it,
old fellow! I'm sick of the road, and would be at
my journey's end. Got two hundred dollars from
my father, and immediately after breakfast sallied
forth: paid bills and visits, and came home.
Found my father sitting with our kinsman, Mr.
——, busily discussing the family origin, root,
branches, and all. We are an old family, they
say, but the direct line is lost after Charles the
Second's reign. Our kinsman is a nice man, with
a remarkably fine face, with which I was greatly
struck. When he was gone, persuaded my father
to come down and take a breathing on the Battery
with me. And a breathing it was with a vengeance. The wind blew tempestuously, the waters,
all troubled and rough, were of a yellow green
colour, breaking into short, strong, angry waves,

whose glittering white crests the wind carried
away, as they sank to the level surface again.
The shores were all cold, distinct, sharp-cut, and
wintry-looking, the sky was black and gloomy,
with now and then a watery wan sunlight running
through it. The wind was so powerful, we could
scarcely keep our legs. My sleeves and skirts
fluttered in the blast, my bonnet was turned front
part behind, my nose was blue, my cheeks were
crimson, my hair was all tangled, my breath was
gone, my blood was in a glow: what a walk ! Met
dear Dr. ——, whom I love. Came in — dined.
After dinner, bethought me that I had not called
upon Mrs. ——, according to promise. Sent for
a coach, and set forth thither; didn't know the
number, so drove up Spring Street, and down
Spring Street, and finally stopped at a shop, got a
directory, and found the address. Sat a few
minutes with her, and at five o'clock left her. The
day was already gone — the *gloamin* come. The
keen cutting wind whizzed along the streets; huge
masses of dark clouds, with soft brown edges lay
on the pale delicate blue of the evening sky. The
moon was up, clear, cold, and radiant; the crowd
had ebbed away from the busy thoroughfare, and
only a few men in great coats buttoned up to their
chins, and women wrapped in cloaks, were scud-

ding along in the dim twilight and the bitter wind towards their several destinations, with a frozen shuddering look that made me laugh. I had got perished in the coach, and seeing that the darkness covered me, determined to walk home, and bade the coach follow me. How pleasant it was : I walked tremendously fast, enjoying the fresh breath of the north, and looking at the glittering moon, as she rode high in the evening sky. How I do like walking alone — being alone; for this alone I wish I were a man. At half-past five, went to the theatre. The house was crammed; play, Hunchback. I missed —— from his accustomed seat, and found that like a very politician he had changed sides. I played abominably ; my voice was weak and fagged. After the play, Katharine and Petruchio. I played that better ; my father was admirable — it went off delightfully. When it was over, they called for my father, and with me in his hand he went on. The pit rose to us like Christians, and shouted and hallooed as I have been used to hear. I felt sorry to leave them : they are a pleasant audience to act to, and exceedingly civil to us, and I have got rather attached to them. New York, too, seems nearer home than any other place, and I felt sorry to leave it. When we had withdrawn, and were going up stairs, we heard three distinct and tremendous cheers. On asking what that meant, we learnt 't was a compliment to us — thank 'em kindly. Came home : found Mr. —— had sent me Contarini Fleming. Began reading it, and could scarce eat my supper for doing so.   *

*   *   *   *   *

*   *   *   *   *

Sunday, 2*d*.

While dressing, received a " sweet note " from Mrs. ——, accompanied with a volume of Bryant's poetry, which, as I like very much, I am her obliged. Swallowed two mouthfuls of bread, and away to church. It was very crowded, and a worthy woman had taken possession of the corner seat in Mr. ——'s pew, with a fidgetting little child, which she kept dancing up and down every two minutes; though in church I wished for the days of King Herod. What strange thoughts did occur to me to-day during service ! 'T is the first Sunday in Advent. The lesson for the day contained the history of the Annunciation. What a mystery our belief is ! how seldom it is that we consider and, as it were, *take hold* of what we say we believe, and when we do so, how bewildered

and lost we become, — how lost among a thousand
wild imaginations, — how driven to and fro by a
thousand doubts, — how wrecked amidst a thousand fears! Surely we should be humble: we
should indeed remember that we *cannot know*, and
not strive for that knowledge which our souls will
lose themselves in seeking for, and our overstrained
minds crack in reaching at.   *   *

   *   *   *   *   *

   *   *   *   *   *

At the end of service they sang Luther's hymn.
I cried with nervous excitement, not at that, but
at my recollection of Braham's singing it with that
terrible trumpet accompaniment, that used to
make my heart stand still and listen. Stayed and
took the sacrament.   *   *   *

   *   *   *   *   *

   *   *   *   *   *

Came home : found a whole regiment of men.
His honour the Recorder, who is my especial
delight, Mr. ——, ——, whom I greatly affection;
to these presently entered Mr. —— and Mr. ——.
They one by one bade me good-by; how disagreeable that is, that good-by. Mr. —— read me
a passage out of one of Jeffrey's letters describing
an English fine lady. The picture is admirable,
and most faithful; they are, indeed, polished,

brilliant, smooth as ice, as slippery, as treacherous, as cold. When they were all gone, Colonel —— gave me to read the descriptive sketch of the French opera, La Tentation, that has been setting all Paris wild. What an atrocious piece of blasphemy, indecency, and folly — what a thoroughly French invention. Mad people! mad people! mad people! Looked over bills, settled accounts, righted desk, tore up papers; among others, sundry anonymous love letters that I had treasured up as specimens of the purely funny in composition, but which began to take up too much room. Dressed for dinner. After dinner sat writing journal, and reading Contarini Fleming.   *

*   *   *   *   *

*   *   *   *   *

Monday, 3d.

Rose at half-past four. The sky was black as death, but in the night winter had dropped his mantle on the earth, and there it lay, cold, and purely white, against the inky sky. Dressed: crammed away all the gleanings of the packing, and in thaw, and sleet, and rain, drove down to the steam-boat. Went directly to the cabin. On my way thither, managed to fall down half-a-dozen steep steps, and give myself as many bruises. I was picked up and led to a bed, where I slept profoundly till breakfast time. Our kinsman, Mr. ——, was our fellow-passenger: I like him mainly. After breakfast, returned to my crib. As I was removing Contarini Fleming, in order to lie down, a *lady* said to me, " Let me look at one of those books;" and without further word of question or acknowledgment, took it from my hand, and began reading. I was a *little surprised*, but said nothing, and went to sleep. Presently I was roused by a pull on the shoulder, and another lady, rather more civil, and particularly considerate, asked me to do her the favour of lending her the other. I said by all manner of means, wished her at the devil, and turned round to sleep once more. Arrived at Amboy, we disembarked and bundled ourselves into our coach, ourselves, our namesake, and a pretty quiet lady, who was going, in much heaviness of heart, to see a sick child. The roads were unspeakable; the day most delightfully disagreeable. My bruises made the saltatory movements of our crazy conveyance doubly torturing; in short, all things were the perfection of misery. I attempted to read, but found it utterly impossible to do so. Arrived at the Delaware, we took boat again; and, as I was sitting very quietly reading Contarini Fleming, with the second volume lying on the stool at my feet, the same unceremonious lady who had *borrowed* it before, snatched it up without addressing a single syllable to me, read as long as she pleased, and threw it down again in the same style when she went to dinner. Now I know that half the people here, if they were to read that in Mrs. Trollope, would say, " Oh, but you know she could not have been a lady; 't is not fair to judge of our manners by the vulgar specimens of American society which a steam-boat may afford." Very true: but granting that she was *not* a lady (which she certainly was not), supposing her to have been a housemaid, or any thing else of equal pretensions to good breeding, the way to judge is by comparing her, not with ladies in other countries, but with housemaids, persons in her own condition of life; and 't is most certain that no person whatsoever, however igno- rant, low, or vulgar, in England, would have done such a thing as that. But the mixture of the republican feeling of equality peculiar to this country, and the usual want of refinement common to the lower classes of most countries, forms a sin- gularly felicitous union of impudence and vulga-

rity to be met with no where but in America. *
Arrived at the Mansion House, which I was quite

* In speaking of the bad and disagreeable results of the
political institutions of this country, as exhibited in the
feelings and manners of the lower orders, I have every
where dwelt upon those which, from my own disposition,
and the opinions and sentiments in which I have been educated, have struck me most, and most unfavourably. But
I should be sorry to be so blind, or so prejudiced, as not to
perceive the great moral goods which arise from the very same
source, and display themselves strongly in the same class of
people: *honesty* and *truth*, excellences so great, that the
most bigoted worshipper of the forms and divisions of societies
in the old world would surely be ashamed to weigh them in
the balance against the deference there paid to rank or
riches, or even the real and very agreeable qualities of
civility and courtesy. Americans (I speak now of the
people, not the gentlemen and ladies, *they* are neither so
honest and true, nor quite so rude,) are indeed independent.
Every man that will work a little can live extremely well.
No portion of the country is yet overstocked with followers
of trades, not even the Atlantic cities. Living is cheap —
labour is dear. To conclude, as the Irish woman said, " It
is a darling country for poor folks; for if I work three days
in the week, can't I lie in my bed the other three if I plase ? "
This being so, all dealings between handicraftsmen and
those who employ them; tradesmen and those who buy of
them; servants and those who are served by them; are
conducted upon the most entire system of reciprocity of
advantage; indeed, if any thing, the obligation appears always
to lie on that party which, with us, is generally supposed to
confer it. Thus, — my shoemaker, a person with whom I
have now dealt largely for two years, said to me the other
day, upon my remonstrating about being obliged regularly

glad to see again. Installed myself in a room,
and while they brought in the packages, finished

---

to come to his shop and unboot, whenever I order a new
pair of walking boots —" Well, ma'am, we can keep your
measure certainly, *to oblige you*, but as a rule we don't do it
for any of our customers, it's so very troublesome." These
people are, then, as I said before, most truly independent;
they are therefore never servile, and but seldom civil, but for
the very same reason they do not rob you; they do not
need to do so; neither do they lie to you, for your favour
or displeasure in no way affects their interest. If you
entrust to their care materials of any sort to make up, you
are sure, no matter how long you may leave them in their
hands, or how entirely you may have forgotten the quantity
originally given, to have every inch of them returned to
you : and you are also generally sure that any question you
ask, with regard to the quality of what you purchase, will
be answered without any endeavour to impose upon you, or
palm upon your ignorance that which is worse for that
which is better. Two circumstances, which have come
under my own knowledge, will serve to illustrate the spirit
of the people ; and they are good illustrations to quote, for
similar circumstances are of daily and hourly occurrence.
   A farmer who is in the habit of calling at our house on
his way to market, with eggs, poultry, &c., being questioned
as to whether the eggs were new-laid, replied, without an
instant's hesitation, " No, not the *very* fresh ones, *we eat
all those ourselves.*"
   On returning home late from the play one night, I could
not find my slippers any where, and, after some useless
searching, performed my toilet for bed without them. The
next morning, on enquiring of my maid if she knew any
thing of them, she replied with perfect equanimity, that

Contarini Fleming. It reminded me of Combes'
book: I wonder whether he is turning phrenolo-
gist at all? those physiological principles were the
bosom friends of the Combes' phrenological ones.
Stowed away my things, made a delicious huge
wood fire, dressed myself, and went down to dinner.
Our kinsman dined with us. Mr. —— came in
while we were at dinner. After dinner, came up
to my room, continued unpacking and putting
away my things till near nine o'clock. When we
went down to tea, my father was lying on the sofa
asleep, and a man was sitting with his back to the
door, reading the newspaper. He looked up as
we came in : it was ——, whom I greatly rejoiced
to see again. During tea, he told us all the Philadelphia gossip. So the ladies are all getting up

---

having walked home through the snow, and got her feet
extremely wet, she had put them on, and forgotten to
restore them to their place before my return. Nobody, I
think, will doubt that an English farmer, and an English
servant, might sell stale eggs, and use their mistress's
slippers; but I think it highly doubtful, that either fact
would have been acknowleged with such perfect honesty
any where but here. As to the servants here, except the
blacks, and the poor Irish bread-hunters who come over,
there are scarcely any to be found : the very name seems
repugnant to an American; and however high their wages,
and easy their situation, they seem hardly to be able to
endure the bitterness of subserviency and subordination.

upon horses, and wearing the " *Kemble* cap," as
they call Lady ——'s device. How she would
laugh if she could hear it ; how I did laugh when
I did hear it.   The Kemble cap, forsooth ! thus it
is that great originators too often lose the fame of
their inventions, and that the glory of a *new idea*
passes by the head that conceived it, to encircle,
as with a halo, that of some mere imitator ; thus
it is that this very big world comes to be called
America, and not Columbia, as it *ought to ;* thus
it is — &c. &c. &c.   He sat for some time.   Saw
poor Mrs. ——.   *   *   *
          *   *   *   *   *
          *   *   *   *   *

She is better, poor thing ; I like her amazingly.

Tuesday, 4*th.*

After breakfast practised for two hours. ——
called and stayed some time. Came up to my
own room ; wrote journal : while doing so a note
containing two cards, and an invitation to " tea,"
from the Miss ——'s was brought to me. Presently I was called down to receive our kinsman,
who sat some time with me, whom I like most
especially, who is a gentleman, and a very nice

person. Came up and resumed my journal: was again summoned down to see young Mr. ——.

* * * * *

* * * * *

When he was gone, finished journal, wrote to Mrs. ——, to my mother, read a canto in Dante, and began to write a novel. Dined at five. After dinner, put out things for this evening, played on the piano, mended habit shirt, dressed myself, and at a quarter to ten went to the theatre for my father. I had on the same dress I wore at Devonshire House, the night of the last ball I was at in England, and looked at myself in amazement, to think of all the strangenesses that have befallen since then. We proceeded to Miss ——'s, and this tea party turned out to be a very crowded dance, in small rooms upon carpets, and with a roasting fire. Was introduced to all the world and his wife. Dr. —— claimed acquaintance with us, and danced with me: I like his manners very much. I have beheld Miss ——, and should doubtless now depart in peace * *

* * * * *

* * * * *

Lord! Lord! what fools men and women do make themselves. Was introduced to one Mr. ——,

Mr. ——'s partner, whom I received graciously
for the sake of the good days on board the Pacific.
Came away at a little after twelve. I never felt any
thing like the heat of the rooms, or heard any thing
so strange as the questions the people ask one, or
saw any thing more lovely than the full moonlight
on the marble buildings of Philadelphia.

Wednesday, 5th.

After breakfast, practised : Mr. and Mrs. ——
called, also Dr. ——. Went and saw poor
Mrs. —— for a little time ; she interests me most
extremely — I like her very, very much. Came
up to my own room; read a canto of Dante.
Was called down to see folk, and found the drawing-room literally thronged. The first face I
made out was Mr. ——'s, for whom I have taken an
especial love : two ladies, a whole load of men,
and Mr. ——, who had brought me a curious
piece of machinery, in the shape of a musical box,
to look at. It contained a little bird, no larger
than a large fly, with golden and purple wings,
and a tiny white beak. On the box being wound
up, this little creature flew out, and perching itself on the brink of a gold basin, began fluttering
its wings, opening its beak, and uttering sundry

very melodious warblings, in the midst of
which, it sank suddenly down, and disappeared,
the lid closed, and there was an end. What a
pity 't is that we can only realise fairy-land through
the means of machinery. One reason why there
is no such thing left as the believing faculty among
men, is because they have themselves learnt to
make magic, and perform miracles. When the
coast was once more clear, I returned to my room,
got out things for the theatre, dined *tête-à-tête*
with D——; my father dined at the public table.
After dinner, came up stairs, read Grahame,
wrote journal, began my novel under another
shape. I can't write prose; (query, can I any
thing else?) I don't know how, but my sentences
are the comicallest things in the world; the end
forgets the beginning, and the whole is a perfect
labyrinth of parenthesis within parenthesis. Perhaps, by the by, without other view, it would
be just as well if I exercised myself a little in
writing my own language, as the grammar hath
it, " with elegance and propriety." At half-past
five, went to the theatre. The play was Romeo
and Juliet; the house not good. Mr. —— played
Romeo.   *   *   *   *

          *   *   *   *   *

          *   *   *   *   *

I acted like a wretch, of course; how could I do
otherwise? Oh, Juliet! vision of the south!
rose of the garden of the earth! was this the
glorious hymn that Shakspeare hallowed to your
praise? was this the mingled strain of Love's
sweet going forth, and Death's dark victory, over
which my heart and soul have been poured out in
wonder and ecstasy?—How I do loathe the stage!
these wretched, tawdry, glittering rags, flung over
the breathing forms of ideal loveliness; these
miserable, poor, and pitiful substitutes for the
glories with which poetry has invested her magnificent and fair creations — the glories with
which our imagination reflects them back again.
What a mass of wretched mumming mimicry acting is! Pasteboard and paint, for the thick breathing orange groves of the south; green silk and
oiled parchment, for the solemn splendour of her
noon of night; wooden platforms and canvass curtains, for the solid marble balconies, and rich dark
draperies of Juliet's sleeping chamber, that shrine
of love and beauty; rouge, for the startled life-
blooa in the cheek of that young passionate
woman; an actress, a mimicker, a sham creature,
me, in fact, or any other one, for that loveliest
and most wonderful conception, in which all that
is true in nature, and all that is exquisite in

fancy, are moulded into a living form. To *act* this! to *act* Romeo and Juliet! horror! horror! how I do loathe my most impotent and unpoetical craft! *   *   *   *   *

*   *   *   *   *

*   *   *   *   *

In the last scene of the play, I was so mad with the mode in which all the preceding ones had been perpetrated, that, lying over Mr. ——'s corpse, and fumbling for his dagger, which I could not find, I, Juliet, thus apostrophised him, — Romeo being dead — " Why, where *the* devil *is* your dagger, Mr. ——?" What a disgusting travesty. On my return home, I expressed my entire determination to my father to perform the farce of Romeo and Juliet no more. Why, it's an absolute *shame* that one of Shakspeare's plays should be thus turned into a mockery. I received a note from young Mr. ——, accompanied by a very curious nosegay in shells; a poor substitute for the breathing, fresh, rosy flowers he used to furnish me with, when I was last here.

Thursday, 6th.

The morning was beautifully bright and warm, like a May morning in England. After break-

fast, practised for two hours: while doing so, was
interrupted by Mr. ——, who came to bid us
good-by. He was going on to New York, and
thence to England.   *   *   *

  *   *   *   *   *

  *   *   *   *   *

He sat some time. When he was gone, and I
had finished my practising, came up to my own
room. Was summoned thence to see my kinsman,
who sat some time with me, and whom I like
of all things. He makes it out (for he seems a
great meddler in these matters) that we are originally Italian people, pirates by name, Campo
Bello; the same family as the Scottish Campbells;
the same family as the Norman Beauchamps:
how I only wish it were true! I have, and
always have had the greatest love and veneration
for old blood; I would rather by far have some
barbarous Saxon giant to my ancestor, than all
the wealth of the earth to my dower. I parted
from my friend with much regret; he has won
my heart fairly. When he was gone, came up to
my own room. The day was brilliant and unclouded; and as I looked into the serene blue sky,
my spirit longed for wings.   *   *

  *   *   *   *   *

  *   *   *   *   *

Dr. —— called this morning, and interested me
by a long account of Webster; in the course of
which, however, he gave me, if possible, a stronger
distaste than I had before, to the form of government in this country, from various results which
he enumerated as inevitably belonging to it. Read
a canto in Dante: it consoles me to read my
Italian, and forget for a time all that *is*. *

    *   *   *   *   *

    *   *   *   *   *

I sat watching the glorious sunset as it came
redly streaming into my room, touching every
thing with glory, and shining through my hair
upon my book. It suggested to me a picture;
and I wrote one for Mrs. ——, who had been
consulting me about a costume in which to sit for
her portrait. Dined at five: my father dined
out. After dinner, sat writing journal till ten,
when he returned. The moon was shining soft
and full, and he asked me if I would take a walk.
I bonneted and booted, and we sallied 'forth to
the Schuylkill. The moon withdrew herself behind a veil of thin white clouds, but left a grey
clear light over the earth, and through the sky.
We reached the Fair Mount bridge at about
eleven. The turnpike was fast, and every body
asleep, so we climbed over the gate, and very

deliberately pursued our way through the strange dark-looking covered bridge, where the glimmering lamps, at distant intervals, threw the crossing beams and rafters into momentary brightness, that had a strange effect contrasted with the surrounding gloom.*   We reached the other side, and turning off from the road, began climbing the hill opposite the breakwater.   The road was muddy in the valley with the heavy rains; and unwilling to wade through the dirt, we clambered along a paling for several yards, and so escaped the mire.   My father steered for the grassy knoll just opposite Fair Mount; and there, screened by a thicket of young cedar bushes, with the river breaking over the broad dam far below us, and the shadowy banks on the other side melting away in the soft grey light, we sat down on a tree trunk. Here we remained for upwards of a quarter of an hour without uttering a syllable; indeed, we had not spoken three words since we set out. My father was thinking, I presume, of —— something; I, of the day of judgment — when these

* The bridges here are all made of wood, and for the most part covered.   Those which are so are by no means unpicturesque objects. The one-arched bridge at Fair Mount is particularly light and graceful in its appearance: at a little distance, it looks like a scarf, rounded by the wind, flung over the river.

thick forests, and wide strong waters, like a shrivelled scroll, are to burn to ashes before the
coming of God's justice. We were disturbed by
a large white spaniel dog, who, coming down from
among the cedar bushes, reminded me of the old
witch stories, and Faust. We arose to depart,
and took our way towards the Market Street
bridge, along the banks of the river. The broken
notes of a bugle horn came at intervals across the
sleeping waters from the opposite shore, where
shone reflected the few lingering lights from the
houses that had not yet shut up for the night. The
moon, faintly struggling through the clouds, now
touched the dark pyramids of the cedar trees that
rose up into the grey sky, and threw our shadows
on the lonely path we were pursuing, now cast a
pale gleam through the rapid clouds that chased
one another like dreams across the sky. The
air was soft and balmy as the night air of mid
August. The world was still; and, except our
footfalls, as we trudged along, no sound disturbed
the universal repose. We did not reach home
till half-past twelve. As we walked down Market
Street, through the long ranges of casks, the only
creatures stirring, except some melancholy night-
loving cat, my father said very calmly, " How I
do wish I had a gimlet."—" What for ?"—" What

fun it would be to pierce every one of these bar-
rels." For a gentleman of his years, this appeared
to me rather a juvenile prompting of Satan; and
as I laughingly expostulated on the wickedness
of such a proceeding, he replied with much innocence, " I don't think they'd ever suspect me of
having done it;" and truly I don't thing they
would. Came home, and to bed. That was a
curious fancy of my father's.

A PICTURE.

Through the half open'd casement stream'd the light
Of the departing sun. The golden haze
Of the red western sky fell warm and bright
Into that chamber large and lone : the blaze
Touch'd slantingly curtain and couch, and threw
A glory over many an antique gem,
Won from the entombed cities that once grew
At the volcano's foot. Mingled with them
Stood crystal bowls, through which the broken ray
Fell like a shower of precious stones, and lay
Reflected upon marble; these were crown'd
With blushing flowers, fresh and glittering yet
With diamond rain drops. On the crimson ground
A shining volume, clasp'd with gold and jet,
And broken petals of a passion flow'r
Lay by the lady of this silent bow'r.
Her rippling hair fell from her pearly round
That strove to clasp its billowy curls : the light

Hung like a glory on their waves of gold.
Her velvet robe, in many a violet fold,
Like the dark pansy's downy leaf, was bound
With a gold zone, and clasp'd with jewels bright,
That glow'd and glanced as with a magic flame
Whene'er her measured breathing stirr'd her frame.
Upon her breast and shoulders lay a veil
Of curious needle-work, as pure and pale
As a fine web of ivory, wrought with care,
Through which her snowy skin show'd smooth and fair.
Upon the hand that propp'd her drooping head,
A precious emerald, like a fairy well,
Gleam'd with dark solemn lustre; a rich thread
Of rare round pearls—such as old legends tell
Th' Egyptian queen pledged to her Roman lord,
When in her cup a kingdom's price she pour'd,—
Circled each soft white arm. A painter well
Might have been glad to look upon her face,
For it was full of beauty, truth, and grace;
And from her lustrous eyes her spirit shone
Serene, and strong, and still, as from a throne.

Friday, 7th.

A break. Found —— in the breakfast room.
The morning was very unpropitious; but I settled
to ride at one, if it was tolerably fine then. He
remained pottering a long time: when he was
gone, practised, habited, went in, for a few minutes,
to Mrs. ——. At one the horses came; but mine

was brought without a stirrup, so we had to wait,
Lord knows how long, till the blundering groom
had ridden back for it.   At length we mounted.
" Handsome is that handsome does," is verity;
and, therefore, pretty as was my steed, I wished
its good looks and itself at the devil, before I was
half way down Chestnut Street.   It pranced, and
danced, and backed me once right upon the
pavement.   We took the Laurel Hill road.   The
day was the perfection of gloom — the road six
inches deep in heavy mud.   We walked the
whole way out: my father got the cramp, and
lost his temper.   At Laurel Hill we dismounted,
and walked down to the river side.   How melancholy it all looked: the turbid rhubarby water,
the skeleton woods, the grey sky, and far winding
away of the dark rocky shores; yet it was fine
even in this gloom, and wonderfully still.   The
clouds did not move, — the water had not the
faintest ripple, — the trees did not stir a branch;
the most perfect and profound trance seemed to
have fallen upon every thing.   ——— and I
scrambled down the rocks towards the water,
expatiating on the capabilities of this place, which
was once a country-seat, and with very little expense might be made a very enchanting as well
as a very comfortable residence; always except-

ing, of course, the chance of fever and ague
during the summer months, when the whole of
the banks of the Schuylkill, high and rocky as
they are, are considered so unhealthy, that the
inhabitants are obliged to leave their houses until
the winter season, when the country naturally
loses half its attractions. At half-past three, we
mounted, and, crossing the river, returned home
by a much better road. My horse, however, was
decidedly a brute, — pulled my arms to pieces,
cantered with the wrong leg foremost, trotted in
a sort of scuttling fashion, that rendered it utterly
impossible to rise in the stirrups, and, instead of
walking, jogged the breath out of my body. I
was fairly done up when we reached home.
Dressed, and dined; —— dined with us. After
dinner, went and sat with Mrs. ——. So it
seems Carolina is in a state of convulsion. Reports have arrived that the Nullifiers and Union-
ists have had a fight in Charleston, and that lives
have been lost. " Bide a wee," as the Scotchman
says; we talk a good deal on the other side the
water of matters that are far enough off; but as
for America, the problem is not yet solved — and
this very crisis (a more important one than has
yet occurred in the political existence of this

country) is threatening to slacken the bonds of
brotherhood between the states, and shake the
Union to its centre. The interests of the northern states are totally different from, and in some
respects opposite to, those of the southern
ones.   *   *   *   *

        *   *   *   *   *

        *   *   *   *   *

The tariff question is the point in debate ; and
the Carolinians have, it seems, threatened to
secede from the Union in consequence of the
policy pursued with regard to that. I was horrified at Dr. ——'s account of the state of the
negroes in the south. To teach a slave to read
or write is to incur a penalty either of fine or
imprisonment. They form the larger proportion
of the population, by far ; and so great is the
dread of insurrection on the part of the white
inhabitants, that they are kept in the most brutish
ignorance, and too often treated with the most
brutal barbarity, in order to insure their subjection.   Oh ! what a breaking asunder of old
manacles there will be, some of these fine days ;
what a fearful rising of the black flood ; what a
sweeping away, as by a torrent, of oppressions
and tyrannies ; what a fierce and horrible retalia-
tion and revenge for wrong so long endured — so

wickedly inflicted. When I came in to tea, at
half-past eight, found Dr. —— there.   *

  * * * * *

When he was gone, sang a song or two like a
crow in the quinsy.   *   *   *

  * * * * *

Wednesday, 12*th.*

After breakfast, went to rehearsal; after rehearsal, went to ——'s. It poured with rain.
Came home; put out things for the theatre;
practised for an hour; finished letter to ——;
wrote journal; dined at three. After dinner,
went and sat with Mrs. ——. Sang to her all
my old Scotch ballads; read the first act of the
Hunchback to her. At half-past five, went to
the theatre. Play, King John; house good: I
played horribly. My voice, too, was tired with
my exertions, and cracked most awfully in the
midst of " thunder," which was rather bad.

  * * * * *

  * * * * *

I had finished early, and came home in my dress
in order to show it to Mrs. ——. She was just
gone to bed, but admitted me.   *   *

  * * * * *

  * * * * *

Sat talking to her until my father came home. So " Old Hickory " means to lick the refractory southerns : why they are coming to a civil war ! However, the grumblers haven't the means of fighting without emancipating and arming their slaves. That they will not and dare not do; the consequence will be, I suppose, that they will swallow the affront, and submit.

Thursday, 13*th.*

While dressing, had the pleasure of witnessing from my window a satisfactory sample of the innate benevolence, gentleness, and humanity of our nature : a child of about five years old, dragging a cat by a string tied to its throat round and round a yard, till the poor beast ceased to use its paws, and suffered itself to be trailed along the ground, after which the little fiend set his feet upon it, and stamped and kicked it most brutally. The blood came into my face ; and, though almost too far for hearing, I threw up the sash, and at the top of my voice apostrophised the little wretch with " Hollo there ! wicked, naughty boy !" He seemed much puzzled to discover whence this appeal proceeded, but not at all at a loss to apply it; for, after looking about with a

very conscience-stricken visage, he rushed into
the house, dragging his victim with him. I came
down, fairly sick, to breakfast. After despatching
it, I put on my bonnet and walked round to the
house where this scene had taken place. I enquired for the child, describing his appearance,
and he was presently brought to me; when I sat
down at the foot of the stairs in the hall, an
spent some time in expatiating on the enormity of
such proceedings to the little ruffian, who, it
seems, has frequently been corrected for similar
ferocities before. I fear my preachment will not
avail much. Came home, put room to rights,
practised for an hour; got ready, and dawdled
about most dreadfully, waiting for D——, who
had gone out with my father. At half-past twelve,
set off with her to the riding school. It was full
of women in long calico skirts, and gay bonnets
with flaunting feathers, riding like wretches;
some cantering, some trotting, some walking —
crossing one another, passing one another in a
way that would have filled the soul of Fossard
with grief and amazement. I put on a skirt and
my riding-cap, and mounted a rough, rugged,
besweated white-brown beast, that looked like an
old trunk more than any thing else, its coat standing literally on end, like " quills upon the fretful

porcupine," with heat and ill condition. 'T is
vain attempting to ride like a Christian on these
heathen horses, which are neither broken, bitted,
nor bridled properly; and poor dumb *creturs*
have no more idea of what a horse ought to be,
or how a horse ought to behave, than so many
cows. My hair, presently, with the damp and
the shaking, became perfectly straight. As I
raised my head, after putting it up under my cap,
I beheld —— earnestly discoursing to D——.
I asked for Tuesday's charger; and the school
having by degrees got empty, I managed to become a little better acquainted with its ways and
means. 'T is a pretty little creature, but 'tis not
half broken, is horribly ill ridden, and will never
be good for any thing — what a pity! At twc
o'clock I dismounted: —— walked home with
us. Went in to see Mrs. ——: she seemed a
good deal better, I thought; sat some time with
her. Mr. —— has sent me back my book of
manuscript music: played and sang half through
it. Came to my room; tried on dresses for Lady
Macbeth, and the Wonder, and dressed for dinner. My father dined out. After dinner, went
in to see Mrs. ——. Sat some time with her
mother, her chicks, and her young doctor of a
cousin, who is quite a civilised mortal. Poor

Mrs. —— was too ill to see me. Came to the drawing-room, wrote journal, played and sang till tea-time. After tea, read the history of Knickerbocker, whereat I was like to have died, through the greate merrimente its rare and excellente pleasantries did cause in me, insomuche that I lay on the sofa screaming, very much like one lunaticke.

Friday, 14*th*.

After breakfast, put out things for the theatre. Practised for an hour; read and marked the Comedy of Errors, which is really great fun: perhaps not funnier than Amphytrion, but the subject is more agreeable a good deal. Read a canto in Dante; got ready for the riding school; found —— and Mr. —— in the drawing-room. As we were going out, the gentlemen did not remain long. When they were gone, D—— and I set off for the riding school. We were hardly there before —— made his appearance: I won-der what he'll do for an *interest*, by the by, when we are gone.   *   *   *
   *   *   *   *   *
   *   *   *   *   *
The school was quite empty, so we had it all to

ourselves. D—— mounted up upon a detestable shambling brute, that wouldn't go *no how*. I had a fancy for making my little fiery charger leap over the bar, and made Mr. —— put it down for me. The beast had no idea of such saltatory proceedings, and jerked himself over it three times most abominably. The fourth time I pushed him at it, he jumped, and I jumped too, out of the saddle on to my feet, having lighted down very comfortably at the horse's head with the reins in my hand, neither hurt nor frightened. This is the first time a horse ever had me off. I got on again, but declined leaping any more. At a quarter to three we returned home. —— walked with us. At the corner of Sansom Street, met young ——. Heaven bless —— from a challenge! Came home; dined: after dinner, went in and sat with Mrs. —— till coffee time. Showed her my dresses, and read her a scene or two of the Hunchback. Went to the theatre at half-past five. Play, the Hunchback — the house was literally crammed. I played very well, except being out in my town scene — an unwonted occurrence with me. After the play, came home, supped, and read the Wonder, which I thought wondrous dull.

Saturday, 1*5th.*

If I were to write a history of Philadelphia, according to the profound spirit of investigation for which modern tourists are remarkable, I should say that it was a peculiarity belonging to its climate, that Saturday is invariably a wet day. At twelve, went to rehearsal, after putting out things for the theatre. Had a long talk with Mr. —— about Pasta, the divine, — the only reality that ever I beheld that was as fair, as grand, as glorious as an imaginary being. Shall I ever forget that woman in Medea? I am thankful I have seen her. After rehearsal, called at Mr. ——'s. Saw and carried off his head of me in Juliet. Certainly the resemblance between myself and Mrs. Siddons must be very strong; for this painting might almost have been taken for a copy of Harlowe's sketch of my aunt in Lady Macbeth: 'tis very strange and unaccountable. Came home; wrote journal: went and sat with Mrs. —— till dinner-time. After dinner, went and sat with her again till coffee-time. Was introduced to Dr. ——, whom I liked very much.

* * * * *

* * * * *

Showed her my dress and my bracelets. Had a long discussion about the precedence of one lady before another among the nobility of European courts, whereat her republican pride seemed highly offended. If Clay *did*, as Dr. —— describes, pass before titled men, at a dinner in England, with his hands in his breeches' pockets, it only follows thence, that he was really ill-bred, and would be thought vulgar if he did it unwittingly, and absurd if he did it intentionally. Went to the theatre at half-past five. The house was wonderful, considering the weather : the play was Fazio. I played pretty well : my dress was *splendid.*

Sunday, 16*th.*

Had only time to swallow a mouthful of breakfast, and off to church; where I heard about as thorough a cock and bull sermon as ever I hope to be edified withal. What shameful nonsense the man talked! and all the time pretending to tell us what God had done, what he was doing, and what he intended to do next, as if he went up into heaven and saw what was going on there, every five minutes. Came home; sat with Mrs. —— for a long time : I am very fond of her.

*   *   *   *   *

*   *   *   *   *

Came to my own room, and studied Violante till dinner-time. How tiresome this pointless prose is to batter into one's head. After dinner, went and sat with Mrs. —— till near tea-time, when I came to the drawing-room. Presently, Mr. —— and Mr. —— called, also Dr. ——. I went to my father's room to apprise him of this invasion of the Goths, and found him very unwell, and labouring under a severe cold. He would not come down; so D—— and I had to entertain these interesting youths what fashion we best might. She gave them tea, and I gave them music, till half-past ten, when they departed.

Monday, 17*th.*

It poured with rain like the very mischief: a sort of continual gushing down from the clouds, combining all the vehemence of a thunder shower, with all the pertinacity of one of our own November drizzles — delightful! Went to rehearse Macbeth. Had a delightful palaver with Mr. ——, who knows all the music that ever was writ, and all the singers that ever sang, and worships Pasta as I do. Came home; put out things for the theatre; dined at three. After dinner, went and sat with Mrs. —— till coffee-time. At half-past five, went to the theatre. In spite of the rain, the house was very full; and in all my life I never saw so large an assembly of people so perfectly and breathlessly still as they were during several of our scenes. I played like a very clever girl as I am; but it was about as much like Lady Macbeth as the Great Mogul. My father laboured his part too much.

Tuesday, 18*th.*

Received letters; one from dear ——, and one from ——. They did as letters from England always do by me, — threw me into a perfect nervous fever. * * * *
* * * * *
* * * * *

After breakfast, went to rehearse the Wonder. Called in on my way on Mr. ——, who is painting a portrait of my father. Saw one or two lovely women's pictures. I wish he would go to England: I think it would answer his purpose very well. At two, went to the riding school: rode till half-past three. The day was bitter cold, with a piercing wicked wind riding through the grey sky. D—— and I walked to pay sundry calls. Met ——, whom we had not seen for two or three days — a most unusual circumstance.

He walked home with us. D—— and I dined
tête-à-tête. On returning home, I found a most
lovely nosegay of real, delicious, fragrant flowers.
Sweet crimson buds of the faint breathing monthly
ly rose; bright, vivid dark green myrtle; the
honey Daphne Odora, with its clusters of pinkey-
white blossoms; and the delicate bells of the tall
white jasmine,— all sweet, and living, and fresh, as
at midsummer: I was blissful! After dinner, I
went in to Mrs. ——. Came back to the drawing-room. ——, who had taken the hint about
our being alone in the evening, came in. I
began making him sing, and taught him the Leaf
and the Fountain: his voice sounded like when
we were nearer home.   *   *   *

   *   *   *   *   *

   *   *   *   *   *

Presently Mr. —— was announced. He was
the author of the flowers.   *   *

  *   *   *   *   *

                    Wednesday, 19th.

After breakfast, —— called. *   *

  *   *   *   *   *

  *   *   *   *   *

Went to rehearsal,— afterwards, to the riding
school.   The school was quite empty, and I alone.

The boy brought me my horse, and I mounted by
means of a chair. As I was cantering along,
amusing myself with cogitations various, ——
came in. He stayed the whole time I rode.   I
settled with him about riding to-morrow, and
came home to dinner. After dinner, went in to see
Mrs. ——: Dr. —— was there, who is a remarkably nice man. She is a very delightful person,
with a great deal of intellect and a wonderful
quantity of fortitude and piety, and a total absence of knowledge of the world, except through
books.   *   *   *   *
       *   *   *   *   *
       *   *   *   *   *

Her children enchant me, and her care of
them enchants me too.   She is an excellent person, with a heart overflowing with the very best
affections our nature is capable of, fulfilled, I
think, to the uttermost. *   *   *
       *   *   *   *   *
       *   *   *   *   *

Stayed with her till time to go to the theatre.
The house was very full: the play was the Wonder — my first time of acting Violante.   My dress
was not finished till the very last moment, — and
then, oh, horror ! was so small that I could not get
into it.   It had to be pinned upon me ; and thus

bebundled, with the dread of cracking my bodice from top to bottom every time I moved, and the utter impossibility of drawing my breath, from the narrow dimensions into which it squeezed me, I went on to play a new part. The consequence was, that I acted infamously, and for the first time in my life was horribly imperfect — out myself and putting every body else out. Between every scene my unlucky gown had to be pinned together ; and in the laughing scene, it took the hint from my admirable performance, and facetiously grinned in an ecstasy of amusement till it was fairly open behind, displaying, I suppose, the lacing of my stays, like so many teeth, to the admiring gaze of the audience; for, as I was perfectly ignorant of the circumstance, with my usual easy *nonchalance*, I persisted in turning my back to the folk, in spite of all my father's pulls and pushes, which, as I did not comprehend, I did not by any means second either. —— was at the play, also Dr. ——, also Henry Clay, who was received with cheers and plaudits manifold. Came home in my dress, and went in to show it to Mrs. —— and her mother, who were both in bed, but marvellously edified by my appearance.

Thursday, 20th.

The day was beautifully brilliant, clear, and
cold — winter, but winter in dazzling array of sunshine and crystal; blue skies, with light feathery
streaks of white clouds running through them;
dry, crisp, hard roads, with the delicate rime
tipping all the ruts with sparkling jewellery; and
the waters fresh, and bright, and curling under
the keen breath of the arrow-like wind. After
breakfast, —— called. Walked out with him to
get a cap and whip for D——. The latter he
insisted on making her a present of, and a very
pretty one indeed it was, with a delicate ivory han-
dle, and a charming persuading lash. Went in
for a short time to Mrs. ——, who entertained
herself with letting all my hair down about my
ears, and pulling it all manner of ways. At
twelve habited, and helped to equip dear D——,
who really looked exceedingly nice in her jockey
habiliments. Went to the school, where we found
—— waiting for us. Mounted and set forth.
We rode out to Laurel Hill. The road was not
very good, but no mud; and the warm, gleesome sunlight fell mellowly over the lovely undulations of the land, with their patches of green
cedar trees, and threadbare cloak of leafless

woods, through which the little birds were careering merrily, as the reviving sunshine came glowingly down upon the world, like a warm blessing. Passed that bright youth, Mr. ——, on the road, riding very like an ass on horseback. When we reached Laurel Hill, we dismounted, tied up the horses, slacked their girths, and walked first up to that interesting wooden monument, where I inscribed my initials on our first ride thither. Afterwards, —— and I scrambled down the rocks to the river side, which D—— declined doing, *'cause vy?*— she'd have had to climb up again. The water was like a broad dazzling river of light and had a beautiful effect, winding away in brightness that the eye could scarce endure, between its banks, which, contrasted by the sunny stream, and blue transparent sky, appeared perfectly black. As I bent over a fine *bluff* (as they here call any mass of rock standing isolated), I espied below me a natural rocky arch, overhanging the river, all glittering with pure long diamond icicles. Thither —— convoyed me, and broke off one of these wintry gems for me. It measured about two feet long, and was as thick at the root as my wrist. I never saw any thing so beautiful as these pendant adornments of the silver-fingered ice god. Toiled up to the house again, where, after brush-

ing our habits, we remounted our chargers, and
came home. The river was most beautiful towards the bridge that they are building: the unfinished piers of which have a very pretty effect,
almost resembling their very opposite, a ruin.
The thin, pale vapour of the steam engine,
employed in some of the works, rising from the
blue water, and rolling its graceful waves far along
the dark rocky shore, had a lovely, fairy-like look,
which even drew forth the admiration of ——,
who, from sundry expressions which have occasionally fallen from him, I suspect to be rather
well endowed with ideality. Reached home at
half-past four. My father dined out. It was
past ——'s dinner time; so we invited him to stay
and dine with us. After dinner, we fell somehow
or another into a profound theological discussion;
—— suddenly proposing for my solution the
mysterious doctrine of the inherent sin of our
nature, and its accompanying doom, death, —
inherited from one man's sin, and one man's
punishment. I am not fond of discoursing upon
these subjects. 'Tis long since I have arrived at
the conviction that the less we suffer our thoughts
to dwell upon what is vague and mysterious in
our most mysterious faith, and the more we confine
our attention and our efforts to that part of it

which is practical and clear as the noon-day, the better it will be for our minds here, and our souls hereafter. Surely they are not wise who seek to penetrate the unfathomed counsels of God, whilst their own natures, moral, mental, nay, even physical, have depths beyond the sounding of their plummet line. —— spoke in perfect sincerity and simplicity of the difficulty he found in believing that which was so "hard a saying;" and as there was not the slightest particle of levity or ridicule in his manner, I spoke as earnestly as I felt and always feel upon this subject, — very strenuously advising him not to strain his comprehension upon matters which baffle human endeavour, which, after all our wanderings and weary explorings, still lead us back to the wide boundless waste of uncertainty; concluding by exhorting him to read his Bible, say his prayers, and go to church if he could, — or, if he could not, at all events to be as good as he could. While we were at tea, young —— and Dr. —— came in. They put me down to the piano, and I continued to sing until past eleven o'clock, when, somebody looking at a watch, there was a universal exclamation of surprise, the piano was shut down, the candles put out, the gentlemen vanished, and I came to bed.

WINTER.

I saw him on his throne, far in the north,
Him ye call Winter, picturing him ever
An aged man, whose frame, with palsied shiver,
Bends o'er the fiery element, his foe.
But him I saw was a young god, whose brow
Was crowned with jagged icicles, and forth
From his keen spirit-like eyes there shone a light,
Broad, glaring, and intensely cold and bright.
His breath, like sharp-edged arrows, pierced the air;
The naked earth crouched shuddering at his feet;
His finger on all murmuring waters sweet
Lay icily,—motion nor sound was there;
Nature seemed frozen—dead; and still and slow
A winding-sheet fell o'er her features fair,
Flaky and white, from his wide wings of snow.

I am sorry to find that I must skip Friday and
Saturday, thereby omitting an account of an interesting ball at Mrs. ——'s, where the floors
were duly chalked, the music very good, the
women very lovely, and where I fell in again with
my dear kinsman, whom I love devotedly, and
whom I jumped half across a quadrille to greet
with extended hands, which must greatly have
edified the whole assembly. Likewise I must
skip a most interesting account of a second polemical conversation with ——; in the course of

which, to my great amazement, he managed to introduce a most vehement abuse of Dr. ——, whose admiration of my singing appears to have troubled him fully as much as the doctrine of original sin,—together with many other things worthy of note, which shall now die in oblivion, and the times return unenlightened to their graves.

Sunday, 23d.

Was only dressed in time to swallow two mouthfuls of breakfast, and get ready for church. —— came to know at what time we would ride, and walked with us to the church door.   *

    *   *   *   *   *

    *   *   *   *   *

After church, came home,—habited; went and sat with Mrs. —— till half-past one. The villanous servants did not think fit to announce the horses till they had been at the door full half an hour, so that when we started it was near two o'clock. D—— seemed quite at her ease upon her gangling charger, and I had gotten up upon Mr. ——'s big horse to see what I could make of him. The day was beautifully bright and clear, with a warm blessed sunshine causing the wintry world to smile. We had proceeded more than half way to Laurel Hill without event, when, driving my heavy-shouldered brute at a bank, instead of lifting up his feet, he thought fit to stumble, fall, and fling me very comfortably off upon the mound. I sprang up neither hurt nor frightened, shook my habit, tightened my girths, and mounted again; when we set off, much refreshed by this little incident, which occasioned a world of mirth and many saucy speeches from my companions to me. At Laurel Hill the master of the house came bowing forth with the utmost courteousness to meet me, expressing his profound sense of the honour I did him in deigning to inhale the air around his abode, and his unspeakable anguish at having been absent, when I had so far condescended before. He was a foreigner, — French or Italian, or *such like*,—which accounts for his civility. Had the horses taken to the stable, and their girths slackened. D—— kept the heights, and —— and I ran, slipped, slid, and scrambled down to the water's edge. The river was frozen over, not, however, strongly enough to bear much, and every jutting rock was hung with pure glittering icicles that shone like jewels in the bright sunshine. Far down the river all was still and lonely, and bright, yet wintry-looking. The flow of the water and its plashing music were

still; there was no breath of wind stirring the
leafless boughs; the sunlight came down, warm
and dazzling upon the silent sparkling world, all
clad in its shimmering ice robe : the air was transparent and clear, and the whole scene was perfectly lovely. Turning to re-ascend the rocks, I
called aloud to D——, and the distinctest, loudest
echo answered me. So perfect was the reflection
of the sound, that at first I thought some one was
mocking me. I ran up a scale as loud, and high,
and rapid as I could; and from among the sunny
fields, a voice repeated the threaded notes as
clearly, as rapidly, only more softly, with a distinctness that was startling. I never heard an
echo that repeated so much of what was sung or
said. I stood in perfect enchantment exercising
my voice, and provoking the hidden voice of the
air, who answered me with a far off tone, that
seemed as though the mocking spirit fled along
the hill tops, repeating my notes with a sweet
gleeful tone that filled me with delight. Oh,
what must savages think an echo is ? How many,
many lovely and wild imaginations are suggested
by that which natural philosophers analyse into
mere conformations of earth and undulations of
air. At length we joined D——, and walked to
the house, where presently appeared the master

of the mansion, with cakes, wine, cordial, preserves, or, as Comus hath it, " a table covered
with all manner of deliciousness." I was at first
a little puzzled by the epithet *cordial* applied to
three goodly-looking *decanters* full of rosy and
golden liquor, and which —— informed me is the
invariable refreshment presented to visiters of both
sexes who ride or drive up to Laurel Hill. To
satisfy my curiosity, I put my lips to some of it,
which proved to be no other than liqueur, an
indifferent sort of noyeau — that which soberest
folks in England take but a thimble-full of after
dinner, by way of *chasse café*, and drunkenest
folk would be ashamed to touch in the morning.
It seems that it is otherwise here; and, indeed,
generally speaking, Americans swallow much more
of all sorts of spirituous nauseousness than we do
in our country. The men take brandy, in a way
that would astound people of any respectability in
England, and in this, as well as many other ways,
contribute to assist the enervating effects of their
climate.* Our host waited himself most atten-

* The time of locking of doors at gentlemen's dinner
parties, and drinking till the company dropped one by one
under the table, has, with the equally disgusting habit of
spitting about the floors, long vanished in England before a
more rational hospitality, and a better understanding of the

tively upon us, and refused all species of remuneration save thanks, which, indeed, he said he

---

very first rule of good breeding, not to do that which is to
offend others. Spirituous liquors are the fashion alone
among the numerous frequenters of the gin palaces of
Holborn, and St. Giles's; even the old-fashioned favourites
of our country gentlemen, port, madeira, and sherry, are
found too heavy and strongly flavoured for the palate of our
modern exquisites,—and the fragrant and delicate wines of
Burgundy, Bordeaux, the Rhine, and its tributary streams,
are the wines now preferred before all others, by persons of
refined taste and moderate indulgence. This in itself is a
great improvement. The gross desire of excitement by a
quantity of powerful stimulants has given place to a temperate enjoyment of things, in themselves certainly the most
excellent in the world. Wine drinking in England is
become altogether a species of *dillettante* taste, instead of
the disgusting excess it used to be; it is indulged in with
extreme moderation, — and so much have all coarse and
thick-blooded drinks gone out of fashion, that even liqueurs
are very seldom taken after coffee but by foreigners. Our
gentlemen have learnt to consider hard and gross drinking
ungentlemanly. I wish I could say the same of American
gentlemen. The quantity and the quality of their potations are
as destructive of every thing like refinement of palate, as
detrimental to their health. Americans are, generally speaking, the very worst judges of wine in the world, always
excepting madeira, which they have in great perfection, and
is the only wine of which they are tolerable judges. One
reason of their ignorance upon this subject is the extremely
indifferent quality of the foreign wines imported here, and
still more powerful reason, is the total loss of all niceness
of taste consequent upon their continual swallowing of

owed me for so far honouring him as to stuff his
cakes and drink his wine. We mounted again,

---

mint julaps, gin slings, brandy cocktails, and a thousand
strong messes which they take *even before breakfast*, and
indifferently at all hours of the day,—a practice as gross in
taste, as injurious to health. Burgundy I have never seen
at an American table: I believe it will not stand the sea-
voyage. Claret they have now in very great perfection,
thanks to Mr. ——, who has introduced it among them,
and deserves to be considered a public benefactor therefore.
Hock is, generally speaking, utterly undrinkable, and champagne (the only foreign wine of which they seem generally
fond), though some of a good quality is occasionally presented to you, is for the most part a very nauseous compound, in which sugar is the only perceptible flavour. Although the American gentlemen do not indeed lock the doors
upon their guests, they have two habits equally fatal to their
sobriety, of which I have heard several Englishmen complain bitterly. The one is mixing their wines in a most
unorthodox manner, equally distressing to the palate and the
stomach; *i. e.* giving you to drink by turns, after dinner,
claret, madeira, sherry, hock, champagne, all and each of
which you are pressed to take as specimens of excellence in
their various ways, forming altogether a vinous hotch-potch,
which confounds alike the taste and the brain. The second
ordeal, to which the sobriety of Englishmen dining out here
is exposed, is at the close of all these various libations,—
which of course last some time,—an instantaneous removal
from the dinner to the supper table, where strong *whisky punch*
effectually *finishes* the wits of their guests, and sends them
home to repent for two days the excess of a few hours.
Perhaps, when the real meaning of the word *society* becomes
better understood in this country, absurd display and dis-

being refreshed, and taking leave of this pearl of
innkeepers, continued our ride long the banks of

---

gusting intemperance will no more be resorted to as its
necessary accompaniments; but of course the *real* material
of which society should be formed must increase a little
first. I have been told that the women in this country
drink. I never saw but one circumstance which would lead
me to believe the assertion. At the baths in New York, one
day, I saw the girl who was waiting upon the rooms carry
mint julaps (a preparation of mint, sugar, and brandy,) into
three of them. I was much surprised, and asked her if this
was a piece of service she often performed for the ladies
who visited the baths? She said, " Yes, pretty often."
Bar-rooms are annexed to every species of public building, —
in the theatres, in the hotels, in the bath-houses, on board
the steam-boats, — and there are even temporary buildings
which serve this purpose erected at certain distances along
the rail-roads. Though the gentlemen drink more than any
other *gentlemen*, the lower orders here are more temperate
than with us. The appearance of a drunken man in the
streets is comparatively rare here; and certainly Sunday is
not, as with us, the appointed day for this disgusting vice
among the lower classes here. Fortunately, most fortunately, it is not with them as with us, the only day on which
the poor have rest, or drunkenness the only substitute they
can find for every other necessary or comfort of life. Our
poor are indeed intemperate. Alas! that vice of theirs will
surely be visited on others; for it is the offspring of their
misery. The effects of habitual intemperance in this country
are lamentably visible in many young men of respectable
stations and easy circumstances; and it is by no means
uncommon to hear of young gentlemen — persons who rank
as such here — destroying their health, their faculties, and

the Schuylkill, until we came to Manayunk, a manufacturing place, where they create cottons, and
which has the additional advantage of being most
lovelily situated upon the banks of the river,
backed by rocky heights, where the cedar bushes,
with their rich dark tufts and the fine bold masses
of grey granite, together with a hundred little
water-courses now hanging from every ridge they
used to flow over in brilliant ice pendants, had a
most beautiful effect.   It was getting late, however, and we pushed on to the bridge; but, lo!
when we reached it, it was under repair and impassable.   What was to be done? the sun had
withdrawn his warm rays from the heavens, — the
lower earth was shadowy and dark, — a rich orange
light hung over the brow of the ridge of hills on
the opposite side of the river, whose current,
rapid and strong, flowed darkly between beautiful
slabs of granite which lay in its path, and round
which the water hurried angrily.   What was to be
done ?   To turn back was disheartening, — to go
on for the chance of a bridge was also to run the
chance of being utterly benighted in paths we
knew nothing of, and on horses which were any

---

eventually their lives, at a most untimely age, by this debasing habit.

thing but safe. However, my evident inclination to the latter course prevailed with my companions. We crossed a narrow bridge, and pursued a sort of tow-path between the canal and the river. The glimmering daylight was fading fast from the sky, and the opposite shores of the river were losing their distinctness of outline, when, from between two beautiful bold masses of rock which overhung its entrance, the wooden bridge appeared. I should like to have lingered in this spot till night-fall, but this was by no means the bargain either with my fellow-travellers or my horse. So on we went over the bridge, and, turning to the left, pursued the river's side, — now close down to its gushing, fretful waters, hurrying from between the rocky impediments of their path, — now high above its course, in the midst of woods growing to the very edge of the precipitous bank, with rocky ridges rising again above us, crowned with the black-looking tufts of the cedar, jagged with icicles, and from which descended, at every ten yards, a trickling rill, which, smoothed over by the glassy ice, rendered our horses' footing, particularly in the twilight, very insecure. We were *in for it;* and when that is the case, 't is vain making lamentations or piteous retrospections : I therefore pushed on with as much care as I

could, of Mr. ———'s tumble-down charger, whose
headlong motion kept me in agonies, leaving ———
to take care of dear D———, whose bones I feared
would ache for this adventure most bitterly.   The
road was perfectly beautiful.   Broad masses of
shadowy clouds hung in the sky, and were reflected
in the waters, together with the pale delicate grey
of evening, and the last amber tinge of sunset.
We did not reach Philadelphia till it was perfectly
dark.   To add to my consternation, too, when we
asked ——— to dine with us, he said that he had an
engagement, for which I began to fear this ill-
starred ride would have kept him too late.

   *   *   *   *   *

   *   *   *   *   *

I came up to my own room, changed my clothes,
and went in to see Mrs. ———.   *   *

   *   *   *   *   *

   *   *   *   *   *

She was completely overpowered with laudanum.
Her head was declined upon a chair.   *

   *   *   *   *   *

   *   *   *   *   *

She looked very lovely, with her beautiful head
bowed, and her dark eyelashes lying on her wan
cheeks.   Her features were contracted with suffering.   I sat watching her with much heartfelt

sadness and interest. I was summoned away, however, to see some gentlemen who were in the drawing-room, whither I adjourned, and where I found Mr. —— and Dr. ——. I was stupid and sleepy, and the gentlemen had the charity not to keep me up, or make me sing.

Monday 24*th, Christmas-eve.*

After breakfast, put out clothes for to-night. When I came down, found —— in the drawing-room with my father : paid him his bill, and pottered an immensity. Went to rehearsal, — afterwards paid all manner of cards with poor dear D——, who puffed and panted through the streets in order not to freeze me, which, however, she did not escape. * * * *
* * * * *
* * * * *

After dinner, went and sat with my poor invalid, whom, in spite of her republicanism, I am greatly inclined to like and admire. Remained with her till coffee-time. Went to the theatre : the play was the Merchant of Venice, — my favourite part, Portia. The house was very full : I played so-soish. * * * *
* * * * *

Tuesday, 25th, Christmas-day.

I wish you a merry Christmas, poor child! away from home and friends. Truly, the curse of the old Scriptures has come upon me; my lovers and my acquaintance are far off from me. After breakfast, practised for an hour; went and saw Mrs. —— ; drove out shopping; saw —— walking with my father. Came home and wrote journal: went out with D—— ; bought a rocking-horse for Mrs. ——'s chicks, whose merry voices I shall miss most horribly by and by. Dragged it in to them in the midst of their dinner. Dined at three. After dinner, went and sat with her till coffee-time. When I came into the drawing-room, found a beautiful work-box sent me by that very youthful admirer of mine, Mr. ——. I was a little annoyed at this, but still more so at my father's desiring me to return it to him, which I know will be a terrible mortification to him. Went to the theatre: the house was crammed with men, and very noisy, — a Christmas audience. Play, Macbeth: I only played so-so. Oh, me! these marks in the stream of time, over which it breaks as over a dam, drawing our attention, which without them would even less often note its rapid, rapid current! They do but become halting posts

for our souls, round which gather the memories
of days and hours escaped and gone from us for
ever. †   *   *   *   *

*   *   *   *   *

*   *   *   *   *

† There is a species of home religion, so to speak, which
is kept alive by the gathering together of families at stated
periods of joy and festivity, which has a far deeper moral
than most people imagine. The merry-making at Christmas,
the watching out the old year, and in the new, the royalty
of Twelfth-night, the keeping of birth-days, and anniver-
saries of weddings, are things which, to the worldly-wise in
these wise times, may savour of childishness or superstition;
but they tend to promote and keep alive some of the
sweetest charities, and kindliest sympathies of our poor
nature. While we are yet children, these days are set in
golden letters in the calendar, long looked forward to, — enjoyed with unmixed delight, — the peculiar seasons of new
frocks, new books, new toys, drinking of healths, bestowing
of blessings and wishes by kindred and parents, and being
brought into the notice of our elders, and, as children used
to think in the dark ages, therefore their betters. To the
older portion of the community, such times were times of
many mingled emotions, all, all of a softening, if not of so
exhilarating a nature. The cares, the toils of the world had
become their portion, — some little of its coldness, its selfishness, and sad guardedness had crept upon them, — distance
and various interests, and the weary works of life had engrossed
their thoughts, and turned their hearts and their feet from the
dear household paths, and the early fellowship of home;
but at these seasons the world was in its turn pushed aside
for a moment, — the old thresholds were crossed by those

Wednesday, 26th.

After breakfast, put out things for theatre.
When I came down to the drawing-room, I found

---

who had ceased to dwell in the house of their birth, — kindred and friends met again, as in the early days of childhood
and youth, under the same roof-tree, — the nursery revel,
and the school-day jubilee, was recalled to their thoughts
by the joyful voices and faces of a new generation, — the
blessed and holy influences of home flowed back into their
souls, at such a time, by a thousand channels, — the heart
was warmed with the kind old love and fellowship, — face
brightened to kindred face, and hand grasped the hand
where the same blood was flowing, and all the evil deeds of
time seemed for a while retrieved. These were holy and
happy seasons. Oh, England! dear, dear England! this sweet,
sacred worship, next to that of God the highest and purest,
was long cherished in your soil, where the word home was
surely more hallowed than any other save heaven.   Far, far
off be the day when a cold and narrow spirit shall quench
in you these dear and good human yearnings, and make the
consecrated earth around our door-stones as barren as the
wide wilderness of life in strange lands.   In this country
I have been mournfully struck with the absence of every
thing like this home-clinging.   Here are comparatively no
observances of tides and times.   Christmas-day is no
religious day, and hardly a holyday with them.   New-year's
day is perhaps a little, but only a little, more so. For Twelfth-
day, it is unknown ; and the household private festivals of
birthdays are almost universally passed by unsevered from the
rest of the toilsome days devoted to the curse of labour.
Indeed, the young American leaves so soon the shelter of

a middle-aged gentleman of very respectable appearance sitting with my father. He rose on my coming in, and, after bowing to me, continued his discourse to my father thus : — " Yes, sir, yes ; you will find as I tell you, sir, the winter is our profitable theatrical season, sir ; so that if any thing should take you to England, you can return again at the beginning of next fall." I modestly withdrew to another end of the room, supposing they were engaged upon business. But my curiosity was presently attracted by the continuation of his discourse. " And recollect, sir, and this lady, your daughter, too, if you please ; that what I have said must not on any account be repeated out of this room. I am myself going immediately to England, and from thence direct to *Jerusalem !*" I stared. " There, sir, is my

---

his home, the world so early becomes to him a home, that the happy and powerful influences and associations of that word to him are hardly known. Sent forth to earn his existence at the very opening time of mind and heart, like a young green-house plant just budding, that should be thrust out into the colder air, the blight of worldliness, of coldness, and of care, drive in the coming blossoms ; and if the tree lives, half its loveliness and half its *usefulness* are shorn from it. These are some of the consequences of the universal doom of Americans, to labour for their bread : there are others and better ones.

real name, ——— : the card I sent up to you is not
my real name. You see, sir, I am an Irishman,
that is to say, in fact, I am really a Jew. *I am
one of those of the tribe of Ephraim who refused to
cross the Red Sea : we were not to be humbugged by
that damned fellow, Moses, — no, sir, we were not !* "
Here my heart jumped into my throat, and my
eyes nearly out of my head with fright and amazement. " Well," continued the poor madman,
" I suppose I may deliver this to the young lady
herself;" giving me a small parcel, which I took
from him as if I thought it would explode and
blow me up. " And now, sir, farewell. Remember, remember my words, — in three years,
perhaps, but *certainly* in ten, *He* that will come,
will come, and it's all up with the world, and the
children of men !" This most awful announcement was accompanied with a snap of his fingers,
and a demi-pirouette. He was then rushing out
of the room, leaving his cloak behind him. My
father called him back to give it him. He bundled
himself into it, exclaimed, " God bless you both !
God bless you both ! — remember, what I have
said requires the profoundest secrecy, as you perceive," and darted out of the room, leaving my
father and myself with eyes and mouth wide open,
gaping in speechless astonishment. At last I

bethought me of opening the little packet the madman had left me. It was a small box, on the cover of which was written, To Miss Kemble, with the compliments of St. George. I then recollected, that some time past I had received some verses, in which love and religion were very crazily blended, signed St. George. But, as I am abundantly furnished with epistles of this sort, I had flung them aside, merely concluding the writer to be gone a short way from his wits. The box contained a most beautiful and curious ornament, something like a Sevigne, highly wrought in gold and enamel, and evidently very costly. I was more confounded than ever, and did not recover from my amazement and fright for a long time. I went in to Mrs. —— to tell her the event. Thence we began talking about young ——'s box; and, upon her advice, I again spoke to my father, and obtained his leave not to send it back; so I indited him a thankful epistle. Practised for a short time, and then went to the riding-school. It was quite empty : I put on my cap and skirt, and was sitting, thinking of many things, in the little dressing-room, when I heard the school-door open, and Mr. —— walked straight up to me.   *   *   *   *

    *   *   *   *   *

    *   *   *   *   *

Dr. —— called to-day. I was quite glad to see him: he gave me all the New York news, and brought with him a gentleman, a friend of his, who nearly made me sick by very deliberately spitting upon the carpet. Mercy on me! I thought I should have jumped off my chair, I was so disgusted. Mr. ——, too, does this constantly.   *   *   *   *

        *   *   *   *   *

        *   *   *   *   *

After dinner, went and sat with Mrs. —— ; was called away to see Mr. ——, whom I thanked for his present.   *   *   *   *

        *   *   *   *   *

        *   *   *   *   *

Went to the theatre at half-past five. The house was very fair, considering the weather, which was very foul. Play, School for Scandal. They none of them knew their parts, or remembered their business — delightful people, indeed! I played only so-so. —— supped with us. He is a very gentlemanly, nice person, and I am told he is extremely amiable.   *   *   *

        *   *   *   *   *

        *   *   *   *   *

He told me sundry steam-boat stories that made my blood curdle; such as, a public brush, a public comb, and a public *tooth-brush.* Also, of a gentleman who was using his own tooth-brush, — a man who was standing near him said, " I 'll trouble you for that article when you 've done with it." When he had done with it, the gentleman presented it to him, and on receiving it again, immediately threw it into the river, to the infinite amazement of the borrower, who only exclaimed, " Well, however, you 're a queer fellow." *

Thursday, 27th.

After breakfast, went to rehearsal. Katharine and Petruchio. After rehearsal, went to the riding-school. It was quite empty, except of Mr. ——, and Mr. ——.   *   *   *

    *   *   *   *   *

    *   *   *   *   *

Came home: found a letter to me from that strange madman. On opening it, it proved a mere envelope, containing a visiting card with the name St. George upon it. After dinner, wrote journal; went and sat with Mrs. —— till coffee-

---

* This happened on board a *western* steam-boat, I beg to observe, if it happened at all.

time. I have had a most dreadful side-ache all
day.   *   *   *   *
    *   *   *   *   *
    *   *   *   *   *

At half-past five, went to the theatre. Play, Much
Ado about Nothing ; farce, Katharine and Petruchio.   *   *   *   *
    *   *   *   *   *
    *   *   *   *   *

At the end I was so tired, and so overcome with
the side-ache, that I lay down on the floor perfectly done up.

                                Friday, 28th.

    After breakfast, ——— called.   Settled to ride, if
possible, to-morrow.   I would give the world for
a good shaking.   I 'm dying of the blue devils :
I have no power to rouse myself.   *
        *   *   *   *   *
        *   *   *   *   *

When ——— was gone, sat down to practise.   Tried
Mrs. Hemans's Messenger Bird, but the words
were too solemn, and too sad : I sobbed instead
of singing, and was a little relieved.   Went in to
see Mrs. ———.   She seemed better ; she was *en
toilette,* in a delicate white wrapper, with her fine

hair twisted up round her classical head. She is
a beautiful person; she is better — an amiable, a
sensible, and a pious one; I am very deeply interested by her; I like her extremely. At half-
past one, went to the riding-school. I met there
a daughter of old Lady ——'s, who introduced
herself to me, and asked leave to stay and see me
ride, which leave I gave her. The bay pony is,
however, fairly ruined. A little wretch not twelve
years old had just been riding it: it had fallen
from all its paces, and went so lame that I gave
up riding, and sat disconsolately enough in the
little dressing-closet, looking through a window
six inches square, at the blessed mild blue heavens, and longing for wings, till my soul was like
to faint.   *   *   *   *
    *   *   *   *   *
    *   *   *   *   *

After dinner, wrote journal. Went in and sat
with Mrs. ——. By the by, that worthy youth,
Mr. ——, dined with us. I got rid of some of
my vapours by sundry hearty laughs at him. I
am sorry to leave Philadelphia on Mrs. ——'s
account. I am growing to her. Oh, Lord! how
soon, how soon we do this! — how we do cling
to every thing in spite of the pitiless wrenches of
time and chance! Her dear babies are delight-

ful to me; their laughing voices have power to excite and make me happy,—and when they come dancing to meet me, my heart warms very fondly towards them.   *   *   *

*   *   *   *   *

*   *   *   *   *

She amuses me much by her intense anxiety that I should be married. First, she wishes —— would propose to me; then she thinks Mr. ——'s estates in Cuba would be highly acceptable; in short, my single blessedness seems greatly to annoy her, and I believe she attributes every thing evil in life to that same. She seemed surprised, and a little shocked, when I said I would accept death most thankfully in preference to the happiest lot in life, — and so I would — I would. Yet death ——. 'T is strange, that Messenger Bird threw more than a passing gloom over me. If the dead do indeed behold those whom they have loved, with loving eyes and fond remembrance, do not the sorrows, the weariness, the toiling, the despairing of those dear ones rise even into the abodes of peace, and wring the souls of those who thence look down upon the earth, and see the wo and anguish suffered here? Or, if they do not feel, — if, freed from this mortal coil, they forget all they have suffered, all that we yet endure, oh! then what fourfold trash is human love! what vain and miserable straws are all the deep, the dear, the grasping affections twined in our hearts' fibres, — mingled with our blood! How poor are all things, — how beggarly is life! Oh! to think that while we yet are bowed in agony, and mourning over the dead,—while our bereaved hearts are aching, and our straining eyes looking to that heaven, beyond which we think they yet may hear our cries, they yet may see our anguish, the dead, the loved, the mourned, nor see, nor hear; or if they do, look down with cold and careless gaze upon the love that lifts our very souls in desperate yearning towards them. Yet one of the two must surely be: either the other life is like this, a life of pain, though not like this, perhaps, a life of selfishness; or this earth, and time, and all they hold, are a more hollow mockery than even I sometimes dream they are. I will not think any more of it. We went to the theatre at half-past five. Play, Hunchback; after it, Katharine and Petruchio. I thought I should have died of the side-ache, — I was in perfect agony. The people here are more civil and considerate than can be imagined. I sent, yesterday evening, for some water-ice: the confectioner had none; when, lo! to-night he brings me some he has made on purpose for me, which he entreats my acceptance of. I admired a very pretty fan, Mrs. —— had in her hand; and at the end of the play, she had it sent to my dressing-room; — and these sort of things are done by me, not once, but ten times every day. Nothing can exceed the kindness and attention which has encountered us every where since we have been in this country. I am sure I am bound to remember America and Americans thankfully; for, whatever I may think of their ways, manners, or peculiarities, to me they have shown unmingled good will, and cordial, real kindness. Remained up, packing, till two o'clock.

TO —— ——

Many a league of salt sea rolls
Between us, yet I think our souls,
Dear friend, are still as closely tied
As when we wandered side by side,
Some seven years gone, in that fair land
Where I was born. As hand in hand
We lived the showery spring away,
And when the sunny earth was gay
With all its blossoms, still together
We passed the pleasant summer weather,
We little thought the time would come,
When, from a trans-Atlantic home,
My voice should greet you lovingly
Across the deep dividing sea.

Oh, friend! my heart is sad: 't is strange,
As I sit musing on the change
That has come o'er my fate, and cast
A longing look upon the past,
That pleasant time comes back again
So freshly to my heart and brain,
That I half think the things I see
Are but a dream, and I shall be
Lying beside you, when I wake,
Upon the lawn beneath the brake,
With the hazel copse behind my head,
And the new-mown fields before me spread.

It is just twilight: that sweet time
Is short-lived in this radiant clime,—
Where the bright day and night more bright,
Upon th' horizon's verge unite,
Nor leave those hours of ray serene,
In which we think of what has been:
And it is well; for here no eye
Turns to the distant days gone by:
They have no legendary lore
Of deeds of glory done of yore,—
No knightly marvel-haunted years,
The nursery tales of adult ears:
The busy present, bright to come,
Of all their thoughts make up the sum:
Little their little past they heed;
Therefore of twilight have no need.

Yet wherefore write I thus? In the short span
Of narrow life doled out to every man,

Though he but reach the threshold of the track,
Where, from youth's better path, strikes out the worse,
If he has breathed so long, nor once look'd back,
He has not borne life's load, nor known God's curse.

And yet, but for that glance that o'er and o'er
Goes tearfully, where we shall go no more;
Courting the sunny spots, where, for a day,
Our bark has found a harbour on its way;
O! but for this, this pow'r of conjuring
Hours, days, and years into the magic ring,
Bidding them yield the show of happiness,
To make our real misery seem less,
Life would be dreary   But these memories start,
Sometimes, unbidden on the mourner's heart;
Unwish'd, unwelcome, round his thoughts they cling,—
In vain flung off, still dimly gathering,
Like melancholy ghosts, upon the path
Where he goes sadly, seeking only death.

Then live again the forms of those who lie
Gather'd into the grave's dark mystery.
Vainly at reason's voice the phantom flies,—
It comes, it still comes back to the fond eyes,—
Still, still the yearning arms are spread to clasp
The blessing that escapes their baffled grasp:
Still the bewildering memory mutters " Gone!"
Still, still the clinging, aching heart loves on.
Oh, bitter ! that the lips on which we pour
Love's fondest kisses, feel the touch no more;
Oh, lonely ! that the voice on which we call
In agony, breaks not its silent thrall;

Oh, fearful! that the eyes in which we gaze
With desperate hope through their thick filmy haze,
Return no living look to bless our sight!
Oh, God! that it were granted that one might
But once behold the secret of the grave, —
That but one voice from the all-shrouding cave
Might speak, — that but one sleeper might emerge
From the deep death-sea's overwhelming surge!
Speak, speak from the grey coffins where ye lie
Fretting to dust your foul mortality!
Speak, from your homes of darkness and dismay, —
To what new being do ye pass away? —
O *do* ye live, indeed? — speak, if on high
One atom springs whose doom is not to die! —
Where have I wandered?   *   *
    *   *   *   *   *
    *   *   *   *   *

Saturday, 29th.

When I came down to breakfast, found a very
pretty diamond ring and some Scotch rhymes,
from Mr. ——, what we call a small return of
favours. I wish my hand was'n't so abominably
ugly,— I hate to put a ring upon it. —— called
to see if we would ride; but D—— had too
much to do; and, after sitting pottering for some
time, I sang him the Messenger Bird, and sent
him away. Went for a few moments to Mrs. ——,

who seemed much better. Went out to pay
sundry bills and visits. Called at Mr. ——'s,
and spent half an hour most delightfully in his
study. His picture of my father is very like, and
very agreeable. 'T is too youthful by a good
deal; but the expression of the face is extremely
good, and upon the whole, except that stern-
looking thing of Kearsley's, 't is the likest thing
I have seen of him. We had a long discussion
about the stage, — the dramatic art; which, as
Helen says, " is none," for, " no art but taketh
time and pains to learn." Now I am a living
and breathing witness that a person may be accounted a good actor, and to a certain degree
deserve the title, without time or pains of any
sort being expended upon the acquisition of the
reputation. But, on other grounds, acting has
always appeared to me to be the very lowest of
the arts, admitting that it deserves to be classed
among them at all, which I am not sure it does.
In the first place, it originates nothing; it lacks,
therefore, the grand faculty which all other arts
possess — creation. An actor is at the best but
the filler up of the outline designed by another,
— the expounder, as it were, of things which
another has set down; and a fine piece of acting
is at best, in my opinion, a fine translation. More-

over, it is not alone to charm the senses that the
nobler powers of mind were given to man; 't is
not alone to enchant the eye, that the gorgeous
pallet of the painter, and the fine chisel of the
statuary, have become, through heavenly inspiration, magical wands, summoning to life images
of loveliness, of majesty, and grace; 't is not alone
to soothe the ear that music has possessed, as it
were, certain men with the spirit of sweet sounds;
't is not alone to delight the fancy, that the poet's
great and glorious power was given him, by
which, as by a spell, he peoples all space, and
all time, with undying witnesses of his own existence; 't is not alone to minister to our senses
that these most beautiful capabilities were sown
in the soil of our souls. But 't is that through
them all that is most refined, most excellent, and
noble, in our mental and moral nature, may be
led through their loveliness, as through u glorious
archway, to the source of all beauty, and all
goodness. It is that by them our perceptions of
truth may be made more vivid, our love of loveliness increased, our intellect refined and elevated,
our nature softened, our memory stored with
images of brightness, which, like glorious reflections, falling again upon our souls, may tend to
keep alive in them the knowledge of, and the

desire after, what is true, and fair, and noble.
But, that art may have this effect, it must be to
   certain degree enduring. It must not be a
transient vision, which fades and leaves but a recollection of what it was, which will fade too.
It must not be for an hour, a day, or a year, but
 biding, inasmuch as any thing earthly may abide,
to charm the sense and cheer the soul of generation after generation. And here it is that the
miserable deficiency of acting is most apparent.
Whilst the poems, the sculptures of the old Grecian
time yet remain to witness to these latter ages
the enduring life of truth and beauty; whilst the
poets of Rome, surviving the trophies of her
thousand victories, are yet familiar in our mouths
as household words; whilst Dante, Boccaccio, that
giant, Michael Angelo, yet live, and breathe, and
have their being amongst us, through the rich
legacy their genius has bequeathed to time;
whilst the wild music of Salvator Rosa, solemn
and sublime as his painting, yet rings in our ears,
and the souls of Shakspeare, Milton, Raphael,
and Titian, are yet shedding into our souls di-
vinest influences from the very fountains of inspiration;—where are the pageants that night after
night, during the best era of dramatic excellence,
riveted the gaze of thousands, and drew forth

their acclamations? — gone, like rosy sunset clouds; — fair painted vapours, lovely to the sight, but vanishing as dreams, leaving no trace in heaven, no token of their ever having been there. Where are the labours of Garrick, of Macklin, of Cooke, of Kemble, of Mrs. Siddons? — chronicled in the dim memories of some few of their surviving spectators; who speak of them with an enthusiasm which we, who never saw them, fancy the offspring of that feeling which makes the old look back to the time of their youth as the only days when the sun knew how to shine. What have these great actors left either to delight the sense, or elevate the soul, but barren names, unwedded to a single lasting evidence of greatness? If, then, acting be alike without the creating power, and the enduring property, which are at once the highest faculty of art, and its most beneficial purpose, what becomes of it when ranked with efforts displaying both in the highest degree? To me it seems no art *, but merely a highly rational,

---

* The evanescent nature of his triumph, however an actor may deplore it, is in fact but an instance of the broad moral justice by which all things are so evenly balanced. If he can hope for no fame beyond mere mention, when once his own generation passes away, at least his power, and his glory, and his reign is in his own person, and during his own life. There is scarcely to be conceived a popularity for

interesting, and exciting amusement ; and I think men may as well, much better, perhaps, spend three hours in a theatre, than in a billiard or bar-room,—and this is the extent of my approbation and admiration of my art. Called on Mrs. ——, whom I like very much. Went to the riding-school to try a new horse, which was ten hands high, all covered with shaggy, angry-looking hair, with a donkey's head, and cart-horse legs, with one of which he peached. —— came to see me mount. Dr. ——'s grey horse was

---

the moment more intoxicating than that of a great actor in his day, so much of it becomes mixed up with the individual himself. The poet, the painter, and the sculptor, enchant us through their works ; and, with very, very few exceptions, their works, and not their very persons, are the objects of admiration and applause : it is to their minds we are beholden ; and though a certain degree of curiosity and popularity necessarily wait even upon their bodily presence, it is faint compared with that which is bestowed upon the actor ; and for good reasons—he is himself his work. His voice, his eyes, his gesture, are his art, and admiration of it cannot be separated from admiration for him. This renders the ephemeral glory which he earns so vivid, and in some measure may be supposed to compensate for its short duration. The great of the earth, whose fame has arisen like the shining of the sun, have often toiled through their whole lives in comparative obscurity, through the narrow and dark paths of existence. Their reward was never given to their hands here,—it is but just their glory should be lasting.

standing in the school with a man's saddle on.
I persuaded —— to put me on it, and I then
sent him away.   *   *   *

*   *   *   *   *

*   *   *   *   *

When he was gone, rode for about an hour without
any pommel, and found I managed it famously. I
slipped my foot out of the stirrup in order to see
if I could sit without both; but this proved rather
too much, for I presently slid very comfortably off.
On my way home, met young ——, with his head
so completely in the clouds, that I had bowed to
him, and was driving on, when he just perceived me,
and fell into a confusion of bows, which he continued long after the coach had passed him.   Found
the usual token of his having been at our house —
a most beautiful nosegay; roses, hyacinths, and
myrtle.   While I was arranging them, I heard a
tremendous shriek of laughter in the hall, which
was followed by the appearance of Mr. ——.
After sitting with him some time, I went and sat
with Mrs. ——.   The amiable Charge d'Affaires
dined with us. After dinner, went to see Mrs.—— ;
but she was too unwell to receive me.   *

*   *   *   *   *

*   *   *   *   *

Saw Dr. ——, who expressed manifold deplor-

ings at my departure : gave him the words of the
Sisters.   At half-past five, went to the theatre :
play, the Wonder.   I acted only so-so : my father
was a *leetle dans les vignes du seigneur.*   When the
play was over, the folk called for us, and we went
on : he made them a neat speech, and I nothing
but a cross face and three courtesies.   How I do
hate this ! 'T is quite enough to exhibit myself to a
gaping crowd, when my profession requires that I
should do so in a feigned semblance ; but to come
bobbing and genuflexioning on, as me myself, to
be clapped and shouted at, and say, " Thank ye
kindly," is odious.   After the play, dressed, and
off to Mrs. ——, with my father and Mr. ——.
On our way thither, the spring of our coach broke,
and we had to go halting along for half an hour,
with a graceful inclination towards the pavement
on one side, which was very pleasant.   There was
quite a brilliant party at Mrs. ——'s. Told Mr.
—— that I had thrown his horse down.   Saw
and spoke to all Philadelphia.   —— was there,
and actually sitting still.   Fell in love with Mr.
——'s youngest son, who is a youth of some ten
years old, and hovers round me with a plenitude
of silent admiration and astonishment that is most
delightful.   Miss —— who is a very pretty creature, (in fact, all American women are pretty

creatures, I never saw any prettier,) sang Dalla Gioga e del Piacer. She sings very well, but pronounces Italian very Americanly, which is a pity. I don't know any thing so necessary to good singing as a good Italian pronunciation, *except* perhaps a good voice, and a good school. They made me sing, and I sang them the galley song, after which Miss —— warbled again. They were surrounding me again, with a shower of " pray do's," when perceiving D—— making towards me, with my boa on her arm, I sat down and sang them, " Yes, aunt, I am ready to go," to their infinite edification. I wonder if Mrs. —— would object to this, I should think not, as —— is not here to catch it again. *   *   *

    *   *   *   *   *

    *   *   *   *   *

Came home, and supped. I had eaten nothing since four o'clock, and was famished; for I do not like stewed oysters and terrapins, which are the refreshments invariably handed round at an American evening party. Did not get to bed till two o'clock. How beautifully bright the heavens are here. The sky has an earnest colour that is lovely and solemn to look at ; and the moon, instead of being " the maiden with white fire laden," has a rich, mellow, golden light, than which nothing can be more beautiful. The stars, too, are more vivid than in our skies, and there is a variety of hues in their light which I never observed before,— some reddish, some violet, and again others of the palest silver.

Sunday, 30th.

After breakfast, Mr. —— called, also ——, to know at what time we would ride. I fixed at twelve, thereby calculating that we should escape the people coming out from church. Went and sat a few minutes with Mrs. ——.   *

      *   *   *   *   *

      *   *   *   *   *

Spent my Sunday morning on my knees, indeed, but packing, not praying. The horses did not come till half-past twelve; so that, instead of avoiding, we encountered the pious multitude. I'm sure when we mounted there were not less than a hundred and fifty beholders round the Mansion House. Rode out to Laurel Hill. The cross road was muddy, so we took the turnpike, which was clean and short, and would have been pleasant enough but for my brute of a horse. Upon my word, these American horses are most unsafe to ride. I never mount one but I recommend myself to the care of Heaven, for I expect to have every bone in my body broken before I dismount again. At Laurel Hill we lunched. While D—— put up her hair, —— and I ran down to the water side. The ice had melted from the river, in whose still waters the shores, and trees, and bridge lay mirrored with beautiful and fairy-like distinctness. The long icicles under the rocky brow beneath which we stood had not melted away, though the warm sun was shining brilliantly on them, and making the granite slab on which we stood sparkle like a pavement of diamonds. I called to the echo, and sang to it scales up, and scales down, and every manner of musical discourse I could think of, during which interesting amusement I as nearly as possible slipped from my footing into the river, which caused both —— and myself to gulp. We left our pleasant sunny stand at last, to rejoin D—— and the lunch, and having eaten and drunken, we remounted and proceeded on to Manayunk, under the bright, warm, blessed sunshine, which came down like a still shining shower upon the earth. The beautiful little water-courses had all broken from their diamond chains, and came dancing and singing down the hills, between the cedar bushes, and the masses of grey granite, like merry children laughing as they run. After crossing the bridge at Flat Rock, I took the van, riding by myself much faster than my companions, whom I left to entertain each other. Several times, as I looked down at the delicious fresh water, all rosy with the rosy light of the clouds, and gushing round the masses of rock that intercepted their channel, I longed to jump off my horse, and go down among their shallow brilliant eddies. The whole land was mellow with warm sunset, the sky soft, and bright, and golden, like a dream. I stopped for a long time opposite the Wissihiccon creek. The stone bridge, with its grey arch, mingled with the rough blocks of rock on which it rested, the sheet of foaming water falling like a curtain of gold over the dam among the dark stones below, on whose brown sides the ruddy sunlight and glittering water fell like splinters of light. The thick, bright, rich tufted cedars basking in the warm amber glow, the picturesque mill, the smooth open field, along whose side the river waters, after receiving this child of the mountains into their bosom, wound deep, and bright, and still, the whole radiant with the softest light I ever beheld, formed a most enchanting and serene subject of contemplation. Further on, I stopped again, to look at a most beautiful mass of icicles, formed by some water falling from a large wooden conduit which belonged to a mill. The long thick masses of silvery white clung in downward pyramids together, and on the ground, great round balls of purest transparent ice, like enormous crystal grapes, lay clustered upon each other. I waited on a little sunny knoll above this glittering fairy work, till my companions joined me, when, leaving D——- to pursue the main road, —— and I turned off, and explored a pretty ravine, down which another mountain stream, half free wild water, half shimmering diamond ice, sparkled in the sunset. We reached Phila-delphia at half-past four, and had again to canter down Chestnut Street just as the folks were all coming from church, which caused no little staring, and turning of heads. My father asked —— to dine with us, but he refused. Mr. —— dined with us. After dinner, went in to pay my last visit to my poor sick friend. I sat with her until summoned to see some gentlemen in the drawing-room. It pained me to part from her; for though she exerted herself bravely, she was very much overcome. I fear she will miss me, poor thing; I had become very much attached to her. I went in to bid Mrs. —— good-by. —— was not gone to bed; I took her in my arms and kissed her, saying I should not see her for a long time again. The tears came into her baby eyes, and she said very sadly, " God bless you, Fanny." How curious a train of associations that word produced in me. It brought ——, and Lord ——, and that beautiful creature his child, before my very eyes. But her father had told little Lady —— to say that, — I am sure he did ; now this little creature blessed me out of her own heart. A child's blessing is a holy thing. Came into the drawing-room. Found Dr. ——, young Mr. ——, and Mr. —— there. Presently, Mr. —— came in, with Baron ——, a man with a thick head, thick white hair, that stood out round it like a silver halo, and gold ear-rings. I sang to them till˙past ten o'clock, and then came to my own room, where I remained up packing and pottering until past two.

Monday, 31*st*.

The river being yet open, thank Heaven, we arose at half- past four o'clock. Dressed sans dawdling for once, and came down.   *

*   *   *   *   *

*   *   *   *   *

D—— and I were bundled into a coach, and

rumbled and tumbled over the stones, through the blackness of darkness down to the steam-boat. —— was waiting for us, and convoyed us safely to the cabin, where I laid myself down, and slept till breakfast-time. My father, Captain ——, Mr. ——, and Baron —— sat themselves down most comfortably to breakfast, leaving us entirely to the charge and care of ——, who fulfilled his trust with infinite zeal. 'T is curious; there was a man on board whom I have now seen every time I have been going to or from New York to Philadelphia, whose appearance was in itself very remarkable, and the subsequent account I received of him perhaps increased the sort of impression it made upon me. He was a man of about from thirty to thirty-five, *I guess*, standing about five feet ten, with a great appearance of strength and activity. His face was that of a foreigner, the features were remarkably well cut, and the piercing black eyes, dark hair, and brown complexion, gave a Spanish character to his countenance. There was a sort of familiar would-be gentlemanly manner in his deportment and address, and a species of slang gentility in his carriage and conversation, that gave me a curiosity to ascertain what on earth he could be. After breakfast, walked up and down deck with ——. —— was on board. I am happy to hear he is thriving: I love all my fellow-passengers; and when I see one of them, my heart warms towards them, as to a bit of the dear old land left behind. After about an hour's steaming, we disembarked to cross the narrow neck of land which divides the Delaware from the Chesapeake. Here we got into a coach holding some twelve of us, to be conveyed over the rail-road by one of Stevenson's engines. Neither the road nor the conveyances are comparable to those of the Liverpool and Manchester rail-way; and instead of those luxurious, roomy coaches, which form the merit of the Liverpool train, we were squeezy and uncomfortable to a degree. The country along this slip of land is flat and very un-interesting, clothed with threadbare young woods, whose thin spare skeletons, without their leafy mantles, looked excessively miserable. The dis-tance from the Delaware to Frenchtown, on the Elk, where we were again to take water, is about sixteen miles, which we did in an hour. The first part of the road lies in Delaware, the latter in Maryland. The Elk, which in this world of huge waters is considered but a paltry ditch, but which in our country would be thought a very decent-sized river, was, a few days ago, frozen up, thereby putting a stop to the steam-boat travelling.

But, fortunately for us, it was open to-day, and presently we beheld the steamer coming puffing up to take us from the pier. This boat — the Charles Carroll — is one of the finest they have. 'T is neither so swift nor so large, I think, as some of the North river boats, but it is a beautiful vessel, roomy and comfortable in its arrangements. I went below for a few minutes, but found, as usual, the atmosphere of the cabin perfectly intolerable. The ladies' cabin, in winter, on board one of these large steamers, is a right curious sight. 'T is generally crammed to suffocation with women, *strewn* in every direction. The greater number cuddle round a stove, the heat of which alone would make the atmosphere unbreathable. Others sit lazily in a species of rocking-chair, — which is found wherever Americans sit down, — cradling themselves backwards and forwards, with a lazy, lounging, sleepy air, that makes me long to make them get up and walk. Others again manage, even upon fresh water, to be very sick. There are generally a dozen young human beings, some naughty, sick, and squalling, others happy, romping, and riotous; and what with the vibratory motion of the rocking-chairs and their contents, the women's shrill jabber, the children's shriller wailing and shouting, the heat and closeness of the air, a ladies' cabin on board an American steam-boat is one of the most over-powering things to sense and soul that can well be imagined. There was a poor sick woman with three children, among our company, two of which were noisy, unruly boys, of from eight to ten years old. One of them set up a howl as soon as he came on board, which he prolonged, to our utter dismay, for upwards of half an hour sans inter-mission, except to draw breath. I bore it as long as I could; but threats, entreaties, and bribes having been resorted to in vain, by all the women in the cabin, to silence him, I at length very com-posedly took him up in my arms, and deposited him on his back in one of the upper berths; whereupon his brother flew at his mother, kicking, thumping, screaming, and yelling. The cabin was in an uproar; the little wretch I held in my arms struggled like a young giant, and though I succeeded in lodging him upon the upper shelf, presently slid down from it like an eel. However, this effort had a salutary effect, for it obtained silence, — the crying gave way to terror, which produced silence, of which I availed myself to sleep till dinner-time. At dinner, —— and Mr. —— took charge of D—— and me, who, seeing that we were to get no dinner till six o'clock, thought fit to eat some lunch. The strange, dark man was sitting opposite us, and discoursing away to his neighbours in a strain and tone in which shrewdness and swagger, and vulgarity and a sort of braggart gallantry, were curiously jumbled. From his conversation, it was evident that he was a seafaring man. He spoke of having been a midshipman on board an American frigate. The question they were debating was that of superstitious prejudice, involving belief in lucky and unlucky days, witches, ghosts, &c. The stranger professed perfect faith in all, and added sundry experiences of his own, at the same time observing, that with regard to sailors, the strong prejudice they have against sailing on certain days often creates the very ill luck they apprehend; for if any danger should occur, 't is all attributed to evil influences against which they have no power, and they are at once deprived of half their energy in labour, and half their courage in peril. When dinner was over, I pointed out this strange man to my father, asking him if he had any idea who he was. " I am told," was his reply, " that he is but just returned from New York, where he has been tried for piracy." This accounted for every thing, — dare-devil look and language, seafaring adventures, and superstitious creed. It is a pleasant mode of

travelling that throws one into contact with such
company.　　*　　　　*　　　　*　　　　*

　　　*　　　　*　　　　*　　　　*　　　　*

Touching pirates, Baltimore, I was told (I
know not how truly), is famous for them. They
have small schooners there of a particularly light
build, and raking masts, which are the prettiest
craft in the world to look at, and the swiftest that
sail sea. The Baltimore clippers are proverbial
for their elegance and fleetness : they are like grey-
hounds on the water. These, I was told, were
frequently owned by gentlemen of rather an am-
biguous character, something between pirate,
smuggler, and wrecker, perhaps a judicious
compound of all three. Their trade is chiefly, I
believe, with and about the West India islands.
I looked at my Spanish-faced friend with redoubled
curiosity : he was the very man for a pirate. We
reached Baltimore at about half-past four. The
Chesapeake bay, like the Delaware river, appeared
to me admirable only as an immense sheet of water.
At some parts that we passed, it was six, at others,
ten, at others, thirteen miles across. The shores
were flat and uninteresting on one side, but on the
other occasionally very picturesque and beautiful,
rising in red-looking cliffs from the water's edge,
and crowned with beautiful green tufts of wood —
cedar, I suppose, for nothing else is green at this

time. The curvings of the shore, too, are very pretty; but owing to the enormous width of the water, my imperfect vision could hardly discern the peculiar features of the land. The day was more lovely than a fine day in early September, in England, — bright, soft, and sunny, with the blue in the sky of the delicate colour one sees in the Sèvres porcelain. As we entered the Patapsco, and neared Baltimore, North Point and Fort M'Henry were pointed out to me. My spirits always sink when I come to a strange place; and as we came along the wharf sides, under the red dingy-looking warehouses, between which the water ran in narrow, dark-looking canals, I felt terribly gloomy. We drove up to Barnham's, the best house in the town; and having found out where to lay my head, I had my fill of crying.*
After dinner, went and lay down; slept profoundly till nine o'clock. On my return to the drawing-room, found ——— there, and Mr. ———, the man who owns the Front Street theatre, but who it seems is only just out of gaol, and has neither actors

* Another house has been opened at Baltimore within the last year, which, though unfinished at the time of our lodging there, promised to be extremely comfortable. The building adjoined, and indeed formed, part of the Exchange; the vestibule of which is the only very beautiful piece of architecture I have seen here. It is very beautiful.

nor scenes to get up a play withal. While he was here, came missives from the proprietors of the Holliday Street theatre, to inform my father that it was lighted up, and requesting him to come and look at it. This was awkward rather. When Mr. —— was gone, I came to my room, where I remained without a fire, cold without and disconsolate within, till past one o'clock. I did not know it was New-Year's eve; and so the waters carried me over this other dam without my looking back at what was past, or forward at what is to come: and why should I? — surely " the thing that hath been, it is that which shall be; and that which is done, is that which shall be done; and there is no new thing under the sun:" sorrow and joy, hoping and fearing, pain and pleasure, laughing and weeping, striving and yielding, — they will all come again and again, and all things will be the same, till all things cease.

Tuesday, January, 1st, } 1833.
New-Year's Day, }

There it lies in its cradle! its pure forehead yet unstained by sin, unfurrowed by care; and not an hour shall have passed without the traces of both becoming visible. And where is the mother gone? where is the fulfilled year? — Gone sorrowing to join the crowd of ancestors, who witness each against me for the unthrift waste I have made of the rich legacies they one by one have bestowed on me. Oh, new-born year! ere half thy hours are spent, how often will my weary spirit have wished them fleeter wings than even those they wear! What secrets are there folded in thy breast, — what undreamt-of chances, — what strange befallings, — what unforeseen sorrows, — what unexpected joys! Perhaps, in the mysterious accomplishments with which thou art laden, my death may be numbered! — perhaps, ere thy course be duly run, the death of Time may be decreed! Oh! this life, and all things in it, remind me of the thin veils of spiders' webs which divided Desire from his aim, and which, though light and transparent, were so numerous, that to lift them all away was hopeless. After breakfast, began writing journal. 'Twas not until dating it that I discovered it was New-year's day. When I did so, and looked at my strange surroundings, at the gloomy wintry sky, and thought of the heathenish disregard with which I was passing over, in this far land, the season of home-gathering and congregating of kin in my own country, I could not refrain from crying bitterly. In spite of the pouring rain, and Mr. ——'s hints to keep us

away, my father, who wished to ascertain the truth
of the reports with regard to the state of his
theatre, set forward thither with me. We found
a very large, handsome house, larger, I think,
than the Park, but dirty, dilapidated, and looking
as if there had been eleven executions in it that
morning. No actors, scarcely any scenes, — in
short, such a state of things as rendered it totally
impossible for us to think of acting there. Came
home; sat diligently crying the whole morning.
The afternoon cleared up, and became soft and
sunny. My father insisted on my taking a walk; so
I bonneted and set out with him. What I saw of the
town appeared to me extremely like the outskirts
of Birmingham or Manchester. Bright-red brick
houses, in rows of three and five, with interesting
gaps of gravel pits, patches of meadow, and open
spaces between, which give it an untidy, straggling
appearance. They are building in every direction,
however, and in less than two years, these little
pauses being filled up, Baltimore will be a very
considerable place; for it covers, in its present
state, a large extent of ground, and contains a vast
population. Immediately after dinner, our host
made his entrée with a piano-forte. I had suggested to Mr. —— that I should be glad of one;
and here it came. I had asked him to return in
the evening, and was glad of the piano, for it helps

the time away. At six o'clock, the managers of
the Holliday Street theatre made their appearance; and my father stating that Mr. —— was
literally unable to fulfil his engagement with us,
entered into arrangements with them, during
which I sat up at a tremendously high window,
looking at the beautiful, serious skies, and radiant
moon, and listening to a tolerable band playing
sundry of Rossini's airs. When these men had
departed, —— came in. I sang and made him
sing till tea-time. After that, he entertained us
with a very long, but not very clear, account of the
various processes of making, polishing, &c. steel,
as practised in his manufactory. His account of
their hard dealings with the poorer manufacturers
was dreadful ; and he himself spoke with horror
of it, saying, " Oh, they are so miserably ground,
poor wretches, they cannot be said to live, — they
barely exist." When I remonstrated with him upon
the wickedness of such proceedings, he replied,
" We are compelled to do it in self-defence : if
we did not use the same means as other manufacturers, we should presently be undersold."
And this is the game playing all over England at
this moment, in every department of her commerce and manufacture, — this cruel oppression
of the poor, this forcing them by a league against

them, as it were, to toil in bitterness for their
scanty daily bread, while those who thus inhu-
manly depreciate their labour, and wring their
hard earnings from their starving grasp, grow
wealthy on their plunder. Are not these the
things for which God has said he will avenge? Is
his abomination of the false balance, and the
stinted measure, and the unjust reckoning, less
than in the days when he said he would visit the
oppressor of the poor, and plead the cause of the
widow and fatherless? Are not these the things
that make a nation rotten at core, and ripe for
decay? Are not these the things for which retribution is laid up, and fourfold restitution will be
demanded?—'T is awful to think of. From this
the conversation grew to the means of obtaining
interest upon money in this country, which the
gentlemen discussed together for a length of time.
I listened to them with many sad thoughts. How
intent they seemed in their discourse; how much
they appeared to value every slightest advantage
of place or circumstance which enabled them to
draw a greater profit from their capital; how
eagerly, how earnestly, they seemed absorbed in
these calculations. I do not know when I have
been so forcibly struck with the worthlessness of
money, and the strange delusion under which all

men seem to be labouring, giving up their lives, as they do, to the hunting of wealth. Are these the cares that should engross the faculties of immortal souls, and rational thinking creatures? That we must live, I know, and that money is necessary to live, I know; but that our glorious capacities of soul, mind, and body, the fitting exercise of which alone, in itself, is happiness, should thus be chained down to the altar horns of mammon, is what I never will believe wise, right, or fitting. I at length spoke, for my heart was burning within me, and burst into an eloquent lamentation on the folly and misery of which the world was guilty in following this base worship as it does. But when I said that I was convinced happiness might and did exist most blessedly upon half the means which men spent their lives in scraping together, my father laughed, and said I was the last person in the world who could live on little, or be content with the mediocrity I vaunted. I looked at my satin gown, and held my tongue, but still I was not convinced. We returned to our music till ten o'clock, when they had some supper, after which they drank a happy new year to England : — poor old England, God bless it ! At about twelve o'clock, —— departed. Sat up a long time at the window, listening to some

serenading, which, in the moonlight, sounded
pleasantly enough.*

Sunday, 6th.

At about half-past ten, Mr. —— called for us,
and we walked up to the cathedral, which is a large
unfinished stone building, standing on the brow
of a hill, which is to be the fashionable quarter of
the town, and where there are already some very
nice-looking houses. The interior of the church
is large and handsome, and has more the look of
a church than any thing I have been inside of in
this country yet. 'T is full eight years since I was
in a Catholic church; and the sensation with
which I approached the high altar, with its golden
crucifix, its marble entablatures, and its glimmering starry lights, savoured fully as much of sadness
as devotion. I have not been in a Catholic place
of worship since I was at school. How well I
remember the beautiful music of the military mass,
the pageants and processions of the feast days at

* This very romantic piece of gallantry (serenading) is
very common in this country. How it comes to be so I
can't quite make out; for it is not at all of a piece with the
national manners or tone of feeling. It's very agreeable,
though, and is an anomaly worth cultivating.

nigh mass, and the evening service, not vespers, but the Salut.* They sang that exquisitely mournful and beautiful *et incarnatus est* of Haydn's, which made my blood all run backwards. One thing disgusted me dreadfully, though the priests who were officiating never passed or approached the altar without bending the knee to it, they kept

* I have heard it several times asserted, that Catholicism was gaining ground extremely in this country. Surely the Preacher sayeth well, " The thing which has been, it is that which shall be, and there is nothing new beneath the sun." Is it not a marvellous thing to think of, that that mighty tree which has overshadowed the whole of the Christian world, under whose branches all the European empires were cradled, and which we have with our own eyes beheld droop, and fade, and totter, as it does at this moment in the old soils, — is it not strange to think of the seed being carried, and the roots taking hold in this new earth, perhaps to send up another such giant shadow over this hemisphere? Its growth here appears to me almost impossible ; for if ever there were two things more opposite in their nature than all other things, they are the spirit of the Roman Catholic religion, and the spirit of the American people. It's true, that of the thousands who take refuge from poverty upon this plenteous land, the greater number bring with them that creed, but the very air they inhale here presently gives them a political faith, so utterly incompatible with the spirit of subjection, that I shall think the Catholic priesthood here workers of miracles, to retain any thing like the influence over their minds which they possessed in those countries, where all creeds, political and polemical, have but one watch-word — faith and submission.

spitting all over the carpet that surrounded and covered the steps to it, interrupting themselves in the middle of the service to do so, without the slightest hesitation. We had a very indifferent sermon : the service was of course in Latin. When it was over, Mr. —— insisted on showing me some paintings which hung on either side the grand entrance. These were a couple of pictures by Paulin Guerin ; the one representing the descent from the cross, the other, the burying of the dead, by St. Charles, in the Holy Land. I do not understand much about bad pictures, but I know good ones when I see them; and I think these were not such. There was no beauty of imagination or poetical conception whatever in them, and there appeared to me to be manifold glaring faults in the execution. I could have sworn to their being French pictures. Was introduced to several people, coming out of church. A little way beyond the cathedral stands Washington's monument, — a *neat and appropriate* pillar, — which, together with a smaller one erected at the head of our street, to the memory of the North Point heroes, has given Baltimore the appellation of the monumental city, which never could have befallen it in any other country under heaven, but this. At eight o'clock, we went to Mrs. ——'s.

They are all in deep mourning, and the circle was very small. They are most agreeable, pleasant people, with a peculiar gentleness of manner, like very high breeding, which I have often observed in Catholics of the better orders. Their conversation appeared to me totally divested of the disagreeable accent which seems almost universal in this country. Mrs. —— talked to me about my aunt Whitelock, and what a charming actress she was, and what an enchanting thrilling voice she had. I spent a delightful evening. Before we went away, Mr. —— showed us a picture of Lady ——, by Lawrence. It looked quite refreshing, with its lovely dark curls unfrizzed, and the form of the neck and arms undisguised by the hideousness of modern fashions. Saw a very good likeness, too, of the Duke of ——. 'T was very like him, though many years younger.

    *   *   *   *   *

    *   *   *   *   *

By the by, somebody said that —— had turned Roman Catholic, and very devout. Some of the Marys and Magdalens of the old Italian painters are very converting pictures, with their tearful melancholy eyes, and golden, glorious, billowy hair. Mrs. —— amused me very much by her account of the slaves on their estates, whom, she said, she found the best and most faithful servants in the world. Being born upon the land, there exists among them something of the old spirit of clanship, and " our house," " our family," are the terms by which they designate their owners. In the south, there are no servants but blacks; for the greater proportion of domestics being slaves, all species of servitude whatever is looked upon as a degradation; and the slaves themselves entertain the very highest contempt for white servants, whom they designate as " poor white trash."

Monday, 7th.

Young —— called, and stayed about an hour with us. At half-past five, took coffee, and off to the theatre. The play was Romeo and Juliet; the house was extremely full : they are a delightful audience. My Romeo had gotten on a pair of trunk breeches, that looked as if he had borrowed them from some worthy Dutchman of a hundred years ago. Had he worn them in New York, I could have understood it as a compliment to the ancestry of that good city; but here, to adopt such a costume in Romeo, was really perfectly unaccountable. They were of a most unhappy choice

of colours, too,— dull , heavy-looking blue cloth,
and offensive crimson satin, all be-puckered, and be-
plaited, and be-puffed, till the young man looked
like a magical figure growing out of a monstrous,
strange-coloured melon, beneath which descended
his unfortunate legs, thrust into a pair of red
slippers, for all the world like Grimaldi's legs *en
costume* for clown. The play went off pretty
smoothly, except that they broke one man's
collar-bone, and nearly dislocated a woman's
shoulder by flinging the scenery about. My bed
was not made in time, and when the scene drew,
half a dozen carpenters in patched trowsers and
tattered shirt sleeves were discovered smoothing
down my pillows, and adjusting my draperies.
The last scene is too good not to be given verbatim : —

ROMEO.   Rise, rise, my Juliet,
    And from this cave of death, this house of horror,
    Quick let me snatch thee to thy Romeo's arms.

Here he pounced upon me, plucked me up
in his arms like an uncomfortable bundle, and
staggered down the stage with me.

JULIET. (*aside.*) Oh, you've got me up horridly! — that'll
never do ; let me down, pray let me down.
    ROMEO. There, breathe a vital spirit on thy lips,
        And call thee back, my soul, to life and love!

JULIET. (*aside*.) Pray put me down; you'll certainly throw me down if you don't set me on the ground directly.

In the midst of " cruel, cursed fate," his dagger fell out of his dress; I, embracing him tenderly, crammed it back again, because I knew I should want it at the end.

ROMEO. Tear not our heart-strings thus!
　　　　They crack! they break!—Juliet! Juliet! (*dies*.)
JULIET. (*to corpse*.) Am I smothering you?
CORPSE. (*to Juliet*.) Not at all; could you be so kind, do you think, as to put my wig on again for me? — it has fallen off.

JULIET. (*to corpse*.) I'm afraid I can't, but I'll throw my muslin veil over it. You've broken the phial, haven't you?
(*Corpse nodded*.)
JULIET. (*to corpse*.) Where's your dagger?
CORPSE. (*to Juliet*.) 'Pon my soul, I don't know.

Sunday, 13th.

By half-past ten we were packed in what in this country is termed an *exclusive extra*, i. e. a stage-coach to ourselves, and progressing towards Washington. The coach was comfortable enough, and the country, for the first twelve or fifteen miles, owing to the abominable account I had heard of it from every body, disappointed me rather agreeably. It was by no means so dreary or desolate as I had been led to expect. There was considerable variety in its outline, and the quantity of cedar thickets scattered over it took away from the comfortless, threadbare look of the wintry woods. Threadbare, indeed, the trees can scarce be called; for the leaves of the black oak, instead of falling as they fade, remain upon the branches, and give the trees more the effect of being lightning-struck, or accidentally blasted, than withered by the fair course of the seasons. I think the effect is more disagreeable than that of absolutely bare, leafless boughs. When near, the trees look singularly deplorable and untidy, although at the distance, the red-brown of the faded oaks mingling with the bright, vivid, green cedars, and here and there a silver-barked buttonwood tree raising its white delicate branches from among them, produce a very agreeable and harmonious blending to the eye. The soil, the banks by the road-side, and broken ridges of ravines, and water-courses, attracted my attention by the variety and vividness of their colours. The brightest red and yellow, and then again pale green, and rich, warm gravel-colour. I wished I had been a geologist. How much pleasure of reflection and contemplation is lost to the ignorant whose outward sense wanders over the objects that surround it, deriving from them but half the delight that they give the wise and well-informed; even fancy is at fault, for fancy itself scarce devises images more strange, and beautiful, and wonderful, than the reality of things presents to those who understand their properties and natures. The waters were all fast frozen up, and one or two little pools, all curdled with ice, and locked up in deep, gravelly basins, looked like onyx stones set in gold. As for the road, we had been assured it was exceedingly good; but mercy on us! I can't think of it without aching. Here we went up, up, up, and there we went down, down, down, — now, I was in my father's lap, and now I was half out of window. The utter impossibility of holding one's self in any one position for two minutes is absolutely ridiculous. Sometimes we laughed, and at other times we groaned, at our helpless and hopeless condition; but at last we arrived, with no bones broken, at about three o'clock, at the capital and seat of government of the United States. * Upon the

* In most European countries, the seat of government and residence of the ruling powers and foreign ambassadors is the capital, and generally the largest, most populous, most wealthy, and most influential city of the kingdom — the place of all others to which travellers would resort to become acquainted with its political, literary, and social spirit. In this,

height immediately above the city is situated the Capitol, a very handsome building, of which the Americans are not a little proud ; but it seems placed there by mistake, so little do the miserable, untidy hovels above, and the scattered, unfinished red-brick town below, accord with its patrician marble, and high-sounding title. We drove to Gadsby's, which is an inn like a little town, with more wooden galleries, flights of steps, passages, door-ways, exits, and entrances, than any building I ever saw : it reminded me of the house in Tieck's Love-charm. We had not been arrived a quarter of

however, as in most other respects, this country differs from all others ; and the spirit of independence, which renders every state a republic within itself, gives to each its own capital, the superior merits of which are advocated with no little pride and jealousy by the natives of the state to which it belongs. Thus, New York, Boston, Philadelphia, Baltimore, Charleston, and New Orleans, are all capitals ; each of them fulfilling in a much higher degree than Washington the foreigner's idea of that word. Indeed I cannot conceive any thing that would more amaze an European than to be transported into Washington, and told he was in the metropolis of the United States ; nor, indeed, could any thing give him a less just idea of the curious political construction, and widely scattered resources, of the country. Washington, in fact, is to America what Downing and Parliament Streets are to London — a congregation of government offices ; where political characters, secretaries, clerks, place-holders, and place-seekers, most do congregate.

an hour, when in walked Mr. —— and Captain
——, and presently Mr. ——. They sat for
some time, discussing, laughing, quizzing, and
being funny, and then departed. Captain ——
was telling us a story about a man somewhere up
in the lost lands, who was called Philemon, and
whose three sons were paganed (christened, I
suppose, one can't say,) Romulus, Remus, and
Tiberius. I thought this was too good to be
true; and D—— and I, laughing over it at dinner,
agreed that we wished any thing of the sort had
happened to us. " Some bread, waiter: what is
your name? " said I to the black who was waiting
upon us. " Horatius ! " was the reply; which
sent me and D—— into fits.

Monday, 14*th.*

When I came in to breakfast, found Mr. ——,
whom I like mainly. While he was here, Dr.
—— and —— came in. I gave the latter a
most tremendous grasp of the hand: it was like
seeing a bit of England to see him. He said to
me, " Oh, how strange it is to see you here; "
which caused my eyes to fill with tears, for Heaven
knows, it feels strange enough. They had hardly

been seated two minutes, when in rushed a boy to
call us to rehearsal. I was as vexed as might be.
They all departed; —— faithfully promising to
come again, and have a long talk about the old
country: we then set forth to rehearsal. The
theatre is the tiniest little box that ever was seen,
— not much bigger, I verily think, than the
baby's play-house at Versailles. When I came
to perceive who the company were, and that
sundry of our Baltimore comrades were come on
hither, I begged to be excused from rehearsing, as
they had all done their parts but a few days before
with me. At about two o'clock, Mr. —— came
to take us to the Capitol. Mr. —— was in the
drawing-room. He had just seen the President;
and it seems, that far from coming to any accommodation with the South Carolinians, there is an
immediate probability of their coming to blows.
They say, the old General is longing for a fight;
and most assuredly, to fight would be better, in
this instance, than to give in; for to yield would
be virtually to admit the right of every individual
state to dictate to the whole government. We
walked up to the Capitol : the day was most beautifully bright and sunny, and the mass of white building, with its terraces and columns, stood out in fine
relief against the cloudless blue sky. We went

first into the senate, or upper house, because
Webster was speaking, whom I especially wished
to hear. The room itself is neither large nor
lofty ; the senators sit in two semi-circular rows,
turned towards the President, in comfortable arm-
chairs. On the same ground, and literally sitting
among the senators, were a whole regiment of
ladies, whispering, talking, laughing, and fidgeting.
A gallery, level with the floor, and only divided
by a low partition from the main room, ran round
the apartment: this, too, was filled with pink, and
blue, and yellow bonnets; and every now and
then, while the business of the house was going
on, and Webster speaking, a tremendous bustle,
and waving of feathers, and rustling of silks, would
be heard, and in came streaming a reinforcement
of political beauties, and then would commence a
jumping up, a sitting down, a squeezing through,
and a how-d'-ye-doing, and a shaking of hands.
The senators would turn round; even Webster
would hesitate, as if bothered by the row, and, in
short, the whole thing was more irregular, and
unbusiness-like, than any one could have imagined. *   Webster's face is very remarkable,

* As the winter resort of all the leading political men of
the Union, Washington presents many attractions in point of
society. Their wives and daughters, frequently the reigning

particularly the forehead and eyes. The former projects singularly, absolutely overhanging the latter, which have a very melancholy, and occasionally rather wild, expression. The subject upon which he was speaking was not one of particular interest, — an estimate of the amount of French spoliations, by cruizers and privateers, upon the American commerce. The heat of the room was intolerable ; and after sitting till I was nearly suffocated, we adjourned to the House of Representatives. On our way thither, we crossed a very beautiful circular vestibule, which holds the centre of the building. It was adorned with

---

beauties of their respective states and towns, generally accompany them thither during the session ; and this congregating of people from all parts of the country, together with the foreign ministers residing there, and the travellers drawn thither from mere curiosity, combine to give more variety to the gaieties of Washington than those of any of the other cities in the Union can boast. The Capitol is a favourite lounge in the morning; and the American lady-politicians are just as zealous in their respective parties as our own. I don't know, however, that they would much relish listening to a long debate from that dismal hole, the lantern of the House of Commons, where one may listen, indeed, and even just manage to see, but where to *be seen* is an utter impossibility : neither do I think that many of them would stand for four long hours, as Miss —— and poor Lady —— did, during Brougham's famous reform bill speech.

sundry memorable passages in American history
done into pictures, by Colonel Trumbull. In the
House of Representatives we were told we should
hear nothing of interest, so turned off, under Mr.
———'s escort, to the library, which is a comfortable, well-sized room, where we looked over
Audubon's Ornithology, a beautiful work, and
saw a man sitting, with his feet upon the table,
reading, which is an American fashion. Met
half the New York world there. After we had
stayed there some time, we went into the House
of Representatives. The room itself is lofty and
large, and very handsome, but extremely ill constructed for the voice, which is completely lost
among the columns, and only reaches the gallery,
where listeners are admitted, in indistinct and
very unedifying murmurs. The members not unfrequently sit with their feet upon their desks.
We walked out upon the terrace, and looked at
the view of the Potomac, and the town, which, in
spite of the enlivening effect of an almost summer's sky, looked dreary and desolate in the
extreme. We then returned home. At half-
past five, we went to the theatre. We were a long
time before we could discover, among the intricate,
dark little passages, our own private entrance,
and were as nearly as possible being carried into

the pit by a sudden rush of spectators making their way thither : I wish we had been; I think I should like to have seen myself very much. The theatre is absolutely like a doll's play-house : it was completely crammed with people. I played ill; I cannot act tragedy within half a yard of the people in the boxes. By the by, a theatre may very easily be too small for tragedies which is admirably adapted to comedies. In the latter species of dramatic representations, the incidents characters, manners, and dresses, are, for the most part, modern, — such as we meet with, or can easily imagine, in our own drawing-rooms, and among our own society. There is little, if any, exaggeration of colouring necessary, and no great exertion of fancy needful either in the actor or audience in executing and witnessing such a performance. On the contrary, comedy, — high comedy, — generally embodying the manners, tone, and spirit of the higher classes of society, the smaller the space, consistent with ease and grace of carriage, in which such personifications take place, the less danger there is of the actor's departing from that natural, quiet, and refined deportment and delivery, which are, in the present day, the general characteristics of polished society. 'T is otherwise with tragic representations.

They are unnatural, not positively, but comparatively unnatural; the incidents are, for the most
part, strange, startling, unusual; and though they
always must be within possibility, in order to
excite the sympathies of beholders, — though
some of them may even be historical facts, — yet
they are, for the most part, events which come
within the probabilities of few of us, and this
renders necessary a degree of excitement and
elevation in the mind of the spectator, foreign to,
and at variance with, the critical spirit of prosaic
reality. Again, the scene of a comedy is generally a drawing-room; and the smaller the stage,
the greater is the possibility of rendering it absolutely like what we all have seen, and are daily in
the habit of seeing; but to represent groves and
mountains, or lakes, or the dwellings of the kings
of the earth, satisfactorily to the spectator's mind,
there must be a certain distance observed, from
which the fancy may take its stand for the best
perception of what is intended. Whereas, in
closer contact with such scenes, not only does their
immediate proximity convey an unpleasing consciousness of the unreality of the whole, but the
near and absolute detail of paint, canvass, and
gilding, is obtruded in a manner that destroys all
illusion, and, by disturbing the effect of the whole

upon the spectator, necessarily weakens that part
which depends solely upon the actor. The same
thing applies to dress. Foil-stone, paste, and
coloured glass, by French ingenuity, have been
manufactured into toys, which, with the help of
distance, may be admitted as representing the splen-
dours of Eastern costume, or even the glittering trap-
pings of those gaudy little superhumans, the fairies.
But nearness utterly dissolves the spell, and these
substitutes for magnificence become palpable im-
positions, and very often most ludicrous ones. I
have often been accused of studying my attitudes;
but the truth is, that most things that are presented to my imagination, instead of being mere
abstractions, immediately assume form and colour,
and become pictures; these I constantly execute
on the stage as I had previously seen them in my
fancy: but as few pictures as large as life admit
of being seen to best effect immediately close to
the spectator, so the whole effect produced by a
graceful attitude, fine colours, or skilful grouping
on the stage, is considerably diminished when the
space is restricted, and the audience brought too
near the performers. So much for little theatres.
—— came in after the play. He told us that as
he was coming out of the theatre, a Kentuckian
accosted him with, " Well, what do you think of

that 'ere *gal?* " — " Oh," hesitatingly replied
——, " I don't quite know." — " Well," retorted
the questioner, " any how, I guess she 's o' some
account ! "

Tuesday, 15*th.*

At eleven o'clock, Mr. —— called. Went with
him to see the original of the Declaration of Independence, also a few medals, for the most part
modern ones, and neither of much beauty or
curiosity. Afterwards went to the War Office,
where we saw sundry Indian properties, — bows
and arrows, canoes, smoking pipes, and what interested me much more, the pictures of a great
many savage chiefs, and one or two Indian women.
The latter were rather pretty : the men were not
any of them handsome ; scorn round the mouth,
and cunning in the eyes, seemed to be the general
characteristic of all their faces. There was a
portrait of Red Jacket, which gave me a most
unpoetical, low-life impression of that great pa-
laverer. The names of many of them delighted
me, — as, *the Ever-awake ; the Man that stands and
strikes ; the North Wind.* One of the women's
names amused me a great deal, — *the Woman that
poke first ;* which title occasioned infinite surmise

among us as to the occasion on which she earned
it. After we had done seeing what was to be
seen, we went on to the President's house, which
is a comfortless, handsome-looking building, with
a withered grass-plot enclosed in wooden palings
in front, and a desolate reach of uncultivated
ground down to the river behind. Mr. ——
gave us a most entertaining account of the levees,
or rather public days, at the President's house.
Every human being has a right to present himself
there ; the consequence is, that great numbers of
the very commonest sort of people used to rush
in, and follow about the servants who carried refreshments, seizing upon whatever they could get,
and staring and pushing about, to the infinite
discomfiture of the more respectable and better
behaved part of the assembly. Indeed, the nuisance became so great, that they discontinued the
eatables, and in great measure got rid of the
crowd. Mr. —— assured me that on one of these
occasions, two *ladies* had themselves lifted up and
seated on the chimney-piece, in order to have a
better view of the select congregation beneath
them. Mr. —— left us to go to the Capitol, and
we came home. ——, Mr. ——, and Captain
—— called. We sat discussing names ; which,
in this country, are certainly more ambitious

than in any other in the world.* Besides Captain ——'s classical family, Mr. —— assured us that he knew of a man whose name was *Return Jonathan Meigs;* and —— swore to one in New York called *Alonzo Leontes Agamemnon Beaugardus.* I have myself seen *a Harmanus Boggs, Aquila Jones,* and *Alpheus Brett;* but I have not been favoured with an acquaintance with any such names as they quoted. —— appears to me altered since I saw him in England. He was always silent, and quiet, and gentle; but there was an air of complacency and contented cheerfulness

* The love of the sublime and beautiful, those aspirations after something more refined, more exalted and perfect than this world affords, in short, that spiritual propensity classed in its many and various manifestations by the phrenologists under the title of *ideality,* will have some vent, and under circumstances most adverse to its existence, will creep out at some channel or another, and vindicate human nature by flourishing in some shape over the narrowest, homeliest, lowliest, and least favourable guise it may put on. Certainly America is not the country of large idealities, — it is the very reverse; if I may create a bump, it is the country of large realities, *i. e.* large acquisitiveness, large causality, large caution, and small veneration and wonder. Nathless some ideality must needs be, and is, and it creeps out in Christian names. I have heard sempstresses called Amanda and Emmeline, and we had a housemaid in New England called Cynthia. Our village carpenter is named Rudolph; and if the spirit of the people appears to me unimaginative and unpoetical, I take great comfort in their fine names.

about him, which I think he has very much lost:
he looks sad and careworn. I was sorry to see
it. After dinner, sat writing journal. Mr. ——
came in and sat some time with us. He is very
clever and agreeable, and I like him greatly.

Wednesday, 16*th*.

After breakfast, went to rehearsal. At half-past
twelve, Mr. —— came to ride with me. The
horse he had gotten for me was base ; but never
mind, the day was exquisitely mild and bright,—
the sort of early spring-feeling day, when in
England the bright gold, and pale, delicate violet
of the crocus buds begin to break the rich, dark
mould, and the fragrant gummy leaves of the lilac
bushes open their soft brown folds. We had a
very pleasant ride through some pretty woodlands
on the opposite side of the river. At half-past
five, went to the theatre. The play was the
Hunchback : the house was crowded. In the last
scene, Master Walter upbraided me thus : —

> The engineer
> Who lays the last stone of his sea-built tow'r,
> And smiling at it, bids the winds and waves
> To roar and whistle now — but in a night

> Beholds the tempest sporting in its place,
> May look *agash* as I did.

Also in the exclamation, —

> Fathers, make straws your children : nature 's nothing,
> Blood nothing: once in other veins it flows,
> It no more *yawneth* for the parent flood
> Than doth the stream that from the stream disparts.

Mr. —— and —— came in after the play. We had a discussion as to how far real feeling enters into our scenic performances. 'T is hard to say : the general question it would be impossible to answer, for acting is altogether a monstrous anomaly. John Kemble and Mrs. Siddons were always in earnest in what they were about; Miss O'Neill used to cry bitterly in all her tragedy parts; whilst Garrick could be making faces and playing tricks in the middle of his finest points, and Kean would talk gibberish while the people were in an uproar of applause at his. In my own individual instance, I know that sometimes I could turn every word I am saying into burlesque, (*never* Shakspeare, by the by,) and at others my heart aches, and I cry real, bitter, warm tears, as earnestly as if I was in earnest.

Thursday, 17*th.*

Sat writing journal till twelve o'clock, when we
went to Mr. ———'s. Took him up, and thence
proceeded to the Presidency to be presented in
due form. His Excellency Andrew Jackson is
very tall and thin, but erect and dignified in his
carriage — a good specimen of a fine old well-
battered soldier. His hair is very thick and grey :
his manners are perfectly simple and quiet, therefore very good ; so are those of his niece, Mrs.
———, who is a very pretty person, and lady of the
house, Mrs. Jackson having been dead some time.
He talked about South Carolina, and entered his
protest against scribbling ladies, assuring us that
the whole of the present southern disturbances
had their origin in no larger a source than the nib
of the pen of a lady. Truly, if this be true, the
lady must have scribbled to some purpose. We
sat a little more than a quarter of an hour ; Mr.
——— was calling at the same time.* We afterwards adjourned to Mr. ———'s house. * *

* I am neither sufficiently interested nor sufficiently well
informed in the politics of this country to have conceived
any opinion of General Jackson, beyond that which the
floating discussions of the day might suggest. Of his merits

* * * * *

* * * * *

Appointed Mr. —— to come down directly and ride with me. Drove with my father and Mr. —— to leave cards on ——, and then walked home. The day was bright and fine, but very cold. Habited, and at about one o'clock Mr. —— called for me. On going to the door, I found him and his horse, and a strange, tall, grey horse for me, and a young gentleman of the name of ——, to whom I understood it belonged, and whom Mr. —— introduced to me as very anxious to join my party. I was a little startled at this, as I did not quite think Mr. —— ought to have brought any body to ride with me without my

---

as a statesman I am totally incapable of judging, or of the effect which his peculiar policy is calculated to have upon the country. When first I came here I heard and saw that he was the man of the people. In the dispute with South Carolina, his firmness and decision of character struck me a good deal; and when, in consequence of the temporary distress occasioned by his alteration of the currency, a universal howl was for a short time raised against him, which he withstood without a moment's flinching, I honoured him greatly. Of his measures I know nothing, but firmness, determination, decision, I respect above all things; and if the old General is, as they say, very obstinate, why obstinacy is so far more estimable than weakness, *especially* in a ruler, that I think he sins on the right side of the question.

leave. However, as I was riding his horse, I was just as well pleased that he was by, for I don't like having the responsibility of such valuable property as a private gentleman's horse to take care of. I told him this, alleging it as a reason for my preferring to ride an indifferent hack horse, about which I had no such anxiety. He replied that I need have none about his. I told him laughingly that I would give him two dollars for the hire of it, and then I should feel quite happy; all which nonsense passed as nonsense should, without a comment. He is a son of —— ; I thought him tolerably pleasant and well informed.

* * * * *

* * * * *

I would have a man who lived in the wretchedest corner of the earth think his own country the first of countries; for 't is noble and natural, one of the most respectable instincts in the human heart. We rode till half-past three. The horse I was upon was, Mr. —— assured me, an English one, but he had been long enough in this world to learn racking and forget every other more christian pace; he tired me dreadfully. After dinner, wrote journal till time to go to the theatre. The play was the School for Scandal; in the fourth act of which Joseph Surface assured me that *I was a plethora ! ! !* — Mr. —— came in and supped with us after the play.   He gave us a very interesting account of a school that had been attempted to be formed in Massachussetts, for the purpose of educating young men of the savage tribes, who were willing to become Christians, and receive instruction. It was obliged, however, to be given up, in consequence of several of them having fallen in love with and married American girls, whom they took away into the woods, many of them after they were there returning to their savage ways of living, which must have placed their wretched Christian wives in a horrible situation.

Friday, 18*th.*

At eleven, Mr. —— called to take D—— and myself to the War Office : I wanted her to see the Indian spoils there.   On our way thither, he read us some very pretty verses which he had written upon the subject of the " woman who spoke first." When we had seen what we wanted to see we returned home, and I began to habit.   While doing so, received a most comical Yankee note, signed by Mr. ——, but written, I am sure, by Captain ——, to apprize me that the former was unwell, but that he, Captain ——, would accompany me on horseback, if I pleased. The note was exquisite. I finished dressing, and then we set off. I charged Captain —— with the note, and he pleaded guilty, — the thing was evident. While we were riding, Captain —— told me sundry most exquisite native morceaux, and one thing that half-killed me with laughing. Mr. ——'s negro servant and Mr. ——'s conversing together about me, one asked the other if he had seen me yet at the theatre, to which Mr. ——'s man replied, " No, sir ; I have had the pleasure of seeing Miss Kemble in private society :" — he brings my horse down every morning for me !

* * * * *
* * * * *

Perhaps, after all, life is worth no more than a laugh, and all its strange mysteries of sin and suffering, its summer dreams of excellence innate and to be acquired, its fond yearning affections, its deep passions, its high and glorious tendings,—all but jests to make the worldly-wise smile, and the believers in them despair. God keep me from such thoughts ! — they are dreadful !   *
* * * * *
* * * * *

After dinner, wrote journal. At half-past five, went to the theatre : the play was the Hunchback,

— the house was very good. I wonder if any body on earth can form the slightest idea of the interior of this wretched little theatre; 't is the smallest I ever was in. The proprietors are poor, the actors poorer; and the grotesque mixture of misery, vulgarity, stage-finery, and real raggedness, is beyond every thing strange, and sad, and revolting, — it reminds me constantly of some of Hogarth's pictures, and passages in Goethe's Wilhelm Meister. After the play, came home and supped. By the by, just as I had done breakfast this morning Judge —— called, who is the most exquisite original I have met with even in this land of their abundance. He gave me a long scolding for getting up so late, and assured me that I meant to settle in this country, at the same time drawing an enchanting picture of rural happiness to the west, — a cottage by a rivulet, with two cows, and just enough to starve upon ! — I think I see myself there. This sentimental prophecy was prefaced by a remark that he knew I was very romantic, and interrupted every two minutes by a dexterous expectoral interjection, which caused me nearly to jump off my chair with dismay.

Saturday, 19*th.*

Giorno d'orrore!—but I wo'n't anticipate. They
have settled to act Much Ado about Nothing,
instead of the Inconstant. I have no clothes for
Beatrice, — but that don't matter. After breakfast, went to rehearsal, and then walked with my
father to see a very pretty model of what is to be
the town-hall. It never will be, for the corpor-
ation are as poor as *Job's kittens,* (Americanism—
communicated by Captain ——,) and the city of
Washington itself is only kept alive by Congress.
Talking of the city of Washington, — 't is the
strangest thing by way of a town that can be
fancied. It is laid out to cover, I should think,
some ten miles square, but the houses are here,
there, and no where: the streets, conventionally,
not properly so called, are roads, crooked or
straight, where buildings are *intended* to be.
Every now and then an interesting gap of a quarter of a mile occurs between those houses that
are built: in the midst of the town, you can't help
fancying you are in the country; and between
wooden palings, with nothing to be seen on either
side but cedar bushes and sand, you are informed
you are in the midst of the town. The Elysian

fields is a broken patch of moorland, sand, and
gravel: the Jardin des Plantes is a nursery-
ground full of slips of shrubs a foot and a half
high; the Tiber, alias Goose Creek, is an unhappy-
looking ditch; — and Washington altogether
struck me as a rambling, red-brick image of futurity,
where nothing *is*, but all things *are to be*. Came
home and habited. At half-past twelve, Captain
—— came for me; just as we were going, ——
called. He was on horseback, and asked leave
to join us, which I agreed to very readily. He
was pilot, and led us round and about through
the woods, and across the waters; all of which, as
Captain —— observed, was in the day's work.
We returned at half-past three. Directly after
dinner, I set out to pay sundry cards. The day
had been heavenly, — bright, and warm, and
balmy; the evening was beautifully soft; and as
I drove over hill and dale, marsh and moorland,
through the city of Washington, paying my cards,
the stars came out one after another in the still
sky, and the scattered lights of the town looked
like a capricious congregation of Jack-o'-lanterns,
some high, some low, some here, some there,
showing more distinctly, by the dark spaces between them, the enormous share that emptiness
has in the congressional city. One of my visits

lay nearly three miles out of town, so that I was not back until six o'clock. As I came rushing along the corridor, I met D—— coming to meet me, who exclaimed, with an air of mingled horror and satisfaction, " Oh, here you are! — here is coffee and Mr. —— waiting for you! " I went into the room, and found a goodly-looking personage, old enough to know better, sitting with my father, who appeared amazingly disturbed, held an open letter in his hand, and exclaimed, the moment I came in, " There, sir, there is the young lady to speak for herself." I courtesied, and sat down. " Fanny," quoth my father, " something particularly disagreeable has occurred, — pray, can you call to mind any thing you said during the course of your Thursday's ride, which was likely to be offensive to Mr. ——, or any thing abusive of this country? " As I have already had sundry specimens of the great talent there is for tattle in the exclusive coteries of this gossiping new world, I merely untied my bonnet, and replied, that I did not at that moment recollect a word that I had said during my whole ride, and should certainly not give myself any trouble to do so. " Now, my dear," said my father, his own eyes flashing with indignation, " don't put yourself into a passion ; compose yourself, and recollect.

Here is a letter I have just received." He proceeded to read it, and the contents were to this
effect — that during my ride with Mr. —— I
had said I did n ot choose to ride an American
gentleman's horse, and *had offered him two dollars
for the hire of his ;* that, moreover, I had spoken
most derogatorily of America and Americans ; in
consequence of all which, if my father did not
give some explanation, or make some apology to
the public, I should certainly be hissed off the
stage, as soon as I appeared on it that evening.
This was pleasant. I stated the conversation as it
had passed, adding, that as to any sentiments a
person might express on any subject, liberty of
opinion, and liberty of speech, were alike rights
which belonged to every body, and that, with a
due regard to good feeling, and good breeding,
they were rights which nobody ought, and I never
would forego. Mr. —— opened his eyes. I
longed to add, that any conversation between me
and any other person was nobody's business but
mine, and his or hers, and that the whole thing
was, on the part of the young gentleman concerned, the greatest piece of blackguardism, and
on that of the old gentleman concerned, the
greatest piece of twaddle, that it had ever been
my good fortune to hear of. " For," said Mr.

———, " not less than *fifty* members of Congress have already mentioned the matter to me." Fifty old gossiping women ! why the whole thing is for all the world like a village tattle in England, among half a dozen old wives round their tea-pots. All Washington was in dismay; and my evil deeds and evil words were the town talk, — fields, gaps, marshes, and all, rang with them. This is an agreeable circumstance, and a display of national character highly entertaining and curious.* It gave

---

* The national vanity of the French, and pride and pre-judice of the English, are proverbial : it is, however, fortu-nate for both that they carry these qualities to such an excess, that it is a matter of extreme difficulty to shake the good opinion which they entertain of themselves. Thus, foreigners may visit England, as Frenchmen have done, and swear that the sun never shines there, and that the only ripe fruit the country affords is roasted apples. John Bull, nothing wrath, wraps himself still closer in his own dear self-approval, and in the plentitude of self-content, drinks his brown stout, and basks by gas-light. On his part, he goes over to Paris, votes the whole *beau pays de France* horrible, because he can't get port wine to drink, or boiled potatoes to eat; in spite of which, Monsieur does not attempt to turn him out of his country, but eats his ragouts, and drinks his chably, and shrugs his shoulders at the savage islander, from the seventh heaven of self-satisfaction. It were much to be desired that Americans had a little *more* national vanity, or national pride. Such an unhappily sensitive community surely never existed in this world ; and the vengeance with which they visit people for saying they don't admire or like them, would

me at the time, however, a dreadful side-ache, and nervous cough. I went to the theatre, dressed, and came on the stage in the full expectation of being hissed off it, which is a pleasant sensation, very, and made my heart full of bitterness to think I should stand, — as no woman ought to stand, — the mark of public insult. However, no such thing occurred, — I went on and came off without any such trial of my courage; but I had been so much annoyed, and was still so indignant, that I passed the intervals between my scenes in

---

be really terrible if the said people were but as mortally afraid of abuse as they seem to be. I would not advise either Mrs. Trollope, Basil Hall, or Captain Hamilton, ever to set their feet upon this ground again, unless they are ambitious of being stoned to death. I live myself in daily expectation of martyrdom; and as for any body attempting to earn a livelihood here who has but as much as said he prefers the country where he was born to this, he would stand a much better chance of thriving if he were to begin business after confinement in the penitentiary. This unhappy species of irritability is carried to such a degree here, that if you express an unfavourable opinion of any thing, the people are absolutely astonished at your temerity. I remember, to my no little amusement, a lady saying to me once, " I hear you are going to abuse us dreadfully; of course, you 'll wait till you go back to England, and then shower it down upon us finely." I assured her I was not in the least afraid of staying where I was, and saying what I thought at the same time.

crying, — which, of course, added greatly to the mirth and spirit of my performance of Beatrice. In the middle of the play, Mr. —— and Captain —— came behind the scenes, and then, indeed, I *was* quite glad to see Englishmen; though their compassionate sympathies for my wrongs, and tender fears lest I should catch cold behind those horrid scenes, very nearly set me off crying again. A soft word, when one is in deep commiseration of one's self, is very apt to open the flood-gates; but I was ashamed to cry before them, so tried to keep my heart-swellings down. When the play was over, came home. Mr. —— came and supped with us. By the by, he called this morning before I went out riding, and expressed many sorrows at our departure. He is a clever and extremely well-informed man, and I like him very much. When he was gone, sat talking over the —— affair. My father was in a greater passion than I think I ever saw him before. I am sure I would not have warranted one of that worthy young gentleman's bones, if he had fallen in with him. I am very glad he did not; for, to knock a man down, even though he does deserve it, is a serious matter rather.

Wednesday, 30*th,*
Philadelphia.

After breakfast, practised for an hour : wrote journal.   Mr. ——, the wild-eyed, flowing-haired, white-waistcoated, velvet-collared, —— —— called upon me.   He sat some time asking me questions; but, since the —— affair, I have grown rather afraid of opening my mouth, and he had the conversation chiefly to himself. Finished journal; dined at half-past three: after dinner, went and sat with Mrs. ——.   One Mr. ——, a Boston man who was at Mrs. ——'s ball last night, was in her room.   I was introduced to him, and he spoke of the ——'s.   *   *   *

*   *   *   *   *

*   *   *   *   *

Sat with them till coffee-time. Went to the theatre at half-past five.   It poured with rain, in spite of which the house was very good: the play was Fazio.   When I came on in my fine dress, at the beginning of the second act, the people hailed me with such a tremendous burst of applause, and prolonged it so much, that I was greatly puzzled to imagine what on earth possessed them.   I concluded they were pleased with my dress, but could not help being rather amused at their vehement and continued clapping, considering they had seen it several times before. However, they ceased at last, and I thought no more about it. Towards the time for the beginning of the third act, which opens with my being discovered waiting for Fazio's return, as I was sitting in my dressing-room working, D—— suddenly exclaimed, " Hark ! — what is that?" —— opened the door, and we heard a tremendous noise of shouts and of applause. " They are waiting for you, certainly," said D——. She ran out, and returned, saying, " The stage is certainly waiting for you, Fanny, for the curtain is up." I rushed out of the room ; but on opening the door leading to the stage, I distinctly heard my father's voice addressing the audience. I turned sick with a sort of indefinite apprehension, and on enquiry found that at the beginning of the play a number of handbills had been thrown into the pit, professing to quote my conversation with Mr. —— at Washington, and calling upon the people to resent my conduct in the grossest and most vulgar terms. This precious document had, it seems, been brought round by somebody to my father, who immediately went on with it in his hand, and assured the audience that the whole thing was a falsehood. I scarce heard what he said, though I stood at the side scene: I was crying dreadfully with fright and indignation. How I wished I was a caterpillar under a green goose-berry-bush!   *   *   *   *

*   *   *   *   *

*   *   *   *   *

Oh, how I did wince to think of going on again after this scene, though the feeling of the audience was most evident; for all the applause I had fancied they bestowed upon my dress, was, in fact, an un-solicited testimony of their disbelief in the accus-ation brought against me. They received my father's words with acclamations; and when the curtain drew up, and I was discovered, the pit rose and waved their hats, and the applause was tremendous. I was crying dreadfully, and could hardly speak; however, I mastered myself and went on with my part, — though, what with the dreadful exertion that it is in itself, and the pain-ful excitement I had just undergone, I thought I should have fainted before I got through with it.

*   *   *   *   *

*   *   *   *   *

Saturday, Feb. 2d.

After breakfast, —— called to see how I did after my walk : he sat for some time. At twelve, went out paying bills and calls ; bought a German eolina ; sat some time with old Mrs. ——, and spent a delightful hour with Mr. —— and his family. He is a most agreeable person, but he thinks too well of acting. · Came home ; dined at three; Mr. and Mrs. —— dined with us. After dinner, went into her room, and remained there till time to go to the theatre. Young —— and Dr. —— came in. The play was the Gamester : it was my benefit, and I am afraid the good folks who addressed that amiable placard to the public will have been rather ill satisfied with their suggestion about my benefit. The house was literally crammed, in consequence of that very circumstance, — crammed is the word. When the curtain drew up, they applauded me without end, and I courtesied as profoundly as I was able ; indeed, I am extremely obliged to this same excellent public, for they have testified most satisfactorily every way the kindest feeling possible for me, and the most entire faith in my good behaviour. I did not play well, my voice was so dreadfully affected by my cough.

Monday, 4th.

Dined at three. After dinner, Mrs. —— came into our room, where I sang and played till time to go to the theatre. The play was the Merchant of Venice, and Katharine and Petruchio for the farce; — my father's benefit: the house was crammed from floor to ceiling as full as it could hold: so much for the success of the hand-bills. Indeed, as somebody suggested, I think if we could find the author of that placard out we are bound to give him a handsome reward, for he certainly has given us two of the finest benefits that ever were seen. I heard that a man said the other day that he should not be surprised if *my father had got the whole of this up himself.* Oh, day and night! that such thoughts should come into any human being's head.* At the end, the people shouted and shriek- ed for us. He went on, and made them a speech, and I went on and made them a courtesy; and

---

* I have been assured, I know not how truly, that the whole of this affair originated with an *Englishman.* This piece of information was given me by a person who said he knew such to be the fact, and also knew the man.

certainly they do deserve the civillest of speeches, and lowest of courtesies from us, for they have behaved most kindly and courteously to us ; and for mine own good part, I love the whole city of Philadelphia from this time forth, for ever more.*

* It may not be amiss here to say one word with regard to the *gratitude* which audiences in some parts of the world claim from actors, and about which I have lately heard a most alarming outcry. Do actors generally exercise their profession to please themselves and gratify their own especial delight in self-exhibition ? Is that profession in its highest walks one of small physical exertion and fatigue (I say nothing of mental exertion), and in its lower paths is it one of much gain, glory, or ease ? Do audiences, on the other hand, use to come in crowds to play-houses to see indifferent performers ? and when there, do they, out of pure charity and good-will, bestow their applause as well as their money upon tiresome performances ? I will answer these points as far as regards myself, and therein express the gratitude which I feel towards the frequenters of theatres. I individually disliked my profession, and had neither pride nor pleasure in the exercise of it. I exercised it as a matter of necessity, to earn my bread, — and verily it was in the sweat of my brow. The parts which fell to my lot were of a most laborious nature, and occasioned sometimes violent mental excitement, always immense physical exertion, and sometimes both. In those humbler walks of my profession, from whose wearisomeness I was exempted by my sudden favour with the public, I have seen, though not known, the most painful drudgery, — the most constant fatigue, — the most sad contrast between real cares and feigned merriments, — the most anxious penurious and laborious existence imaginable. For the part of my questions which regarded the audiences, I

Mr. —— came round to the stage door to bid us good-night; and as we drove off, a whole parcel

---

have only to say, that I never knew, saw, heard, or read of any set of people who went to a play-house to see what they did not like; this being the case, it never occurred to me that our houses were full but as a necessary consequence of our own attraction, or that we were applauded but as the result of our own exertions. I was glad the houses were full, because I was earning my livelihood, and wanted the money; and I was glad the people applauded us, because it is pleasant to please, and human vanity will find some sweetness in praise, even when reason weighs its worth most justly. Thus I cannot say that in general I had any great *gratitude* towards my audiences. Once or twice, however, that feeling was excited between me and my witnesses, and the circumstance of which I have spoken in my journal was one of the instances. But this was a different matter altogether. I was no longer before an audience labouring for their approbation as an actress. I was dragged before so many judges in my own person, to answer for words spoken in private conversation. The same clapping of hands with which they rewarded my exertions in my profession, was the only method by which they could intimate the " not guilty," which was their judgment upon the appeal that had been made to them against me; but with this difference, that I never felt *obliged* to them, or *grateful* for their applause before, and did feel obliged and grateful for their verdict then. Now, as regards the benefit-nights of actors, I do not observe that even on these occasions much *gratitude* is owing to the people who attend them; for I know, and so does every member of the profession, that the oldest and best actor on any stage, — the one who for a series of years has appeared

of folk, who had gathered round the door to see us
depart, set up a universal hurrah ! How strange

---

before audiences to whom his private respectability and worth
were well known, — the longest established *favourite* of the
public (as they are termed), will assuredly have empty
houses on his benefit-nights, if, trusting to the feeling of
that public, to whom he owes so much gratitude, he failed
to secure the assistance of whatever star (tragedian, panto-
mimist, or dancing dog, it matters not which), happens to be
the newest object of attraction. I speak all this more particularly as regards this country, for it is here that I have
heard most of this species of cant. Gratitude is a good
word and an excellent thing, and neither in speaking or acting should it be misapplied. In the aristocratical lands over
the water, this nonsense about patronage might surprise one
less; but in America it seems strange there should be any
mistake about a simple matter of traffic — 't is nothing in
life else. We give our health, our strength, our leisure, and
our pleasure, for your money and your applause, neither of
which do we beg or borrow from you. This being the case,
where lies the obligation, and where the gratitude? As to
the pretty speeches which actors make when called from behind the curtain, they always appeared to me very much of the
same order as advertisements in newspapers — A. D. returns
his grateful acknowledgments to the public for their liberal
support, &c. &c. That calling performers on after a play is
a foreign, not an English, custom, and, to my mind, one
more honoured in the breach than in the observance. Extraordinary occasions might warrant extraordinary demonstra-
tions; but it is a pity to make that a common ceremony,
which, rarely granted, would be a gratifying testimony of
feeling, and excite rational *gratitude* in those on whom it
was conferred.

a thing it is, that popular shout.   After all, Pitt
or Canning could get no more for the finest oratory
that human lips ever uttered, or the wisest policy
that human brain ever devised.   Sometimes they
got the reverse; but then the *hereafter* — there's
the rub !   Praise is so sweet to me that I would
have it lasting : above all, I would wish to feel
that I deserved it.   I must do so if I am to value
it a straw; and acting, even the best that ever was
seen, is, to my mind, but a poor claim to approbation.   I think the applause of an audience in a
play-house should be reckoned with the friendly
and favourable opinions of a good-natured tipsy
man,—'t is given under excitement.   Oh Lord !
how unsatisfactory all things are.

> *Wednesday,* 13*th,*
> *New York.*

After dinner, —— came in.   He sat himself
down, and presently was overhead in reminiscences.
His account of Tom Paine's escape from the Con-
ciergerie, on the eve of being guillotined, was
extremely interesting.   His own introduction to,
and subsequent acquaintance with, that worthy,
was equally so, and his summing up was highly

characteristic. " I tell ye, madam, the saving of
that man's life was an especial providence, that he
might come over to this country, where his works
have done so much harm, and might have done so
much more, and just exemplify the result of his
own principles put into practice in his own person, and show that the glorious light of reason,
and the noble natural gifts of man, of which he
preached so much, would neither prevent a man's
becoming a drunkard and a spendthrift, nor a
debased, degraded being. If Paine had been
guillotined, madam, he would have been a martyr,
and his works would have had ten times the
power of evil they had before. But he lived to
be a miserable, low unthrift, and sot, and died
neglected and despised by all reputable and respectable individuals, and I say again, it was a
manifest providence that he did so." We left
the gentlemen to their wine for a short time, but
were presently summoned back. —— had gone
to the theatre. —— began his history to me,
and it was, word for word, a repetition of Galt's
book, except that occasionally it was more touching. The pity of all this is, the man's own consciousness that he is a lion. His vanity is almost
as amusing as his recollections are curious and
interesting; and though the tears were in my eye

several times while he described the blessed time
he lived with his sweet Phebe, yet at others, I
could scarce help exclaiming, in the words of his
own countryman, " Heigh, cretur, cretur ! thou
hast unco plause o' thysel' ! " He ended his narrative with a eulogy of women that would have
warmed the heart of a stone ; and to my utter
surprise, addressed Mr. —— with, " Out upon
ye, bachelors, all ! ye throw away your lives, and
your life's happiness ! " This last attack of ——'s
seemed too much for Mr. —— ; and, as I turned
to him with the tears in my eyes, to desire he would
not laugh, which he was doing very heartily, he said
he couldn't stand it any longer, and went away,
apparently more amused than edified by ——'s
appeal.

Thursday, 14*th.*

St. Valentine's day ! I wish all these pretty,
golden days, which, like the flowers in the sun-
dial of Linnæus, were wont so gaily to mark the
flight of time, were not becoming so dim in our
calendars ; I wish St. Valentine's day, and May
morning, and Christmas day, and New-Year's
day, were not putting off their holyday suits to
wear the work-day russet of their drudging fel-

lows; I wish we were not making all things, of all sorts, so completely of a neutral tint. *

* * * * *

* * * * *

I wouldn't be in the Reform Parliament of England for ten thousand pounds! ——, and ——, the bruiser, and the bankrupt! Oh, shame, England, shame! — Poor England!

A RHAPSODY.

White lady, sitting on the sea,
Tell to me, oh, tell to me,
How long shall thy reigning be,
White lady, sitting on the sea?

Long as the oak with which I'm crown'd
Shall bear one leaf above the ground,
Round which the crawling ivy's grasp
Its cursed tendrils does not clasp;
Long as one foot remains to stand
Firm on its own ancestral land;
Or one true man be left to claim
The burden of a noble name;
Long as one Gothic shrine shall rise
With 'scutcheon'd tomb, and banner'd stall,
Or the blest glances of the skies,
Through storied casements dimly fall;
Long as one heart shall beat to hear
Legends of the old, valiant time;

Long as the Sabbath wind shall bear
The music of one haunting chime.

> White lady, sitting on the sea,
> Tell to me, oh, tell to me,
> When shall thy downfalling be,
> White lady, sitting on the sea?

When the vile kennel mud is thrown
Upon the ermine of the king,
And the old worships are cast down
Before a rabble's triumphing;
When toothless —— is young again
To do the mischief he but dreams,
And little —— shall make more plain
The good that glitters through his schemes;
When the steam engine of the north
Leaves making essays and wry faces;
And patriot Whigs forget the worth
Of pensions, power, pride, and places;
When on the spot where Burke and Pitt
Earn'd their high immortality,
Boxers and bankrupts boldly sit,
Then, then shall my downfalling be.

Monday, 18*th.*

After breakfast, went to rehearsal; came home
and stitched at my *Françoise de Foix* head-dress.
My father is extremely unwell; I scarce think he
will be able to get through his part to-night.

After dinner, practised, and read a canto in Dante. It pleases me when I refer to Biagioli's notes, to find that the very lines Alfieri has noted, are those under which I have drawn my emphatic pencil marks. At half-past five, went to the theatre. The play was Macbeth, for my benefit : the house was very full, and I played very ill. My father was dreadfully exhausted by his work. I had an interesting discussion with Mr. —— about the costume and acting of the witches in this awful play. I should like to see them acted and dressed a little more like what they should be, than they generally are. It has been always customary, — heaven only knows why, — to make low comedians act the witches, and to dress them like old fish-women. Instead of the wild unearthly appearance which Banquo describes, and which belongs to their most terrible and grotesquely poetical existence and surroundings, we have three jolly-faced fellows, — whom we are accustomed to laugh at, night after night, in every farce on the stage, — with as due a proportion of petticoats as any woman, letting alone witch, might desire, jocose red faces, peaked hats, and broomsticks, which last addition alone makes their costume different from that of Moll Flagon. If I had the casting of Macbeth, I would give the witches to the first melo-dramatic actors on the stage, — such men as T. P. Cooke, and O. Smith, who understand all that belongs to picturesque devilry to perfection, — and give them such dresses, as, without ceasing to be grotesque, should be a little more fanciful, and less ridiculous than the established livery; something that would accord a little better with the blasted heath, the dark, fungus-grown wood, the desolate, misty hill-side, and the flickering light of the caldron cave. †

* * * * *

* * * * *

† I would recommend Retsch's etchings of Macbeth to the study of all representatives of the witches : there is great sublimity and fearfulness in their figures and attitudes. By the by, in looking over those unique etchings (I mean *all* those he has executed), the colossal genius of Shakspeare is brought more fully in its vastness to our conviction ; for the genius of the artist, — which has fallen no whit behind the first work of one of the first men of this age, — sinks in utter impotence under the task of illustrating Shakspeare. The wonder, and the beauty, and the pity of Faust, are as strong and true in the outlines of Retsch, as in the words of Goethe — the drawings equal the poem; 't is the highest praise they can receive: and it is only when we turn from these perfect works, to contemplate his outlines of Shakspeare, that we feel, by the force of comparison, how unutterably beyond all other conceptions are those of Shakspeare. Retsch's etchings, both of Hamlet and Macbeth, are, compared with his German illustrations, failures. Hamlet is the better of the two; but he seems to have quailed under the other in utter

Wednesday, 20*th.*

After breakfast, —— and Mr. —— came. —— gave me the words and tune of a bewitching old English ballad. Mr. —— called and sat some time with me : I like him mainly, — he's very pleasant and clever. That handsome creature, Mme. ——, called with her daughter and her son-in-law. Mr. —— and —— dined with us. After dinner, came to my own room, sang over ——'s ballad, and amused myself with writing one of my own. At half-past five, took coffee, and off to the theatre. The house was very full; play, the Stranger : I didn't play well : I 'd a gown on that did not fit me, to which species of accident our *art* is marvellously subservient; for a tight arm-hole shall mar the grandest passage in Queen Constance, and too long or too short a skirt keep one's heart cold in the balcony scene in Juliet. Came home ; supped; finished marking the Winter's Tale. What a dense fool that fat old Johnson must have been in matters of poetry ! his notes upon Shakspeare make one swear, and his summing up

---

inability— Macbeth himself falls far short of all that he should be made to express; and as to Lady Macbeth, Retsch seems to have thought he had better not meddle with her.

of the Winter's Tale is worthy of a newspaper
critic of the present day, — in spirit, I mean, not
language ; Dr. Johnson always wrote good English. — What dry, and sapless, and dusty earth
his soul must have been made of, poor fat man !
After all, 't is even a greater misfortune than fault
to be so incapable of beauty.   *   *

      *   *   *   *   *
      *   *   *   *   *

BALLAD.

The Lord's son stood at the clear spring head,
  The May on the other side,
" And stretch me your lily hand," he said,
  " For I must mount and ride.

" And waft me a kiss across the brook,
  And a curl of your yellow hair ;
Come summer or winter, I ne'er shall look
  Again on your eyes so fair.

" Bring me my coal-black steed, my squire,
  Bring Fleetfoot forth !" he cried ;
" For three-score miles he must not tire,
  To bear me to my bride.

" His foot must be swift, though my heart be slow ;
  He carries me towards my sorrow ;
To the Earl's proud daughter I made my vow,
  And I must wed her to-morrow."

The Lord's son stood at the altar stone, —
   The Earl's proud daughter near:
" And what is that ring you have gotten on,
   That you kiss so oft and so dear?

" Is it a ring of the yellow gold,
   Or something more precious and bright
Give me that ring in my hand to hold,
   Or I plight ye no troth to-night."

" It is not a ring of the yellow gold,
   But something more precious and bright;
But never shall hand, save my hand, hold
   This ring by day or night."

" And now I am your wedded wife,
   Give me the ring, I pray." —
" You may take my lands, you may take my life,
   But never this ring away."

They sat at the board; and the lady bride
   Red wine in a goblet pour'd;
" And pledge me a health, sweet sir," she cried,
   " My husband and my lord."

The cup to his lips he had scarcely press'd,
   When he gasping drew his breath,
His head sank down on his heaving breast,
   And he said, " It is death! it is death! —

" Oh, bury me under the gay green shaw
   By the brook, 'neath the heathery sod,
Where last her blessed eyes I saw,
   Where her blessed feet last trod! "

Saturday, 23d.

We came home at two. —— and the horses were waiting for me: we mounted and rode down to the Hoboken ferry, where we crossed. The day was like an early day in spring in England; a day when the almond trees would all have been in flower, the hawthorn hedges putting forth their tender green and brown shoots, and the primroses gemming the mossy roots of the trees by the water-courses. The spring is backwarder here a good deal than with us: to be sure, it is sudden compared with ours, — as my poetising friend hath it, —

> " Not with slow steps, in smiles, in tears advancing,
>   But with a bound, like Indian girls in dancing."

I do not like this : I like to linger over the sweet hourly and daily fulfilment of hope, which the slow progress of vegetation in my own dear country allows one full enjoyment of; to watch the leaf from the bark, the blossom from the bud; the delicate, pale-white, peeping heads of the hawthorn, to the fragrant, snowy, delicious flush of flowering; the downy green clusters of small round buds on the apple trees, to the exquisite, rosy-tinted clouds of soft blossoms waving against an evening sky. The melted snow had made the roads all but impassable; however, the day was delightfully mild and sunny, and therefore we did not get chilled by the very temperate rate at which we were obliged to proceed. We turned off to look at the Turtle Pavilion, and pursuing the water's edge, got up upon a species of high dyke between some marshes that open into the river. Our path, however, was presently intercepted by a stile, and as the horses were not quite of the sort one could have risked a leap with, —— got off and endeavoured to lead his charger round the edge of the steep bank, but the brute refused that road, and we were forced to turn back; and, after floundering about over some of the roughest, worst ground imaginable, we e'en went out of the Hoboken domain at the gate where we entered, and pursued that beautiful road overlooking the Hudson, under that fine range of cliffs which are the first idea, as it were, of the Palisadoes. We took the lower road down into the glen below Weehawk. The sun shone gloriously: the little fairy stream that owns this narrow glade was singing and dancing along its beautiful domain with a sweet, gleesome voice, and a succession of little sparkling breaks and eddies that looked like

laughter. We left the muddy road, and turned
our horses into the stream; but its bed was very
stony and uneven, and we were obliged to turn
out of it again. We rode like very impudent
persons up to the house on the height. The house
itself is too unsheltered for comfort either in
summer or winter, but the view from its site is
beautiful, and we had it in perfection to-day.
Standing at an elevation of more than a hundred
feet from the river, we looked down its magnificent, broad, silvery avenue, to the Narrows —
that rocky gate that opens towards my home.
New York lay bright and distinct on the opposite
shore, glittering like a heap of toys in the sunny
distance: the water towards Sandy Hook was
studded with sails; and far up on the other side
the river rolled away among shores that, even in
this wintry time of bare trees and barren earth,
looked gay and lovely in the sunshine. We turned
down again; but after crossing the bridge over the
pretty brook, we took an upper path to the right,
and riding through some leafless, warm, sunny
woodlands, joined the road that leads to the Wee-
hawken height, and so returned to New York.
On our way, discussing the difference between religion as felt by men and women, —— agreed
with me, that hardly one man out of five thousand

held any distinct and definite religious belief. He said that religion was a sentiment, and that as regarded all creeds, there was no midway with them; that entire faith or utter disbelief were the only alternatives; for that displacing one jot of any of them made the whole totter, —which last is, in some measure, true, but I do not think it is true that religion is *only* a sentiment. There are many reasons why women are more religious than men. Our minds are not generally naturally analytical— our educations tend to render them still less so: 't is seldom in a woman's desire (because seldom in her capacity) to investigate the abstract bearings of any metaphysical subject. Our imaginations are exceedingly sensitive, our subservience to early impressions, and exterior forms, proportionate; and our habits of thought, little enlarged by experience, observation, or proper culture, render us utterly incapable of almost any logical train of reasonings. With us, I think, therefore, faith is the only secure hold; for disbelief, acting upon mental constructions so faulty and weak, would probably engender insanity, or a thousand species of vague, wild, and mischievous enthusiasms.* I believe, too, that women are more

---

* I wonder how long it will be before men begin to consider the rational education of the mothers of their children

religious than men, because they have warmer and deeper affections. There is nothing surely on earth that can satisfy and utterly fulfil the capacity for loving which exists in every woman's nature. Even when her situation in life is such as to call forth and constantly keep in exercise the best affections of her heart, as a wife, and a mother, it still seems to me as if more would be wanting to

---

a matter of some little moment. How much longer are we to lead existences burdensome to ourselves and useless to others, under the influence of every species of ill training that can be imagined? How much longer are the physical evils under which our nature labours to be increased by effeminate, slothful, careless, unwholesome habits? How much longer are our minds, naturally weakened by the action of a highly sensitive nervous construction, to be abandoned, or rather devoted to studies the least likely to strengthen and ennoble them, and render them independent, in some measure, of the infirmities of our bodies? How much longer are our imaginations and feelings to be the only portions of our spiritual nature on which culture is bestowed? Surely it were generous in those who are our earthly disposers to do something to raise us from the state of half-improvement in which we are suffered to linger. If our capacities are inferior to those of men, — which I believe, as much as I believe our bodies to be inferior to theirs in strength, swiftness, and endurance, — let us not be overwhelmed with all the additional shackles that foolish and vain bringing up can add; let us at least be made as strong in body and as wise in mind as we can, instead of being devoted to spiritual, mental, and physical weakness, far beyond that which we inherit from nature.

fill the measure of yearning tenderness, which, like an eternal fountain, gushes up in every woman's heart; therefore I think it is that we turn, in the plenitude of our affections, to that belief which is a religion of love, and where the broadest channel is open to receive the devotedness, the clinging, the confiding trustfulness, which are idolatry when spent upon creatures like ourselves, but become a holy worship when offered to Heaven.*   Nor is it only from the abundance and overflowing of our affections that we are devout; 't is not only from our capacity of loving, but also from our capacity of suffering, that our piety springs.   Woman's physical existence, compared with that of man, is one of incessant endurance.   This in itself begets a necessity for patience, a seeking after strength, a holding forth of the hands for support; thus, the fragile frame, the loving heart, and the ignorant mind, are in us sources of religious faith.   But it often happens that those affections, so strong, so deep, so making up the sum and substance of female existence, instead of being happily employed, as I have supposed above, are converted into springs of acute

---

* Was it not Mme. de Sévigné who said with such truth and bitter satire, " Mme. de —— s'est jetée dans la dévotion, c'est a dire, elle a changé d'amant ? "

suffering. These wells of feeling hidden in the soul, upon whose surface the slightest smile of affection falls like sunlight, but whose very depths are stirred by the breath of unkindness, are too often unvisited by the kindly influence of kindred sympathies, and go wearing their own channels deeper, in silence and in secrecy, and in infinite bitterness, — undermining health, happiness, the joy of life, and making existence one succession of burden-bearing days, and toilsome, aching, heavy hours. It is in this species of blight, which falls upon many women, that any religious faith becomes a refuge and a consolation, more especially that merciful and compassionate faith whose words are, " Come unto me, all ye that labour and are heavy laden, and I will give you rest." To that rest betakes itself the wearied spirit, the wounded heart ; and it becomes a blessing beyond all other blessings ; a source of patience, of fortitude, of hope, of strength, of endurance ; a shelter in the scorching land, — a spring of water in the wilderness.   *   *   *   *

*   *   *   *   *

*   *   *   *   *

Saturday, April 13*th.*

At a quarter after four, drove down to the boat. —— was waiting to see us off, and —— presently made his appearance to see us on. Owing to the yesterday's boat not having sailed, it was crowded to-day, and freighted most heavily, so as to draw an unusual quantity of water, and proceed at a much slower rate than common. At a few minutes after five, the huge brazen bell on deck began to toll; the mingled crowd jostled, and pushed, and rolled about; the loiterers on shore rushed on board; the bidders-farewell on board rushed on shore; D—— and I took a quiet, sunny stand, away from all the confusion, and watched, from our floating palace, New York glide away like a glittering dream from before us. A floating palace indeed it was, in size and in magnificence: I never saw any thing to compare with the beauty, and comfort, and largeness of all its accommodations. Our Scotch steam-boat, the United Kingdom, is a cockboat to it, and even the splendid Hudson boat, the North America, is far inferior to it in every respect, except, I believe, swiftness, —but then these Boston boats have sometimes

very heavy sea to go through.* Besides the ladies'
cabin, this boat is furnished with half a dozen
state rooms, taken from the upper deck, — an
inexpressible luxury.   Into one of these our night-
bags were conveyed, and we returned to the deck
to watch the sun down.   A strong and piercing
wind blew over the waters, and almost cut me in
half as I stood watching the shores, which I did
not wish to lose by going in.   However, I might
have done so, and lost but little; for after passing
Hell-gate, where the rocks in the river and the
banks have rather a picturesque appearance, there
was neither form nor comeliness in the flat, wearisome land to either side; and the only objects
which detained me on deck were the bright blue

---

* The cleanliness of the table furniture, and the neatness
of the attendants, is one of the most essential comforts of
these boats. The linen, and knives and forks, &c. at our meals,
were remarkably clean and bright.   On more than one occasion, too, being rather late for the public breakfast, we have
been indulged with a small separate table in the quiet recess
at the end of the great eating and sleeping cabin, — a favour
only to be appreciated by people unaccustomed to any
ordinaries, much less steam-boat dinner-tables with sometimes near two hundred guests.   On board all the other
boats, the only alternative is to have what you eat brought to
you into the ladies' cabin.   To those who have once breathed
the atmosphere of a " ladies' cabin," it will be difficult to
imagine how such an alternative should not be productive of
an amazing saving of the boat's provisions.

waters themselves, all shining in the sunset, and those lovely little boats, with one mast and two glittering sails, scudding past us like fairy craft upon the burnished waves. At about eight, we were summoned down to tea, which was a compound meal of tea and supper. The company were so numerous that they were obliged to lay the table twice. We waited till the crowd had devoured their feed, and had ours in comparative peace and quiet. An excellent man, by name ——, an officer in the American army, made himself known to me, considering, as he afterwards told me, his commission to be a sufficient right of introduction to any body. He was a native of Boston, and was returning to it, after an absence of *fourteen years.*   *

  *   *   *   *   *
  *   *   *   *   *

Sunday, 14*th.*

The morning was beautifully bright and clear. While dressing, heard the breakfast bell, and received sundry intimations to descend and eat; however, I declined leaving my cabin until I had done dressing, which I achieved very comfortably at leisure, during which time the ship weathered Point Judith, where the Atlantic comes in to the shore between the termination of Long Island

and the southern extremity of Rhode Island.
The water is generally rough here, and I had
been prophesied an agreeable little fit of sea sickness; but no such matter, — we passed it very
smoothly, and presently stopped at Newport, on
Rhode Island, to leave and take up passengers.
The wind was keen and bracing; the morning
beautifully bright and sunny; the blue waters, all
curled and crisped under the arrow-like wind,
broke into a thousand sapphire ridges tipped with
silver foam, that drove away in sparkling showers
before the bitter breath of the north. We entered
Providence river in a few moments, and steamed
along between Rhode Island and the main land,
until we reached Providence, a town on the shore
of Rhode Island, where we were to leave the boat,
and pursue our route by coach to Boston. I
walked on deck with Captain —— for an hour
after breakfast, breasting the wind, which almost
drove us back each time we turned up the deck
towards the prow. After my walk, went in,
righted my hair, which the wind had dressed *à la
frantic*, and came and sat in the sun with Brewster's book, — which I like mainly, — till we
reached Providence. The boat was so heavily
laden that she drew an enormous quantity of
water, and was fairly aground once, as we were

nearing the pier. When the crowd of passengers had ebbed away, and we had seen them pack themselves into their stages and drive off, we adjourned to our exclusive extra, which, to our great sorrow, could not take all our luggage after all. The distance from Providence to Boston is forty miles; but we were six hours and a half doing it over an excellent road. The weather was beautiful, but the country still sad and wintry-looking. The spring is backwarder here than in New York by full three weeks: the trees were all bare and leafless, except the withered foliage of the black oaks, and the face of the country, with its monotonous rises, and brooks flowing through flat fields, reminded me of parts of Cumberland. Every now and then, however, we came to a little lakelet, or, as they call them here, pond, of the holiest, deepest dark-blue water, sparkling like a magic sapphire, against smooth, bright, golden, sandy shores, and screened by vivid thickets of cedar bushes. They were like little bits of fairyland, and relieved the wearisomeness of the road. As we approached Boston, the country assumed a more cultivated aspect, — the houses in the road-side villages were remarkably neat, and pretty, and cottage-like, — the land was well farmed; and the careful cultivation, and stone walls, which perform the part of hedges here, together with the bleak look of the distances on each side, made me think of Scotland. We entered Boston through a long road with houses on each side, making one fancy one's self in the town long before one reaches it. We did not arrive until half-past six. Went to my own room and dressed for dinner. When I came to the drawing-room, found the ——'s : dear —— was half crazy at seeing us again. After dinner, came to my room with her, and righted all my clothes, and established myself; after tea, returned to the same work, and, at about half-past ten, came to bed. Here we are in a new place ! — how desolate and cheerless this constant changing of homes is : the Scripture saith, " There is no rest to the wicked ; " and truly I never felt so convinced of my own wickedness as I have done since I have been in this country.

Monday, 15th.

Went over to the theatre to rehearse Fazio. Mr. ——, however, met us at the door, and assured me there was no necessity for my doing so till to-morrow. —— came early to see me, and stayed all the morning. Mr. —— called this morning, — I was quite glad to see him, — and Mrs. ——, whom I thought beautiful. Tried to finish letter to ——, but was interrupted about a dozen times. At about half-past four, the horses came to the door. The afternoon was lovely, and the roads remarkably good: I had a fine, handsome, spirited horse, who pulled my hands to pieces for want of being properly curbed. We rode out to *Cambridge*, the University of Massachussetts, about three miles distant from Boston. The village round it, with its white cottages, and meeting roads, and the green lawns and trees round the college, reminded me of England. We rode on to a place called Mount Auburn, a burial-ground which the Bostonians take great pride in, and which is one of the lions of the place. The entrance is a fine, solid, granite gateway, in a species of *Egyptian* style, with this inscription engraved over it: " Then shall the dust return to the earth as it was, and the spirit shall return unto God, who gave it." * The whole place is

---

* My astonishment was unfeigned, when, upon an after inspection, I found this very lofty gateway was constructed of *painted wood*. What! a cheat, a sham thing at the threshold of the grave! — surely, thereabouts pretences should have an end. Sham magnificence, too, is sad; an iron railing, or a wooden paling, would, to my mind, have been a thousand times better than this *mock granite*. Let us hope that this is

at present in an unfinished state, but its capabilities are very great, and, as far as it has progressed, they have been taken every advantage of. The enclosure is of considerable extent, — about one hundred acres, — and contains several high hills and deep ravines, in the bottom of which are dark, still, melancholy-looking meres. The whole is cut, with much skill and good taste, by roads for carriages, and small, narrow footpaths. The various avenues are distinguished by the names of trees, as, Linden walk, Pine walk, Beech walk; and already two or three white monuments are seen glimmering palely through the woods, reminding one of the solemn use to which this ground is consecrated, which, for its beauty, might seem a pleasure-garden instead of a place of graves. Mr. —— delighted me very much: he told me he was looking for a plot of earth in this cemetery which he intended to dedicate to poor English people, who might come out here, and die without the means of being decently laid to rest. We looked, with this view, at a patch of ground on the slope of a high hill, well shadowed over with

---

merely a temporary entrance, — there is *real* granite enough to be had at Quincy; and if the living can't afford it, why the dead will never miss it, — and any thing would be better than an imitation gateway.

trees, and descending to a great depth to a dark
pond, shining in the hollow like an emerald.
'T was sad and touching to gaze at that earth, with
the thought that amidst strangers, and in a strange
land, the pity of a fellow-countryman should here
allot to his brethren a grave in the quiet and
solemn beauty of this hallowed ground.   Our
time was limited ; so, after lingering for a short
space along the narrow pathways that wind
among the dwellings of the dead, we rode home.
We reached Boston at a quarter to seven.   My
father and D—— were already gone to the theatre. I dressed, and went over myself immediately.
The play was begun : the house was not very full.
The managers have committed the greatest piece
of mismanagement imaginable, — they advertise
my father alone in Hamlet to-night, and instead
of making me play alone to-morrow night, and so
securing our attraction singly before we act together, we are *both* to act to-morrow in Fazio, which
circumstance, of course, kept the house thin
to-night.   My father's Hamlet is very beautiful.
'T is curious, that when I see him act I have none
of the absolute feeling of contempt for the profession that I have while acting myself. What
he does appears, indeed, like the work of an artist ;
and though I always lament that he loves it as he

does, and has devoted so much care and labour to it as he has, yet I certainly respect acting more while I am seeing him act than at any other time.* Yet surely, after all, acting *is* nonsense, and as I sit here opposite the churchyard, it seems to me strange to think, that when I come down into that darkness, I shall have eaten bread, during my life, earned by such means. The Ophelia was perfectly beautiful: I think I scarcely ever saw a more faultless piece of mortality

---

* The spirit of man of its own dignity ennobles whatever it devotes itself to. The most trivial actions may become almost heroical from the motive which prompts them, and the most absurd ceremonies of superstition sincerely practised, may excite pity, but neither contempt nor ridicule. If such a thing as an enthusiastic shoemaker were to be met with, there is no doubt but his feeling of his craft would elevate it into something approximating an art, and his work would bear witness to his veneration for it. At the time when the stage was in its highest perfection, its members had *all* a great love and admiration for their profession; many of them were men of education and mental accomplishment, and brought to bear upon their labour all the intellectual stores which they possessed. They respected their own work, and it was respectable; they thought acting capable of elevation, of refinement, of utility, and their faith in it invested it with dignity. Of this class were all my father's family. *One* reason why the stage and every thing belonging to it has fallen to so low an ebb now, is because actors have ceased to care for their profession themselves, — they are no longer artists, — acting is no longer an art.

in point of outward loveliness. The eyes
and brow of an angel, serene and calm, yet
bright and piercing; a mouth chiselled like a
Grecian piece of sculpture, with an expression of
infinite refinement; fair round arms and hands, a
beautifully moulded foot, and a figure that seemed
to me perfectly proportioned. It did not perhaps
convey to me the idea of such absolute loveliness
as ——'s figure did; but altogether I think I
never saw a fairer woman — it was delightful to
look at her. *   The audience are, upon the whole,
cold; — very still and attentive, however, and when
they do warm it is certainly very effectually, for
they shout and hurrah like mad.   *

*   *   *   *   *

Wednesday, 27th.

Somebody very civilly has sent me that beautiful
book, Rogers's Italy: it set me wild again with

* Besides the advantage of possessing the very prettiest
collection of actresses I ever saw, the theatre at Boston has
decidedly the best company I have played with *any where* out
of London. Some of the old leaven alluded to in the last
note exists amongst the ladies and gentlemen of the Tremont
theatre : they do not seem to despise their work, and it is,
generally speaking, well done therefore. Our pieces were all
remarkably well got up there; and the green-room is both
respectable and agreeable.

my old frenzy for the south of Europe.   Wrote to
—— ; after dinner, practised for an hour; at half-
past five, off to the theatre. The house was
crammed : the play, the Stranger. It is quite
comical to see the people in the morning at the
box-office : our window is opposite to it, and 't is a
matter of the greatest amusement to me to watch
them.   They collect in crowds for upwards of an
hour before the doors open, and when the bolts
are withdrawn, there is a yelling and shouting as
though the town were on fire. In they rush,
thumping and pummelling one another, and not
one comes out without rubbing his head, or his
back, or showing a piteous rent in his clothes.   I
was surprised to see men of a very low order
pressing foremost to obtain boxes, but I find that
they sell them again at an enormous increase to
others who have not been able to obtain any ; and
the better to carry on their traffic, these worthies
smear their clothes with molasses, and sugar, &c.,
in order to prevent any person of more decent
appearance, or whose clothes are worth a cent,
from coming near the box-office : this is ingenious,
and deserves a reward.   Our other window looks
out upon a large churchyard, in the midst of
which stands a cenotaph, erected by Franklin in
honour of his father. Between the view of the

play-house, and the view of the burial-ground, my contemplations are curiously tinged. This house (the Tremont) is admirably quiet and comfortable.

Thursday, 18*th*.

After breakfast, went to rehearsal, — the School for Scandal, — however, half the people weren't there, so the rehearsal was nought. Came home, and at half-past eleven, rode out; the day was beautifully bright: we rode to a beautiful little mere, called Jamaica Pond, through some country very like Scotland. We turned from the road into a gentleman's estate, and rode up a green rise into an enclosed field, which commanded an extensive view of the country below. But the spring tarries still, and though her smile is in the sky, the trees are leafless, and blossomless, and wintry-looking still. We came in by a pretty village called Roxbury, about two miles and a half distant from Boston : here we stopped to get a nosegay for my Lady Teazle, at a very pretty green-house, kept by a mechanic, who has devoted his leisure hours to the pleasurable and profitable pursuits of gardening. We returned to town at about half-

past two.   I ran into the drawing-room, and found
—— sitting with my father.   *   *

        *   *   *   *   *

        *   *   *   *   *

Saturday, 20th.

Walked up to the State House.   The day was
any thing but agreeable; a tremendous high wind,
(easterly of course, — 't is the only wind they have
in Boston,) and a burning sun tempered only by
clouds of dust, in which, every two minutes, the
whole world, — at least, as much as we could see
of it, — was shrouded.   On entering the hall of
the State House we confronted Chantry's statue
of Washington, which stands in a recess immediately opposite the entrance.   I saw that, how
many years ago, in his study at Pimlico!   We
proceeded to mount into the cupola, whence a very
extensive view is obtained of the city and its surroundings, — and a cruel height it was!   I began
it at full speed, like a wise woman, but before I
got to the top was so out of breath, that I could
hardly breathe at all: defend me from such alti-
tudes! — and after all, the day was hazy and not
favourable for our purpose; the wind came in
through the windows of the lantern like a tor-

nado; and, as my father observed, after the
exertion of ascending, 't was the very best place
in the world for catching one's death of cold.
We came down as quickly as we could. At about
twelve, we rode to Mount Auburn. The few days
of sunshine since we were last there have clothed
the whole earth with delicate purple and white
blossoms, a little resembling the wood anemone,
but growing close to the soil, and making one
think of violets with their pale purple colour: they
have no fragrance whatever. We afterwards rode
on to a beautiful little lake called Fresh Pond,
along whose margin we followed a pretty woody
path: a high bank covered with black-looking
pines rose immediately on our right, and on our
left the clear waters of the rippling lake came
dancing to and fro along the pebbly shore, which
shone bright and golden under their crystal folds.
We stood with our hats off to receive the soft wind
upon our brows, and to listen to the chiming of
the water upon the beach, the most delicious sound
in all nature's orchestra. We then turned back
and rode home. By the by, on our way out to
Mount Auburn we took the Charleston road, and
rode over Bunker Hill. They have begun a
monument upon the spot where General Warren
was killed, to commemorate the event. I felt

strangely as I rode over that ground. Mr. ———
was the only American of our party, but though
in the minority, he had rather the best of it.
And this is where so much English blood was
shed, thought I; for after all, 't was *all* English
blood, — do as they can, they can never get rid
of their stock; and deeply as oppression and
resistance have dug the grave in which all kindred
feeling seems for a time to have been buried, —
't is only, I believe and trust, for a time, — buried
in blood and fierce warfare, to spring up again in
peace and mutual respect.   England and America
ought not to be enemies, 't is unnatural while the
same language is spoken in both lands.   Until
Americans have found a tongue for themselves,
they must still be the children of old England, for
they speak the words her children speak by the
fireside of her homes.   Oh, England ! noble,
noble land !   They may be proud of many things,
these inheritors of a new world, but of nothing
more than that they are descended from Englishmen ; that their fathers once trod the soil
whereon has grown more goodness, more greatness, more beauty, and more truth, than on any
other earth under God's sun.   *   *

*   *   *   *   *

*   *   *   *   *

At half-past four, we went to dine with the ———'s. Their house is very pretty and comfortable. When first we went in, we were shown into a couple of drawing-rooms, in which there were beautiful marble copies of one or two of the famous statues. One of Canova's dancing girls, the glorious Diana, a reclining figure of Cleopatra, — an exquisite thing, — the crouching Venus, and the lovely antique Cupid and Psyche.

*   *   *   *   *

*   *   *   *   *

'T is strange that feelings should pass from our hearts and minds as clouds pass from the face of heaven, as though they had never been there ; — yet not so, after all ; they do not pass so tracklessly, — they do leave faint shadows behind ; they leave a darker colour upon the face of all existence : sometimes they leave a sad conviction of wasted capabilities, and time, precious time, expended in vain. Yet not in vain : even though our feelings change, — pass, perhaps, to our own consciousness — cease altogether, — 't is not in vain — life is going on — experience and solemn wisdom may come with the coming time ; and existence is, after all, but a series of experiments upon our spiritual nature. Our trials vary with our years ; and though we deem (too often

rightly) that suffering and disappointment are
but barren thorns, whereon grows neither fruit
nor flower, 't is our sin that they are so, for they
are designed to bear an excellent harvest. " Sweet
are the uses of adversity ; " so he has said who
knew all things, and so indeed to the wise they
are.

Tuesday, 30th.

We rode down to the " Chelsea Ferry," and
crossed over the Charles river, where the shore
opposite Boston bears the name of that refuge for
damaged marine stores. The breath of the sea was
delicious, as we crossed the water in one of the
steam-boats constantly plying to and fro, and on
the other side, as we rode towards the beach, it
came greeting us delightfully from the wide waters. When we started from Boston, the weather
was intensely hot, and the day promised to be like
the day before yesterday, a small specimen of
the dog-days. We had about a five miles' ride
through some country that reminded me of Scotland: now and then the dreary landscape was
relieved by the golden branches of a willow tree,
and the delicate, pale peach blossoms, and tiny white
buds in the apple orchards, peeping over some stone

dyke, like a glance over the wall from the merry
laughing spring. So we reached Chelsea beach,
a curving, flat, sandy shore, forming one side of a
small bay which runs up between this land and a
rocky peninsula that stretches far out into the
ocean, called Nahant. At the extremity of the
basin lay glimmering a white, sunny town, by
name *Lynn* ; — 't is quite absurd the starts and
stares which the familiar names cause one for
ever to make here. This small bay is beautifully
smooth and peaceful, the shore is a shelving reach
of hard, fine sand, nearly two miles long, and the
wild waves are warded off in their violence from
it by the rocky barrier of Nahant. How happy
I was to see the beautiful sea once more, — to be
once more galloping over the golden sands, — to
be once more wondering at and worshipping the
grandeur and loveliness of this greatest of God's
marvellous works. How I do love the sea ! —
my very soul seems to gather energy, and life,
and light, from its power, its vastness, its bold,
bright beauty, its fresh, invigorating airs, its
glorious, triumphant, rushing sound. The thin,
thin rippling waves came like silver leaves spreading themselves over the glittering sand with just a
little, sparkling, pearly edge, like the cream of a
bright glass of champagne. Close along the

shore the water was of that pale, transparent green colour, that blends so delicately with the horizon, sometimes at sunset; but out beyond, towards the great deep, it wore that serene and holiest blue that surrounds one in mid-ocean, when the earth is nearly as far below as the heaven seems high above us. For a short time my spirits seemed like uncaged birds; I rejoiced with all my might, — I could have shouted aloud for delight; I galloped far along the sand, as close in to the water's restless edge as my horse would bear to go. But the excitement died away, and then came vividly back the time when last I stood upon the sea beach at Cramond, and lost myself in listening to that delicious sound of the chiming waters—I was many years younger then.

      *   *   *   *   *

      *   *   *   *   *

The end of my ride was sadder than the beginning, for at first my senses alone took cognizance of what surrounded me, and afterwards my soul looked on it, and it grew dark. We rode two miles along the beach, and stopped at a little wooden hut, where, Mr. —— told me, sportsmen, who come to shoot plover along the flats by the shore, resort to dress their dinners and refresh themselves. Here we dismounted : lay in the sun

on the roof with the fresh, sweet, blessed breath
of heaven fanning us. My horse thought proper
to break his bridle and walk himself off through
the fields: they followed him with corn, and
various inducements; —— and I, mean time, ran
down to the water, collecting interesting relics,
muscle shells, quartz, pebbles, and sea-weed;
finally, we remounted and returned home. The
weather had changed completely, and become
quite bleak and cold : the variations of the climate
in this place are terrible. As we rode down a
pleasant lane towards the Salem road, we met a
large crowd of country-people busily employed in
raising the framework of a house. In this part of
the country, the poorer class of people build their
houses, or rather, the wooden frames of their
houses, entirely before they set them up. When
the skeleton is entirely finished, they call together
all their neighbours to assist in the raising, which
is an event of much importance, and generally ends
in a merry-making. The filling up the outline of
the habitation, which they do with boards here, is
an after work : the frame seems to be the material
part of the building, and slight enough too, I
thought, for protection against these bitter east
winds. We reached home at about half-past two.
The play was Much Ado about Nothing : the

house was spoilt by the fair which the ladies have
been getting up for the blind here, and which was
lighted and open for inspection previous to to-
morrow, when the sale is to take place. *

* * * * *

* * * * *

LINES.

* * * and I
Am reading, too, my book of memory:
With eyelids closed, over the crested foam,
And the blue, marbled sea, I seek my home.
All present things forgotten, on the shore
Of the romantic Forth I stand once more;
Once more I hear the waves' harmonious strife;
Once more, upon the mountain coast of Fife,
I see the checker'd lights and shadows fall.
Upon the sand crumbles the ruin'd wall
That guards no more the desolate demesne,
And the deserted mansion.   High between
The summer clouds the Ochil hills arise;
And far, far, like a shadow in the skies,
Ben Lomond tow'rs aloft in sovereign height.
O, Cramond beach! are thy sands still as bright —
Thy waters still as sunny, — thy wild shore
As lonely and as lovely as of yore? —
Haunts of my happy time! as wandering back
Along my life, on memory's faithful track,
How fair ye seem, — how fair, how dear ye are!
Ye need not to be gazed at from afar;

Deceptive distance lends no brighter hue ;
Your beauty and your peacefulness were true.
Not yours the charms from which we wearied stray,
And own them only when they 're far away.
O, be ye blest for all the happiness
Which I have known in your wild loneliness.
Old sea, whose voice yet chimes upon my ear, —
Old paths, whose every winding step was dear, —
Dark, rocky promontories, — echoing caves,
Worn hollow by the white feet of the waves, —
Blue, lake-like waters, — legend-haunted isle,
Over ye all, bright be the summer's smile ;
And gently fall the winter on your breast,
Haunts of my youth, my memory's place of rest.

Wednesday, May 1st.

Mr. —— came in the morning, and I settled
to call down at eleven for Mrs. —— to go to the
fair. We drove to Faneuil Hall, a building opposite the market, which was appropriated to the
uses of the fair ; but the crowd was so dense round
the steps, that we found it impossible to approach
them, and wisely gave up the attempt, determining
to take our drive, and then come back and try our
later fortune. We drove down to the Chelsea
beach. The day was bleak and cold, though
bright, with a cutting east wind. After taking a

good race along the bright, creaming edge, we
returned to the carriage, and drove into town again
to the fair, which we managed at last to enter.
The whole thing was crowd, crush, and confusion,
to my bewildered eyes.　We got upon a platform
behind the stalls, and squeezed our way to Mrs.
———'s shop, where my father had desired me to
buy him a card-case, which I did.　I found ———
installed in her stall.　——— joined us, and Mr.
———, who drew me away to his wife's table,
where I bought one or two things, and having
emptied my purse, came away.　After dinner, Mr.
——— came in : he showed us some things he had
bought at the fair.　I thought the prices enormous,
but the money is well spent in itself, or rather, on
its ultimate object, and the immediate return is of
no import.

Thursday, 2d.

After breakfast, went over to rehearsal; at half-
past eleven, went out to ride: the day was heavenly,
bright, and mild, with a full, soft, sweet spring
breeze blowing life and health over one.　The
golden willow trees were all in flower, and the air, as
we rode by them, was rich with their fragrance.　The
sky was as glorious as the sky of Paradise: the whole

world was full of loveliness; and my spirits were in most harmonious tune with all its beauty. We rode along the chiming beach, talking gravely of many matters, temporal and spiritual; and when we reached the pines, I dismounted, entreated for a scrap of paper, and, in the miserable little parlour of this miserable little mansion, sat down and scribbled some miserable doggrel to ease my heart. How beautiful the scene around me was ! — the bright, boundless sea, smooth as a sapphire, except at the restless, rippling edge; the serene, holy sky looking down so earnestly and gently on the flowering earth ; the reviving breeze, dipping like a bird its fresh wings into the water, — how beautiful all things did seem to me, — how full of witnesses of the great power and goodness that created them. Why is it that clouds ever come between us and God when there are seasons like this, when we seem to sit at his very feet, — when his glory and his mercy seem the atmosphere we are breathing, and our whole existence is lifted, for a time, into the reality of all we hope and pray for? Yet these are but passing emotions: they are not, indeed, the very spirit of God, — they are but reflections of his image, caught from the glorious mirror of nature. The sky becomes cloudy, — the sea stormy ; the blos-

soming and the bearing seasons pass away, and
winter comes apace, with withered aspect, and
bitter, biting breath; the face of the universe becomes dark, and the trust, and faith, and joy of
our souls, fade into doubt, disbelief, and sorrow.
Infirmity and imperfection pluck us back from
our heavenward flight, and the weight of our mortality drags us down fast, fast again towards the
earth.   These fair, outward creatures, and the
blessed emotions they excite, will pass away, —
must — do pass away, — and where is the abiding
revelation of God to which we shall turn?   It
lives for ever, in the still burning light of a strong
and steadfast soul; in the resolute will and high
unshaken purpose of good; in the quiet, calm,
collected might of reason; in the undying warmth
and brightness of a pure and holy heart. *

    *   *   *   *   *

    *   *   *   *   *

My ride did me ten thousand goods.   As we were
riding through Mrs. ——'s farm, a little boy
came running to meet me with his hand full of
beautiful flowers, which he stood upon tiptoe to
thrust into my hand, and, without waiting to be
thanked, rushed back into the house.   I was delighted: the flowers were exquisite, and the
manner of the gift very enchanting.   Altogether,

I do not know when I have been so completely
filled with pleasurable emotions as during this
ride.   *   *   *   *

      *   *   *   *   *

      *   *   *   *   *

LINES.

To the smooth beach, the silver sea
Comes rippling in a thousand smiles,
And back again runs murmuringly,
To break around yon distant isles.
The sunshine, through a floating veil
Of golden clouds, looks o'er the wave,
And gilds, far off, the outline pale,
Of many a rocky cape and cave.
The breath of spring comes balmily
Over the newly blossom'd earth;
The smile of spring, on sea, and sky,
Is shedding light, and love, and mirth.
I would that thou wert by my side,
As underneath the rosy bloom
Of flowering orchard trees I ride,
And drink their fragrant, fresh perfume;
I would that thou wert by my side,
To feel this soft air on thy brow,
And listen to the chiming tide
Along that smooth shore breaking now;
I would that thou wert here to bless,
As I do now, the love and care,
That with such wealth of loveliness,
Have made life's journeying-land so fair.

*   *   *   *
*   *   *   *
*   *   *   *

I have taken several enormous rides round Boston,
and am more and more delighted with its envi-
rons, which are now in full flush of blossoming,
as sweet, and fresh, and lovely as any thing can
be.   On Saturday, rode to the Blue Hills, a distance of upwards of twelve miles.   The roads
round this place are almost as good as roads in
England, and the country altogether reminds me
of that dear little land.*   These Blue Hills were,

---

* To the English traveller, around whose heart the love
of country and the influences of early association may yet
cling, New England appears to me, of all the portions of the
United States which I have visited, most likely to afford
gratification ; and the *Yankees*, — properly so called, — the
Americans with whom he will find, and towards whom he
will feel most sympathy.   They do us the honour to call
themselves *purely English* in their origin ; they alone, of the
whole population of the United States, undoubtedly were
so ; and in the abundant witness which their whole character, country, and institutions bear to that fact, I feel an additional reason to be proud of England, — of Old England,
for these are her children, — this race of men, as a race incomparably superior to the other inhabitants of this country.
In conversing with New Englandmen, in spite of any passing, temporary bitterness, any political difference, or painful
reference to past times of enmity, I have always been struck
with the admiring, and in some measure, tender feeling with
which England, as the mother-country, was named.   Nor is

a few years ago, a wilderness of forest — the favourite resort of rattlesnakes; but the trees have

---

it possible to travel through the New England states and
not perceive, indeed, a spirit (however modified by different
circumstances and institutions) yet most truly English in its
origin. The exterior of the houses, — their extreme neatness and cleanliness, — the careful cultivation of the land,
— the tasteful and ornamental arrangement of the ground
immediately surrounding the dwellings, that most English of
all manifestations, — above all, the church spires pointing
towards heaven, from the bosom of every village, — recalled
most forcibly to my mind my own England, and presented
images of order, of industry, of taste, and religious feeling,
nowhere so exhibited in any other part of the Union. I
visited Boston several times, and mixed in society there, the
tone of which appeared to me far higher than that of any I
found elsewhere. A general degree of cultivation exists
among its members, which renders their intercourse desirable and delightful. Nor is this superior degree of education
confined to Boston; the zeal and the judgment with which
it is being propagated throughout that part of the country
is a noble national characteristic. A small circumstance is
a good illustration of the advance which knowledge has
made in these states. Travelling by land from New Haven to
Boston, at one of the very smallest places where we stopped
to change horses, I got out of the carriage to reconnoitre
our surroundings. The town (if town it could be called)
did not appear to contain much more than fifty houses :
amongst the most prominent of these, however, was a bookseller's shop. The first volumes I took up on the counter
were Spurzheim's volume on education, and Dr. Abercrom-
bie's works on the intellectual and moral faculties. I saw

been partly cleared, and though 't is still a wild, desolate region, clothed with firs, and uncheered by a human habitation, its more savage tenants have disappeared with the thick coverts in which they nestled, and we rode to the summit of the highest hill without seeing any thing in the shape of Eve's enemy.   At the top, by the by, we did find some species of building in decay and ruin. Whoever perched himself up there had no mind to be overlooked, and must have been fond of fresh air.   The view from the mountain is magnificent, yet I do not believe the elevation to be very extraordinary ; although, as I looked down, it seemed to me as though the world was stretched at my feet; and I thought of the temptation of our Saviour.   The various villages, with their blossoming orchards, looked like patches of a snow-scene ; the river wound, like a silver snake,

more pictures, more sculptures, and more books in private houses in Boston than I have seen any where else.   I could name more men of marked talent that I met with there than any where else.   Its charitable and literary institutions are upon a liberal scale, and enlightened principles.   Among the New Englanders I have seen more honour and reverence of parents, and more witnesses of a high religious faith, than among any other Americans with whom I have lived and conversed.

all round the fields; the little lakes lay diminished to drops of bright blue light; and the lesser mountains rose below us like the waves of a dark sea. The whole was strange and awful to me: — the savage loneliness of the place, its apparent remoteness from the earth, and its walkers, filled me with a solemn sensation. Had I been there alone, I do not know a place where I should sooner have expected to meet some of the wandering spirits of mid-air, — shapes, and sights, and beings of another order from those of the world, that lay like a map below me. The mountain itself is formed of granite, of which large slabs appeared through the turf and brushwood. I looked in vain for what I found in such abundance on the Portland hill, the sweet, wild thyme. I thought I should find some of it among the stony rifts, where it loves to cling, but I was disappointed. Indeed, I met with a much more severe disappointment than that. The turf was thickly strewn with clumps of violets, the very same in form and colour as our own sweet wood violet. I stooped in an ecstasy to gather them, but found they were totally senseless — mere pretences of violets. A violet without fragrance! a wild one, too! — the thing's totally unnatural. I flung the little purple cheat away in a rage. I have since found cowslips with the same entire absence of fragrance. The heat and cold of this climate chill or wither every thing; and almost all the flowers which are most common and sweet, growing in the moist soil of England, seem reared with difficulty here, and lose their great fragrance, their soul, as it were, under the extreme influences of this sky.* There were many wild things growing on this mountain, that for beauty, and delicacy of form and colour, would have found honourable place in our conservatories; but they had not the slightest perfume, and I took no delight in them. A scentless flower is a monster; and though I acknowledge with due admiration the pale beauty of that queen of flowers, the camelia, I never see it in its cold, pearl-like pride

---

* There are, I believe, no primroses, no wild thyme, and no heather, that grow naturally in this country. I do not remember to have seen either wild honeysuckle or clematis, both of which are so abundant with us. The laurestinus, rosemary, southernwood, and monthly roses, all of which are so common in England, growing out of doors all the year round, are kept in hot-houses during the winter, even as far south as Philadelphia. The common garden flowers — roses, pinks — are far less abundant and less fragrant than with us. Sweet peas, and mignionette, are comparatively scarce; serynga, and laburnum, I have never seen at all: but so little care is bestowed upon ornamental gardening, that I do not know whether this dearth of flowers is the fault of the climate, or the consequence of the utter neglect in which flower-gardens are held here.

of bloom, that it does not strike me like a fine lady — an artificial creature, fair indeed to behold, but without the very property of a flower — sweetness. Oh, the lilies of the valley, — the primroses, — the violets, — the sweet, sweet hawthorn, — the fresh fragrant blush rose, — the purple lilac bloom, — the silver serynga, — the faint breathing hyacinths, — the golden cowslips, of a morning, at the close of May in England ! — the fulness of sweetness that loads the temperate air, as it breathes over the fresh lawns of that flower-garden !   *

*   *   *   *   *

*   *   *   *   *

I took another long ride to a quarry ten miles distant from Boston, whence the granite, which is much used in Boston for building, is drawn.   I started at six in the morning, and rode about twenty miles before breakfast, which I think was a piece of virtue bordering upon heroism : to be sure, I had my reward, for any thing so sweet as the whole world, at about half-past six, I never beheld. The dew was yet fresh upon tree and flower, — the roads were shady and cool, — the dust had not yet been disturbed ; a mild, soft, full breeze, blew over the flowery earth, and the rosy apple blossoms stirred on the rocking boughs against the serene and smiling sky.   They have in this country neither nightingales, thrushes, linnets, nor blackbirds, at least, none with the same notes as ours; but every now and then, from the snowy cherry trees, there came a wild snatch of trilling melody, like the clear ringing song of a canary bird. My companion did not know the minstrel by his note; but I never heard a more brilliant and joyful strain, or one more fitted to the bright hour of opening day,—always excepting the lark's, that triumphant embodied spirit of song.* The blackbird's song is to me the sweetest in the world, — sad and soft, and rich as the sunsets through which it is heard. The quarry which we visited is an extensive vein of fine, dark-coloured granite. We dismounted and walked among the workmen to see them at their various processes. This quarry, and one at a short distance, merely supply the blocks of granite, which, being detached from the main stone, are piled upon cars, and sent down an inclined plane to the rail-road, by means of a powerful chain, which acts at once as a support and check, suffering the load to proceed slowly down the declivity, and at the same time sending up from the bottom, upon another track,

* Lacking the nightingale and the lark, I think they want the two perfect specimens of natural music.

the empty car from which the granite has been unloaded below, as the buckets of a well are drawn up and down. A very serious accident occurred here, by the by, to a party of gentlemen, among whom Mr. —— was one. They had placed themselves in the empty car at the bottom of the inclined plane, and were being slowly drawn up, as the car loaded with granite descended on the other track. Just as they were approaching the summit, the chain by which the car was drawn up gave way, and it rolled backwards down the plane with fearful velocity, and starting off the track of the rail-road, pitched down into a ravine full of rocks and blocks of granite, over which the road passes like a bridge at the foot of the quarry. I believe one of them was killed, and the others most terribly injured. The rough blocks of granite are conveyed by horses, in the same rail-road cars, to smaller quarries below, where they are wrought and shaped for their appointed uses. After looking down from the summit of the granite rock upon the country which lay smiling for many a sunny mile of flowery earth and sparkling sea below, and wandering about the works, which are interesting and curious, we remounted and rode home over turfy wood-paths, through tangled thickets of pine, fir, and cedar, whose warm fragrance was beginning to be drawn forth by the morning sun. We disturbed in our path a poor woodcock, who was sitting with her young : it was a pity to see the poor thing flutter about her treasure, and go trailing a little way into the brushwood, to entice us away from them. Poor mother ! what a tempest of fear and agony was in your downy breast. I was very sorry we had frightened her, poor creature. The country we rode through was extremely pretty, — so, indeed, I think all the country round Boston is ; the only deficiency is water, — running water, I mean ; for there are several beautiful pools in this vicinity, — and, turn which way you will, the silver shield of the sea shining against the horizon is a lovely feature of the landscape. But there are no rivulets, no brooks, no sparkling, singing water-courses to refresh one's senses, as one rides across the fields and through the woodlands. —— called on us on Sunday last. He is very enchanting : I wish it had been my good fortune to see him oftener. One of the *great men* of this country, he would have been a first-rate man all the world over ; and, like all first-rate people, there is a simplicity and a total want of pretension about him that is very delightful. He gave us a description of Niagara, which did what he complained no description of it ever does, — conveyed to us an exact idea of the natural position and circumstances which render these falls so wonderful; whereas, most describers launch forth into vague and untangible rhapsodies, which, after all, convey no express idea of any thing but water in the abstract, he gave me, by his few simple words, a more *real* impression of the stupendous cataract than all that was ever writ or spoken of waterfalls before, not excepting Byron's Terni. Last Saturday, I dined at ——'s ; where, for my greater happiness, I sat between —— and ——. I remember especially two bright things uttered ; the one by the one, the other by the other of these worthies. Mr. ——, speaking of Knowles's Hunchback, said, " Well, after all, it's no great matter. The author evidently understands stage effect and dramatic situations, and so on ; but as for the writing, it's by no means as good as Shakspeare." I looked at the man in amazement, and suggested to him that Shakspeare did not grow upon every bush. Presently, Mr. —— began a sentence by assuring me that he was a worshipper of Shakspeare ; and ended it by saying that Othello was disgusting, King Lear ludicrous, and Romeo and Juliet childish nonsense : whereat I swallowed half a pint of water, and nearly my tumbler too, and remained silent ; for what could I say? However, in spite of this, I owe —— some gratitude; for he brought —— to see me the other day, whose face is more like that of a good and intellectual man than almost any face I ever saw. The climate of this place is dreadful! The night before last, the weather was so warm, that, with my window open, I was obliged to take half the clothes off my bed : last night was so cold, that, with window shut, and additional covering, I could scarce get to sleep for the cold. This is terrible, and forms a serious drawback upon the various attractions of Boston; and to me it has many. The houses are like English houses : the Common is like Constitution Hill; Beacon Street is like a bit of Park Lane; and Summer Street, now that the chestnut trees are in bloom, is perfectly beautiful. But for the climate, I should like to live in Boston very much : my stay here has been delightful. It is in itself a lovely place, and the country round it is charming. The people are *intellectual,* and have been most abundantly good-natured and kind to me.   *

*   *   *   *   *

*   *   *   *   *

I have finished ——'s sermons, which are most excellent. I think he is one of the purest English prose writers now living. I revere him greatly;

yet I do not think his denial of the Trinity is consistent with the argument by which he maintains the truth of the miracles. I have begun the Diary of an Ennuyée again : that book is most enchanting to me, — merely to read the names of the places in which one's imagination goes sunning itself for ever, is delightful.

New York.

I have seen ——, who, in his outward man, bears but little token of his inward greatness. Miss —— had prepared me for an exterior over which debility and sickness had triumphed now for some years; but, thought I, there must be eyes and a brow ; and there the spirit will surely be seen upon its throne. But the eyes were small grey eyes, with an expression which struck me at first as more akin to shrewdness of judgment, than genius and the loftier qualities of the mind ; and though the brow and forehead were those of an intellectual person, they had neither the expanse nor conformation I had imagined. The subject of our conversation, though sufficiently natural for him to choose, addressing one of my craft, did not appear to me to be a happy one for his own powers, — perhaps I thought so because

I differed from him. He talked about the stage and acting in as unreal, and, in my opinion, mistaken, a manner as possible. Had he expressed himself unknowingly about acting, that would not have surprised me; for he can have no means of judging of it, not having frequented the theatre for some years past: and those who have the best means of forming critical judgments upon dramatic subjects, for the most part talk arrant nonsense about them. Lawrence was the only man I ever heard speak about the stage who did so with understanding and accuracy. I have heard the very cleverest men in England talk the greatest stuff imaginable about actors and acting. But to return to ———: he said he had not thought much upon the subject, but that it appeared to him feasible and highly desirable to take detached passages and scenes from the finest dramatic writers, and have them well declaimed in comparatively private assemblies, — this as a wholesome substitute for the stage, of which he said he did not approve; and he thought this the best method of obtaining the intellectual pleasure and profit to be derived from fine dramatic works, without the illusion and excitement belonging to theatrical exhibitions. My horror was so unutterable at this proposition, and my amazement so extreme that he should make it, that I believe my replies to it were all but incoherent. What! take one of Shakspeare's plays bit by bit, break it piece-meal, in order to make recitals of it! — destroy the. marvellous unity of one of his magnificent works, to make patches of declamation! If the stage is evil, put it away, and put away with it those writings which properly belong to it, and to nothing else; but do not take dramatic compositions, things full of present action and emotion, to turn them into recitations, — and mutilated ones, too. Get other poems to declaim, no matter how vivid or impassioned in their descriptions, so their form be not dramatic. It is not to be supposed that the effect proper and natural to a fine dramatic conception can be preserved when the language is merely declaimed without the assistance of distance, dress, scenic effects, — all the appertainings that the author has reckoned upon to work out his idea. —— mentioned the dagger soliloquy in Macbeth, as an instance which would admit of being executed after his idea; saying, that that, well read by any person in a drawing-room, would have all the effect necessary or desirable. I remember hearing my aunt Siddons read the scenes of the witches in Macbeth; and while doing so, was obliged to cover my eyes, that her

velvet gown, modern cap, and spectacles might
not disturb the wild and sublime images that her
magnificent voice and recitation were conjuring
up around me. If a man professes to tell you a
story, no matter what, — say the story of Romeo
and Juliet, — and sits in a modern drawing-room,
in modern costume, it matters not, — *he* is no part
of his story, — you do not connect him with his
narrative, — his appearance in no way clashes
with your train of thought, — you are not thinking of him, but of the people he is talking about.
But if a man in a modern drawing-room, and in
modern costume, were to get up, and begin re-
citing the balcony scene in Romeo and Juliet, I
think the case would be altered. However, never
having heard such a proposal before, I had not
thought much about it, and only felt a little
stunned at the idea of Shakspeare's *histories* being
broken into fragments.*

---

* Among the many signs of the total decay of dramatic
mind and spirit in this age, a frequent piece of criticism passed
upon modern plays appears to me a very conclusive one —
" Such a play is exceedingly full of dramatic effect, but there's
no poetry in it." " Such a playwright understands situation
and character, but really reading his plays you find no poetry
in them." I have heard this bright comment passed repeatedly upon the best dramatic composition of modern times,
— the Hunchback; a play whose immense popularity every

Thursday.

At a little after ten, —— came to take us to see the savages. We drove down, D——, my father,

---

where is the surest and truest warrant of its excellence, — a play containing the most dramatic situations, the most pathetic and comic effects, and by far the finest conception of a female character of any play since the old golden dramatic age. I do not hesitate to say that this is a most false piece of criticism, induced alone by a want of perception of what are the requisites in a dramatic poem, and a total absence of true dramatic feeling. First, in the ingredients of a fine play, comes the fiction, — the invention; to this belong those same much sneered at stage effects, and theatrical situations; next comes the skilful and powerful delineation of individual character; *lastly* comes the item of a poetical diction. *One* alone has united these in their utmost perfection; for such another the world may look in vain. But I think the play-goers of Shakspeare's time would have been tolerably satisfied with a most interesting fiction, and a true and vigorous delineation of character; and let me ask, is there no poetry besides that of words? — is there no poetry in the fable of a play — none in the faithful portraying of a human being's mind and passions? As for all pretty speeches, lengthy descriptions, abstract disquisitions, — unless things placed in the mouth of characters to whose identity such mental manifestations belong, — they are inadmissible in a right good play, and should by all means be confined to the pages of those anomalous modern growths — plays for the closet. In all our elder dramatists, Shakspeare alone ex-

he, and I, to their hotel. We found, even at that
early hour, the portico, passage, and staircase,
thronged with gazers upon the same errand as
ourselves. We made our way, at length, into the
presence chamber ; a little narrow dark room, with
all the windows shut, crowded with people, come
to stare at their fellow wild beasts. Upon a sofa
sat Black Hawk, a diminutive, shrivelled looking
old man, with an appearance of much activity in
his shrunk limbs, and a calmness and dignified
self-composure in his manner, which, in spite of
his want of size and comeliness, was very striking.
Next to him sat a young man, the adopted son
of his brother the prophet; whose height and
breadth, and peculiar gravity of face and deportment, were those of a man nearly forty, whereas
he is little more than half that age. The undisturbed seriousness of his countenance was explained
to me by *their keeper*, thus : he had, it seems, the
day before, indulged rather too freely in the delights of champagne, and was suffering just retribution in the shape of a head-ache, — unjust retri-

---

cepted, the main quality of a play, the story, is often defective
to an excess, not only in morality, but in probability and consistency ; and the same defects exist in the delineation of character in many of their noblest plays.

bution I should say, for in his savage experience
no such sweet bright poison had ever before been
recorded, *I guess*, by the after pain it causes. Next
to him sat Black Hawk's son, a noble, big young
creature, like a fine Newfoundland puppy, with a
handsome, scornful face, which yet exhibited more
familiarity and good-humoured amusement at
what was going on than any of the rest. His
hair was powdered on the top, and round the ears
with a bright vermilion-coloured powder, and
knots of scarlet berries or beads, I don't know
which, hung like ear-rings on each side of his face.
A string of glass beads was tied round his naked
throat; he was wrapped in a large blanket, which
completely concealed his form, except his legs and
feet, which were clothed in common leather shoes,
and a species of deerskin gaiter. He seemed much
alive to what was going on, conversed freely in his
own language with his neighbour, and laughed
once or twice aloud, which rather surprised me, as
I had heard so much of their immovable gravity.
The costume of the other young man was much
the same, except that his hair was not adorned.
Black Hawk himself had on a blue cloth surtout,
scarlet leggings, a black silk neck handkerchief,
and ear-rings. His appearance altogether was
not unlike that of an old French gentleman. Be-

side him, on a chair, sat one of his warriors, wrapped in a blanket, with a cotton handkerchief whisped round his head. At one of the windows apart from their companions, with less courtesy in their demeanour, and a great deal of sullen savageness in their serious aspects, sat the great warrior, and the prophet of the tribe—the latter is Black Hawk's brother. I cannot express the feeling of commiseration and disgust which the whole scene gave me. That men such as ourselves, creatures with like feelings, like perceptions, should be brought, as strange animals at a show, to be gazed at the livelong day by succeeding shoals of gaping folk, struck me as totally unfitting. The cold dignity of the old chief, and the malignant scowl of the prophet, expressed the indecency and the irksomeness of such a situation. Then, to look at those two young savages, with their fine muscular proportions, and think of them cooped up the whole horrible day long, in this hot prison-house full of people, made my heart ache. How they must loathe the sight of these narrow walls, and the sound of these strange voices; how they must sicken for their unmeasured range of wilderness! The gentleman who seemed to have the charge of them pressed me to go up and shake hands with them, as every body else in the room did; but I refused to do so from literal compassion,

and unwillingness to add to the wearisome toil
they were made to undergo. As we were departing, however, they reiterated their entreaties that
we would go up and shake hands with them,—so
I did. Black Hawk and the young men received
our courtesy with great complaisance; but when
we went to the great warrior and the prophet, they
seemed exceedingly loath to receive our hands,
the latter particularly, who had, moreover, one of
the very worst expressions I think I ever saw upon
a human countenance. I instinctively withdrew
my hand; but when my father offered his, the
savage's face relaxed into a smile, and he met his
greeting readily. I wonder what pleased him
about my father's appearance, whether it was his
large size or not. I had a silver vinaigrette in my
pouch, which I gave Black Hawk's son, by way
of keepsake: it will make a charming present for
his squaw.

Sunday, June 30th.

Rose at four, but after looking at my watch, resumed my slumbers until six, when I started up,
much dismayed to find it so late, and presently,
having dressed as fast as ever I could, we set off
for the steam-boat. The morning was the brightest

possible, the glorious waters that meet before New
York were all like rivers of light blazing with the
reflected radiance of the morning sky.   We had
no sooner set foot on board the steam-boat, than
a crowd of well-known faces surrounded us : I
was introduced to Mr. ——, and Mr. —— the
brother of our host at Cold Spring.   Mr. ——
came and stood by me for a considerable time after
we started.   It is agreeable to talk to him, because
he has known and seen so much ; traversed the
world in every direction, and been the friend of
Byron and Shelley ; a common mind, that had enjoyed the same opportunities, (that's impossible, by
the by, no common mind would have sought or
found them,) must have acquired something from
intercourse with such men, and such wide knowledge of things ; but he is an uncommon man, and
it is very interesting to hear him talk of what he
has seen, and those he has known.   *

    *   *   *   *   *

    *   *   *   _   *   *

. When we reached West Point, Mr. —— was
waiting with his boat to convey us over to Cold
Spring ; and accordingly bidding our various acquaintance and companions farewell, we rowed
over out of the course of the river, into a sunny
bay it forms among the hills, to our kinsman's
abode.

Mr. ——'s place is a lovely little nook, situated
on the summit of a rise on the brink of the placid
curve of water formed here by the river, and which
extends itself from the main current about a mile
into the mountains, ending in a wide marsh. The
house, though upon a hill, is so looked down upon,
and locked in by the highlands around it, that it
seems to be at the bottom of a valley. From the
verandah of his house, through various frames
which he has had cut, with exceeding good judgment, among the plantations around the lawn, exquisite glimpses appeared of the mountains, the
little bay, the glorious Hudson itself, with the
graceful boats for ever walking its broad waters,
their white sails coming through the rocky passes
where the river could not be detected, as though
they were sailing through the valleys of the earth.
The day was warm ; but a fresh breeze stirred the
boughs, and cooled the air. My father and D——
seemed overcome with drowsiness, and lay in the
verandah with half-closed eyes, peeping at the
dream-like scene around them. I was not inclined
to rest; and Mr. —— having promised to show
me some falls at a short distance from the house,
he, his brother, and I set forth thither. We
passed through the iron works : 't was Sunday,
and every thing, except a bright watercourse,

laughing and singing as it ran, was still. They took me over the works; showed me the iron frames of large mill-wheels, the machinery and process of boring the cannon, the model of an iron forcing-pump, the casting-houses, and all the wonders of their manufactory. All mechanical science is very interesting to me, when I have an opportunity of seeing the detail of it, and comprehending, by illustrations presented to my eyes, the technical terms used by those conversing with me. We left these dark abodes, and their smouldering fires, and strange, powerful-looking instruments, and, taking a path at the foot of the mountains, skirted the marsh for some time, and then struck into the woods, ascending a tremendous stony path, at the top of which we threw ourselves down to pant, and looked below, through a narrow rent in the curtain of leaves around us, on the river, and rocks, and mountains, bright with the noonday splendour of the unclouded sky. After resting here a few moments, we arose, and climbed again, through the woods, across a sweet clover-field, to the brow of the hill where stands the highland school, a cheerful looking cottage, with the mountain tops all round, the blessed sky above, and the downward sloping woods, and lake-like river below. Passing through the ground surrounding it, we joined a road skirting a deep ravine, from the bottom of which the waters called to me. I was wild to go down, but my companions would not let me: it was in vain that I strained over the brink, the trees were so thickly woven together, and the hollow so deep, that I could see nothing but dark boughs, except every now and then, as the wind stirred them, the white glimmer of the leaping foam, as it sprang away with a shout that made my heart dance. We followed the path, which began to decline; and presently a silver thread of gushing water ran like a frightened child across our way, and flung itself down into the glen. At length we reached the brown golden-looking stream. Mr. —— was exhorting us to take an upper path, which he said would bring us to the foot of the fall; but I was not to be seduced away from the side of the rivulet, and insisted upon crossing it then and there, through the water, over moss-capped stones, across fallen trees, which, struck by the lightning, or undermined by the cold-kissing waters, had choked up the brook with their leafy bridges. So striving on, as best we might, after wading through the stream two or three times, we reached the end and aim of our journey, the waterfall. We stood on the brink of a pool, about forty feet across, and varying in depth from three to seven or eight feet: it was

perfectly circular, and, except on the south, where
the waters take their path down the glen, closed
round with a wall of rock about thirty feet high,
in whose crevices trees with their rifted roots hung
fearlessly, clothing the grey stone with a soft curtain of vivid green. Immediately opposite the
brook, and at the north of the pool, the water came
tumbling over this rocky wall in three distinct
streams, which, striking the projecting ledges of
iron-looking stone, at different angles, met within
eight or ten feet of the pool, and fell in a mingled
sheet of foam. The water broke over the rocks
like a shower of splintered light; the spray sprang
up in the sunlight, and fell again all glittering into
the dark basin below, that gleamed like a magic
jewel set in the mossy earth. On the edge of the
rocks, beside the waterfall, a tree stood out among
its greenly mantled fellows, bare, broken, and
scathed to the very roots with lightning. Its
upper half had fallen aslant one branch of the
waterfall, and lay black and dripping over the
pure white torrent; half falling down its course,
half stayed by some rocky ledges on which it
rested. As I gazed up in perfect ecstasy, an
uncontrollable desire seized me to clamber up
the rocks by the side of the fall, and so reach the
top of it. My companions laughed incredulously

as I expressed my determination to do so; but
followed where I led, until they became well
assured that I was in earnest. Remonstrance,
and representation of impossibility, having been
tried in vain, Mr. —— prepared to guide me,
and Mr. —— with my bag, parasol, and bonnet
in charge, returned to the edge of the pool to
watch our progress. Away we went over the
ledges of the rocks, with nothing but damp leaves,
and slippery roots of trees, for footing. At one
moment, the slight covering of mould on which I
had placed my foot crumbled from beneath it, and
I swung over the water by a young sapling which
upheld me well, and by which I recovered footing
and balance. We had now reached the immediate
side of the waterfall, and my guide began ascending
the slippery slanting rocks down which it fell. I
followed: in an instant I was soaked through with
the spray, my feet slipped, I had no hold, he was
up above me, the pool far below. With my head
bowed against the foam and water, I was feeling
where next to tread, when a bit of rock, that my
companion had thought firm, broke beneath his
foot, and came falling down beside me into the
stream. I paused, for I was frightened : I looked
up for a moment, but was blinded by the water,
and could not see where my guide was; I looked

down the slanting ledge we had climbed, over
which the white water was churning angrily:
" Shall I come down again? " I cried to Mr. ——,
who was anxiously looking up at our perilous
path. " Give me your hand," shouted his brother,
above me; I lifted my head, and turned towards
him, and a dazzling curtain of spray and foam
fell over my face. " I cannot see you," I replied;
" I cannot go on; I do not know what to do."
" Give me your hand! " he exclaimed again; and
I, planting one foot upon a ledge of rock so high
as to lift me off the other, held up my arm to
him: but my limbs were so strained from his
height above me, that I had no power to spring
or move, either up or down. However, I felt
my presence of mind going: I knew that to
go down was impossible, except headlong; the
ascent must therefore be persevered in. " Are
you steady, quite, quite steady? " I enquired; he
replied, " Yes; " and holding out his hand, I
locked mine in it, and bade him draw me up.
But he had not calculated upon my weight; my
slight appearance had deceived him; and, as I
bore upon his arm, we both of us slipped. I
turned as sick as death; but only cried out, " Recover yourself, recover yourself, I am safe;" which
I was, upon a rocky rim about three inches wide,

with my arm resting on the falling stump of the
blasted tree. He did recover his balance; and,
again holding out his hand, drew me up beside
where he was sitting, on the edge of the rocks, in
the water. We pledged each other in the clear
stream; and, standing on the top of our hardly-
gained eminence, in the midst of the rushing
brook, I wrang my handkerchief triumphantly
at Mr. ——; which was rather a comical consideration, as I was literally dripping from head to
foot. No Naïad ever looked so thoroughly watery,
or could have taken more delight in a ducking.
As soon as he saw us safe, he scrambled up through
the woods to the road; and we doing the same,
we presently all met on the dusty highway, where
we congratulated each other on our perseverance
and success, and laughed very exceedingly at my
soaked situation. We determined not to pass
through the highland school ground, but kept
the main road for the advantage of sun and wind,
the combined influences of which presently dried
my frock and handkerchief. When I reached
home, ran up stairs, and dressed myself for dinner,
which we sat down to at about four. After dinner,
came up to my room and slept very profoundly,
until summoned to coffee, which we drank in the
verandah. At about eight o'clock, the sun had left

the sky ; but his warm mantle lay over the western
clouds, and hung upon the rocks and woody mountain sides.   A gentle breeze was stirring the trees
round where we sat; and through the thick
branches of a chestnut tree, as they waved to and
fro, the silver disk of the full moon looked placidly
down upon us.   We set out strolling through the
woods : leisurely as foot could fall, we took our
way through the twilight paths ; and when we
reached the Roman Catholic chapel our host is
building by the river side, the silent, thoughtful
mountains were wrapped in deep shadows, and
the broad waters shone like a sheet of silver in
the moonlight.   We sat down on the cannon lying
on the pebbly shore, and Mr. —— ran off to order
the boat, which presently came stealing round over
the shining waters.   We got in, —— rowing, and
they put me at the helm ; but, owing to Mr. ——'s
misdirections, who seemed extremely amused at
my awkwardness, and took delight in bothering
poor ——, by making me steer all awry, we made
but little progress, and that rather crab-wise;
backing, and sideling, and turning, as though the
poor boat had been a politician.   *   *

   *   *   *   *   *

   *   *   *   *   *

Full of my own contemplations, I kept steering

round and round, and so we wandered, as pur-
poseless as the night air over the smooth waters,
and beneath the shadows of the solemn hills, till
near eleven o'clock, when we made for shore, and
slowly turned home. We sat for a length of time
under the verandah: the gentlemen were discussing the planetary system, as accepted in the
civilised world; and Mr. —— maintained, with
sufficient plausibility, that we knew nothing at all
about it, in spite of Newton: for that, though
his theories were borne out by all observation,
it did not follow, therefore, that another theory
equally probable might not exist; that because he
had found out one way of accounting for the construction and motion of the heavenly bodies, there
was no other possible way in which they were
constructed and impelled; because one means is
sufficient, he argued, it does not thence follow,
that 't is the only sufficient means. Mr. ——
maintained that there was, at least, strong pre-
sumption in favour of Newton's systems; because
they are borne out by our observation of results,
and also because hitherto no other better method
of accounting for what we perceive has been discovered. And so they went on, the end of all being,
to my mind, as usual, utter unsatisfactoriness;

and, as the musquitoes were stinging me, I left
them to their discussions, and came to bed.

Monday, July 1st.

Major —— and Mr. —— came over from West
Point : they were going to prove some cannon that
had not yet been fired ; and some time passed in
the various preparations for so doing. At length,
we were summoned down to the water-side, to see
the success of the experiment. The cannon lay
obliquely one behind the other, at intervals of
about six yards, along the curve line of the little
bay ; their muzzles pointed to the high gravelly
bank into which they fired. The guns were double-
loaded, with very heavy charges ; and as soon as
we were safely placed, so as to see and hear, they
were fired. The sound was glorious : the first
heavy peal, and then echo after echo, as they
rimbombavano among the answering hills, who
growled aloud at the stern voice waking their still
and noonday's deep repose. I pushed out in the
boat, from shore, to see the thick curtain of smoke
as it rolled its silver, and brassy, and black volumes over the woody mountain-sides ; parting in
jagged rents as it rose ; through which the vivid
green, and blessed sky, smiled in their peaceful

loneliness. They ended in discharging all the
cannon at once; which made a most glorious
row, and kept the mountains grumbling with its
echoes for some minutes after the discharge. All
the pieces were sound; which was highly satisfactory, as upon each one that flaws in the firing
Mr. —— loses the cost of the piece. Just as the
smoke cleared off from the river, we saw the boat
making to shore; and, presently, Mr. ——, his
wife, and children, and a young Mr. ——, landed.
After introductions, and one or two questions,
Mrs. —— went up to her cottage to put things in
order there; Mr. —— betook himself to Frois-
sart and the shade; Mr. —— to his business; and
D ——, my father, Mr. —— and myself, set forth
to the fountain in the glen. The weather was intensely hot; the thermometer above ninety in the
shade; it was about half-past twelve; and we toiled
and gasped on like so many Indians up the steep
path. The walk had been so laborious, that
neither D—— nor my father were willing, at first,
to admit that the object was a sufficient one. We
sat for some time by the dark shady pool; and
they, by degrees, recovered their breath and complacency, and began to perceive how beautiful
the place really was. My father said the waterfall looked like a fine lace veil torn by the rocks;

which pleased me, because it did look like that. Mr. —— proposed an admirable plan, that of walking down the water's side, and taking a boat upon the Hudson; and so avoiding the long hot walk home. We called at the highland school; where the worthy man who keeps it received us with infinite civility, put us into a delicious cool room, and gave us some white hermitage and water to drink, which did us all manner of good.* We then descended to the river : after some delay and difficulty, got a boat and rowed home.

*   *   *   *   *

*   *   *   *   *

* Of the mental process which the pupils at this highland school undergo, I can say nothing, being totally unacquainted with the system of education adopted there ; but a more advantageous residence for the cultivation of health, strength (for physical education), or the developement of all those pious and poetical tendings of the human soul and mind which are fostered and ripened by the sublime influence of natural beauty and grandeur, cannot be imagined. The gentlemen at the head of this establishment are New Englanders. The observations I made upon the superior intelligence and cultivation of the natives of that part of the United States have been borne out constantly by the fact, that there is hardly any establishment in the States I have visited, in any way connected with education, or the dissemination of information, which is not conducted partially or entirely by New Englanders.

LINES.

Here be the free gifts of the morning for thee ;
Dog-roses, with their thorns all strung with pearls,
And a large round diamond in each rosy cup :
Their leaves are the colour of Aurora's cheeks.
Here is a pale white flower, without a name,
At least to me, who am a stranger here :
It has a delicate almond smell, and grew
Among thick boughs, and leaves that guarded it.
Poor thing ! I took it from its shelter for thee.
Here be some lilac heads of clover, sweet
As the breath of love : they lay amongst the hay
In a new-mown meadow, glittering in the sun.
Here are the leaves of the wild vine, that shine
Like glass without, and underneath are white
And soft as a swan's breast.   There is an oak branch ;
I gather'd it, because it grows at home,
And in this strange land look'd as sad and loving
As a friend's face : when it is wither'd, keep it.
They are all heavy with the tears of the night,
Who weeps, because she may not meet the sun ;
And when he comes down from the mountain tops,
Parting the forests with his hands of fire,
He drinks her weeping, kissing all the flowers
With passionate love, which makes them look so blushing.

Tuesday, 2d.

Packed up my bag, took a cup of tea, went and gathered some flowers, and gave the poor lamb some heads of clover ; bade a very unwilling farewell to the pretty place, and rowed over to West Point, where Mr. —— was waiting for us. We breakfasted at ten, and went down to meet the boat. Young Mr. —— came over to see us off, and brought me some lovely fresh flowers. Mr. —— and Mr. —— were both at the embarking post. When the boat came up, the rush to and from it was, without exception, the most frightful thing I ever saw. The ——'s were landing ; and I just spoke to her, as she was borne past by the throng. Safely on board, I again found myself surrounded by familiar faces : I took out my work, and Mr. —— sat down by us. As a nuisance, which all unsought-for companionship is, he is quite the most endurable possible ; for he has seen such things, and known such people, that it is greatly worth while to listen to him. Every thing he says of Byron and Shelley confirms my own impression of them. The scenery of the Hudson, immediately beyond West Point, loses much of its sublimity, though no beauty. The river widens, and the

rugged summits of the highlands melt gradually
into a softer and more undulating outline. The
richness, and swelling, and falling of the land
reminded me occasionally of England. The yellow grain was giving diversity and warmth to the
green landscape; and the shadowy woods fencing
the corn fields threw over the whole picture a
sheltering, peaceful charm. On the left, we presently began to see the blue outline of the Catskill
mountains, towering into the hot sky, and looking most blessedly cool and dark amid the fervid
glowing of the noonday world. Mrs. —— came
on board at one of the stopping places. I was
quite glad to see her sweet face, and hear her
gentle voice again. Mr. —— was greatly smitten
with her calm look of repose, and lulling speech,
and took to her vehemently. She told me long
stories, like fairy tales, of caverns lately discovered
in the bosom of these mountains; of pits black
and fathomless; of subterranean lakes in gloomy
chambers of the earth; and tumbling waters,
which fall down in the dark, where men heard,
but none had dared to go. How I should like to
go there! Oh, who will lead me into the secret
parts of the earth; who will guide me to the deep
hiding-places where spirits are — where the air of
this upper world is not breathed, and its sounds

are unknown — where the light of the sun is unseen, and the voice of human creatures unheard? how I should like to go there! At about half-past three in the afternoon, the sky became suddenly and thickly overcast: the awning which sheltered the upper deck was withdrawn, and every preparation made for a storm. The pale, angry-looking clouds lay heaped like chalk upon a leaden sky; and presently one red lightning dipped down into the woods like a fiery snake falling from the heavens. At the same time, a furious gust of wind and torrent of rain rushed down the mountain side. We scuttled down to the lower deck as fast as ever we could; but the storm met us at the bottom of the stairs, and in an instant I was drenched. Chairs, tables, every thing was overturned by the gust; and the boat was running with water in every direction. It thundered and lightened a little; but the noise of the engine was such, that we scarce heard the storm. I stood by the door of the furnace, and dried leisurely; talking the while to Mr. ——, who is sun-burnt enough to warm one through with a look. During our progress, one of the wheels (or paddles, as they are properly called) took it into its head to knock its case to pieces, and banged the boards about in a strange way. Accident the

second : — one of the men, a black, who was employed in tending the fire, got so dreadfully heated
with the intense furnace, that he rushed out of the
engine-room, and swallowed two or three draughts
of cold water.   The effect was instantaneous : he
fell down in violent internal spasms, and died,
poor wretch ! before we arrived at Albany.   We
reached that town at about half-past five in the
afternoon, and went to a house the ——'s recommended to us.   At about seven, they gave us
dinner ; and immediately after I came up to my
own room.   I was so exhausted with fatigue, and
a violent cold and cough, that I literally fell down
on the floor, and slept till dark.   As we came up
the river, we passed Dr. ——'s place, Hyde Park,
which has the reputation of being the best-kept
private estate in America : the situation of the
house, on the edge of a ridge, appeared to me,
from the river, rather too much exposed.

Saturday, 6th.

My father had settled to go to the Cohoes
Falls.   *   *   *   *
          *   *   *   *   *
          *   *   *   *   *
When we were in the steam-boat, going up to

Troy *, —— put a letter into my hands, which
he told me was written by the mother of Alle-
gra, Byron's child.   The letter was remarkable
only for more straightforwardness and conciseness
than is usual in women's letters.   I do not know
whether —— gave it me to read on that account
alone, or because it contained allusions to wild and
interesting adventures of his own: perhaps there
was a mingling of motives.   There never was, by
the by, a *homogeneous* motive, as Brewster would
say, in the human breast.   We reached Troy in
about twenty minutes, and walked up into the town
to procure some species of vehicle for our progress
to the falls.   There was none ready; and, while
one was being procured, a man, who was standing
near us, very civilly invited us to come into his
shop and sit down; which we did very readily.   The
situation of the warehouses, on the side near the
river, of the main street of Troy, is exceedingly
pretty.   They are, for the most part, large, long

---

* Troy! and that Troy has a Mount Ida!   The names of
places in this country are truly astonishing.   Troy, Syracuse,
and Rome are pretty well in this way; but the state of New
York alone, I believe, boasts of a Manlius, a Homer, a Virgil,
an Ovid, a Cicero, and a Socrates, whose second appearance
in this world is in all the glories of flaming red bricks, new
boards, and white paint.   Did Pythagoras admit of men
becoming towns as well as beasts?   I forget.

rooms, opening to the street at the one end ; and
on the other, looking down, from a considerable
height, upon the Hudson. The shop we were in
was a china store ; and the nice cold crockery-
ware made one cool to look at it : the weather was
roasting. Mr. —— left us to gather information,
and kindly brought me back word that the population of Troy was five hundred, *or* five thousand,
I really forget which ; and, for my journal, it
don't much matter ; and that the storekeeper
assured him the Trojans were an exceedingly
refined and literary set of folks ; and that the society, in point of these two advantages, was no
whit behind Boston : there 's for Boston ! — We
obtained a coach, and crossed a ferry, such as I
had never seen before, worked by horses. Poor
wretches ! they reminded me of ——'s steeds
Martyre et Souffrance. Mr. —— observed that
they led the life of the majority ; and so they do,—
Labour and suffering that custom renders endurable, and that ends by grinding down every faculty
of mind or soul : we're a blessed pack of drudges,
and deserve to be just what we are. After crossing
the ferry, we drove about five miles through some
gentle smiling lands, that made one feel very charitable. The Cohoes is, I believe, a Dutch name
for a hill just above a turn in the Mohawk ; where,

after some shallow, rapid, hasty running over a
rocky bed, the river flings itself down over a
broad barrier, between thirty and forty feet high,
with the most delightful gushing sound in the
world.   The foam looked very nice, and soft, and
thick, and cold : I longed to be in the middle of
it.   *   *   *   *   *

   *   *   *   *   *

   *   *   *   *   *

After wandering about for some time, we sat ourselves down on a high grassy knoll just above the
falls.   *   *   *   *   *

   *   *   *   *   *

   *   *   *   *   *

We returned in time, as we flattered ourselves,
to meet the steam-boat which leaves Troy for
Albany at four; but, just as we were crossing
the ferry, the steamer ran past us, leaving us,
with eyes and mouths wide open, very much bothered as to how we were to get down to Albany.
D—— proposed a row-boat, and the sense of the
company seemed to agree thereto; but, upon driving to the inn where we hired our carriage, and
enquiring for such a conveyance, we were assured
that there was no such thing to be had : whereupon my father, good easy man ! believed there
was not, and got into the coach again.   Mr. ——,

however, had absconded, and remained gone so
long, that I began to think he had, perhaps,
started to swim down the river ; when he presently
appeared, informing us that he had gotten a boat
for us. We jumped readily out of the coach;
and, though my father had actually made a bargain
for the hire of it, to convey us to Albany, with the
innkeeper, and, moreover, given him the money,
the righteous man refunded the dollars; which,
Falstaff knows, is a displeasing thing to do:
" I hate that paying back ! " Our row back
was delightful : the evening was calm and lovely
beyond description ; the sun had lost his fierce-
ness, and the warm air clasped the fresh woods
tenderly; the waters were unbroken as a mirror;
the very spirit of love and peace possessed the
world: the effect of all which was to send me
into a very sound sleep. *   *   *

     *   *   *   *   *

     *   *   *   *   *

We reached Albany in very good time for dinner. Mr. —— dined with us : what a savage
he is, in some respects ! He's a curious being :
a description of him would puzzle any one
who had never seen him. A man with the
proportions of a giant for strength and agility;
taller, straighter, and broader than most men ;

yet with the most listless, indolent carelessness of
gait; and an uncertain, wandering way of drop-
ping his feet to the ground, as if he didn't know
where he was going, and didn't much wish to go
any where.   His face is as dark as a Moor's;
with a wild, strange look about the eyes and forehead, and a mark like a scar upon his cheek : his
whole appearance giving one an idea of toil, hardship, peril, and wild adventure.   The expression
of his mouth is remarkably mild and sweet; and
his voice is extremely low and gentle.   His hands
are as brown as a labourer's : he never profanes
them with gloves, but wears two strange magical-
looking rings : one of them, which he showed me,
is made of elephant's hair.   *   *

  *   *   *   *   *

  *   *   *   *   *

Occasionally, in his horror of one class of pre-
judices, he embraces the opposite ones : perhaps
the extreme of any evil, in this world of imperfect
means, can only be effectually resisted by its reverse extreme.

        Monday, 8th.

After breakfast, went to rehearsal : Mr. ——
came with us.   The actors were one and all read-

ing their parts: the lady who played Charlotte
was the only exception—she was perfect. As I
sat on the stage, between my scenes, a fat, good-
tempered, rosy, bead-eyed, wet-haired, shining-
faced looking man accosted me; and having ascertained that I was myself, proceeded to accuse
me of having, in Mrs. Haller, pronounced the
word "industry" with the accent on the middle
syllable, as "in*dus*try;" adding, that he had already quoted my authority to several people for
the emphasis, and begging to know my "exquisite
reason" therefore. It was in vain that I urged
that it must have been a mistake if I said so; that
I never meant to say so, if I did say so; that if I
did say so, I was very wrong to say so; that I was
very sorry for having said so; that I never would
say so again. Between each of my humblest apo-
logies my accuser merely replied, "But you *did*
say in*dus*try," with an inflexible pertinacity of condemnation, which was not a whit softened by my
sincere confessions. Presently, the worthy creature,
adverting to the letter in the Mirror about General
Jackson, begged that as I had passed the fourth
of July, that glorious anniversary, in Albany, I
would illustrate its celebration by some remarks
in the style of that admirable composition. Great

was the fat man's surprise, and evident his contempt for me, when I disclaimed the authorship
of that document. Greater still waxed both, when
I assured him that on the fourth of July I positively walked out of the town, to avoid the noise
in it. After this, he remained gazing at me in silent
amazement; and, as soon as he had sufficiently
recovered from it to move, he took up his hat,
and briefly wished me " good morning." Mr.
—— told me the man was a newspaper editor;
but I think he looked too fat and fresh, and good-
tempered for that. When we returned home, sat
down to write journal.   *   *   *

    *   *   *   *   *

    *   *   *   *   *

The play was the Gamester: the house was very
full. Mr. —— did not know one syllable of his
part, and bothered me utterly. At the end of
the play, they called for my father, and civilly
desired we would act the Hunchback; as, however, we had not the dresses for it with us, he declined, but promised we would return hereafter.

    *   *   *   *   *

    *   *   *   *   *

Tuesday, 9th.

After breakfast, the day being extremely fine, Mr. —— urged us to go out, and take a walk; so forth we set, my father and I leading the way, and D—— and Mr. — following.   *

*   *   *   *   *

*   *   *   *   *

We crossed the river, and, following the first road like a flock of geese errant, arrived at the top of a delightful breezy knoll, opposite a tiny waterfall, the rocks and basin of which were picturesque; but the water had been turned off to turn a mill. The hill where we stood commanded a beautiful view of the Hudson, Albany, and the shores stretching away into sunny indistinctness. My father, and D——, and Mr. ——, sat down under some oak trees: I ran off to explore the stream.   *

*   *   *   *   *

*   *   *   *   *

After looking about in every direction, I returned to my friends: we strolled away through the woods and along the high road, with the sweet smell of mellow hay keeping us company the while. We halted at an orchard corner, near a pleasant-look-

ing farm, where we all agreed we should like to
live.   *   *   *   *   *
      *   *   *   *   *
      *   *   *   *   *

Mr. —— killed us with laughing with an account
he gave us of some of Byron's sayings and doings,
which were just as whimsical and eccentric as un-
amiable, but very funny.   To-morrow we start
for Utica: Mr. —— comes with us: I am glad of
it — I like him.

Wednesday, 10*th.*

   Just as we were getting into the railroad coach
for Schenectady, a parcel was put into my hand:
it was a letter from ——, and Pellico's " Mie Pri-
gioni :" I was glad of it. At Schenectady we dined.
By the by, I must not forget to mention the civility we met with from the people who kept the
house.   There have been so many instances given
of the discomfort and discourteousness which travellers encounter in America, that it is but justice
to record the reverse when one meets with it. For
my own part, with very few exceptions, I have
hitherto met with nothing but civility and attention of every description.   We have almost always commanded private sitting, and single sleep-

ing rooms; have had our meals served in tolerable comfort and decency; and even on board the steamboats, where every thing is done by shoal, I have found that, in spite of being an inveterate dawdle, and never ready at any of the bell-ringings, I have always had a place reserved for me, and enough to eat, without fighting for it. But to return to our Schenectady hosts. The house was very full; and, while waiting for the canal boat to avoid the gaping crowds with which all the rooms were filled, D—— and I walked out into the verandah, when a pretty lassie, the daughter, I conclude, of the house, invited us into a very nice private parlour, belonging to the family, where I found a fine piano, books, music, and all civilisation as well as civility. We proceeded by canal to Utica, which distance we performed in a day and a night, starting at two from Schenectady, and reaching Utica the next day at about noon. I like travelling by the canal boats very much. Ours was not crowded; and the country through which we passed being delightful, the placid, moderate gliding through it, at about four miles and a half an hour, seemed to me infinitely preferable to the noise of wheels, the rumble of a coach, and the jerking of bad roads, for the gain of a mile an hour. The only nuisances are the bridges over the

canal, which are so very low, that one is obliged
to prostrate one's self on the deck of the boat, to
avoid being scraped off it; and this humiliation
occurs, upon an average, once every quarter of an
hour. Mr. —— read Don Quixote to us: he
reads very peculiarly; slowly, and with very
marked emphasis. He has a strong feeling of
humour, as well as of poetry : in fact, they belong
to each other; for humour is but fancy laughing,
and poetry but fancy sad. The valley of the Mohawk, through which we crept the whole sunshin-
ing day, is beautiful from beginning to end; fertile,
soft, rich, and occasionally approaching sublimity
and grandeur in its rocks and hanging woods.
We had a lovely day, and a soft, blessed sunset,
which, just as we came to a point where the canal
crosses the river, and where the curved and wooded
shores on either side recede, leaving a broad smooth
basin, threw one of the most exquisite effects
of light and colour I ever remember to have seen
over the water and through the sky. The sun
had scarce been down ten minutes from the horizon, when the deck was perfectly wet with the
heaviest dew possible, which drove us down to
the cabin. Here I fell fast asleep, till awakened
by the cabin girl's putting her arms affectionately
round me, and telling me that I might come and

have the first choice of a berth for the night, in the horrible hen-coop allotted to the female passengers. I was too sleepy to acknowledge or avail myself of the courtesy; but the girl's manner was singularly gentle and kind. We sat in the men's cabin until they began making preparations for bed, and then withdrew into a room about twelve feet square, where a whole tribe of women were getting to their beds. Some half undressed, some brushing, some curling, some washing, some already asleep in their narrow cribs, but all within a quarter of an inch of each other: it made one shudder. As I stood cowering in a corner, half asleep, half crying, the cabin girl came to me again, and entreated me to let her make a bed for me. However, upon my refusing to undress before so much good company, or lie down in such narrow neighbourhood, she put D—— and myself in a small closet, where were four empty berths, where I presently fell fast asleep, where she established herself for the night, and where D——, wrapped up in a shawl, sat till morning under the half-open hatchway, breathing damp starlight.

Thursday, 11*th.*

D——'s exclamations woke me in the morning: the day was breaking brightly, and the dewy earth was beginning to smile in the red dawn, when we approached Little Falls, a place where the placid, gentle character of the Mohawk becomes wild and romantic, and beautifully picturesque. The canal is for some space cut through the solid rock, and the banks, high and bold, were crowned with tangled woods, and gemmed with wild flowers, and the delicate, vivid tufts of fern. It was exceedingly beautiful; and though I believe I missed some part of the scenery immediately surrounding Little Falls, the approach to it, which is of the same nature, enchanted me extremely. When we arrived at Utica, I gave the nice cabin girl my silver needle-case: her tenderness and care of me the night before made it impossible for me to offer her money. She took my gift, and, throwing her arms round my neck, kissed me very fervently for it. I was struck with her manner, which had appeared to me, in discharge of her common duties, reserved, and rather dignified. This exhibition of feeling surprised me, therefore; and, together with her dark eyes, hair, and complexion, made me think she must have foreign blood in her veins. I asked her, but she said no: American by birth, English by descent: certainly she had neither the face nor bearing of the one or the other. She was a very singular and striking looking person. As for Mr. ———, he fell in love with her forthwith, and, I think, had half a mind to settle on the Mohawk, and make her his fellow farmer. At Utica we dined; and after dinner I slept profoundly. The gentlemen, I believe, went out to view the town, which twenty years ago *was not,* and now is a flourishing place, with fine-looking shops, two or three hotels, good broad streets, and a body of lawyers, who had a supper at the house where we were staying, and kept the night awake with champagne, shouting, toasts, and clapping of hands: so much for the strides of civilisation through the savage lands of this new world. The house was full, and we could not get a room to ourselves; so we sat in a corner of the large dining-room. Passed the evening in writing journal. Mr. ——— showed me his of Sunday last.

Friday, 1*2th.*

We all breakfasted early together, and immediately after breakfast got into an open carriage
and set off for Trenton. D—— and my father
sat beside each other, —— and I opposite them ;
Mr. —— on the box ; and so we progressed.
The day was bright and breezy : the country was
all smiling round us in rich beauty ; the ripening
sheets of waving grain ; the sloping fields, with
here and there the grey tomb-stone of a forest
tree ; the vivid thickets bounding the pale harvest
plots ; the silvery-looking fences, with their irregular lines relieved against the dark woods ; the
clear sky above ; — all was lovely. About seven
miles from Utica, we stopped to water the horses
at a lonely road-side house : we alighted, and
without ceremony strolled into the garden, — a
mere wilderness of overgrown sweet-briar, faint
breathing dog-roses, and flaunting red poppies,
overshadowed by some orchard trees, from which
we stole sundry half-ripe cherries. The place
was desolate, I believe ; yet we lingered in it, and
did not think it so. We got into the carriage
again : the remaining eight miles of our journey
were as beautiful and as bad as the preceding

ones had been. I thought of our dark drive back
through these miry and uneven ways. At last
we reached the house at which visiters to the
Falls put up: a large, comfortable dwelling enough,
kept by a couple of nice young people, who live
in this solitude all the year round, and maintain
themselves and a beautiful big baby by the profits
they derive from the pilgrims to Trenton. We
ordered dinner, and set forth to the Falls, with
our host for guide. We crossed a small wood
immediately adjoining the house, and, descending
several flights of steps connected by paths in the
rocky bank, we presently stood on the brink of
the channel, where the water was boiling along,
deep, and black, and passing away like time. We
followed along the rocky edge: the path is not
more than a foot wide, and is worn into all manner
of unevenness and cavities, and slippery with the
eternal falling of the spray. —— walked before
me : we dared not turn our heads, for fear of
tumbling into the black whirlpool below. We
walked on steadily, warning each other at every
step, and presently we arrived at the first fall,
where the rest of our party were halting. I can't
describe it : I don't know either its height or
width; I only know it was extremely beautiful,
and came pouring down like a great rolling heap

of amber. The rocks around are high to the
heavens, scooped, and singularly regular; and the
sides of the torrent are every now and then paved
with large smooth layers of rock, as even and regular in their proportions as if the fairies had done
the work. After standing before the tumbling
mass of water for a length of time, we climbed to
the brink above, and went on. Mr. —— flung himself down under a roof of rock by the waterfall.
My father, D——, and the guide went on out of
sight, and —— and I loitered by the rapid waters,
flinging light branches and flowers upon the blood-
coloured torrent, that whirled, and dragged, and
tossed them down to the plunge beneath. When
we came to the beautiful circular fall, we crept
down to a narrow ridge, and sat with our feet
hanging over the black caldron, just opposite a
vivid rainbow that was clasping the waterfall. We
sat here till I began to grow dizzy with the sound
and motion of the churning darkness beneath us,
and begged to move, which we did very cau-
tiously. I was in an agony lest we should slip
from the narrow dripping ledges along which we
crawled. We wandered on, and stopped again
at another fall, upon a rocky shelf overhanging
the torrent, beside the blasted and prostrate trunk
of a large tree. I was tired with walking, and

—— was lifting me up to seat me on the fallen tree, when we saw Mr. —— coming slowly towards us. He stopped and spoke to us, and presently passed on; we remained behind, talking and dipping our hands into the fresh water. At length we rejoined the whole party, sitting by a narrow channel, where the water looked like ink. Beyond this our guide said it was impossible to go : I was for ascertaining this by myself; but my father forbade me to attempt the passage further. I was thirsty; and the guide having given me a beautiful strawberry and a pale blue-bell, that he had found, like a couple of jewels in some dark crevice of the rocks, I devoured the one, and then going down to the black water's edge, we dipped the fairy cup in, and drank the cold clear water, with which abundant draught I relieved my father's thirst also.* Around the

* These beautiful little delicate wild flowers seem to love the dewy neighbourhood of waterfalls : it is only at Trenton, and the Chaudière in Canada, that I remember to have seen them at all in this country. Some poor Scotch peasants, about to emigrate to Canada, took away with them some roots of the " bonny blooming heather," in hopes of making this beloved adorner of their native mountains the cheerer of their exile in the wild lands to which they were going. The heather, however, refused to grow in the Canadian soil, and the poor emigrants had not the melancholy pleasure of

place where we were resting, the rocks rose like
circular walls up to the very sky. From their overhanging edges, tiny threads of water fell upon the
rocky pavement beneath, with a silver glancing,
and a clear, plashing tone, that sounded even amid
the hoarse talking of the dark waters below.   In
some mould among these cliffs, at their very highest
edge, a tree had struck its roots, and, growing
upside down, stretched its drooping green arms to
the hurrying stream below, that would not tarry.
We had walked, I suppose, a mile and a half along
the water's side, and in this distance its course is
broken by six beautiful cataracts.   The variety of
the colour of the water, occasioned by the various

---

seeing its sweet, familiar bloom round their new dwellings.
The person who told me this said that the circumstance had
been related to him by Walter Scott, whose sympathy with
the disappointment of these poor children of the romantic
heatherland betrayed itself even in tears.   When I visited
the beautiful falls of the Chaudière, our party was enlivened,
and the picturesque effect of the scene much heightened, by
some of the Highland band belonging to the regiment quar-
tered in Quebec.   I could not help wondering, as I gathered
the blue bells, which grew profusely round the cataract,
whether these poor fellows looked upon the emblem of their
distant country with any of the feelings which I lent them ;
and the whole brought back to my mind the heather that
would not gladden the exile's eyes in a foreign soil, and the
compassion of Scott for his countrymen's disappointment.

depths of its channel, and the different tints of the
rocks over which it flows, is singular. Where the
river expands, its rapid broken waves were of the
darkest red-brown, like coffee; or rather, indeed,
redder than that, like a deep blood colour; reaching the walls of rock, over which they fall into a
lower bed, they became pouring masses of amber
and diamonds, or soft, thick heaps of whitest foam;
and then again, in the deep narrow channels which
received their headlong leaping, all was black as
blackest night, and the waters were sucked away
under the hollow rocks in inky eddies, that made
me think of drowning with double horror. The
several falls are very various in their height and
forms, but they are all beautiful, most beautiful;
not a place to visit for a day, but to live the summer away in.   *   *   *   *
        *   *   *   *   *
        *   *   *   *   *

When we were all rested, we rose to retrace
our steps: our guide was a man of some cultivation, and of much natural refinement, with a
strong feeling of the exquisite beauty of the scenes
in which he was living. These falls are upon his
own land, belong to him, and he pointed out to
us a spot beside the torrent where he said he had
read all Byron's works: this pleased me. Re-

turning, I thought the path even more difficult than it was before : there is a chain fastened along the rock where it narrows, for the security of persons walking : this has been put up since the lamentable loss of a young girl, who, following her party along this slippery path, missed her footing, and was swept into a foaming whirlpool, whence nothing could ever emerge. Our guide told us of another terrible accident which happened not long before we were there. A young lady and her lover were going along the water side, and, in order to retain hold of her hand, he walked upon a narrow ridge, where he could hardly balance himself : the girl said, " Oh, if you walk there, I shall let you go :" she did so, and in the same instant he slipped from the rock and was dragged away to that dark death.*

* I do not know that the sense of danger has ever been so vivid in my mind as while walking along this narrow edge of eternity. Nothing around Niagara appeared to me half so full of peril as the path along the Trenton Falls, although I have hung over the brink of the last rock that vibrates on the very verge of that great abyss, and explored, entirely alone, the path under the huge watery curtain that falls from Table Rock. I do not know whether the mention of the late accidents at Trenton affected my imagination, and caused me to exaggerate the danger; but it appeared to me almost miraculous that every body passing along those narrow, dripping, uneven ledges did not share the fate of the two unfortunate persons I have mentioned.

The chain upon the rock was about as high as my shoulder; but when the river is swollen, it constantly rises above the chain: at which time, it is scarce possible to go any distance along its banks. This had been the case a short time before we were there. We returned to the house, and dined. After dinner, had a gossip with Mrs. ——, and a romp with her beautiful baby. I strolled into the garden: it was in disorder, and looked like a wilderness; but I saw some roses drooping their full bosoms to the earth, and I went to fetch them. Our host came with me: he said he had but little leisure to cultivate his garden, and could not well afford to have it kept in better order; that it supplied them with nearly all they required; and that, with his other occupations, he had hardly time to make it more than useful. I questioned him about the number of visiters who came to the falls. He said in summer there was a constant succession of them; but that in winter no one came there. Upon my expressing some surprise that people did not come, and remain for some weeks at least, in so beautiful a place, he told me that the generality of visiters were quite satisfied with an hour's stroll by the water; and that some had arrived at his door, alighted from their carriage, dined, sauntered round the house,

and, *without even going down to the river*, returned
to Utica quite satisfied with having been at Trenton. I was amazed. But the utter insensibility
of the generality of Americans to the beauty and
sublimity of nature is nothing short of amazing;
and in this respect they literally appear to me to
want a sense. I have been filled with astonishment and perplexity at the total indifference with
which they behold scenes of grandeur and loveliness that any creature, with half a soul, would
gaze at with feelings almost of adoration. But in
these glorious tabernacles of nature, where God's
majesty seems, as it were, visibly resting on his
works, I have seen Americans come and stare,
and stand for a moment, and depart again, apparently impressed with nothing but the singularity
of the man or woman who could remain there
longer than they did. What can be the cause of
this?—Is it possible that a perception of the beautiful in nature is a result of artificial cultivation?—
is it that the grovelling narrowness of the usual
occupations to which the majority addict themselves has driven out of them the fine spirit, which
is God's altar in men's souls?—is it that they
become incapable of beauty? Wretched people!
They remind me, by contrast, as I see them toiling along the crowded streets of their cities, those

dens of Mammon, of Wordsworth's noble description of him, —

> " Who walked in glory and in joy,
>   Behind his plough, upon the mountain side."
>   *   *   *   *   *
>   *   *   *   *   *

At about sunset, I wandered into the wood, to the top of the steps leading to the waterfall; where I could hear, far below, its sweet voice singing as it passed away. I remained standing here till the carriage was announced. Just before we went away, our host gave me a small piece of crystal. It is found among the rocks here, which, I believe, present many curious geological phenomena; which I leave to the learned to describe. The strata are the most beautifully regular possible; and, upon their broad, smooth, surfaces, a thousand theories sit; which I hope I did not disturb, as I walked over them in the plenitude of my ignorance, admiring God's masonry. Oh, fair world ! — oh, strange, and beautiful, and holy places — where one's soul meets one in silence — and where one's thoughts arise, with the everlasting incense of the waters, from the earth, which is *His* footstool, to the heavens, which are *His* throne. It grew dark long before we reached Utica: half the way, I sang; the other half, I slept, in spite of ruts five fathoms deep, and all the joltings of these evil ways. To-morrow we start on our way to Niagara ; which, Mr. —— says, is to sweep Trenton clean from our memories. I do not think it.

Saturday, 1*3th.*

Left Utica at six o'clock, in our exclusive extra : we were to go on as far as Auburn, a distance of seventy-six miles. The day was very beautiful, but extremely hot. At Vernon, where we stopped to breakfast, we overtook the ——'s : we had a very good breakfast; and, I think, for the first time since our land journey from Baltimore to Philadelphia, last winter, we were waited on by women. Found a case of musical glasses : sat on the floor, in great delight, amusing myself with them : while the stage was getting ready, —— and I began wandering about; but the place did not look promising, and the heat was intense. We sat ourselves down under the piazza of the tavern, and I gave him the words of " To that lone Well." In about an hour, we set off again. The country was very rich and beautiful ; and, at every knoll, backed by woodlands, and skirted by golden grain

fields. Mr. —— exclaimed, " Come, we will
have a farm here." He and my father were to
smoke, reflect, and enjoy life; I was to sing,
whenever I happened to please, and enjoy life too ;
D—— was to brew, to bake, wash, iron, plough,
manage the house, look after the cattle, take care
of the poultry, mind the dairy ; in short, do every
thing on earth that was to be done, and enjoy life
too : all which arrangements afforded us matter of
converse on the way, and much amusement. Then
my father and Mr. —— had long argumentations
about acting : the latter is a vehement admirer of
Kean; and of course, that being the case, matter of debate was not wanting. It was all extremely
pleasant and profitable ; and while the sun shone,
and we all kept our tempers, nothing could do
better. —— amused me by telling me portions
of ——'s book, the Adventures of a younger
Son, with which he had been extremely charmed;
and which I remember beginning on board ship,
as we crossed from England.   *   *

*   *   *   *   *

*   *   *   *   *

At about half-past three, we arrived at a place
called *Syracuse ! ! !* — where, stopping to change
horses, my father observed that here there
were two different routes to our point of destina-

tion; and desired our driver to take that which passes through Skaneateles, a very beautiful village, situated on a lake so called. However, to this the master of the inn, who was also, I believe, proprietor of the coach, seemed to have some private objection ; and while my father was yet speaking, very coolly shut the coach-door in his face, and desired the driver to go on in the contrary direction. The insolence of the fellow enraged my father extremely; and it was rather astonishing, that's the fact: but the deuce is in't if, in a free country, a man may not choose which way his own coach shall go, in spite of the folk who pay him for the use of it. We had to pocket the affront; and, what was much more disagreeable, to travel an ugly, uninteresting road, instead of a picturesque and pretty one. We had not proceeded many miles after this occurrence, and were just recovering our equanimities, when the said vehicle broke down. We were not overturned or hurt, only tilted a little on one side. The driver, however, did not seem to think it safe to proceed in this condition: the gentlemen got out, and searched the hedges and thickets for a piece of oak sufficiently strong and stout to repair, at least for the moment, the damage: we were not at the time within reach of any house. At last, they procured what they wanted; and, having propped up the carriage after the best fashion they could, we proceeded at a foot pace to the next village. Here, while they were putting our conveyance into something like better order, —— and I wandered away to a pretty bright watercourse, which, like all water in this country, was made to turn a mill. The coach being made sound once more, we packed ourselves into it, and progressed. The evening was perfectly sultry. I never shall forget, at a place where we stopped to water the horses, a cart-full of wretched sheep and calves, who were, I suppose, on their way to the slaughter-house, but who, in the mean time, seemed enduring the most horrible torture that creatures can suffer. They were jammed into the cart so as to be utterly incapable of moving a single limb; the pitiless sun shone fiercely upon their wretched heads, and their poor eyes were full of dust and flies. I never saw so miserable a spectacle of suffering. I looked at the brutal-looking man that was driving them, and wondered whether he would go to hell, for tormenting these helpless beasts in this fashion.

The sun set gloriously. Mr. —— began talking about Greece, and getting a good deal ex-

cited, presently burst forth into " The isles of
Greece ! the isles of Greece ! " which he recited
with amazing vehemence and earnestness. He
reminded me of Kean several times : while he
was declaiming, he looked like a tiger. 'T is
strange, or, rather, 't is not strange, 't is but natural, how, in spite of the contempt, and even
hatred, which he often expresses for England,
and every thing connected with it, his thoughts
and plans, and all the energies of his mind, seem
for ever bent upon changes to be wrought *in* England — freer government, purer laws, more equal
rights. He began to talk about Cromwell : he
wanted, he said, to have a play written out of
Cromwell's life. We talked the matter over with
infinite zeal, and established most satisfactorily,
that to accomplish such a thing, as it ought to be
done, would be quite one of the most difficult
tasks in the world. Nobody but a religious and
political enthusiast could do it : a poet, unless
himself a republican Englishman and fanatical
sectarian, hardly could : it must be unlike all other
works of art — not an imitation of truth, but truth
itself. Schiller is the only man I can imagine who
could have attempted it with any chance of success : and I even doubt whether he would have

made of it the firebrand our friend wants.* Towards evening the heat became more and more oppressive. Our coach was but ill cobbled, and leaned awfully to one side. I fell asleep lying in my father's lap; and when we reached Auburn, which was not until nine o'clock, I was so tired,

---

* Thank God! a firebrand, which shall throw England into confusion and anarchy, is not, indeed, of easy make. Italy, crushed under the heel of her northern rulers; or France, blown about with every breath of opinion, may rush into revolutions for a ballad or an opera. The misery of the one, and the miserable excitability of the other nation, render it easy to rouse, in the former, the spirit of retribution; in the latter, the desire of change. But Englishmen, who are neither slaves nor weathercocks, are less easily stirred to wild excesses of political excitement. Let who will steer, the old ship is too well ballasted to sink. Whoever rules, whatever party may be at the head of her government, England is sound at heart: there is a broad foundation of moral good and intelligence in the nation, which will not be shaken or upturned, let factions erect or pull down what temporary trophies they please, to their own short-lived and selfish triumphs. The file of the mechanic may still gnaw angrily at the iron crown of the aristocracy; interests of classes may still jar, parties wrangle, and the eternal warfare between those who climb, and those who stand upon the topmost round of the ladder, may still be waged. And so be it: in none of these is there fear or danger; but rather a wholesome action of power against power; a checking, winnowing, purifying, and preserving influence. Moral evil, vice; and mental evil, ignorance; are the roots of decay: surely England is far from the day of her downfalling.

so miserably sleepy, and so tortured with the side-ache, from the cramped position in which I had been lying, that I just crawled into the first room in the inn where we alighted, and dropped down on the floor fast asleep. They roused me for supper; and very soon after I betook myself to bed. The heat was intolerable; the pale feet of the summer lightning ran along the black edges of the leaden clouds, — the world was alight with it. I could not sleep: I never endured such suffocating heat.

Sunday, 14*th.*

Rose at eight: the morning was already sultry as the hottest noon in England. After breakfast, I wandered about the house in search of shade; went into an empty room, opened the shutters, and got out upon a large piazza, or, rather, colonnade, which surrounded it. The side I had chosen was defended by the house from the fierce sunlight; and I walked up and down in quiet and loneliness for some time. Not far from the house stood the prison, one of the state prisons of the country; a large grey building, which appeared like a huge block of granite, unsheltered by a single tree or bush, and dim with the hazy heat of the atmosphere. Being Sunday, we were not able to visit it; but the person who kept the house where we were, a very intelligent and civil man, gave us some account of it, and fully corroborated the fact which Stuart mentions, — that when the prison took fire, and all the criminals confined in it were liberated to assist in saving the building, in spite of the general confusion and total absence of restraint or observation, which for some time left them the most easy opportunity of escape, not one of them took advantage of this accident to recover their liberty, but every prisoner returned voluntarily, after the fire was got under, to his cell. This seems miraculous, and speaks more for the excellence of the system pursued in these establishments than all the disquisitions in the world. At about ten, our exclusive extra having driven to the door, we packed ourselves into it, and proceeded towards Geneva, where we were to dine. The sky, however, presently became overcast; and, towards noon, the world was absolutely shrouded in a lead-coloured pall. The air was stifling : it was impossible to draw one's breath; and a quarter of a degree more of heat would certainly have occasioned suffocation. We were all gasping. Sud-

denly the red lightning tore open the heavy
clouds, the thunder rolled round the heavens, the
rain came down in torrents : we were away from
all shelter, and obliged to proceed through the
storm.   The leather curtains of our coach were
speedily unrolled and buttoned down ; but this
formed but a miserable shelter against the furious
rain.   Our carpet-bags, which were on the outside of the carriage, were soaked through; and
we ourselves were soon in nearly as bad a plight.
The rain came in rivulets through the crevices of
our insufficient shelter, and the seats and bottom
of the coach were presently standing pools.   We
arrived between twelve and one o'clock at Cayuga;
and here we drew up before the inn door, to
await the end of the storm.   The rain was still
so violent, that we preferred remaining in the
coach to getting out and being still more thoroughly drenched.   The thunder growled sulkily
at a distance, and the lightning glared rapidly
from side to side.   By degrees, the over-swollen
clouds, having emptied themselves, rolled away ;
the rain became less violent ; the mist and heavy
vapour parted from off the face of the earth, and
the lake appeared blending with the sky amid
the indistinct and hazy outlines of the half-
shrouded country.   While we were sitting listen-

ing to the storm, silence had fallen upon us all: a thunder-storm is apt to prove an interruption to conversation. During this pause, Mr. —— took out his pencil, and wrote upon a scrap of paper a very eloquent Mahomedan description of the attributes of God. I do not know whether it was his own, or an authentic Mahomedan document: it was sublime.   *   *

    *   *   *   *   *

    *   *   *   *   *

The storm having abated, we proceeded on our way; crossed a bridge a mile and some roods long, over the Cayuga lake; which, however, was still so veiled with scowling mist and clouds, that we could discern none of its features. At about three o'clock we reached Geneva, a small town situated on a lake called Seneca Water. Here we dined. —— had most providentially brought silver forks with him: for the wretched two-pronged iron implements furnished us by our host were any thing but clean or convenient. After dinner, the weather having become mild and bright, we went up to a piazza on the second floor, which overlooked the lake and its banks: the latter are very picturesque; and the town itself, climbing in terraces along the side of a steep acclivity, rising from the water, has a very good effect. The lake at this point did not appear very wide; for we could distinguish, from where we stood, minute objects on the opposite shore.

After resting ourselves for a short time, we again took to our coach, and pursued our route towards Canandaigua, where we were to pass the night. The afternoon was bright and beautiful, the road tolerable, and the country through which we passed fertile and smiling.

As the evening began to come on, we reached Canandaigua Lake, a very beautiful sheet of water, of considerable extent; we coasted for some time close along its very margin. The opposite shore was high, clothed with wood, from amidst which here and there a white house looked peacefully down on the clear mirror below : the dead themselves can hardly inhabit regions more blessedly apart from the evil turmoil of the world, than the inhabitants of these beautiful solitudes.* Leaving

---

* I have had occasion to observe, in a former note, that foreigners travelling through this country see only the least desirable society of the various cities they visit. There is another class of Americans, whom they rarely, if ever, become acquainted with at all; by far the most interesting, in my opinion, which the country affords. I speak of those families

the water's edge, we proceeded about a quarter
of a mile, and found ourselves at the door of the

---

thickly scattered through all the states, from whose original
settlers many of them are immediately descended; who
reside upon lands purchased by their grandfathers in the
early days of the *British colonies ;* and who, living remote
from the Atlantic cities, and the more travelled routes between them, are free from all the peculiarities which displease
an European in the societies of the towns, and possess
traits of originality in their manners, minds, and mode of life,
infinitely refreshing to the observer, wearied of the eternal
sameness which pervades the human congregations of the
Old World.

In mixing with the commercial fashionables and exclusives
of the American cities, the European is at once amused and
annoyed with the assumption of a social tone and spirit at
variance with the whole *make* of the country. He is told
that he is in the best society of the place, and with perfect
justice condemns this best society as, probably, the worst he
ever saw : a society assuming the airs of separate rank
where no rank at all exists, attempting to copy the luxury
and splendour of the residents of European capitals, without possessing one tithe of their wealth to excuse the
extravagance, or enable them to succeed in the endeavour,
and presenting the most incongruous and displeasing mixture
possible of pretension, ignorance, affectation, and vulgarity.
I have before said, that even in the cities there are circles of
a very different order; but yet freer from all these drawbacks
is the society formed by the class of people of whom I have
spoken above, and whom I should designate as the gentry

inn at Canandaigua; the principal among some
houses surrounding an open turfed space, like an
English village green, across which ran the high
road. My father, Mr. ——, and I went up to a
sort of observatory at the top of the house, from
whence the view was perfectly enchanting. The
green below, screened on three sides with remarkably fine poplar trees, and surrounded by neat
white houses, reminded me of some retired spot
in my own dear country. Opposite us, the land
rose with a gentle wooded swell; and to the left,
the lake spread itself to meet the horizon. A
fresh breeze blew over the earth, most grateful
after the intense heat of the morning, and the
sky was all strewed with faint rosy clouds, melting

---

of this country; using that term in the best sense in which
it was once used in England.

Among this large but widely scattered portion of the
community, should the European traveller's good fortune
lead him, he will find hospitality without ostentation, purity
of morals independent of the dread of opinion, intellectual cultivation unmixed with the desire of display, great simplicity
of life and ignorance of the world, originality of mind
naturally arising from independence and solitude, and *the
best*, because the most natural, manners. Of such, I know,
from the lower shores of the Chesapeake, to the half savage
territory around Michilimakinack.

away one by one into violet wreaths, among which the early evening star glittered cold and clear.

We came down to supper, which was served to us, as usual, in a large desolate-looking public room. After this, we came to the sitting-room they had provided for us, a small comfortable apartment, with a very finely-toned piano in it. To this I forthwith sat down, and played and sang for a length of time : late in the evening, I left the instrument, and my father, Mr. ——, and I took a delightful stroll under the colonnade, discussing Milton; many passages of which my father recited most beautifully, to my infinite delight and ecstasy. By and by they went in, and —— came out to walk with me.

Certainly this climate is the most treacherous imaginable : the heat this morning had been intolerable, and to-night a piercing cold wind had arisen, that would have rendered winter clothing by no means superfluous. We walked rapidly up and down, till the bleak blast became so keen, that we were glad to take refuge in the house. Our unfortunate carpet bags and their contents are literally drenched : many of my goods and chattels will never recover this ablution; among others, I am sorry to say, ——'s beautiful satchel.

Monday, 1*5th.*

Our breakfast, which was extremely comfortable and clean, was served to us in our private room ; a singular favour : one, I hope, which will become a custom as the country is travelled through by greater numbers. Before breakfast, D—— had been taking a walk about the pretty village, and trying to beg, borrow, or steal some flowers for me. The master of the inn, however, succeeded better than she did ; for he presently made his appearance with a very beautiful and fragrant nosegay, which I found, to my utter dismay, had been levied from a gentleman's private garden in my name. My horror was excessive at this, and was scarcely diminished when I discovered, upon enquiry, that they had been gathered from Mr. ——'s garden ; that gentleman having large property and a fine residence here. He was not in Canandaigua himself ; but, as we drove past his house, I left cards for his lady, who must have thought my demand on her green-house one of the greatest impertinencies extant. It was nine o'clock when we left Canandaigua : we were all a little done up with our two previous days; and it was unanimously settled that we should proceed only to Rochester, a distance of between thirty and forty miles, which we accomplished by two o'clock.

Rochester, upon whose site, I understand, twenty years ago there stood hardly a house, is now a large and populous manufacturing town. The progress of life in this country is amazing. From day to day the wilderness becomes inhabited, peopled, civilised; and where yesterday the majestic woods were standing, and the silent waters gliding in all the solemn solitude of unexplored nature, to day the sound of the forge and anvil is heard, the busy feet of men pass and repass, their mingled voices resound, their dwellings arise; the wheels of a thousand mechanical miracles clash, creak, and jar; the vapours of a thousand steam-engines mingle with the hitherto lonely clouds; and the huge fins of a thousand steam-boats beat the waters, carrying over their hitherto undisturbed surface the vast produce of industry. The labours, the arts, the knowledge, the wealth, the wonders of education and civilisation! It is something that fills one with admiration, in the old, and eke the new sense of the word.

The inn at which we alighted was large and comfortable : in the drawing-room I found a very tolerable piano-forte, to which I instantly betook myself. By the time we had seen our bed-rooms, and ordered dinner, we found we should have leisure, before it was ready, to walk to the falls of the Genesee (the river on which Rochester stands), which have some celebrity for their beauty. A man from the hotel volunteered to be our guide, and joined our party. We walked up the main street, which was crowded and full of business. From this, presently turning off, we followed a wider road, with houses and pretty flower-gardens on each side, and reached, after half a mile's walk, a meadow skirted by a deep ravine, through which the river ran; from whence we looked immediately upon the falls. They would be, and were, I doubt not, once beautiful; for the barrier of rock, over which the river throws itself into the valley below, is of considerable breadth and height; but, alas! the waters have been turned off to turn mills, and a thin curtain, which falls over the rocks like a vapoury sheet of blue smoke, is all that remains of the Genesee falls; whilst, from a thousand dingy-looking mills and manufactories, the poor little rivulets of labouring water come rushing through narrow dirty channels, all stained and foaming and hot from their work, to throw themselves into the thin bosom of their parent stream. Truly, mills and steam-engines are wonderful things, and I know that men must live ; but I wish it were not expedient to destroy what God has made so very beautiful, in order to make it useful. Our guide perceiving our admiration was a good deal excited by the picturesque beauty of the scene, fell into a species of rhapsody, which terminated thus : " Yes, sir, when I see the waters thus falling *from the bottom to the top ;* I say, sir, when I look at the water falling from *the bottom to the top,* I can compare it to nothing — but — but — but — wool out of a cotton mill ! " This was an unlooked for climax, and gave us all a violent inclination to laugh in the face of the orator ; which, however, would have been exceedingly wrong ; for so sincere was the good man in his enthusiasm, that he was not in the least aware of the miraculous proceeding which he twice, with much emphasis, ascribed to the *upward falling* water.†

* * * * *

* * * * *

† This spot is famous as the scene of the last exploit of a singular individual, known by the name of Sam Patch. An

We waited in this meadow for the passing of a train
of rail-road carriages, which run between Rochester and a small village about three miles distant,
where the river was said to be very beautiful.
We hailed them as they went by, and proceeded
in them to their destination. The view itself,
from this point, though romantic and pretty, was
scarce worth going out of the way for; the walk
back, however, was delightful. The river runs
here through a deep gully, the banks rising pre-
cipitously above a hundred feet on each side of it.
On one side they are beautifully and thickly
wooded; the other presents a bare wall of reddish
rock lying in very regular strata. About a mile
and a half below the falls, the channel of the river
contracts itself, and the water, forcing its way
through some irregular rocky projections, forms
a very pretty miniature cataract. We walked

Irishman by birth, I believe, he came over to this country
to earn his bread, and hit upon a very ingenious method of
doing so, *i. e.* jumping for large wagers down cataracts;
which daring feat he performed successfully more than once.
But, like the Sicilian diver of old, poor Sam Patch took one
plunge too many; and, after leaping with impunity from the
rocks immediately below the Falls of Niagara, he found his
death in the Genesee — attempting the leap, it is said,
while in a state of intoxication.

along the high margin of the glen, upon some very thick soft turf, looking down upon the deep bed of the water, and enjoying a delicious fresh breeze. 'T is curious enough, that upon this strip of turf, close to the high road, under the shelter of a group of trees, we found a couple of tomb-stones. They were carefully railed round, and bore the names of a man and his wife, without, however, assigning any cause for their choice of a burial-place so public and unhallowed. The last mile of our walk was by no means so agreeable as the previous part had been. Nearing the town, we had to leave the brink of the river and follow the dusty track of the rail-road. When we reached Rochester, we dined; after which I went and lay down, and slept till tea-time. When I came down to tea, found the gentlemen profoundly busied : —— writing home, Mr. —— journalising, my father poring over maps and road-books, to find out if we could not possibly get as far as Niagara to-morrow.

Tuesday, 16*th.*

Had to get up before I 'd half done my sleep. At six, started from Rochester for Murray, where

we purposed breakfasting.   Just as we were nearing the inn, at this same place, our driver took it
into his head to give us a taste of his quality. We
were all earnestly engaged in a discussion, when
suddenly I felt a tremendous sort of stunning blow,
and as soon as I opened my eyes, found that the
coach was overturned, lying completely on its side.
I was very comfortably curled up under my father,
who, by Heaven's mercy, did not suffocate me;
opposite sat D——, as white as a ghost, with her
forehead cut open, and an awful-looking stream
of blood falling from it; by her stood Mr. ——,
also as pale as ashes: —— was perched like a
bird above us all, on the edge of the doorway,
which was open. The first thing I did, was to
cry as loud as ever I could, " I 'm not hurt, I 'm
not hurt ! " which assurance I shouted sufficiently
lustily to remove all anxiety from their minds.
The next thing was to get my father up; in ac-
complishing which, he trampled upon me most
cruelly. As soon as I was relieved from his moun-
tainous pressure, I got up, and saw, to my dismay,
two men carrying Mr. —— into the house. We
were all convinced that some of his limbs were
broken : I ran after as quickly as I could, and
presently the house was like an hospital. They

carried him into an upper room, and laid him on a bed; here, too, they brought D——, all white and bleeding. Our hand-baskets and bags were ransacked for salts and eau de Cologne. Cold water, hot water, towels, and pocket handkerchiefs, were called into requisition; and I, with my clothes all torn, and one shoulder all bruised and cut, went from the one to the other in utter dismay. Presently, to my great relief, Mr. —— revived; and gave ample testimony of having the use of his limbs, by getting up, and, in the most skilful manner, plastering poor D——'s broken brow up. —— went in quest of my father, who had received a violent blow on his leg, and was halting about, looking after the baggage and the driver, who had escaped unhurt.* The chief cause of our misfortune was the economy with

---

* Although nobody, I believe, ever travelled a hundred miles by land in this country without being overturned, the drivers deserve infinite credit for the *rare occurrence* of accidents. How they can carry a coach at all over some of their roads is miraculous; and high praise is due to them both for care and skill, that any body, in any part of this country, ever arrives at the end of a land journey at all. I do not ever remember to have seen six-in-hand driving except in New England, where it is common, and where the stage-drivers are great adepts in their mystery.

which the stage-coaches are constructed in this
thrifty land; that is, they have but one door, and,
of course, are obliged to be turned round much
oftener than if they had two: in wheeling us,
therefore, rapidly up to the inn, and turning the
coach with the side that had a door towards the
house, we swung over, and fell.   While the coach
was being repaired, and the horses changed, we,
bound up, bruised, and aching, but still very
merry, sat down to breakfast.   Mr. ——, who
had been merely stunned, seized on the milk and
honey, and stuffed away with great zeal: poor
D—— was the most deplorable of the party, with
a bloody handkerchief bound over one half her
face; I only ached a little, and I believe ——
escaped with a scratch on his finger; so, seeing it
was no worse, we thanked God, and devoured.
After breakfast, we packed ourselves again in our
vehicle, and progressed.   Mr. —— had procured
for me a bunch of flowers; and I amused myself
with making a wreath of them.   Our route lay
over what is called the Ridge road; a very remarkable tract, pursuing a high embankment,
which was once the boundary of Lake Ontario;
though the waters are now distant from it upwards of seven miles.   The theories of the geolo-

gists respecting the former position of the lake are very singular; though borne out by similar instances of natural convulsions, and also by the very features of the land. The country through which we journeyed to day was wilder and less cultivated than any we have yet seen. A great deal of forest land, consisting of close, thin, tall, second-growth, springing around the stump of many a huge tree; thick tangled underwood; marsh and damp green wilderness, where the grass and bushes trailed about in rank luxuriance; and piles of felled timber, with here and there a root yet smoking, bore witness to the first inroads of human cultivation. None of the trees that were standing were of any girth, or comparable in size and beauty to our park trees; but some of the stumps were of large size, and must have been the foundations of noble forest pillars. Our road, after leaving the Ridge road, was horrible: for some length of time before we reached Lockport, we were dragged over what is called a *corduroy road;* which consists merely of logs of wood laid close to each other, the natural inequalities of which produce a species of jolting incomparably superior to any other I ever felt, and administering but little comfort either to our bruised bones or apprehensive nerves.

We reached Lockport at about four o'clock.
There had been rain in the course of the morning,
but the evening was clear, though very cold. The appearance of Lockport is very singular: a collection
of new white houses, that look as though they were
but this instant finished, standing in a half-cleared
wilderness. All round the town, if such it may be
called, stretch the remains of the once pathless
woods, half cleared, half savage-looking yet ; and,
as far as the eye can reach, the country presents
a series of dreary slopes, covered with prostrate
trees, heaps of hewn timber, smoking stumps, and
blackened trunks — a sort of forest stubble-land —
a very desolate looking thing indeed. The house
where we stopped appeared to be hardly finished.
We ordered dinner, and I forthwith began
kindling a fire, which was extremely welcome to us
all. I was very much bruised with our morning's
overturn, and went and lay down in my bed-room,
where I presently slept profoundly.

Wednesday, 17*th.*

At nine o'clock, we started from Lockport :
before doing so, however, we went down to the

canal side to look at the works, which are here very curious and interesting. —— ran into a bookseller's shop, and got ——'s book for me, which he was going to pounce upon without knowing what it was; and ——, for some reasons best known to himself, snatched it away from him, saying it was a book which he was sure he would not like. The road between Lockport and Lewistown is very pretty; and we got out and walked whenever the horses were changed. At one place where we stopped, I saw a meek-eyed, yellowish-white cart-horse, standing with a man's saddle on his back. The opportunity was irresistible, and the desire too — I had not backed a horse for so long. So I got up upon the amazed quadruped woman's fashion, and took a gallop through the fields, with infinite risk of falling off, and proportionate satisfaction. We reached Lewistown at about noon, and anxious enquiries were instituted as to how our luggage was to be forwarded, when on the other side; for we were *exclusive extras ;* and for creatures so above common fellowship there is no accommodation in this levelling land. A ferry and a ferry-boat, however, it appeared, there were, and thither we made our way. While we were waiting for the boat, I climbed out on the branches of a huge oak, which grew over the banks of the river, which here rise nearly a hundred feet high.   Thus comfortably perched, like a bird, 'twixt heaven and earth, I copied off some verses which I had scrawled just before leaving Lockport. The ferry-boat being at length procured, we got into it. The day was sultry; the heat intolerable.

The water of this said river Niagara is of a most peculiar colour, like a turquoise when it turns green.   It was like a thick stream of verdigris, full of pale, milky streaks, whirls, eddies, and counter-currents, and looked as if it were running up by one bank, and down by the other.   I sat in the sun, on the floor of the boat, revising my verses.   *   *   *   *

*   *   *   *   *

*   *   *   *   *

Arrived on the other side, *i. e.* Canada, there was a second pause, as to how we were to get conveyed to the Falls.   My father, ——, and D—— betook themselves to an inn by the road-side, which promised information and assistance; and —— and I, clambering up the heights of Queenston, sat ourselves down under some bushes, whence we looked towards Lake Ontario, and where he told me the history of the place; how his countrymen had thumped my countrymen upon this spot, and how the English general Brock had fallen near where we sat. A monument, in the shape of a stone pillar, has been erected to his memory; and to the top of this —— betook himself to reconnoitre; which ambitious expedition I felt no inclination to share. After he had been gone some time, I thought I perceived signs of stirring down by the inn door: I toiled up the hill to the base of the pillar to fetch him, and we proceeded down to the rest of the party. An uneasy-looking, rickety cart without springs was the sole conveyance we could obtain, and into this we packed ourselves. —— brought me some beautiful roses, which he had been stealing for me, and —— gave me a glass of milk; with which restoratives I comforted myself, and we set forth. As we squeaked and creaked (I mean our vehicle) up the hill, I thought either my father's or ——'s weight quite enough to have broken the whole down; but it did not happen. My mind was eagerly dwelling on what we were going to see: that sight which —— said was the only one in the world which had not disappointed him. I felt absolutely nervous with expectation. The sound of the cataract is, they say, heard within fifteen miles when the wind sets favourably : to-day, however, there was no wind; the whole air was breathless with the heat of midsummer, and, though we stopped our waggon once or twice to listen as we approached, all was profoundest silence. There was no motion in the leaves of the trees, not a cloud sailing in the sky; every thing was as though in a bright, warm death. When we were within about three miles of the Falls, just before entering the village of Niagara, —— stopped the waggon; and then we heard distinctly, though far off, the voice of the mighty cataract. Looking over the woods, which appeared to overhang the course of the river, we beheld one silver cloud rising slowly into the sky, — the everlasting incense of the waters. A perfect frenzy of impatience seized upon me : I could have set off and run the whole way; and when at length the carriage stopped at the door of the Niagara house, waiting neither for my father, D——, nor ——, I rushed through the hall, and the garden, down the steep footpath cut in the rocks. I heard steps behind me ; —— was following me : down, down I sprang, and along the narrow footpath, divided only by a thicket from the tumultuous rapids. I saw through the boughs the white glimmer of that sea of foam. " Go on, go on; don't stop," shouted ——; and in another minute the thicket was passed: I stood upon Table Rock. —— seized me by the arm, and, without speaking a word, dragged me to the edge of the rapids, to the brink of the abyss. I saw Niagara.—Oh, God! who can describe that sight?

THE END.